# HANDBOOK OF RESEARCH ON BUSINESS ANGELS

HANDBOOKS IN VENTURE CAPITAL

**Series Editor:** Hans Landström, *Professor in Business Administration, Sten K. Johnson Centre for Entrepreneurship, Lund University, Sweden*

Titles in the series include:

Handbook of Research on Venture Capital
*Edited by Hans Landström*

Handbook of Research on Venture Capital: Volume 2
A Globalizing Industry
*Edited by Hans Landström and Colin Mason*

Handbook of Research on Business Angels
*Edited by Hans Landström and Colin Mason*

# Handbook of Research on Business Angels

*Edited by*

Hans Landström

*Professor in Business Administration, Sten K. Johnson Centre for Entrepreneurship, Lund University, Sweden*

Colin Mason

*Professor of Entrepreneurship, Adam Smith Business School, University of Glasgow, UK*

HANDBOOKS IN VENTURE CAPITAL

Edward Elgar
PUBLISHING

Cheltenham, UK • Northampton, MA, USA

Published by
Edward Elgar Publishing Limited
The Lypiatts
15 Lansdown Road
Cheltenham
Glos GL50 2JA
UK

Edward Elgar Publishing, Inc.
William Pratt House
9 Dewey Court
Northampton
Massachusetts 01060
USA

A catalogue record for this book
is available from the British Library

Library of Congress Control Number: 2016938586

This book is available electronically in the **Elgar**online
Business subject collection
DOI 10.4337/9781783471720

Printed on elemental chlorine free (ECF)
recycled paper containing 30% Post-Consumer Waste

ISBN 978 1 78347 171 3 (cased)
ISBN 978 1 78347 172 0 (eBook)

Typeset by Servis Filmsetting Ltd, Stockport, Cheshire
Printed and bound in the USA

# Contents

# Contributors

**Frances M. Amatucci**, School of Business, Slippery Rock University of Pennsylvania, USA.

**Miguel Atienza**, Economics Department, Economics and Business Faculty, Universidad Católica del Norte (UCN), Chile.

**Sofia Avdeitchikova**, The Ratio Institute, Stockholm, Sweden.

**Tiago Botelho**, Norwich Business School, University of East Anglia, UK.

**Cécile Carpentier**, School of Accounting, Laval University, Québec, Canada and Cirano, Montréal, Canada.

**Veroniek Collewaert**, Vlerick Business School, Ghent, Belgium and Katholieke Universiteit Leuven, Leuven, Belgium.

**Lars Hornuf**, Department of Economics, University of Trier and Max Planck Institute for Innovation and Competition, Munich, Germany.

**Henrik Keinonen**, Vendep Ltd and Department of Economics, Hanken School of Economics, Helsinki, Finland.

**Tom Lahti**, Department of Entrepreneurship and Management, Hanken School of Economics, Vaasa, Finland.

**Hans Landström**, Sten K. Johnson Centre for Entrepreneurship, Lund University, Sweden.

**David Lingelbach**, Merrick School of Business, University of Baltimore, USA.

**Manhong Liu**, Research Center on Fictitious Economy and Data Science, Chinese Academy of Sciences, Beijing, China.

**Colin Mason**, Adam Smith Business School, University of Glasgow, UK.

**Andrew Maxwell**, Canadian Innovation Centre and Lassonde School of Engineering, York University, Toronto, Canada.

**Diamanto Politis**, Sten K. Johnson Centre for Entrepreneurship, Lund University, Sweden.

**Gianni Romaní**, Management Department, Entrepreneurship and SME

Center, Economics and Business Faculty, Universidad Católica del Norte (UCN), Chile.

**William Scheela**, College of Business, Communications and Technology, Bemidji State University, Minnesota State University System, USA.

**Armin Schwienbacher**, Université Côte d'Azur–SKEMA Business School, France.

**Roger Sørheim**, Norwegian University of Science and Technology (NTNU), Norway.

**Jean-Marc Suret**, School of Accounting, Laval University, Québec, Canada and Cirano, Montréal, Canada.

**Yi Tan**, Antai College of Economics and Management, Shanghai Jiaotong University, Shanghai, China.

**Jiani Wang**, School of Finance, Capital University of Economics and Business, Beijing, China.

This book is dedicated to Professor Emeritus William J. Wetzel Jr
to recognize his seminal contribution to the field of
business angel research.

# 1 Business angels as a research field

*Hans Landström and Colin Mason*

## 1.1 THE AIMS OF THE BOOK

This is the third volume of the Edward Elgar Publishing book series 'Handbooks in Venture Capital'.[1] This volume focuses on Business Angels (BAs), that is, 'high net worth individuals, acting alone or in a formal or informal syndicate, who invests his or her own money directly in an unquoted business in which there is no family connection and who, after making the investment, generally takes an active involvement in the business, for example, as an advisor or member of the board of directors' (Mason and Harrison, 2008, p. 309).

Our knowledge of BAs is now more than three decades old and our understanding of the phenomenon has gradually increased over this time (Landström, 2007; Landström and Mason, 2012). Nevertheless, some researchers have pointed out that this knowledge and understanding is highly fragmented – the field seems to have moved from providing 'no answers' to presenting 'a flora of answers' about the nature and activity of BAs (Shane, 2009). It is therefore important to take stock and synthesize our knowledge about BAs. This is the purpose of this volume of the *Handbook of Research on Business Angels*.

A further need for this *Handbook* arises from the expectations that politicians and policy-makers have been directed to the BA market over the past two decades as a solution to the financial gaps that have been identified among new and entrepreneurial ventures around the world. Consequently, the BA market has, and continues to attract, considerable interventions by policy-makers. However, most of these policy initiatives have been made without being anchored in the knowledge that has been developed about the market. Thus, a further objective of this *Handbook* is to compile and synthesize our knowledge in a way that is helpful to policy-makers.

## 1.2 THE IMPORTANCE OF BUSINESS ANGELS

As a phenomenon, private individuals who invest in high-risk projects have existed since the origin of economic activity in society. For example, entrepreneurs raising capital from private individuals can be found as early the First Babylonian Era in the seventeenth to eighteenth centuries BC as well as in early medieval Europe. One extraordinary example is the investment made by Queen Isabella of Spain to finance the voyage of Christopher Columbus – an investment that could be regarded as highly profitable for Spain. Investments by private individuals were also influential in the evolution of the industrial revolution during the nineteenth and early twentieth centuries. For example, in the USA, groups of private investors were responsible for financing the development of several new industries, such as railroads, steel, petroleum and glass. These kinds of investments are not unique to the USA; similar activities can be found in many other countries (Rind, 1981; Benjamin and Margulis, 2001; Gompers and Lerner, 2003).

Following the arguments by Avdeitchikova and Landström in Chapter 3 we will contend that the contributions made by BAs go beyond the amount of capital they provide to businesses. The fact that BAs provide small amounts of capital in the early stages of venture development gives them a critical role in the financial system. But, in addition, BAs are often associated with an active involvement in the venture in which they invest, providing the venture with access to key non-financial resources, such as skills, knowledge, experience and a network. An investment made by a BA may also leverage additional finance from other sources. BAs predominantly invest equity capital and therefore contribute to a strengthening of the balance sheet of their investee ventures that may enable them to go on to raise debt finance. Their investment may also give positive signals to other investors either to co-invest or provide follow-on financing. At a more aggregated level, it has been shown that BAs play an important role in the entrepreneurial eco-system of regions, thereby improving the conditions for venture growth.

## 1.3 THE EVOLUTION OF THE RESEARCH FIELD

Originally, the term 'angel' was used to describe individuals who helped to finance theater productions on Broadway ('theater angels'). These 'angels' invested in such productions mainly for the pleasure of rubbing shoulders with their favorite actors. These were high-risk investments, the angels lost their money if the production was a flop but shared in the profits if it was successful (Benjamin and Marqulis, 2001; Mason, 2007). William Wetzel Jr (1981, 1983) from the University of New Hampshire in the USA was one of the first to coin the term 'business angels' for people providing the same kind of risk investments to young entrepreneurial ventures.

William Wetzel can be regarded as the pioneer of research on BAs, publishing a seminal study of BAs in New England (Wetzel, 1981, 1983, 1986) in the early 1980s. But even before this, in the 1950s and 1960s, policy-makers and researchers had started to pay attention to the BA market. The financial problems experienced by many technology-based ventures at that point in time provided a starting point for studies on BAs. For example, in the late 1950s the Federal Reserve in the USA undertook a couple of studies that focused on the initial financing of new technology-based ventures (Rubenstein, 1958) that identified BAs as an important external source of finance. The first PhD thesis with an interest in BAs was presented by Hoffman in 1972 at the University of Texas at Austin (Hoffman, 1972).

However, it was the pioneering work by Professor William Wetzel that led to an increasing interest in BAs. Wetzel's study was based on the widely held perception that new technology-based ventures experienced problems when raising small amounts of early-stage financing. But this conflicted with anecdotal evidence that 'business angels' played a role in solving this problem. Little was known about the characteristics of BAs and the flow of BA capital. Wetzel's objective was therefore to 'put some boundaries on our ignorance' on BAs and their investments. His study made the BA market visible and revealed its importance. Specifically, it showed that BAs represented a substantial pool of funds for entrepreneurial ventures, and were motivated by both financial and non-financial incentives to make investments. However, the market was relatively inefficient in bringing entrepreneurs and investors together, the effect of which was to discourage entrepreneurs from searching for finance and angels in seeking investment opportunities, resulting in potential investments from not occurring.

Wetzel's New Hampshire research promoted efforts to replicate the study in California (Tymes and Krasner, 1983), and in US Small Business Administration (US SBA) studies of the Sunbelt region (Gaston and Bell, 1986), Great Lake region (Aram, 1987) and the East Coast (Haar et al., 1988). Gaston (1989a) provided a synthesis of these US SBA studies. In this so-called first generation of BA studies, researchers focused their attention on two main questions:

- How large is the BA market? (market scale)
- What characterizes the BAs? (attitudes, behavior and characteristics)

Estimating the size of the BA market is challenging. Indeed, Wetzel (1983, p. 26) argued that the size of the market is 'unknown and probably unknowable.' However, despite various conceptual and methodological problems several scholars have attempted to estimate the size of the market (for example, Wetzel, 1986, 1987; Gaston, 1989b; Mason and Harrison, 2000; Sohl, 2003; Avdeitchikova and Landström, 2005). The conclusion that can be drawn from these studies is that estimations of the BA market are problematic in various ways, and have to be considered to be very crude estimates of the markets in different regions. Nevertheless, they showed that across US regions and in various countries the BA markets were large, with investments by BAs in early-stage ventures exceeding those made by the institutional venture capital industry (Freear and Wetzel, 1990). Moreover, these results seem to be consistent over time.

Alongside the size of the market, another key issue was to identify the types of individuals making the investments and to describe their attitudes, behavior and characteristics (ABC of BAs). The early studies showed that the 'typical' angel investor was a middle-aged male with a reasonable net income and net worth, with previous start-up experiences, who makes about one investment a year, usually close to home. The primary method of finding new investment opportunities is through friends and business associates, and they prefer high-technology and manufacturing ventures. Their investment decision is motivated by the prospect of financial returns, coupled with strong personal (non-financial) driving forces. They are hands-on investors adding value to the ventures in which they invest.

The pioneering works conducted in the USA during the 1980s encouraged researchers in other countries to undertake their own studies of their BA markets and to make international comparisons of the BA markets. Studies were conducted in Canada (Riding and Short, 1987), the UK (Mason and Harrison, 1994), Sweden (Landström, 1993), Finland (Lumme et al., 1998), Australia (Hindle and Wenbam, 1999), Japan (Tashiro, 1999), Norway (Reitan and Sørheim, 2000) and Germany (Brettel, 2003; Stadler and Peters, 2003). Although the conditions for an active BA market differ from country to country, the conclusion from these international studies was that there were many similarities in the attitudes, behavior and characteristics of BAs irrespective of geographical context (Kelly, 2007) as well as over time (Månsson and Landström, 2005). However, despite many common characteristics, research has repeatedly indicated that the BA market is highly heterogeneous. Hence, there have been various attempts to describe the market in more nuanced ways, notably by developing various classifications of BAs (for example, Gaston, 1989a; Coveney and Moore, 1998; Sørheim and Landström, 2001; Lahti, 2011).

These early studies of the market scale and characteristics of BAs were important, not only because they made the BA market visible, which, in turn, stimulated interest amongst entrepreneurs, high net worth individuals and policy-makers, but also provided the basis for further research. On the back of these demographic studies researchers increasingly started to take the next step in increasing understanding of the BA market. Progress was also stimulated by the Babson Entrepreneurship Research Conference, initiated in 1981, which provided an opportunity to present research on BAs (and subsequently published in *Frontiers of Entrepreneurship Research*) and the growing number of publication opportunities, not least the establishment of a new academic journal dedicated to venture capital and other forms entrepreneurial finance: *Venture Capital: An International Journal of Entrepreneurial Finance*, in 1999. These second generation studies focused on three main issues:

- the investment decision-making process of BA
- policy issues to improve the BA market
- theoretical understandings of BA.

A major focus of research during the 1990s (and subsequently) has been on understanding the way in which BAs made their investments and specifically their investment decision-making process and criteria for selecting investments (for example, Riding et al., 1994; Landström, 1995, 1998; Mason and Rogers, 1997). This research showed that the investment decision is a multi-stage process, and that BAs are highly selective, rejecting some 90 percent of the opportunities that they see in the initial screening stage. The trustworthiness of the entrepreneur is critical in their appraisal.

For several decades the institutional venture capital marked had a focus on governmental interventions (Lerner, 2009) – on the grounds that high technology-based ventures needed substantial amounts of capital. However, in the 1990s it became obvious that new and technology-based ventures also needed small amounts of money to get off the ground. The high overhead costs of venture capital funds meant that it was uneconomic for them to make small investments. However, BAs were able to make small investments because they did not cost their time in the same way. As a consequence, the BA market became a major focus for policy intervention – starting in the UK in the early 1990s and around ten years later in the rest of Western Europe (Mason, 2009; OECD, 2011). Several studies from this era addressed the two major problems associated with the BA market: (a) how to increase the number of BAs and (b) how to address the market inefficiencies arising from the invisible character of the market that made it difficult for investors and entrepreneurs to find each other. Several studies examined the case for, and effectiveness of, Business Angel Networks (BANs) – analogous to 'dating sites' – as a mechanism through which BA and entrepreneurs could connect with each other (Harrison and Mason, 1996a, 1996b; Collewaert et al., 2010).

Another stream of research that was undertaken during the 1990s explored the extent to which different theoretical frameworks could explain the activities of BAs and the BA market. Several theoretical frameworks were applied in the BA context, notably, decision theory (Landström, 1995; Feeney et al., 1999), agency theory (Landström, 1992; Fiet, 1995; van Osnabrugge, 2000), social capital theory (Sætre, 2003; Sørheim, 2003) and signaling theory (Prasad et al., 2000). The conclusion that can be drawn from these studies is that the theoretical approaches that have mainly been borrowed from other disciplines only partly seem to explain the behavior of BA and the characteristics of the BA market.

A third generation of BA studies has emerged over the past 10–15 years. These studies are rather eclectic. First, a considerable amount of research has continued to investigate the investment decision-making by BAs but with a much narrower focus. For example, Parhankangas and Ehrlich (2014) have looked at how entrepreneurs could use impression management tools to seduce investors. Mitteness et al. (2012) have looked at the impact of the entrepreneur's passion on the angels' interest in investing. Related studies by Mason and Harrison (2003) and Clark (2008) have examined the reactions of angels to the entrepreneur's pitch. Other studies have looked at investment decision-making beyond the initial screening stage (Maxwell et al., 2011, 2014). Other stages of the investment process remain neglected, notably the negotiation and contracting stage where the study by Kelly and Hay (2000, 2003) remains the only significant contribution, and the exit stage that is only now attracting some attention (Mason and Botelho, 2016; Mason et al., 2016). A second theme has been a focus on specific types of angel – notably founder angels (Festel and De Cleyn, 2013), super angels and women angels (Harrison and Mason, 2007; Sohl and Hill, 2007). Third, some studies have sought to introduce a time dimension, examining angel investment trends over time, and specifically following the global financial crisis (Månsson and Landström, 2005; Sohl, 2006; Mason and Harrison, 2015).

## 1.4 THE CURRENT STATE OF KNOWLEDGE OF BUSINESS ANGELS

This *Handbook of Research on Business Angels* seeks to capture and document our current knowledge of BAs. It is divided into five parts: the characteristics of business angel markets; the business angel investment process; international dimensions; policy issues; and new developments.

### 1.4.1 The Characteristics of Business Angel Markets

The first part of the book elaborates on some characteristics of the BA markets. Identifying BAs and accessing data have been challenges of undertaking research on BAs ever since Wetzel's pioneering research. More recently, as research has gathered momentum, a further challenge has emerged concerning the definition of BAs. The Global Entrepreneurship Monitor has been a key source of this definitional confusion by introducing the concept of 'informal investment,' which combines both investment in the businesses of family members – so-called love money – and BA investment. The challenges are reviewed by Colin Mason in Chapter 2. He reviews the definitional issues, stressing that love money and angel investing are conceptually different and emphasizing the key features of BAs: they are investing their own money, investing in private unquoted companies, investing directly and are motivated by commercial returns. However, the emergence of managed angel groups has challenged the continued validity of some aspects of this definition. He then goes on to review the various ways in which researchers have sought to identify BAs, either for sampling purposes or to estimate the size of the market. Each of the sources reviewed significant deficiencies. Mason is therefore of the same view as Wetzel, that the population of BAs 'is unknown and probably unknowable' (Wetzel, 1983, p.26). However, he does see the emergence of angel groups as an important development, comprising a significant investment category in their own right and which is visible, in contrast to solo angels who operate informally and so remain largely invisible. He therefore advocates that efforts should be made to collect investment information from such groups on a regular basis. This is already being done by some national angel associations, such as Canada's National Angel Capital Organisation.[2]

In Chapter 3 Sofia Avdeitchikova and Hans Landström revisit one of the original topics in BA research: to measure the scope of the BA market and evaluate its impact on the economy, especially the financial contributions of BA at the macro (market) level. This is an issue that has considerable policy relevance. Most policy initiatives to support the BA activities have been introduced without any strong empirical justification nor evidence to inform on the appropriateness of different types of policy measures. In this chapter, the authors summarize our knowledge about the size of the BA market in different countries. The authors then turn their attention from the size of the market to its 'significance'; in other words, shifting from a concern with measuring the size of the market to a concern with the relative importance of BAs for funding new and growing ventures in the economy. Avdeitchikova and Landström propose two sets of indicators to evaluate the significance of the BA market – one that focuses on the supply perspective, that is, the relative importance of BA finance compared to other sources, and the other focuses on the demand perspective, that is, the extent to which BA finance is available in relation to the demand for capital in the small and medium-sized enterprises (SME) sector.

Previous studies of BAs have shown that the population is very heterogeneous, with various studies developing typologies to describe different categories of investor. In Chapter 4 Roger Sørheim and Tiago Botelho provide critical review of previous research on BA categorizations to highlight the key contributions. The authors note that previous studies have categorized BAs using a wide range of variables, mostly grouping investors according to investors' characteristics and often derived from data rather than theory. The main contribution of these studies has been to develop a more sophisticated and nuanced view of the definition and behavior of BAs – which breaks free from an oversimplified stereotypical view of BAs. However, in many cases the categorizations are fragmented, lacking a theoretical anchor, supply-side driven and rather static. The authors conclude that these studies have not significantly influenced policy-makers and policies to target different categories of BA.

BA investing has traditionally been a male-dominated activity. However, over time, there has been an increase in the total number of women BAs worldwide. In Chapter 5 Frances M. Amatucci provides a gender-based review of the changes occurring in the BA market. Recent reports from the USA show a significant growth of the number of women BAs who are now estimated to represent 15–20 percent of the BA market in the USA, but comprise a significantly lower proportion in other countries. Amatucci argues that there are several barriers that can prevent women from becoming BA investors. For example, women are more conservative and less experienced investors, less likely to be 'cashed out' entrepreneurs, with different social networks than men, and have different types of family responsibilities. When women become BAs they invest sectors that have often been overlooked by male BAs, and they tend to invest in women-led ventures. Amatucci identified a number of favorable trends that will continue to drive the growth in the number and proportion of women BAs. These include an increase in the number of high net worth women, an increase in the number of women-led angel investment funds and the proliferation of programs to train women BAs.

### 1.4.2 The Business Angel Investment Process

The BA investment process is the focus of the second part of the book. The investment process includes the BA investment decision, their contributions to the ventures after the investment has been made and also the 'dark side' of the relationship between the entrepreneur and investor.

From the entrepreneur's perspective, attracting investment from a BA is not an easy task. Of course, there are many reasons for this. In Chapter 6 Andrew Maxwell argues that entrepreneurs need to understand what drives BAs and how they make investment decisions. Such understanding will improve their prospects of raising finance. Thus, the aim of this chapter is to summarize and synthesize the research on the BA's investment decisions. In particular, Maxwell focuses attention on recent research that has explored the critical stage of the investment decision process when the entrepreneur and BA first meet.

BAs are regarded as 'smart' investors who make value added contributions to their investee businesses that go beyond their financial investments. Most studies of the value added process provide empirical descriptions of the hands-on support provided by BAs. However, a more comprehensive and theoretical overview of the process is lacking and theoretical progress remains slow. In Chapter 7 Diamanto Politis provides a review and synthesis of the available research evidence on the hands-on involvement of BAs after they have made their investment. Her analysis is based on a framework that comprises four interrelated dimensions of the value added process: behavior, context, reception and impact. This results in three main themes that provide insights into the process of adding value. The first theme addresses the involvement of BAs in the ventures in which they invest and how this involvement translates into a set of potential value adding benefits. The second theme addresses how and to what extent the set of potential benefits that the portfolio ventures receive may translate into benefits for the venture development process. The third theme addresses how situational contingencies may influence the value added of BAs.

As recognized in Chapter 7, BAs are active investors who create long-term relationships with the entrepreneurs in the ventures in which they invest. However, in-depth knowledge on how BAs and entrepreneurs work together to create an effective investment relationship is lacking. Nevertheless, we know that the BA–entrepreneur relationship is not always 'rosy' – there is also a dark side of the relationship in which various kinds of conflicts can arise. In Chapter 8 Veroniek Collewaert elaborates on this issue by providing a review on our knowledge about the conditions, triggers, contingencies and outcomes of conflicts in the BA–entrepreneur relationship. Collewaert shows that both extremes – the absence of conflict and extremely high levels of conflict – are rare in the BA–entrepreneur relationship. When conflicts do occur the causes have many roots, from scarce resources, personal differences, to goal incompatibilities. The impact of a conflict could have performance-related outcomes as well as individual affect- and attitude-related outcomes. Collewaert recognizes that not all conflicts are equally good or bad – rather, it depends on the type of conflicts that occur and various moderating influences such as team and task characteristics.

### 1.4.3 International Dimensions

This third part takes an international perspective on BA activity, looking primarily at the BA markets in China, Southeast Asia, sub-Saharan Africa and Latin America. In the first of these chapters, Jiani Wang, Yi Tan and Manhong Liu (Chapter 9) elaborate on the BA market in China, which has developed significantly since its emergence at the end of the 1990s. The increasing numbers of successful cashed-out entrepreneurs emerging from the internet and high-tech has resulted in the emergence of angel investment. Currently, there are numerous angel groups and matchmaking services that have served to enhance the market. The authors show that the investment behavior of Chinese BAs is very similar to that in western countries, but Chinese BAs are younger, invest more infrequently and lack an understanding of BA investing. The authors also emphasize the need to understand the role of the government in the BA market in improving the regulation and environment of BA investments.

Southeast Asia, which includes the emerging economies of Brunei, Cambodia, Indonesia, Lao PDR, Malaysia, Myanmar, Philippines, Thailand and Vietnam as well as the developed economy of Singapore, represents one of the most rapidly growing regions globally. Entrepreneurship has played a major role in this impressive growth. According to the Global Entrepreneurship Monitoring research the population of these countries shows an above-average intention to become entrepreneurs. But in spite of impressive economic growth and entrepreneurial activity, there have been very few studies on the impact of BA financing. This lack of research arises because many BAs operate in the informal economy and hence prefer a low profile, making them even more invisible compared to their western counterparts. In Chapter 10 William Scheela reviews the studies that have been conducted on the BA markets in Southeast Asia. He argues that BAs in Southeast Asia exhibit differences as well as similarities to their counterparts in western economies. There are apparent similarities as most BAs are experienced and hands-on investors, actively use their networks and co-invest with other BAs. However, there are obvious differences, notably in terms of the absence of a fully developed institutional framework to support BA investing. Singapore is the exception in this respect with a business environment supported by well-developed institutions.

The response of many BAs is to focus more strongly on family relationships, and be more socially focused in their investment strategy. An additional issue raised by Scheela is the definition of BAs. The traditional way of defining BA seems to fit, except in Thailand and for the Chinese Philippines that make what are more family-like investments. This raises concerns about the definition of a BA in studies that are conduced outside western countries.

Definitional concerns are also an issue when researching BAs in sub-Saharan Africa. In Chapter 11 David Lingelbach focuses attention on this subject in his review of our knowledge of BA in sub-Saharan Africa. He emphasizes the need to consider the institutional context and the heterogeneity between countries as well as the differences from western countries. In this chapter, Lingelbach argues that the recent increase in gross domestic product (GDP) growth in several African economies, combined with a slow reduction in the level of violence, has contributed to an increase in entrepreneurial activity and, as a consequence, we can expect an increase in BA investments. However, these activities will not mimic the behavior of BAs in developed economies, but will evolve a practice that is suited to local conditions. National levels of BA investing activity are likely to continue to vary, influenced by formal and informal institutions.

In Chapter 12 Gianni Romaní and Miguel Atienza discuss the emergent BA markets in Latin America – comprising a heterogeneous group of countries, the largest of which are Argentina, Brazil, Chile, Colombia and Mexico. These countries are increasingly aware of the importance of entrepreneurship as engines of economic development. Most Latin American governments are fostering a series of policies to encourage entrepreneurship and innovation, including the creation of Business Angel Networks. At the same time, wealthy individuals are starting to invest in entrepreneurial ventures. However, Romaní and Atienza show that the BA market in Latin America is still incipient, and its development is influenced by the experience of successful companies in the USA such as Amazon and Google, which were initially funded by BA investors. In some Latin American countries, the progress of the BA market has had significant support from public policies and ultilateral organizations. Changes in the institutional frameworks during the last decade have contributed to greater political and economic stability. Nevertheless, the region has not yet a critical mass of BAs. There are several remaining obstacles for the progress of the BA markets. For example, cultural issues such as a lack of trust, makes the relationship between entrepreneurs and BAs insecure. A lack of long-term vision and a risk aversion among Latin American investors and institutional obstacles, such as a lack of clarity in defining the rules of the game, represent further barriers.

### 1.4.4 Policy Issues

Worldwide, governments have implemented numerous initiatives to promote BA investment activity. However, assessment of these initiatives produce mixed results, hence discussion about their effectiveness continues to be debated. A popular approach to increase BA investment activity involves changing their risk–return ratio through the introduction of various kinds of tax incentives. The most common form of tax incentive is a front-end tax relief that has the effect of reducing the real cost of the investment. In the fourth section of the book, Cécile Carpentier and Jean-Marc Suret (Chapter 13) review and compare the evidence on the effectiveness of different tax programs around the world. This reveals that there is very limited evidence that tax incentives for BAs are effective, with tax expenditures generally being higher than the tax revenues that are generated by the investments. Carpentier and Suret attribute the failure of the programs to their poor design. However, it needs to be acknowledged that there are inconsistencies in the results of the assessments of the programs. These may be attributable to the choice of hypotheses and method in the assessments. Hence, there is the need for further research on the effectiveness of tax initiatives for BAs.

In Chapter 14 Tom Lahti and Henrik Keinonen focus on another initiative that has become popular among policy-makers around the world in order to foster BA activities, namely, Business Angel Networks (BANs). BANs have been established to increase the transparency and improve the efficiency of the BA market by providing a channel of communication that enables entrepreneurs seeking finance to come into contact with BAs, and at the same time enable BAs to receive information on investment opportunities without the need to compromise their anonymity if so desired. In this chapter the authors describe the development of BAN activities in different countries and evaluate their benefits and drawbacks. The chapter identifies different kinds of BANs and the different ways that BANs can provide their deal-brokering service and deliver supplementary functions such as training of entrepreneurs and BAs, advisory service, contract templates and the development of good practice. Evaluations of BANs have shown both positive impacts on investment activity as well as negative effects, hence there is no conclusive answer to whether there is a need for public sector interventions to support the establishment and operation of BANs.

### 1.4.5 New Developments

In the fifth section, in the final chapter (Chapter 15), Lars Hornuf and Armin Schwienbacher review our knowledge of crowdinvesting (or equity crowdfunding). Crowdfunding has emerged over the past decade as a new and promising means of financing new ventures. Crowdfunding includes a broad range of activities, including donations, pre-purchase and other reward-based forms of funding by the crowd as well as debt and equity financing. In this chapter Hornuf and Schwienbacher focus on a subcategory of crowdfunding that can be defined as 'crowdinvesting' – internet-based investment in new ventures by the crowd with the intention to obtain some residual claim on future cash flow of a venture. As a new development in the market it raises questions regarding the boundaries between crowdinvestors and BAs. The aims of this chapter are to describe the function of crowdinvesting, and to analyze the similarities and differences between crowdinvesting and angel investing. The authors argue that in many cases, crowdinvestors are likely to complement rather than substitute BAs and venture capital funds. They all tend to fill funding gaps at the lower end of the market and co-invest with professional investors in the same round.

## 1.5 BUSINESS ANGEL RESEARCH: SOME FUTURE DIRECTIONS

Although considerable progress has been made in BA research since the first generation studies of the early 1980s, many unanswered questions remain. Meanwhile, the way in which the angel market has evolved and the different features that have emerged as it has spread internationally have also generated new questions and challenged the ongoing relevance of existing knowledge. This final section therefore summarizes the suggestions that each of the contributors have made for future research in their research areas.

The first part of the book elaborates on the characteristics of the BA market. In Chapter 2 Mason is optimistic that the growth of the so-called visible market of angel investing, comprising Business Angel Networks and managed angel groups, will go some way toward overcoming the data deficiencies that characterize angel investing. He advocates that efforts are made by researchers, national angel associations and governments to collect information on a regular basis on the investments that angels make through these networks. On the other hand, he is pessimistic that the inherent problems arising from the invisibility and anonymity of angels can be overcome to accurately document investment activity in the invisible market unless government instigates changes in the way that shareholding information is reported and makes accessible information on the users of tax schemes. He does see a role for the Global Entrepreneurship Monitor to adjust its methodology for collecting investment data so that angel investments can be separately identified from other types of informal investing.

The chapter by Avdeitchikova and Landström (Chapter 3) discusses how we can measure the scope of the BA market and evaluate its impact on the economy. In this respect there are some key issues for future research, for example:

- How to measure the scope and significance of BA, not only on the national level, but also at the regional level.
- Methodology needs to be improved, for example, using register-based data such as tax data to capture the BA (informal investors) market in a country.

In Chapter 4 Sørheim and Botelho argue that the BA market is very heterogeneous and in order to understand the market we need more effective ways of identifying different categories of investors:

- Future categorizations need to incorporate different kinds of 'proximity' into studies of BA categorizations, for example, social, technology, cognitive and cultural proximities.
- We also need categorization studies from a demand-side perspective, addressing the manner in which entrepreneurial ventures experience the process and contributions of different categories of BA.
- There is a need for research on BA categories in different geographic regions to counter the current dominance of studies from the USA and Europe.

In Chapter 5 Amatucci takes a closer look at our knowledge of one significant category of BA – women. This is a fairly new research topic, hence there are several interesting issues for future research:

- There is an increasing number of high net worth women worldwide, but we know little about whether the source of net wealth (inherited or self-generated) influences angel investment behavior.
- There are many barriers for women making BA investments. What are these barriers, what consequences do they have and how could these barriers be removed?
- There are an increasing number of women angel investor groups, which raise questions regarding women angel group dynamics, the effects that these groups have on the investment process and the financial performance of the investments.

The second part of the book takes a close look at the BA investment process. In Chapter 6 Maxwell examines the BA's investment decision. Even though there has been considerable research on this topic, there is still a lot more to know. Maxwell suggests the following topics for future research:

- There is a need to understand the various stages of the investment decision process, and to find alternative ways to describe the process.
- More and more investments are made in syndicates and groups; it is therefore essential to investigate the impact of group decision-making on the investment decision.
- In the growth of the venture, the entrepreneur might have many financial options, of which BA funding is only one. Understanding these alternative options and the reasons why entrepreneurs choose one source rather than another is important.

In Chapter 7 Politis synthesizes our knowledge with regards the way BAs add value beyond their financial investment in the ventures in which they have invested. She suggests the following topics for future research:

- The involvement of BAs and how this involvement translates into value adding benefits: how important are the frequency of contacts, different forms of involvement and active involvement? How do the various forms of involvement serve as complements or substitutes to each other, and how do various forms of involvement cluster together? To what extent do various forms of involvement produce different kinds of value added benefits?
- The translation of potential benefits into valuable and helpful effects on the venture development process: how do the frequency and forms of contacts by BAs impact business performance? Do different roles have different impacts on different performance indicators?
- The influence of situational contingencies on the value added by BAs: for example, what is the relative influence of macro (country and regional) versus micro (individual or firm) level contingencies on the hands-on involvement of BAs?

In Chapter 8 Collewaert elaborates on the 'dark side' of the relationship between the entrepreneur and BA when different kinds of conflicts arise in the relationship. The areas for future research that she suggests include the following:

- Questions related to: How does conflict arise? What are the consequences of BA–entrepreneurs conflicts? How do BAs and entrepreneurs deal with their conflicts?

- To measure conflicts is difficult, often using some form of subjective 'conflict scale,' so it is important to develop alternative measures.
- Going beyond conflicts to study the role of trust in the BA–entrepreneur post-investment interaction.

The third part of the book takes an international perspective on BA investing. One general issue that is discussed by all authors in this part is related to the lack of good quality data and the need to improve the databases on BAs. But there are also more specific questions. In Chapter 9 Wang, Tan and Liu emphasize the importance of tracking the development and characteristics of the BA market in China in terms of market size, factors impacting BA investment decision-making, factors impacting BA performance, legal barriers to the BA market, the relationship between BAs and entrepreneurs and assessing public policy interventions.

In Chapter 10 Scheela argues for more research on BAs in Southeast Asia, extending research to more countries in the region and developing larger databases within each country. He identifies the need for both macro studies – similar to the Global Entrepreneurship Monitor data – to collect data on BAs in order to identify characteristics and trends in BA investing and micro studies to better understand the BA investment process in terms of similarities and differences between the countries and to develop policy recommendations.

Lingelbach argues in Chapter 11 that Africa provides a unique research setting that is characterized by dominant elite coalitions who often block innovations that can erode the rents on which their position in the social order depends, extreme economic shocks in the form of commodity booms and busts, famines and migrations and institutional diversity, all of which lends itself to comparative research. In this context, Lingelbach suggests the following research questions:

- How important is BA investing in the African context? What are the similarities and differences in BA investing between sub-Saharan African and other emerging economies?
- How do BAs structure their investments? How do BAs connect to venture capitalists?
- In what way do Africa's distinctive institutional environments shape angel investing activity? How are BAs investing markets organized in Africa?

In Chapter 12 Romaní and Atienza discuss the research on the BA markets in Latin America. This continent has not attracted much attention, which opens up a broad range of research possibilities, for example:

- Business Angel Network (BAN) activities, for example, case studies of BANs and best practices as well as successful BA investments, studies of the discontinuity of BANs, the causes and potential viable alternatives.
- Cultural aspects of BA investments, for example, the analysis of trust, and incentives that can increase the number of BAs in Latin America.
- Comparative studies between countries in Latin America and also with more developed countries.
- The geography of BA investment is of particular interest in Latin America as there is a high degree of spatial concentration of the population, and there exists differences in the level of fiscal, administrative and political decentralization in each country.

The fourth part of the book reviews our knowledge of policy interventions that have been undertaken in order to promote BA activities. In Chapter 13 Carpentier and Suret review the evidence of the effectiveness of different tax programs. They conclude by identifying three important questions that are not addressed in earlier research and that could be fruitful avenues for future research:

- Even if tax incentive programs attempt to improve investors' rate of return, we do not know whether this objective has been reached.
- The tax incentives programs are generally open to all taxpayers or qualified investors, but we do not know what kind of investors are attracted by these tax incentives.
- The assumption that back-end incentives provide the most positive outcomes and are less costly than front-end incentives needs to be tested.

In Chapter 14 Lahti and Keinonen take a closer look at another policy initiative that has become popular among policy-makers to foster BA activities – Business Angel Networks (BANs). The authors suggest the following topics for future research:

- We need to know more about the management of the BANs, and particularly the impact of the human and social capital of the BAN management on the quality of the services provided by the BAN.
- From various studies we know that BANs operate differently in different spatial contexts. Research is needed that examines the effects of the maturity of the market on the way that BANs operate and on their performance.

- From the perspective of the cost-effectiveness of public support, BANs should be compared with providing tax initiatives to BAs.

The focus of the final part of the book is on crowdfunding, a new phenomenon in the BA market. Crowdfunding is an emerging instrument for financing of new ventures that offers considerable potential. In Chapter 15 Hornuf and Schwienbacher review our knowledge on crowdinvesting. They conclude that very little is known about crowdinvesting, mainly due to lack of data, hence there are considerable avenues for future research:

- Risk and expected return of crowdinvesting for the crowd, the types of firms that are created by crowdinvestors and realistic exit routes for crowdinvestors.
- Issues related to the crowd more directly, for example, what motivates the crowd to invest in new ventures, and are their motivations different from BAs?
- Questions related to the structure of the platforms and contracts: Do some contract forms attract more investors and potentially larger funds? Do investor restrictions imposed by platforms affect crowd participation?

In summary, the important role that BAs play throughout the world in financing entrepreneurial businesses means that they should be a major focus for entrepreneurship researchers. Our contributors have indicated that while considerable progress has been made in understanding the BA market, there remains a large number of topics where further research is needed. For example, the changing organization of the market, specifically the importance of managed angel groups and the emergence of crowdinvesting, challenges the ongoing relevance of the existing body of research and raises new questions. In addition, the internationalization of angel investing challenges our existing definitions and research and also raises new questions. Governments have recognized the importance of BAs and introduced a variety of initiatives to stimulate their investment activity. This also raises a variety of research questions. Finally, the challenge in BA research – especially in comparison to venture capital and other parts of the entrepreneurial finance market – is the lack of databases that enable sophisticated statistical analysis. However, it would be an extremely retrograde step for the research agenda to be dictated by data availability. We therefore encourage scholars to use their ingenuity and creativity to overcome data problems to engage in the research agenda that is outlined here.

## NOTES

1. The first volume in the series, Landström (2007), *Handbook of Research on Venture Capital*, focused on the knowledge accumulation within the field of institutional venture capital, corporate venture capital and informal venture capital. In the second volume, Landström and Mason (2012), *Handbook of Research on Venture Capital: Volume 2*, we paid particular attention to the global development of venture capital.
2. http://www.nacocanada.com/naco-academy/research/angel-activity-reports/.

## REFERENCES


Aram, J.D. (1987), *Informal Risk Capital in the Great Lakes Region*, Washington, DC: Small Business Administration.

Avdeitchikova, S. and H. Landström (2005), 'Informal venture capital: scope and geographical distribution in Sweden', Paper presented at the 2005 Babson Entrepreneurship Research Conference, Glasgow, Scotland.

Benjamin, G.A. and J. Margulis (2001), *The Angel Investor's Handbook*, Princeton, NJ: Bloomberg Press.

Brettel, M. (2003), 'Business angels in Germany: a research note', *Venture Capital*, **5**(3), 251–68.

Clark, C. (2008), 'The impact of entrepreneurs' oral "pitch" presentation skills on business angels' initial screening investment decisions', *Venture Capital*, **10**(3), 257–79.

Collewaert, V., S. Manigart and R. Aernoudt (2010), 'Assessment of government funding of Business Angel Networks in Flanders', *Regional Studies*, **44**(1), 119–30.

Coveney, P. and K. Moore (1998), *Business Angels: Securing Start-up Finance*, Chichester: Wiley.

Feeney, L., G. Haines and A. Riding (1999), 'Private investor's investment criteria: insights from qualitative data', *Venture Capital*, **1**(2), 121–45.

Festel, G.W. and S.H. De Cleyn (2013), 'Founding angels as an emerging subtype of angel investment model in high-tech businesses', *Venture Capital*, **15**(3), 261–82.

Fiet, J. (1995), 'Reliance upon informants in the venture capital industry', *Journal of Business Venturing*, **10**, 195–223.

Freear, J. and W.E. Wetzel Jr (1990), 'Who bankrolls high-tech entrepreneurs?', *Journal of Business Venturing*, **5**(2), 77–89.

Gaston, R.J. (1989a), *Finding Private Venture Capital for Young Firms: A Complete Guide*, New York: Wiley.

Gaston, R.J. (1989b), 'The scale of informal venture capital markets', *Small Business Economics*, **1**, 223–30.

Gaston, R. and S.E. Bell (1986), *Informal Risk Capital in the Sunbelt*, Washington, DC: Small Business Administration.

Gompers, P. and J. Lerner (2003), 'Equity financing', in Z.J. Acs and D.B. Audretsch (eds), *Handbook of Entrepreneurship Research*, Boston, MA: Kluwer, pp. 267–98.

Haar, N., J. Starr and I. Macmillan (1988), 'Informal risk capital investors: investment patterns on the East Coast of the USA', *Journal of Business Venturing*, **3**, 11–29.

Harrison, R. and C. Mason (eds) (1996a), *Informal Venture Capital: Evaluating the Impact of Business Introduction Services*, Hemel Hempstead: Prentice Hall.

Harrison, R.T. and C.M. Mason (1996b), 'Developing the informal venture capital market: a review of the Department of Trade and Industry's informal investment demonstration project', *Regional Studies*, **30**(8), 765–71.

Harrison, R.T. and C.M. Mason (2007), 'Does gender matter? Women business angels and the supply of entrepreneurial finance', *Entrepreneurship Theory and Practice*, **31**(3), 445–72.

Hindle, K. and R. Wenban (1999), 'Informal venture capitalists: an explorative profile', *Venture Capital*, **1**(2), 169–86.
Hoffman, C.A. (1972), 'The venture capital investments process: a particular aspect of regional economic development', PhD thesis, University of Texas at Austin.
Kelly, P. (2007), 'Business angels research: the road traveled and the journey ahead', in H. Landström (ed.), *Handbook of Research on Venture Capital*, Cheltenham, UK and Northampton, MA, USA: Edward Elgar, pp. 315–31.
Kelly, P. and M. Hay (2000), 'Deal-makers: reputation attracts quality', *Venture Capital*, **2**(3), 183–202.
Kelly, P. and M. Hay (2003), 'Business angel contracts: the influence of context', *Venture Capital*, **5**(4), 287–312.
Lahti, T. (2011), 'Categorization of angel investments: and explorative analysis of risk reduction strategies in Finland', *Venture Capital*, **13**(1), 49–74.
Landström, H. (1992), 'The relationship between private investors and small firms: an agency theory approach', *Entrepreneurship and Regional Development*, **4**, 199–223.
Landström, H. (1993), 'Informal risk capital in Sweden and some international comparisons', *Journal of Business Venturing*, **8**, 525–40.
Landström, H. (1995), 'A pilot study on the investment decision-making behavior of informal investors in Sweden', *Journal of Small Business Management*, **33**(3), 67–76.
Landström, H. (1998), 'Informal investors as entrepreneurs', *Technovation*, **18**, 321–33.
Landström, H. (ed.) (2007), *Handbook of Research on Venture Capital*, Cheltenham, UK and Northampton, MA, USA: Edward Elgar.
Landström, H. and C. Mason (eds) (2012), *Handbook of Research on Venture Capital: Volume 2*, Cheltenham, UK and Northampton, MA, USA: Edward Elgar.
Lerner, J. (2009), *Boulevard of Broken Dreams*, Princeton, NJ: Princeton University Press.
Lumme, A., C.M. Mason and M. Suomi (1998), *Informal Venture Capital: Investors, Investments and Policy Issues in Finland*, Boston, MA: Kluwer Academic Publishers.
Månsson, N. and H. Landström (2005), 'Business angels in a changing economy: the case of Sweden', *Venture Capital*, **8**(4), 281–301.
Mason, C. (2007), 'Informal sources of venture finance', in S. Parker (ed.), *The Life Cycle of Entrepreneurial Ventures, Volume 3*, New York: Springer, pp. 258–300.
Mason, C.M. (2009), 'Public policy support for the informal venture capital market: a critical review', *International Small Business Journal*, **27**(5), 536–56.
Mason, C.M. and T. Botelho (2016), 'The role of the exit in the initial screening of investment opportunities: the case of business angel syndicate gatekeepers', *International Small Business Journal*, **34**, 157–75.
Mason, C.M. and R.T. Harrison (1994), 'The informal venture capital market in the UK', in A. Hughes and D.J. Storey (eds), *Financing Small Firms*, London: Routledge, pp. 64–111.
Mason, C.M. and R.T. Harrison (2000), 'Informal venture capital and the financing of emergent growth businesses', in D. Sexton and H. Landström (eds), *Handbook of Entrepreneurship*, Oxford: Blackwell, pp. 221–9.
Mason, C.M. and R.T. Harrison (2003), 'Closing the regional equity gap? A critique of the Department of Trade and Industry's regional venture capital funds initiative', *Regional Studies*, **37**(8), 855–68.
Mason, C.M. and R.T. Harrison (2008), 'Measuring business angel investment activity in the United Kingdom: a review of potential data sources', *Venture Capital*, **10**(4), 309–30.
Mason, C.M. and R.T. Harrison (2015), 'Business angel investment activity in the financial crisis: UK evidence and policy implications', *Environment and Planning C: Government and Policy*, **33**(1), 43–60.
Mason, C. and A. Rogers (1997), 'Understanding the business angel's investment decision', Venture Finance Research Project, Working Paper No. 14, Southampton University.
Mason, C., R. Harrison and T. Botelho (2016), 'Business angels and beyond: the changing nature of the early risk capital market', in J.G. Hussain and J.S Scott (eds), *International*

*Research Handbook on Entrepreneurial Finance*, Cheltenham, UK and Northampton, MA, USA: Edward Elgar, Chapter 7.
Maxwell, A., S.A. Jeffrey and M. Lévesque (2011), 'Business angel early stage decision making', *Journal of Business Venturing*, **26**, 212–25.
Maxwell, A.L., M. Levesque and S. Jeffrey (2014), 'The non-compensatory relationship between risk and return in business angel investment decisions', *Academy of Management Proceedings*, **2014**(1), 10463.
Mitteness, C., R. Sudek and M.S. Cardon (2012), 'Angel investor characteristics that determine whether perceived passion leads to higher evaluations of funding potential', *Journal of Business Venturing*, **27**(5), 592–606.
OECD (2011), *Financing High Growth Firms. The Role of Angel Investors*, Paris: OECD Publishing.
Parhankangas, A.-L. and M. Ehrlich (2014), 'How entrepreneurs seduce business angels: an impression management approach', *Journal of Business Venturing*, **29**(4), 543–64.
Prasad, D., G. Bruton and G. Vozikis (2000), 'Signaling value to business angels: the proportion of the entrepreneur's net worth invested in a new venture as a decision signal', *Venture Capital*, **2**(3), 167–82.
Reitan, B. and R. Sørheim (2000), 'The informal venture capital market in Norway: investor characteristics, behavior and investment preferences', *Venture Capital*, **2**(2), 129–41.
Riding, A. and D. Short (1987), 'On the estimation of investment potential of informal investors: a capture/recapture approach', *Journal of Small Business and Entrepreneurship*, **5**(4), 26–40.
Riding, A., L. Duxbury and G. Haines (1994), *Financing Enterprise Development: Decision-making by Canadian Angels*, Ottawa: Carleton University.
Rind, K.W. (1981), 'The role of venture capital in corporate development', *Strategic Management Journal*, **2**(2), 169–80.
Rubenstein, A.H. (1958), *Problems of Financing and Managing New Research-based Enterprises in New England*, Boston, MA: Federal Reserve Bank of Boston.
Sætre, A. (2003), 'Entrepreneurial perspectives on informal venture capital', *Venture Capital*, **5**(1), 71–94.
Shane, S. (2009), *Fool's Gold: The Truth Behind Angel Investing in America*, Oxford: Oxford University Press.
Sohl, J. (2003), 'The private equity market in the USA: lessons from volatility', *Venture Capital*, **5**(1), 29–46.
Sohl, J.E. (2006), 'Angel investing: changing strategies during volatile times', *Journal of Entrepreneurial Finance*, **11**(2), 27–47.
Sohl, J.E. and L. Hill (2007), 'Women business angels: insights from angel groups', *Venture Capital*, **9**(3), 207–22.
Sørheim, R. (2003), 'The pre-investment behavior of business angels: a social capital approach', *Venture Capital*, **5**(4), 337–64.
Sørheim, R. and H. Landström (2001), 'Informal investors: a categorization with policy implications', *Entrepreneurship and Regional Development*, **13**(4), 351–70.
Stadler, H. and H.H. Peters (2003), 'Business angels in Germany: an empirical study', *Venture Capital*, **5**(3), 269–76.
Tashiro, Y. (1999), 'Business angels in Japan', *Venture Capital*, **1**(3), 259–73.
Tymes, E. and O. Krasner (1983), 'Informal risk capital in California', in J. Hornaday, J. Timmons and K. Vesper (eds), *Frontiers of Entrepreneurship Research*, Wellesley, MA: Babson College, pp. 347–68.
van Osnabrugge, M. (2000), 'A comparison of business angels and venture capital investment procedures: an agency theory-based analysis', *Venture Capital*, **2**(2), 91–109.
Wetzel Jr, W.E. (1981), 'Informal risk capital in New England', in K.H. Vesper (ed.), *Frontiers of Entrepreneurship Research*, Wellesley, MA: Babson College, pp. 217–45.
Wetzel Jr, W.E. (1983), 'Angels and informal venture capital', *Sloan Management Review*, **24**(4), 23–34.
Wetzel Jr, W.E. (1986), 'Informal risk capital: knowns and unknowns', in D. Sexton and

R. Smilor (eds), *The Art and Science of Entrepreneurship*, Cambridge, MA: Ballinger, pp. 85–108.
Wetzel Jr, W.E. (1987), 'The informal venture capital market: aspects of scale and market efficiency', *Journal of Business Venturing*, **2**(4), 299–313.

# PART I

# THE CHARACTERISTICS OF BUSINESS ANGEL MARKETS

# 2 Researching business angels: definitional and data challenges

*Colin Mason*

## 2.1 INTRODUCTION

Some 25 years ago Ian Macmillan and Jerome Katz noted that 'as our understanding of entrepreneurship grows our curiosity about newly discovered processes is frequently outstripping our ability to study them (Macmillan and Katz, 1992, p. 1). This is because the person or event is difficult to find or, more properly, is obscured. We may not be able to observe the event, for example, because it is rare. Alternatively, it may be that we are unable to identify the individual(s) involved in the event. This may arise because the individual(s) wishes to remain anonymous. Business angels were identified as an example of a category of individuals in the entrepreneurial domain who are obscure and hence elusive.

The challenges involved in undertaking research on business angels have been apparent from the outset. William Wetzel Jr, the pioneer of angel research who introduced the term 'business angel' in his study of 'Informal risk capital in New England' (Wetzel, 1981), defined them as 'financially sophisticated individuals of means, often with previous investment or management experience with entrepreneurial ventures' (p. 281) who provide risk capital informally to start-up and emerging growth industries. However, he observed that the population of business angels 'is unknown and probably unknowable' (Wetzel, 1983, p. 26) on account of their invisibility, desire for anonymity and the undocumented nature of their investing. Unlike the institutional venture capital market, there are no lists or directories of business angels. This has had several consequences. Researchers have had to identify business angels through a variety of imperfect sources with no way in which to test for the 'representativeness' of the samples that have been generated. Indeed, many studies have been based on 'samples of convenience' with significant recognised or, more commonly, unrecognised, biases. The difficulty of finding business angels has, in turn, meant that most samples are small, which adds to the representativeness problem and limits the potential for the use of quantitative research techniques. Moreover, the lack of control groups and large enough samples of angels have prevented the use of hypothesis testing (Shane, 2009). In some respects, these challenges have been reduced as angel investing becomes more institutionalised with the emergence of angel networks and groups and therefore more visible. However, this has created a new set of issues concerning the representativeness of those angels who engage with these organisations. This evolution in angel investing and its expansion to other countries with different cultural and institutional settings have also resulted in greater diversity in types of investors and approaches to investment, which has complicated what was originally a straightforward definition of business angels.

These issues of definition and data are addressed in this chapter. In the context of the growing definitional confusion, the next section considers definitional issues – how do we define business angels? Who should be included in, and excluded from, studies of business angels? The following sections review the various ways in which researchers have sought to identify business angels and their investment activity. They provide a critical review of data sources and approaches used in previous scholarly studies of business angels and the issues that arise in terms of representativeness and bias.

## 2.2 DEFINITIONAL ISSUES

In the 35 years since business angels have been recognised as a focus of research and policy attention definitional issues have become more problematic. There are three reasons for this. First, the angel population is heterogeneous, with research identifying several different types of angel investor, some of whom deviate to a lesser or greater extent from the conventional definition (for example, Coveney and Moore, 1998; Sørheim and Landström, 2001; Infometrics Ltd, 2004; Avdeitchikova, 2008; Lahti, 2011). As Shane (2009, p. 53) notes: 'angels aren't all wealthy, high income, well-educated, older, retired', the typical stereotype of angels. Specifically, only a minority of angels meet the wealth and experience requirements to be defined as an 'accredited investor' under securities legislation that provides a regulatory framework for angel investing to protect both the angel and the entrepreneur. Accredited investors are defined as requiring reduced need for protection and hence able to receive exclusive deal flow from financial intermediaries. Second, the maturing of the informal venture capital market has been characterised by the development of more ways in which investors can make investments in unquoted companies, notably through various forms of angel groups, syndicates and networks and other intermediaries, the effect of which is to dilute the original distinctiveness of angel investing from other forms of investing. Third, and perhaps most significant, the Global Entrepreneurship Monitor (GEM) has introduced definitional imprecision by reporting on what it terms 'informal investment' to describe *all* non-institutional risk capital investments in unquoted businesses. This includes investments made in the businesses of family members and those of friends as well as business angel investments (in businesses owned by 'strangers'), with business angel investment being the smallest category. These investments are dominated by close family members (49 per cent) and other relatives (9 per cent) and friends and neighbours (26 per cent) and work colleagues (8 per cent). Only 7 per cent of informal investments are made by 'strangers', who could be seen as constituting business angels (Bygrave and Hunt, 2005).

It is essential that business angels should be seen as conceptually distinct from 'love money' invested by family and friends. Angel investment is primarily commercially oriented, with the caveat that some business angels are willing to trade off some commercial returns against altruistic considerations (Wetzel, 1981; Sullivan, 1994), whereas love money is not. Indeed, 51 per cent of all informal investors expected a zero or negative return from their investments, while 'strangers' was the only category of investor who expected a positive return on their investment. Investments by strangers were also more than twice the size of the investments made by other types of informal investor (Bygrave and Hunt, 2005). Love money is also more likely to be a one-off investment. Moreover, an angel investment is not constrained whereas love money is, by definition, restricted to situations in which there is a family or friendship connection between the investor and the entrepreneur. Adding to the definitional confusion is that a clear distinction can be made between immediate family members and others, whereas the definition of a friend is much more problematic: surveys of 'pure' business angels have consistently identified social, as well as business, networks as sources used to identify potential investment opportunities. To complicate matters even further, the same individual can make both 'love money' and angel investments.

Government efforts to stimulate business angel investing through the tax system can create further definitional complications. Considering just the UK experience – the Enterprise Investment Scheme (EIS) and its predecessor, the Business Expansion Scheme (BES) – both attracted a proportion of passive investors, often investing through intermediaries, and enabling investments in asset-backed businesses, neither of which would be regarded as meeting the definition of angel investing. The introduction of social investment tax relief, similar to the EIS, enabling individuals making an eligible investment in a social enterprise to deduct 30 per cent of the cost of their investment from their income tax liability, is breaking the link with the commercial orientation of business angel investing.

The first essential step before we can go on to consider means of identifying business angels is to bring some greater clarity to definitional and measurement issues. There are four features that are regarded as being fundamental to business angels and their investments and distinguish this form of investing from other types of investment (Mason, 2006).

- First, angels are *investing their own money*. This feature of angel investing has never been questioned, although it does occasionally arise as an issue, notably when an angel syndicate changes from investing the money of its members to investing other people's money (for example, Knighton, 1996) or sets up a side-car fund into which non-syndicate members can invest and which invests alongside syndicate members.
- Second, business angels are *investing in private unquoted companies* as opposed to businesses that are quoted on a stock market (and are therefore willing to accept the potential loss of liquidity that goes with such investments).
- Third, angels are making *direct investments*. This was originally intended to convey the point that no intermediary was involved. However, with the emergence of angel groups this attribute is no longer always present. Instead, the sense of this aspect should be that business angels are *making their own investment decisions*. Even if the opportunity is presented to an angel group, the angels still have to make their own individual decision whether or not to invest (Sudek, 2006). Conversely, situations in which an individual has invested in a pooled investment vehicle, where the allocation of this money to specific investments is made by a manager (even if the investee companies were unquoted), would be regarded as retail (or collective) investing rather than angel investing.
- Finally, angel investing primarily involves seeking *commercial returns*. US research has established that 'typical' business angels may be motivated in part by non-financial considerations and may even be willing to trade off such considerations against financial return (Wetzel, 1981; Sullivan, 1994). This suggests that 'socially motivated' investors can be accommodated within the conventional business angel definition as long as they perceive their investee business(es) to be an investment rather than charity and that they make their own investment decision. Other motives include satisfaction from being involved in starting a new business (which might be termed psychic income), as a hobby (for example, because retirement is boring), to

'buy' a job for themselves and to support the community (Shane, 2009).

A further feature of the standard definition of a business angel investment is that it is a hands-on investment. This conflicts with empirical evidence that a significant and increasing minority of angels take a passive role in their investments. It is important here to distinguish between investors and investments. Investors who are passive in some deals, typically because there are co-investors present, and hands-on in other deals, should certainly be regarded as business angels. However, it might be questionable whether an investor who is passive in every investment can be defined as a business angel – yet many members of angel groups will be in this position. Accordingly, this aspect might be modified to say that 'the investor, *or a co-investor*, will play a hands-on role': the definition of a business angel investor in this case will rely on the other characteristics being met.

There are a number of additional definitional issues. The first concerns investing in family businesses. As discussed earlier, a strong case can be made for arguing that investments in businesses owned by family members should be excluded on the grounds that they are conceptually distinct from business angel investments. This is not to deny the importance of the role of the family in funding entrepreneurial ventures. Indeed, the availability of family funding is likely to be an important factor in explaining several aspects of new firm formation, such as why some individuals are able to start businesses while others do not, the ability of some businesses to successfully negotiate the start-up process, and local and regional variations in business start-up and survival rates. It is axiomatic that access to finance from family members is constrained by ties of blood and marriage, and so it is only available to other family members. Accordingly, it does not constitute a market. This source of potential funding is closed off to entrepreneurs who are unfortunate enough to come from impoverished families. Moreover, investing in a family member's business is unlikely to be made for commercial reasons. Investment in businesses owned by friends is rather more problematic. However, it would be inappropriate to restrict the definition of business angel investments to those in which the investor and entrepreneur are strangers since, according to Atkin and Eseri (1993), many angel deals arise from chance encounters with friends and associates. Thus, the key criterion for non-family investments is that they should have a commercial orientation.

A second issue concerns whether the focus should only be on 'active' angels. The population of business angels is not fixed or static. Rather, being a business angel is a transitory state. A 'virgin' angel is someone who is looking to make their first investment. Most studies have identified these as comprising a significant minority of respondents. Since most of these studies have been based on the membership of an angel network that typically requires payment, this can be regarded as a strong indicator that these individuals have a high level of commitment to making investments (although this does not succeed in totally eliminating the 'voyeur' element). However, this assumption may be harder to sustain when respondents are allowed to self-define themselves as angels. Another problematic category is 'dormant' angels – individuals who have made one or more investments but are not currently looking to make new investments, perhaps because they have no further liquidity (but may become active investors again once they realise cash from a successful exit event). A further category is latent investors – individuals who would not describe themselves as active investors but who will invest opportunistically if suitable deals 'pop up'. Including 'virgin' angels, 'dormant' angels and 'latent angels' has the potential to overestimate the population of angels and the amount of funding available. So, if, as Atkin and Eseri (1993) suggest, angel investing involves a lot of opportunism then the appropriate basis for any definition should be on the basis of their activity rather than their intentions. Nevertheless, the assessment of potential investment (from latent, dormant and virgin angels) has important policy implications, specifically arising from an understanding of the determinants of their 'conversion' into active investors and, as a consequence, increases the supply of entrepreneurial risk capital in the market.

A third, and related, issue concerns amounts of money available for investment. It is clear from studies that have asked investors to report how much money they have available to make further investments that these numbers need to be treated with considerable scepticism. Many angels do not allocate a fixed sum to this type of investing and make adjustments depending on the number of suitable opportunities available. If an angel found a good investment that exceeded the funds they had for investment then they may bring in a co-investor (Mason and Rogers, 1997). A study undertaken on behalf of the NatWest Bank noted that the potential amounts that individuals had available was depended on their liquidity, the opportunity and the follow-on financing needs of their existing portfolio (Innovation Partnership, 1993). Finally, investors may indicate an 'in principle' commitment of funds to this investment activity but never actualise it, because of changes in personal circumstances, changes in investment preferences or difficulty in finding investment opportunities.

A fourth important insight from previous research is the skewed nature of the business angel population. Based on the amount invested some studies have referred to a 'dual population' – Hindle and Wenban (1999) used the terms 'seraphim' (the highest order of angels) and 'cherub' (a second order angel) to denote the two distinct categories of angels that they identified in Australia. A category of 'super-angels' has also been identified. These are defined as angel investors who have the capacity to invest in excess of hundreds of thousands of dollars per year, year on year (Sudek et al., 2011). This has two implications. First, the size distribution of investments (whether by investor or transaction) is positively skewed: there are many investors who have invested small amounts but relatively few angels who have invested large amounts. However, the aggregate distribution of amounts invested is negatively skewed. The relatively small number of angels making large investments contribute disproportionately to total investment activity. Second, the frequency of investing is also positively skewed. Most angels have made relatively few investments (less than five) but there are a minority of much more active investors who have a disproportionate effect on overall market activity. Particular data sources may be biased to particular ends of the distribution. Specifically, business angels who are members of business angel networks may be biased towards the right hand of the distribution – comprising more frequent investors. Indeed, the debate between Mason and Harrison and Stevenson and Coveney over their starkly contrasting estimates of business angel activity stemmed from their contrasting approaches to identifying business angels that involved over-sampling from the extremes of the distribution. Mason and Harrison (1994, 1997) over-sampled from the left hand of the distribution while Stevenson and Coveney (1994, 1996) over-sampled from the right-hand tail because they surveyed subscribers to a high price investment opportunities magazine that was not cost-effective for small, infrequent investors to purchase. One of the implications is that diverse data sources should be used to identify business angels in order to reduce the effect of the bias in any individual source (Mason and Harrison, 1997).

Fifth, the way in which the angel market is evolving, notably with the creation of managed angel groups (Sohl, 2007; Mason et al., 2013), raises new definitional issues. Angel groups do not invest as a whole; rather, each angel decides independently whether to invest.[1] However, there are variations between angel groups. The key distinction is between those groups in which each member takes an active role in the investment opportunity identification, screening and investment processes and those that operate on a 'core–periphery' basis, with a small core of active investors offering passive members of the group the opportunity to invest in deals that they are offered but had no role in identifying, evaluating or negotiating and will not play any hands-on role in the investee businesses (for example, see Gregson et al., 2013). This second group might be considered to have diverged from some aspects of the conventional definition of a business angel. Nevertheless, as the members are investing their own money on a deal-by-deal basis and making a basic investment decision (yes or no) they can still be considered to be business angels. Rather more problematic are those groups that operate on the basis of angels pooling their investment funds and devolving the investment decisions to the syndicate leaders. The reality of angel investing is therefore that it operates on a spectrum, occupied at one end by the solo investor who makes his or her own investment decision to invest directly, and at the other end by investors who are part of angel groups who simply say 'yes' or 'no' to the investment opportunities that they are offered and play no direct hands-on role in the investee company. The hands-off investor who invests in a pooled fund, and delegates the decision on which investments to make, would not be considered to be a business angel on the basis of the definition adopted here.

Finally, another new development – crowdfunding, or, to be precise, crowdinvesting or equity crowdfunding – also has the potential to confuse the definition of business angels. It can be argued that equity crowdfunding platforms allow anyone to be a business angel, particularly if there is no minimum size of investment. However, at least in the USA crowdfunding platforms are limited to accredited investors. There is clearly an overlap, with one survey reporting that 22 per cent of business angels had also invested via a crowdfunding platform (Mason and Botelho, 2014). However, as Hornuf and Schwienbacher (see Chapter 15, this volume) point out, there are some significant differences between crowdinvesting and angel investing, notably, the use of a standardised contract by the platform, the limited scope to undertake personal due diligence on the investment beyond what the platform provides, the limited types of investment instruments available to invest and hence the limited scope for downside protection. Crowdinvesting is also unlikely to enable investors to play a hands-on role in their investee businesses. However, as crowdinvesting matures it may become more common to see business angels playing a complementary role with equity crowdfunding platforms, co-investing with the crowd (and thereby raising the proportion of the funding target that the business has reached), providing follow-on funding to businesses that were initially crowdfunded (although anecdotal evidence indicates that some angels would be uncomfortable investing in a business that already has multiple shareholders) or co-investing alongside a crowdfunding platform as part of a funding 'bundle' (Baldock and Mason, 2014).

It is important that researchers as far as possible operate to a common definition of business angels, albeit with the recognition that this definition may need to evolve. The definition of business angels as 'high net worth individuals who invest their own money, along with their time and expertise, directly in unquoted companies in which they have no family connection, in the hope of financial gain' (Mason, 2006, p. 261) has been used in several studies, indicating broad acceptance. It captures the key distinctive features of business angels but, as the preceding discussion has indicated, is sufficiently flexible to accommodate changes in the nature of angel investing.

## 2.3 IDENTIFYING BUSINESS ANGELS: A REVIEW OF SAMPLING STRATEGIES

As noted earlier, the various directories and databases of venture capital firms do not have any equivalent in the world of business angels. They typically do not go out of their way to indicate that they are business angels, nor is there any need for them to do so. As a consequence, they are largely invisible. Researchers have therefore had to use various indirect approaches to identify samples of business angels but with no way to test for their representativeness. With the emergence of institutions such as angel networks and angel groups an important part of the angel market is now at least semi-visible, with angels being potentially contactable via the managers of these intermediary organisations. Indeed, many studies have been based on such 'samples of convenience' but without considering the biases that might be involved. Furthermore, the difficulty of finding business angels has meant that most samples are small, which adds to the representativeness problem and makes it problematic to extrapolate from sample results to derive population estimates of activity with any degree of robustness.

This section reviews the various approaches used by researchers to identify business angels. The structure of this discussion reflects the emerging division of the angel market between the traditional invisible market comprising angels operating on their own and in ad hoc groups and an emerging visible market comprising angels investing via networks and groups. We discuss each of these markets separately.

### 2.3.1 Invisible Market

**Snowball sampling**

Snowball sampling is possibly the most common approach in the early studies of business angels. For example, in their study of business angels in Ottawa, Riding and Short (1989) used three sources for snowball sampling: professional advisers, local entrepreneurs and other investors. Other studies using snowball sampling include Tymes and Krasner (1983), Landström (1993), Mason and Rogers (1997) and Lumme et al. (1998). It involves the identification of an initial, generally small, set of respondents who are then asked to provide connections to others. This approach therefore involves relatively little effort in comparison to other approaches and generally has a high response rate (Sørheim and Landström, 2001). However, the key disadvantage is that it will reproduce any biases in the initial set of contacts because respondents are likely to refer to others with similar characteristics.

**Mailing lists**

One of the limitations of snowball sampling is that it generates small samples. Mailing lists comprising individuals who match the key characteristics of business angels has been the most common approach used by the early angel studies that sought to achieve larger numbers of responses than normally achievable through snowball sampling. This includes mailing lists that were purchased from list brokers, memberships of associations and contacts of various types of intermediaries and gatekeepers.

Wetzel (1981) pioneered this approach, using the following lists: high income investors, presidents of major New England companies, colleague alumni from top New England professional schools; New England certified public accountants (CPAs), attorneys and bank chief executive officers (CEOs); participants in the 1980 White House Conference on small business; subscribers to *Inc Magazine*; owners of Mercedes Benz cars; and gatekeepers of various professional associations for small businesses, bankers and securities dealers. Haar et al. (1988) used a similar approach, mailing questionnaires to MBA alumni, members of a venture group, dentists, subscribers to an entrepreneurial magazine and members of a business angel network. Postma and Sullivan (1990) mailed questionnaires to accountants, attorneys, brokers, health care professionals, top management of local businesses, commercial bankers and members of entrepreneurship networking groups. In the UK Mason and Harrison (1994) used contacts of an investment syndicate, owner managers of small and medium-sized enterprises (SMEs), high income groups, investors in junior market stocks. Reitan and Sørheim (2000) used members of the national share investment association, contacts of a private consulting firm specialising in capital raising and investor forums to identify business angels in Norway. Riding et al. (1993) used the contacts of intermediary organisations such as boards of trade, chambers of commerce and regional development associations to identify angel investors in Canada. Lumme et al. (1998) relied, in part, on science park managers and venture capital fund managers to identify business angels in Finland. The inherent bias in any particular individual list can be offset by the use of multiple lists.

The general consensus is that such lists are ineffective in identifying business angels, generating extremely low response rates. For example,

Mason and Harrison (1994) achieved just 60 usable responses from over 4000 mailings. However, there is considerable variation in responses, with some lists – primarily those with an 'investor' orientation – generating much higher rates. For example, Møen et al. (2008) achieved a 15.8 per cent response rate from mailing to a variety of lists dominated by members of the Norwegian Share Investment Association. But as there is no way of differentiating between non-respondents who are business angels from those who are not, it is questionable whether a response rate is actually meaningful. A further concern is that using mailing lists is tautological – the selection of mailing lists is informed by a view of what business angels look like (for example, high net worth, entrepreneurs, active stock market investors and so on) but the responses are then used to provide a profile of business angels (high net worth, entrepreneurs and so on). Respondents to surveys based on mailing lists may therefore not be representative of the business angel population – but since the population in unknown and probably unknowable (Wetzel, 1981) it is impossible to be sure. All of this suggests that mailing lists are problematic as a means of generating samples of business angels.

**General surveys of the adult population**

General surveys of the population offer an alternative approach that avoids the limitations inherent in both snowball surveys and the use of mailing lists, overcomes the invisibility of angels and can also generate larger samples. Population surveys have the advantage of representativeness and if sufficiently extensive can also generate large samples. However, because business angels are relatively rare, general surveys may be unable to generate a sample that is sufficiently large to capture the diversity of the angel population.

The angel literature features studies based on two different population surveys. The first is the Global Entrepreneurship Monitor (GEM), an international research programme involving scholars from over 50 countries. It is best known for identifying levels of entrepreneurial activity in each of the countries involved in the programme. This is based on asking respondents in a telephone survey whether they are in the process of starting a business or have started a business within the previous 42 months. GEM also asks respondents whether they have invested in someone else's firm in the previous three years (excluding buying publicly traded shares and mutual funds) and, if so, how much did they invest and what was the relationship with the business owner. Sample sizes are at least 2000 in each country, surveys are administered by professional market research companies and conducted by telephone and samples weighted to be representative of the adult population.

As discussed earlier, several studies have used GEM in an effort to gain a better understanding of informal venture capital investing. Bygrave et al. (2003) examined informal investing in 18 GEM countries for which there was data for more than 40 investors. The prevalence ranged from under 2 per cent to over 6 per cent (in the USA and New Zealand, respectively), with an average of 3.4 per cent. Some 48 per cent of investors invested in a relative's business, 29 per cent in a friend or neighbour's business, 11 per cent in a work colleague's business and 8 per cent in a stranger's business. Bygrave and Reynolds (2004) have made a separate analysis of informal investing in the USA from 1998 to 2003. The prevalence of informal investing was 5 per cent, and the annual amount invested was $108 billion, almost 1 per cent of gross domestic product (GDP). More than 50 per cent of informal investing goes to a relative's business, 29 per cent to a friend or neighbour's business, 6 per cent to a work colleague's business and 9 per cent to a stranger's business. Wong and Ho (2007) have also used GEM to examine informal investing in Singapore. They note that 42 per cent of investments are in businesses started by family members. The remainder are dominated by investments in businesses started by friends and neighbours: only 2 per cent of investors have provided finance to entrepreneurs with whom they are not personally acquainted. Thus, it is clear that regardless of country, informal investment is dominated by investments in the businesses of family members, with investments in the businesses of friends and neighbours and work colleagues also significant, some of which may qualify as business angel investment as we have defined it. The inability to unequivocally separate out these two conceptually discrete categories of investment makes this data source a very imperfect basis for examining business angel investment trends.

A significant development in the use of GEM data is offered by Maula et al. (2005) who studied informal investors in Finland, pooling three years of GEM data for the years 2000 to 2002. The prevalence rate of informal investors was 2.9 per cent. Half of the investments were in the businesses of close family or other relatives. The key contribution of this study was to separately distinguish investments in businesses owned by close family from other investments. They found that the predicated determinants of investing provided a better explanation for investing in firms owned by other than close family members. One of the advantages of this approach is the pooling of data over, in this case, three years. This offers the ability to run more robust sophisticated analyses using pooled cross-sectional data.

GEM, as presently constituted, therefore has a number of limitations and deficiencies that reduces its potential for generating evidence on business angel investment activity. First, whereas it identifies investors the information on their investments is limited. Second, GEM covers both business angel investment and affinity investment in the businesses of family and friends. It is therefore capturing and measuring a much broader range of investment activity than just business angels. Moreover, investors can have dual status – they can make investments in the businesses of close family investors as well as in businesses owned by non-family members. However, GEM allocates investors to a binary category based on their most recent investment. Third, given the rarity of business angels even a comparatively large sample size, such as UK GEM, still contains relatively few angels. This has implications for the sample errors of estimates of changes in the scale of the market over time, with year-on-year changes in investment activity having to be fairly large to register as statistically significant.

An alternative approach is offered by Avdeitchikova et al. (2008) who have undertaken a random population survey in an effort to identify business angels in Sweden. A market research company was contracted to undertake the initial screening survey of more than 40,000 individuals (more than 10 times the size of the GEM sample) to identify business angels. The screening question was as follows: 'Have you invested money in unquoted companies that did not belong to yourself or to a member of your family within the past five years.' Just over 24,000 answered this screening question, a 59.9 per cent response rate. From this survey 861 responded affirmatively to the screening question, implying that they were business angels, 3.6 per cent of the total. Social security numbers – which provided current contact details – were obtained for 548 of these respondents who were contacted to ask if they would agree to a further interview by the researchers: 401 were successfully contacted. What is interesting is that 123 of these individuals were found not to meet the definition of a business angel, suggesting flaws in the initial screening survey. A further 32 declined to participate. This left 278 respondents who met the criteria and were interviewed, with information obtained on their investment history, personal background and three most recent investments. This information was used to extrapolate to the full population, making an adjustment to allow for those respondents who on closer examination were not angels. Extrapolation was made on the basis of the median, rather than the mean, value of investments. This was a one-off survey, with no time series information and would be expensive to replicate on a regular basis.

General population surveys are therefore able to generate an unbiased sample of business angels that is representative of the general population. If background information is available for the entire sample, then it is also possible to undertake a non-respondent analysis to examine response bias. Moreover, such studies can be replicated over time to generate longitudinal data. Nevertheless, the approach has some significant limitations. First is the high cost of implementing a population survey of sufficient size. This can be mitigated to some extent, as in the case discussed here, by participating in an omnibus survey, but that creates a new set of constraints. Second, respondents may misunderstand the definition of a business angel used in the screening question and as a result misrepresent themselves as business angels. In the Swedish case respondents were incorrectly defining themselves as business angels on the basis of investments in their own companies, in family businesses and in publicly traded companies (Avdeitchikova et al., 2008). A further implication of this study is that other population-based surveys such as GEM that do not use the double screening question may significantly overestimate the number of business angels in the population and hence the size of the market (Avdeitchikova et al., 2008). Third, the relative rarity of business angels requires a large sample to generate a reliability at ±2 per cent and a 95 per cent confidence level (Farrell et al., 2008). Fourth, even though this approach can be expected to generate a fairly representative sample of business angels the heterogeneity of the business angel population means that it may not generate sufficient numbers to capture specific sub-groups in the business angel population – for example, super-angels (Sudek et al., 2011), founder angels (Festel and De Cleyn, 2013) or women angels (Harrison and Mason, 2007; Sohl and Hill, 2007). For the same reason, this approach may be weak in revealing geographical variations in the presence of angels and their investment activity.

**Targeted population sub-groups**

As an alternative to mailing lists, several studies have focused on specific populations thought likely to contain high proportions of business angels. This subsection discusses three populations that have been targeted by researchers.

The first population is company owners. It is well established from the earliest studies that a majority of business angels are, or have been, entrepreneurs. Canada's SME Financing Data Initiative comprises both a demand side survey and a supply side survey. The demand side survey is a weighted sample of firms with up to 499 employees and less than CAN$50 million in gross revenues (with certain sectors excluded – financing and leasing companies, co-operatives, subsidiaries, not-for-profit organisations, government and other public sector organisations). The surveys have occurred on a biennial basis since 2001 and have provided the basis for several reports on SME financing. As part of this survey the sampled SME owners are asked 'whether, excluding publicly traded shares, market funds or stock, did the majority owners of this business make any investments in any other business at any time since [year]?'. The responses have been analysed by Riding (2006, 2008); 13.9 per cent of respondents could be defined as business angels, investing at arm's length in businesses that were not owned by family and friends. As some businesses take an active role in the businesses in which they invest, some of the 37.5 per cent of respondents who had operational roles in businesses that they invested that were not owned by family and friends were also likely to be business angels. From this evidence Riding was able to estimate the significance of business angels in Canada and the annual amount that they invest.

The logic and rigour makes this a very appealing methodology. It utilises an existing survey of SMEs. Unlike other firm-based surveys it is able to calculate estimates for both the flow and stock of angel capital. However, these figures are sensitive to the estimate of the proportion of business angels who are business owners that is used to scale-up the estimates to the entire population. But perhaps the main concern with this approach is evidence from previous research that some angels are cashed-out entrepreneurs who have sold their business and so are no longer business owners.

A second approach is to sample from business registrations – the broad array of registrations of incorporations, partnerships and sole proprietors that are overseen by government bodies. These registers provide specific details of all legally operating companies (Farrell et al., 2008). This approach was used by Farrell (1998) in a study on behalf of the Atlantic Canada Opportunities Agency (ACOA) which sought to identify business angels amongst those individuals who are closely associated with newly incorporated companies – entrepreneur, director, agent, lawyer or investor. Her sample was drawn from the more than 35,000 new company incorporations in Atlantic Canada in the period 1992 to 1997. However, she was only able to interview 328 individuals from the 1408 incorporations sampled. Reasons for this high attrition rate were as follows: unable to find a phone number (45 per cent); disconnected phone line (7 per cent); no response (9 per cent); call back never fulfilled (28 per cent); and reached but refused (11 per cent). Of the 328 interviewed, 95 (20 per cent) had invested their own money in a new or expanding business that was largely operated and managed by someone else. These individuals provided information on themselves and their investments. One in ten new incorporations had a business angel investor. From all of this information it was possible to make an estimate of business angel investment activity in Atlantic Canada. Farrell extended this approach for her PhD by making contact with a further 1101 principals from a further sample of newly incorporated companies in Atlantic Canada (Farrell and Howorth, 2003). This sample contained 141 business angels (12 per cent) divided almost equally between novice and habitual investors. These investors were grouped into three categories:

- Those who had made just one investment that was in a family firm (33 investors).
- Those who had made both family and arm's length investments (16 investors).
- Those who had only invested at arm's length (92 investors).

This approach avoids most of the biases that are inherent in other studies. However, there may be fees to pay to access the data (Farrell et al., 2008). The disadvantage is that it cannot identify angels who have chosen not to be listed as a director in their investee companies. As passive investors are least likely to become directors this source may be biased to those angels who adopt a hands-on approach to their investments.

Information that is held by securities regulators may also be a means of targeting business angels. For example, securities legislation may relieve some firms from the costly necessity of developing a prospectus when raising private equity to reduce the cost and time involved in raising finance from private individuals. Such firms would be permitted to offer and sell their shares to 'accredited investors' without the need to meet the prospectus and ongoing disclosure requirements of securities legislation (Preston, 2007). Accredited investors are defined in terms of net worth or income. Such investors would appear to offer a rigorous and well-focused means of defining business angels. Indeed, a simple headcount by the securities authority would provide an indication of trends in numbers of business angels and a regular survey of such investors could gather information on investment activity. However, only one study has used this type of data. Robinson and Cottrell (2007) have studied 'informal' investors who are exempt under the Alberta (Canada) securities legislation (which is a provincial responsibility). They are of three types:

- Family, friends and business associates of the principals of the firm ('relational investing').
- Offering Memorandum and Short Form Offering Prospectus – which covers individuals with small pools of capital for investing in early stage businesses on an ad hoc basis ('opportunity-based investing').
- Sophisticated and Accredited investors – which covers individuals who are able to make informed investment decisions and those who meet minimum income and asset tests and so are able to absorb an

investment loss (such investors would meet the typical definition of a business angel).

Firms that rely on exemptions to sell securities to Albertans are required to file an exemption report with the provincial securities commission. Robinson and Cottrell (2007) used this data to compare the investment behaviour of these three types of investor.

**Firm surveys**

A very different approach used in three regional studies funded by the US Small Business Administration (SBA) in the mid 1980s was to identify business angels through the firms in which they had invested. These studies covered: (1) mid-Atlantic, South Central and Southeast states (Gaston and Bell, 1986); (2) urban areas contiguous to the eastern Great Lakes (Arum Research Associates, 1987; Arum, 1989); and (3) all regions not covered in the previous studies (Gaston and Bell, 1988). Uniformity of design, procedures and key results permitted merger of these three surveys into a single database on informal investment in the USA that was used by Gaston (1989a) to profile the US informal venture capital market and by Gaston and Bell (1988) and Gaston (1989b) to estimate the scale of angel investing in the USA.

The procedure for gathering data involved two stages. First, a representative sample of 240,000 businesses with less than 500 employees was selected from the Dun and Bradstreet file. These businesses were asked if they had any business angels and, if so, to provide their contact details. Second, questionnaires were sent directly to the 2900 individuals who had been identified in this way: 551 were completed and returned, of which 435 were usable. These questionnaires provided information on both investors and businesses receiving informal investment. The stock of investors was estimated by multiplying the total number of firms in the USA by the proportion that were identified as having business angels, adjusting to take account of the average number of investors per firm, multiple investments made by investors and the average holding period. All of these measures were derived from the questionnaires completed by investors. This estimated figure for the stock of investors was multiplied by the average annual investment rate of investors to derive an estimate of annual investment activity. This figure was multiplied by the average size of equity investment to calculate the annual dollar level of investments. The process was replicated to estimate the value of loans and loan guarantees provided by investors. On the basis of this approach Gaston (1989b) estimated that business angels in the USA in the 1980s were providing capital to over 40 times the number of firms receiving institutional venture capital, and that the amount of capital they invested almost exceeded all other sources of external equity capital for new and growing businesses combined.

There are two main criticisms of this approach. First, it requires a huge upfront investment in the firm survey to generate a relatively small number of usable responses from angels. This reflects a combination of the rarity of informal investing and low response rates. In the case of the eastern Great Lakes region study, 40,000 firms were randomly selected (out of 470,000 small businesses). This led to the identification of 200 firms that had investors. This produced 68 responses, 55 of which were usable, after extensive chasing, involving up to four telephone calls per investor (Arum Research Associates, 1987). Second, the component statistics that are used to calculate the national estimate of informal investment activity are all based on estimates. Moreover, the approach used does not permit the measurement of statistical confidence limits. Gaston (1989b) sought to defend the validity of the approach by testing his estimate for plausibility against other information.

**Investment data**

It might have been expected that angel investors could be identified from either commercial or government databases. Wong (2002) notes that there are no commercial databases that record angel investment information. Angel investments can therefore only be identified on an ad hoc basis. Moreover, the coverage of commercial databases is skewed to large angel investments. Incorporated companies are required to file details of investments received, where such investment results in the issue of shares. In the UK this information is filed with Companies House. This source has been used to study the Scottish risk capital market (Harrison and Don, 2004, 2006; Harrison et al., 2010; Harris and Mason, 2012). Vo (2013) has also used the Company Share register in British Columbia. However, investor share information has several problems. First, angel investors are not flagged up. Hence, short of examining every entry – which is impractical given the number of companies involved – it is necessary to have external information to indicate that a share issue has taken place. With this information, attention can be focused on relevant companies. However, a second problem is that companies file under their incorporated name. Occasionally companies will operate under different brand names. Market comment on deals usually quotes the latter. This means that a widely publicised deal may be difficult or impossible to check. Companies also change names, form complex groups and transfer businesses between themselves, making tracking more difficult. Third, while all incorporated companies are under a legal obligation to file details of investments the obligation refers only to the issue of shares. But it is common practice to divide an investment between an equity instrument and one or more debt instruments. The latter – which may sometimes represent 95 per cent or more of a deal – will be invisible to an outside observer. Fourth, considerable market intelligence information is required to effectively search the company filings. It is sometimes difficult to distinguish accurately between founders and business angels in the filings. An early business angel investor may become actively involved for a year or two and look like a founder to the outside world, but like an investor to the original entrepreneurs. Specifically, while name and address details are provided, there is no indications as to the provenance of the investor shareholders and their relationship to the business. Additional and sometimes extensive work is required to classify investors, identify 'insiders' (principals in the business) from 'outsiders' and separate family investors (who may not, of course, share surnames in common) from non-connected investors. And finally, a small number of business angels will use investment vehicles to manage their investments. In some cases, these vehicles may be based offshore to conceal their activities and/or manage their tax liabilities. While many of these vehicles can be accurately attached to given individuals, some cannot, muddying the distinction between angel and institutional investment.

### 2.3.2 The Visible Market: Angel Networks and Groups

The angel market has shifted over the past 30 years from one of total invisibility to the present situation in which it has split into two segments, one that is visible and the other that remains invisible. The emergence of a visible segment reflects the partial institutionalisation of the market. The initial institutions were business angel networks, established to overcome the high search costs of entrepreneurs seeking business angels and business angels seeking investment opportunities (Wetzel, 1984; Harrison and Mason, 1996a, 1996b; Collewaert et al., 2010). The earliest Business Angel Networks (BANs) were established as economic development initiatives with their costs underwritten by government agencies. Subsequently, private sector BANs were established. They were fee-based, with the fee related to the size of the investment and therefore tended to focus on larger deals (Mason and Harrison, 1997). With the decline in public sector support for BANs, especially in the UK, the number of BANs has declined. Since the turn of the twenty-first century there has been a growth of a second type of institution, the managed angel group. A key driver in their emergence was the decline in venture capital funds that angels used to look to for follow-on funding for their portfolio businesses, forcing angels in make follow-on investments. By joining with other angels this provided the necessary 'deep pockets' to be able to make follow-on investments. Other benefits included the opportunity for angels to diversify, superior deal flow and the opportunity to benefit from the collective skills and experience of other members of the group in the evaluation of investment opportunities and value-added contributions after the investment had been made. Angel groups have also been attractive to more passive angels who lack the time, networks or skills to invest independently, thereby increasing the supply of angel capital. Typically, angel groups have a manager – either a hired professional or one of the members of the group – who will seek deal flow and undertake the initial screening. Angels make their own investment decisions whether to invest in those deals that pass this stage (Sudek, 2006; Mason et al., 2013).

BANs and angel groups are generally visible and accessible and have membership records that it may be possible to access as sources of data or for survey purposes. As such, they represent a relatively low cost mechanism for collecting data, and are used in this context. However, there are also several significant limitations. In particular, the coverage of the market is incomplete – with only a minority of business angels who are members of networks and groups. However, the proportion of angels who are members of angel networks and groups is unknown.

BANs have been widely used to generate samples of business angels for closer study, particularly in the UK. For example, Mason and Harrison (2002a) surveyed members of the National Business Angel Network to examine the barriers that angels encountered in making investments. In another study based on questionnaires that BANs sent out to their members Mason and Harrison (2002b) reported on the returns that angels have received from their investments. A further study of women business angels was based on questionnaires sent by BAN managers to their members (Harrison and Mason, 2007). Other studies that have used angel networks to access samples of angels include Kelly and Hay (2000, 2003), Paul et al. (2003, 2007) and Stedler and Peters (2003). A related approach has been to attract responses from angels attending investment conferences (Mason and Harrison, 2000, 2003) and investment forums organised by angel networks (Clark, 2008).

The longitudinal nature of BAN data has been used to examine changes in the angel market. Two studies can be noted. First, Freear et al. (1993) used the investor registration forms for the period 1985 to 1992 for the Venture Capital Network (VCN), based in New England, one of the earliest established BANs that sought to introduce investors and business angels using computer software. The forms profiled investor characteristics and preferences, investments and the extent of their involvement in their investee businesses. Simple analysis of this data was effective in highlighting the declining pace of angel investment activity over this period, one of economic decline.

Second, in the UK information was collected and reported on investments made through BANs on an annual basis from 1993–94 through to 2003, initially on behalf of the British Venture Capital Association and then for the National Business Angel Network (NBAN), and linked to the publication by these organisations of an annual directory of angel networks. Response rates by BANs were generally very high (over 90 per cent) and the quality of the information provided was good. This is because many BANs were remunerated by a success fee so had a vested interest in tracking the outcomes of the introductions that they made. Some BANs were also very involved in the investments as an honest broker. Missing information was only a significant problem in two situations: breaking down amounts invested when there were two or more investors and knowledge about the co-investors in a deal. Data collection ceased after 2003 following the demise of NBAN. Mason (2006) used this data to provide a detailed analysis of business angel investment trends from 1993–94 to 2003. This highlighted the increasing volume of activity on all indicators (investors, deals, amount) from 1993–94 to 1997–98; the increasing amounts invested from 1997–98 to 2001 but static trends in investors and investments; and the decline in number of investors and amount invested in 2001 and 2002 but some recovery in 2003. In terms of investment characteristics, the main trends were as follows:

- Increase in the average size of investments up to 2001, then a decline.
- Increasing number of deals involving groups of angels and a dramatic decline in solo investors.
- A gradual shift to bigger deal sizes in parallel with a growth in smaller individual investments.
- An increasing focus on technology investments in terms of their share of the total number of investments.

More detailed analysis of the UK's business angel market was produced in two annual reports published by the Department for Business, Innovation and Skills (BIS) based on data provided by the networks and groups that were members of the UK Business Angels Association (UKBAA) (Mason and Harrison, 2010, 2011). This showed that angel investing had held up since the onset of the 2008 Global Financial Crisis. It also highlighted an increase in the proportion of deals in which angels invested alongside other investors (Mason and Harrison, 2015).

Angel groups are now emerging as significant players in the provision of start-up and early stage venture capital. Some groups are members of their national venture capital associations (for example, BVCA in the UK; NVCA in the USA) and their investments are reported as part of the association's annual report on investment activity. One side-effect of this is to disguise the extent to which venture capital funds have shifted away from making early stage investments. Jeffrey Sohl has pioneered the collection and reporting of angel group investment activity in the USA (for example, Sohl, 2012). The National Angel Capital Association of Canada has published five annual reports on angel investment activity based on information provided by its member groups.[2]

Researchers are increasingly using angel groups to access samples of angels, particularly for studies of investment decision-making (Sudek, 2006; Mitteness et al., 2012; Kerr et al., 2014; Parhankangas and Ehrlich, 2014; Carpentier and Suret, 2015). In many cases the angels are drawn from just one group. Several studies have been based on Tech Coast Angels. This practice is dubious. More generally, it can be questioned whether angels who join angel groups are distinctive from those who continue to operate on their own. Specifically, it seems likely that they will attract a proportion of passive investors. There may also be an age bias. There is evidence that older angels have joined angel groups after some time investing, presumably on their own, in the invisible market, whereas younger angels are more likely to start their investment career as part of an angel group (Mason and Botelho, 2014). Moreover, members of groups typically have less involvement in the investment process. The initial screening is usually carried out by the group's manager. Third, there is evidence that angels in groups are more likely to be influenced in their investment decision by the opinions of the group manager and other angels in the group (Mason and Botelho, 2014), which, in turn, might lead to 'group think'.

Notwithstanding the tip-of-the-iceberg issue, investment data from business angel networks and groups provides a unique and valuable insight into investment trends in a significant and growing segment of the angel market. They also provide a convenient sampling source if access can be negotiated with the individuals who perform the 'gatekeeping' function. However, such samples are likely to be unrepresentative of the wider population of angels.

## 2.4 CONCLUSION

Business angels play a critical role in supporting an entrepreneurial economy. Various studies suggest that they are the largest external source of start-up finance after family and friends, their investments fill the size, stage and sector gaps left by venture capital funds, and in many regions are virtually the only source of risk capital. Business angels are often responsible for providing the initial funding for young companies that achieve fast growth. Indeed, many angel syndicates have the capability to do multiple rounds of financing, sufficient to take the company to a trade sale or initial public offering (IPO) without the need to 'pass the baton' to venture capital funds. As experienced business people, in many cases as successful entrepreneurs, business angels also contribute valuable non-financial assistance to the businesses in which they invest. Policy-makers therefore need to understand how the business angel market works and be able to measure, monitor and, if appropriate, respond to trends in business angel investment activity. However, the invisibility of business angels and their investment activity is a major barrier to the development of information on business angel investment activity with our knowledge-base largely restricted to various ad hoc studies, mainly conducted by academic researchers. These are largely cross-sectional rather than longitudinal, small-scale, based on samples of convenience and increasingly use inconsistent definitions of business angel activity. In view of the priority that most governments give to removing financial barriers to small business growth there is an urgent need for better statistical information on business angel investment activity. Without improved statistical information there is a risk of inappropriate policy intervention.

This chapter has highlighted two major constraints on research on business angels. The first is the lack of a consistent definition of a business angel. There is a clear need for researchers to agree that business angels are a distinctive type of investor and reach consensus on their attributes. The adoption of GEM's unhelpful category of 'informal investment' needs to be resisted. It also requires a consensus on the definition of a business angel – that is, what should be measured. Although the definition of 'business angels' has become increasingly fuzzy at the edges, the key features that distinguish business angels from other types of 'informal' investors remain robust, namely:

- investing their own money
- making their own investment decision
- commercial considerations dominate the investment decision (although some investors may trade off part of the commercial return for non-financial considerations)
- excludes within-family investments
- involves 'hands-on' involvement with the investee company (if not by the investor then by a co-investor).

The collection of data must therefore be based on this rigorous definition of business angels.

The second constraint on research on angels is the lack of suitable data on both investors and their investments. This arises from their invisibility. Problems in identifying business angels have implication for sample sizes, the representativeness of samples and the types of analysis that are possible, comparability between studies and replication. The angel market place is becoming more organised and, as a consequence, more visible with the emergence of managed networks and groups. Indeed, these groups are now a significant investment category in their own right. There are over 240 angel groups and platforms that are members of the Angel Capital Association that covers the USA and Canada; these groups have over 13,000 member-accredited angel investors.[3] This growing significance would suggest that researchers and policy-makers should seek to work with angel groups and national angel associations where they exist to record the investments of angel groups on an annual basis and subject their investment processes and practices to greater scrutiny. However, there are three dangers. First, the focus may switch to the investment activity of the groups, with the group members being ignored. Second, researchers will use angel groups as samples of convenience (as is already the case) and ignore the distinctiveness of angels who have joined groups and the differences in the investment activities of group members and solo angels. Third, angels in the invisible market may become ignored. The existence of angel groups therefore does not avoid the need to continue to investigate angel activity in the invisible market. However, this will require imaginative thinking if the present data limitations are to be overcome. Governments could be lobbied to change the way that shareholding information is reported and for information on the users of tax schemes to be made accessible. Legal and accountancy professional bodies could be lobbied to report angel investments. GEM should also be encouraged to adjust its methodology for collecting investment data so that angel investments can be separately identified from other types of informal investing.

## NOTES

1. Several of these angel groups have been profiled in the scholarly literature (May and Simmons, 2001; Cerullo and Sommer, 2002; May, 2002; Payne and McCarty, 2002; May and O'Halloran, 2003; Gregson et al., 2013).
2. http://www.nacocanada.com/naco-academy/research/angel-activity-reports/.
3. http://www.angelcapitalassociation.org/directory/.

## REFERENCES


Arum Research Associates Inc. (1987), *Informal Risk Capital in the Eastern Great Lakes Region*, Washington, DC: US Small Business, Office of Advocacy.

Arum, J.D. (1989), 'Attitudes and behaviors of informal investors toward early stage investments, technology-based ventures and coinvestors', *Journal of Business Venturing*, **4**, 333–47.

Atkin, R. and M. Esiri (1993), 'Informal investment: investor and investee relationships', Paper presented at the 16th National Small Firms Policy and Research Conference, Nottingham, 17–19 November.

Avdeitchikova, S. (2008), 'On the structure of the informal venture capital market in Sweden: developing investment roles', *Venture Capital*, **10**(1), 55–85.

Avdeitchikova, S., H. Landström and N. Månsson (2008), 'What do we mean when we talk about business angels? Some reflections on definitions and sampling', *Venture Capital*, **10**(4), 371–94.

Baldock, R. and C. Mason (2014), 'Government intervention in the entrepreneurial finance market: the case of the UK's Angel Co-Fund', Paper presented at the 2014 ISBE Conference, Manchester, November.

Bygrave, W.D. and S.A. Hunt (2005), *Global Entrepreneurship Monitor: 2004 Financing Report*, Wellesley, MA and London: Babson College and London Business School.

Bygrave, W.D. and P.D. Reynolds (2004), 'Who finances startups in the USA? A comprehensive survey of informal investors, 1999–2003', Paper presented at the Babson-Kaufman Entrepreneurship Research Conference, University of Strathclyde, Glasgow, 3–5 June.

Bygrave, W.D., M. Hay, E. Ng and P. Reynolds (2003), 'A study of informal investing in 29 nations composing the Global Enterprise Monitor', *Venture Capital*, **5**, 101–16.

Carpentier, C. and J.-M. Suret (2015), 'Canadian business angel perspectives on exit: a research note', *International Small Business Journal*, **33**, 582–93.

Cerullo, B. and B. Sommer (2002), 'Helping healthcare entrepreneurs: a case study of Angel Healthcare Investors, LLC', *Venture Capital*, **4**, 325–30.

Clark, C. (2008), 'The impact of entrepreneurs' oral "pitch" presentation skills on business angels' initial screening investment decisions', *Venture Capital*, **10**, 257–79.

Collewaert, V., S. Manigart and R. Aernoudt (2010), 'Assessment of government funding of business angel networks in Flanders', *Regional Studies*, **44**(1), 119–30.

Coveney, P. and K. Moore (1998), *Business Angels: Securing Start-up Finance*, Chichester: Wiley.

Farrell, A.E. (1998), *Informal Venture Capital Investment in Atlantic Canada: A Representative View of Angels?*, St Mary's University, Halifax, Canada.

Farrell, E. and C. Howorth (2003), 'Definitional and sampling concerns regarding business angel research', Paper presented at the Babson-Kauffman Entrepreneurship Research Conference, Babson College, Wellesley, MA, March.

Farrell, E., C. Howorth and M. Wright (2008), 'A review of sampling and definitional issue in informal venture capital research', *Venture Capital*, **10**(4), 331–53.

Festel, G.W. and S.H. De Clyn (2013), 'Founding angels as an emerging subtype of the angel investment model in high-tech businesses', *Venture Capital*, **15**(3), 261–82,

Freear, J., J.E. Sohl and W.E. Wetzel Jr (1993), 'Angel profiles: a longitudinal study', Paper presented at the Babson Entrepreneurship Research Conference, University of Houston, June.

Freear, J., J.E. Sohl and W.E. Wetzel Jr (1994), 'Angels and non-angels: are there differences?', *Journal of Business Venturing*, **9**, 109–23.

Gaston, R.J. (1989a), *Finding Venture Capital for Your Firm: A Complete Guide*, New York: John Wiley and Sons.

Gaston, R.J. (1989b), 'The scale of informal capital markets', *Small Business Economics*, **1**, 223–30.

Gaston, R.J. and S.E. Bell (1986), *Informal Risk Capital in the Sunbelt Region*, Washington, DC: US Small Business, Office of Advocacy.

Gaston, R.J. and S.E. Bell (1988), *The Informal Supply of Capital*, Washington, DC: US Small Business, Office of Advocacy.
Gregson, G., S. Mann and R. Harrison (2013), 'Business angel syndication and the evolution of risk capital in a small market economy: evidence from Scotland', *Management and Decision Economics*, **34**(2), 95–107.
Haar, N., J. Starr and I.C. Macmillan (1988), 'Informal risk capital investors: investment patterns on the East Coast of the USA', *Journal of Business Venturing*, **3**, 11–29.
Harris, J. and C. Mason (2012), *The Risk Capital Market 2009–2011*, Edinburgh: Edinburgh House Publishing Ltd for Scottish Enterprise.
Harrison, R.T. and G. Don (2004), *The Equity Risk Capital Market in Scotland: A Benchmark Analysis and Report*, Glasgow: Scottish Enterprise.
Harrison, R.T. and G. Don (2006), *The Equity Risk Capital Market for Young Companies in Scotland 2000–2004*, Glasgow: Scottish Enterprise.
Harrison, R.T. and C.M. Mason (1996a), 'Developing the informal venture capital market: a review of DTI's Informal Investment Demonstration Projects', *Regional Studies*, **30**, 765–72.
Harrison, R.T. and C.M. Mason (eds) (1996b), *Informal Venture Capital: Evaluating the Impact of Business Introduction Services*, Hemel Hempstead: Prentice Hall.
Harrison, R.T. and C.M. Mason (2007), 'Does gender matter? Women business angels and the supply of entrepreneurial finance', *Entrepreneurship Theory and Practice*, **31**, 447–74.
Harrison, R.T., G. Don, K. Glancey and M. Greig (2010), 'The early stage risk capital market in Scotland since 2000: issues of scale, characteristics and market efficiency', *Venture Capital*, **12**(3), 211–39.
Hindle, K. and R. Wenban (1999), 'Australia's informal venture capitalists: an exploratory profile', *Venture Capital*, **1**, 169–86.
Infometrics Ltd (2004), *New Zealand's Angel Capital Market: The Supply Side*, Wellington: Ministry of Economic Development.
Innovation Partnership (1993), *Private Investor Networks*, a study commissioned by the National Westminster Bank plc, Manchester.
Kelly, P. and M. Hay (2000), 'Deal makers: reputation attracts quality', *Venture Capital*, **2**(3), 183–202.
Kelly, P. and M. Hay (2003), 'Business angel contracts: the influence of context', *Venture Capital*, **5**(4), 287–312.
Kerr, W.R., J. Lerner and A. Schoar (2014), 'The consequences of entrepreneurial finance: evidence from angel financings', *Review of Financial Studies*, **27**(1), 20–55.
Knighton, E. (1996), 'The role and potential of a formal investor syndicate: Priory Investments Limited', in R.T. Harrison and C.M. Mason (eds), *Informal Venture Capital: Evaluating the Impact of Business Introduction Services*, Hemel Hempstead: Prentice Hall, pp. 197–208.
Lahti, T. (2011), 'Categorization of angel investments: an explorative analysis of risk reduction strategies in Finland', *Venture Capital*, **13**(1), 49–74.
Landström, H. (1993), 'Informal risk capital in Sweden and some international comparisons', *Journal of Business Venturing*, **8**(6), 525–40.
Lumme, A., C. Mason and M. Suomi (1998), *Informal Venture Capital: Investors, Investments and Policy Issues in Finland*, Dordrecht, Netherlands: Kluwer Academic Publishers.
Macmillan, I.C. and J.A. Katz (1992), 'Idiosyncratic milieus of entrepreneurial research: the need for comprehensive theories', *Journal of Business Venturing*, **7**(1), 1–8.
Mason, C.M. (2006), 'The informal venture capital market in the United Kingdom: adding the time dimension', in J. Butler (ed.), *Research on Entrepreneurship and Management, Volume 5, Venture Capital and Entrepreneurship*, Greenwich, CT: Information Age Publishing, pp. 137–71.
Mason, C. and T. Botelho (2014), *The 2014 survey of Business Angel Investing in the UK: A Changing Market Place*, Adam Smith Business School, University of Glasgow.
Mason, C.M. and R.T. Harrison (1994), 'The informal venture capital market in the UK', in A. Hughes and D.J. Storey (eds), *Financing Small Firms*, London: Routledge, pp. 64–111.

Mason, C.M. and R.T. Harrison (1997), 'Business angels in the UK: a response to Stevenson and Coveney', *International Small Business Journal*, **15**(2), 83–90.
Mason, C.M. and R.T. Harrison (2000), 'Influences on the supply of informal venture capital in the UK: an exploratory study of investor attitudes', *International Small Business Journal*, **18**(4), 11–28.
Mason, C.M. and R.T. Harrison (2002a), 'Barriers to investment in the informal venture capital sector', *Entrepreneurship and Regional Development*, **14**, 271–87.
Mason, C.M. and R.T. Harrison (2002b), 'Is it worth it? The rates of return from informal venture capital investments', *Journal of Business Venturing*, **17**, 211–36.
Mason, C.M. and R.T. Harrison (2003), '"Auditioning for money": what do technology investors look for at the initial screening stage?', *Journal of Private Equity*, **6**(2), 29–42.
Mason, C.M. and R.T. Harrison (2010), *Annual Report on the Business Angel Market in the United Kingdom: 2008/09*, London: Department of Business, Innovation and Skills.
Mason, C.M. and R.T. Harrison (2011), *Annual Report on the Business Angel Market in the United Kingdom: 2009/10*, London: Department of Business, Innovation and Skills.
Mason, C.M. and R.T. Harrison (2015), 'Business angel investment activity in the financial crisis: UK evidence and policy implications', *Environment and Planning C; Government and Policy*, **33**(1), 43–60.
Mason, C. and A. Rogers (1997), 'The business angel's investment decision: an exploratory analysis', in D. Deakins, P. Jennings and C. Mason (eds), *Entrepreneurship in the 1990s*, London: Paul Chapman Publishing, pp. 29–46.
Mason, C., T. Botelho and R. Harrison (2013), 'The transformation of the business angel market: evidence from Scotland', Working Paper, Adam Smith Business School, University of Glasgow.
Maula, M., E. Autio and P. Arenius (2005), 'What drives micro-angel investments?', *Small Business Economics*, **25**(5), 459–75.
May, J. (2002), 'Structured angel groups in the USA: the Dinner Club experience', *Venture Capital*, **4**, 337–42.
May, J. and E.F. O'Halloran (2003), *Cutting Edge Practices in American Angel Investing*, Charlottesville, VA: Darden School, Batten Institute, University of Virginia.
May, J. and C. Simmons (2001), *Every Business Needs an Angel: Getting the Money You Need to Make Your Business Grow*, New York: Crown Business.
Mitteness, C.R., M.S. Baucus and R. Sudek (2012), 'Horse vs. jockey? How stage of funding process and industry experience affect the evaluations of angel investors', *Venture Capital*, **14**(4), 241–67.
Møen, O., R. Sørheim and T. Erikson (2008), 'Born global firms and informal investors: examining investor characteristics', *Journal of Small Business Research*, **46**(4), 36–54.
Parhankangas, A. and M. Ehrlich (2014), 'How entrepreneurs seduce business angels: an impression management approach', *Journal of Business Venturing*, **29**(4), 543–64.
Paul, S., G. Whittam and J. Johnston (2003), 'The operation of the informal venture capital market in Scotland', *Venture Capital*, **5**(4), 313–35.
Paul, S., G. Whittam and J. Wyper (2007), 'Towards a model of the business angel investment process', *Venture Capital*, **9**(2), 107–25.
Payne, W.H. and M.J. McCarty (2002), 'The anatomy of an angel investing network: Tech Coast Angels', *Venture Capital*, **4**, 331–6.
Postma, P.D. and M.K. Sullivan (1990), *Informal Risk Capital in the Knoxville Region*, Kentucky, TN: Center for Excellence for New Venture Analysis, College of Business Administration, University of Tennessee.
Preston, S.L. (2007), *Angel Financing for Entrepreneurs*, San Francisco, CA: Jossey Bass.
Reitan, B. and R. Sørheim (2000), 'The informal venture capital market in Norway – investor characteristics, behaviour and investment preferences', *Venture Capital*, **2**, 129–41.
Riding, A. (2006), 'Estimating informal investment in Canada', Paper presented at a SME FRI Workshop, Ottawa, 21 September.
Riding, A.L. (2008), 'Business angels and love money investors: segments of the informal market for risk capital', *Venture Capital*, **10**(4), 355–69.

Riding, A.L. and D.M. Short (1989), 'Informal investors in the Ottawa-Carleton region: experiences and expectations', *Entrepreneurship and Regional Development*, **1**(1), 99–112.
Riding, A.L., P. Dal Cin, L. Duxbury, G. Haines and R. Safrata (1993), *Informal Investors in Canada: The Identification of Salient Characteristics*, Ottawa: Carleton University.
Robinson, M.J. and T.J. Cottrell (2007), 'Investment patterns of informal investors in the Alberta private equity market', *Journal of Small Business Management*, **45**(1), 47–67.
Shane, S. (2009), *Fool's Gold: The Truth Behind Angel Investing*, Oxford and New York: Oxford University Press.
Sohl, J.E. (2007), 'The organisation of the informal venture capital market', in H. Landström (ed.), *The Handbook of Research on Venture Capital*, Cheltenham, UK and Northampton, MA, USA: Edward Elgar, pp. 347–68.
Sohl, J.E. (2012), 'The changing nature of the angel market', in H. Landström and C. Mason (eds), *The Handbook of Research on Venture Capital: Volume 2*, Cheltenham, UK and Northampton, MA, USA: Edward Elgar, pp. 17–41.
Sohl, J.E. and L. Hill (2007), 'Women business angels: insights from angel groups', *Venture Capital*, **9**(3), 207–22.
Sørheim, R. and H. Landström (2001), 'Informal investors – a categorisation with policy implications', *Entrepreneurship and Regional Development*, **13**, 351–70.
Stedler, H. and H.H. Peters (2003), 'Business angels in Germany: an empirical study', *Venture Capital*, **5**(3), 269–76.
Stevenson, H. and P. Coveney (1994), *Survey of Business Angels*, Henley-on-Thames, UK: Venture Capital Report Ltd.
Stevenson, H. and P. Coveney (1996), 'A survey of business angels', in R. Blackburn and P. Jennings (eds), *Small Firms: Contributions to Economic Regeneration*, London: Paul Chapman Publishing, pp. 37–48.
Sudek, R. (2006), 'Angel investment criteria', *Journal of Small Business Strategy*, **17**(2–3), 89–103.
Sudek, R., A. May and R. Wiltbank (2011), *Angel Investing: Catalyst for Innovation*, Salem, OR: Angel Resource Institute, Willemette University.
Sullivan, M.K. (1994), 'Altruism and entrepreneurship', in W.D. Bygrave, S. Birley, N.C. Churchill et al. (eds), *Frontiers of Entrepreneurship Research*, Babson Park, MA: Babson College, pp. 373–80.
Tymes, E.R. and O.J. Krasner (1983), 'Informal risk capital in California', in J.A. Hornaday, J.A. Timmons and K.H. Vesper (eds), *Frontiers of Entrepreneurship Research*, Babson Park, MA: Babson College, pp. 347–68.
Vo, D. (2013), 'The geography of angel investment', PhD thesis, University of Victoria, Canada.
Wetzel, W.E. (1981), 'Informal risk capital in New England', in K.H. Vesper (ed.), *Frontiers of Entrepreneurship Research*, Wellesley, MA: Babson College, pp. 217–45.
Wetzel Jr, W.E. (1983), 'Angels and Informal Risk Capital', *Sloan Management Review*, **24**(4), 23–34.
Wetzel Jr, W.E. (1984), 'Venture Capital Network Inc: an experiment in capital formation', in J. Hornaday, F. Tarplay J.A. Jr, Timmons and K.H. Vesper (eds), *Frontiers of Entrepreneurship Research*, Babson Park, MA: Babson College, pp. 111–25.
Wong, A. (2002), 'Angel finance: the other venture capital', University of Chicago Graduate School of Business, Working Paper, available at http://ssrn.com/abstract=941228.
Wong, P.K. and Y.P. Ho (2007), 'Characteristics and determinants of informal investment in Singapore', *Venture Capital*, **9**(1), 43–70.

# 3 The economic significance of business angels: toward comparable indicators

*Sofia Avdeitchikova and Hans Landström*

## 3.1 THE ROLE OF BUSINESS ANGELS IN THE ECONOMY: THE POTENTIAL FOR IMPACT

The importance of access to early-stage finance for fostering high-growth innovative entrepreneurship has been widely acknowledged in the literature. Business angels are believed to be one of the most important sources of funding for such early-stage, high-risk, high-potential ventures. However, their contribution to firms and to the economy may well go beyond that. In principle, four types of contribution can be distinguished:

1. Increasing the supply of financial capital. In countries where evidence of the scope of business angel activity is available, the data indicates that business angels provide as much or more capital to firms as formal venture capital investors and finance a great many more ventures (for example, Gaston, 1989; Mason and Harrison, 2000; Sohl, 2012). Thus, business angels contribute directly to increasing the flow of finance to firms. Furthermore, not just the quantity of finance provided by business angels is important, but also the type of finance. By primarily providing small amounts of finance in the early stages of a firm's development, business angels play a unique role in the small and medium-sized enterprise (SME) finance landscape.
2. Contributing to a venture's ability to attract more financing. As business angels mainly invest equity capital, their investments contribute to strengthening the firm's balance sheet, in contrast to loan financing that weakens a company's finances. Business angel investment can also send positive signals to other investors and the market (provided that the firm succeeds in attracting the 'right' business angel), reducing some of the informational asymmetry and leading to lower perceived risk for other financiers (cf. Elitzur and Gavious, 2003; Conti et al., 2011). This may in turn imply a larger pool of financing opportunities for these firms, better valuations (in cases of equity) and more favorable interest rates (in cases of loans).
3. Increasing the 'quality' of firms through value-adding activities.

Business angel investment is often associated with the active involvement of the investor, which can take the form of advising, coaching, providing access to the investor's network and so on. It can also be assumed that business angels add value faster and in a more flexible manner than many other investors such as venture capitalists and banks. Thus, firms that receive business angel funding potentially gain access to non-financial value, which can result in better prospects for development and growth (for example, increased productivity, profitability and level of innovation) compared to firms that use more traditional sources of funding.

4. Strengthening the entrepreneurial eco-system. Scholars have started to draw attention to business angels' role in entrepreneurial eco-systems (Zacharakis et al., 2003). As they are often active or former entrepreneurs themselves, many business angels are well networked in their local communities. Therefore, when a business angel acts by connecting firms to competence, intermediaries and so on, the entrepreneurial eco-system itself may benefit, which contributes to improved conditions for firm growth in the region. An eco-system with a high level of angel investing can also be perceived as more attractive for innovative start-ups, which can lead to increased start-up rates and growth of firms.

This brief overview illustrates that the contribution of business angels to funding entrepreneurial ventures can be discussed on different levels and that there are both input and effect dimensions to be considered. By the input dimension we mean the activities of business angels – what do business angels do? What is the nature of their contribution to the firms? How much do they invest and what do they invest in? By the effect dimension we mean – what are the outcomes of business angel financing? Does it have a positive impact on firms/regions/industries/countries?

In this chapter, we focus on the financial contributions of business angels at the macro (market) level. Thus, we do not cover their non-financial contribution; these aspects can be found in Chapter 7 in which Politis focuses on business angels as smart investors and in Chapter 8 where Collewaert discusses the business angel–entrepreneur relationship. Furthermore, we do not cover the effect dimension, as our focus is on the extent of business angel investing and not on the outcomes that it creates.

Due to its importance, the business angel market has attracted considerable interest among policy-makers around the world in recent decades (Mason, 2009; OECD, 2011; also see Chapter 13 by Carpentier and Suret on tax incentives). However, most of the policy initiatives to support business angel investment have been taken without policy-makers having a strong empirical basis to guide their actions. Thus, there is a great need for policy-makers and politicians to be able to measure the scope and significance of the business angel market (Mason and Harrison, 2008). For example, it is important to monitor the changes in the number of business angels and their investments that could threaten the entrepreneurial 'eco-system'. It is also essential to determine the need for interventions to support the market. However, the invisibility of the market makes it difficult to obtain information about its size (see Chapter 2 by Mason for this discussion), which implies a risk of inappropriate policy interventions.

The research results so far have provided little guidance for policy-makers regarding the state of the business angel market and what (if any) policy response is required to support it. In this chapter, we take one step in the direction of 'making sense' of the existing evidence. We differentiate between the size and the significance of the business angel market. To date, most studies have focused on measuring the size of the market, that is, estimating the extent of business angel investment activity. However, we shall argue that we need to move beyond talking about the extent of business angel activity and increase our understanding of its significance, here defined as relative (actual or potential) importance for funding new and growing ventures. Discussing the significance of business angels in relative terms enables us to understand business angel financing in the context of the overall supply of and demand for venture financing in a country, make cross-national comparisons and draw more informed policy lessons.

In the present chapter, we start by reviewing current knowledge about the scope of business angel investing in different countries. We then change focus to the significance of business angel activities in their national contexts. We propose two sets of indicators of the significance of business angels – from the supply and the demand side, as well as discussing their informational value, availability and the required quality of data necessary to construct such indicators. We use four countries (France, Norway, the UK and the USA) to demonstrate how the indicators can be calculated and what they reveal. However, our purpose is not to make any strong statements about the business angel markets in these specific countries; the examples provided are of an illustrative nature. Finally, we discuss how these findings can provide guidance for policy-makers.

## 3.2 REVIEW OF THE SCOPE OF BUSINESS ANGEL ACTIVITIES

Business angel research is now more than three decades old. It has provided important insights into the functioning of business angel financing and our level of understanding of the phenomenon has gradually increased (Landström, 2007; Landström and Mason, 2012). Nevertheless, some researchers have pointed out that the field seems to have moved from providing no answers to presenting a plethora of answers about the nature and activity of business angels (Shane, 2009). In particular, no clear picture has yet emerged of just how significant this source of funding is for financing entrepreneurship.

Why our knowledge of the significance of the business angel market has not progressed further is explained by three factors. First, as discussed in Chapter 2, accessing data on business angel investments has been a challenge in itself, as in most countries there are no official registers of business angel activity and, as a consequence, most studies have been cross-sectional and based on small non-representative samples. Second, a variety of definitions have been used by different scholars, which has inhibited the build-up of a consistent knowledge-base. Third, the results of different studies have rarely been put into a wider context of the access to finance system on a country level, or the regional entrepreneurial eco-system for that matter, making it difficult to understand and interpret the results. For a more comprehensive discussion about the definitions and methodologies in business angel research, see Chapter 2 by Mason.

### 3.2.1 Early Attempts to Measures the Scope of Business Angel Activities

In his seminal work on business angels in 1983, William Wetzel Jr noted that the population of business angels 'is unknown and probably unknowable' (Wetzel, 1983, p. 26). More than 30 years later, Wetzel's observation still holds, as it has been shown in many studies over the years that the extent of business angel investment activity is difficult to measure.

In one of the first attempts to measure the scope of the activities, Wetzel (1987) 'played with existing numbers,' using a variety of fragmented data on high-income families and the financing of business, concluding that:

> if the average net worth of millionaires is between $1 million and $2 million, then, excluding borrowed funds, the total wealth controlled by the one million or more US millionaires is between $1 trillion and $2 trillion. If the average millionaire commits 10% of his or her net worth to venture investing, the total informal venture capital pool is between $100 and $200 billion. If only one-fourth of US millionaires have any interest in venture investing, the pool of informal venture capital controlled by these 250,000 individuals lies in the $25 to $50 billion range, about twice the capital managed by professional venture investors . . . it appears that each year over 100,000 individual investors finance between 20,000 and 50,000 firms for a dollar investment totaling $5 billion and $10 billion. The typical firm financed by angels raises about $250,000 from three or more investors. (Wetzel, 1987, p. 305)

Obviously, these are rough estimates, but the figures served a useful purpose at the time when there was a need to provide some numerical estimation of the scale of business angel markets in order to highlight the significance of the market for policy-makers and politicians. Since Wetzel's seminal attempt to measure the scope of the market, many researchers have tried to generate estimates of the size of the business angel markets in various countries. The estimates of the size of the business angel market in some of these studies are presented in Table 3.1.

The results presented in Table 3.1 reveal that the estimates of the business angel markets vary considerably between studies, making it obvious that robust estimates of the size of the business angel markets are lacking.

*Table 3.1 Early estimates of business angel activity*

| Country | Estimated size of the BA market | Study |
|---|---|---|
| USA | Two million families holding investments of US$300 billion in privately held businesses. | Ou (1987) |
| | 720,000 private investors making 490,000 investments totaling US$32.7 billion in equity and US$23 billion in debt finance to 87,000 companies. | Gaston (1989) |
| | 250,000 business angels in the USA who invested US$10–20 billion a year in over 30,000 companies. | Wetzel (1994) |
| | 300,000 to 350,000 business angels investing about US$30 billion a year in 50,000 companies. | Sohl (2003) |
| | In 2009, business angels invested US$17.6 billion in 57,225 companies. Over the period 2002–09, business angel investors invested on average US$21 billion in approximately 50,000 companies annually. | Sohl (2012) |
| UK | 20,000 to 80,000 business angel investors investing £500 million to £2 billion. | Mason and Harrison (2000) |
| | In 2008/09 business angels in the UK invested about £426 million. | Mason and Harrison (2011) |
| Canada | Canadian business angels invested US$200 to US$400 million. | Short and Riding (1988) |
| | Business angels in eastern Canada invested US$60–75 million annually. | Farrell (1998) |
| | During 2004, 15,800 business angels invested approximately CAN$1.9 billion. | Riding (2008) |
| | In 2005, the Canadian business angel market was estimated at US$3.5 billion. | Riding (2005) |

Our knowledge has mainly been based on ad hoc studies using various definitions of business angels (or informal investors), and employing different sampling techniques (see discussion by Mason in Chapter 2). However, bearing these definitional and sampling concerns in mind, previous research has shown that in many countries business angels seem to be the single largest source of external capital, after family money, for firms in the early stages of development, and business angels not only provide capital but also significant non-financial inputs, for example, mentoring, advice, networks and other forms of added value (see Chapter 7 by Politis in this volume). Not least, it has been demonstrated that business angels invest as much or more capital in a greater number of firms than formal venture capitalists, especially early-stage firms.

### 3.2.2 Contemporary Studies on the Scope of Business Angel Activities

The scope of business angel investing is likely to change over time and be affected by changes in market conditions. In the past two decades, the boom and bust of the IT bubble in the late 1990s and early 2000s, the financial crisis of 2008/09 and the subsequent credit crunch, as well as the development of a technological infrastructure that facilitates direct equity investments in unquoted businesses through different web platforms are all likely to have had a significant impact on business angels' investment activity. Thus, the data on business angel investment activity is not easily comparable over time. The market is fairly volatile, and even within a period of a few years there can be considerable variations in the level of angel activity, echoing changes in market liquidity, perceived market conditions and availability of other types of finance (Månsson and Landström, 2006; Mason and Harrison, 2015). In this respect, short-term fluctuations in angel investment activity can be greater than those of institutional investors, reflecting the inherent difference in the functioning of these sources of finance. While venture capitalists need to invest the fund's equity during the lifetime of the fund, business angels do not have such pressure, making it easy for them to hold off investing in 'bad' times.

Furthermore, when making international comparisons, we need to be aware that countries can be influenced in different ways by global macroeconomic and societal trends. Equally, national context factors play an important role in the scope and functioning of the business angel market, such as the structure of national financial markets, tax systems, regulations affecting angel investment and technological advancement, as well as governmental policies aimed at promoting investment.

A couple of attempts have also been made in recent years (post-2008/09 crisis) to measure the scope of business angel investment activity and we focus on these contemporary estimates later in this chapter. We summarize the estimates below and in the next subsection attempt to place them in their national context and develop comparable indicators of the significance of business angel finance.

### 3.2.3 Overview of Contemporary Studies in the UK, the USA, France and Norway

In their work on business angels' investment activity in the UK during the recent financial crisis, Mason and Harrison (2011) estimated that business angel activity in the UK amounted to £317.7 million annually in the period 2009/10. The estimate is based on extrapolating from the 'visible market', that is, investors who are part of business angel networks/syndicates, based on a presumed degree of participation. The estimate relies on data provided by the British Business Angel Association and LINC Scotland, adjusted for undercounting and complemented by a questionnaire. For the period 2008/09 they provided an estimate of £426 million. However, the latter may involve a certain degree of double-counting, thus it cannot be concluded that there was a decline (Mason and Harrison, 2015). The study does not apply a specific definition of business angels and instead relies on a self-defined population – investors who are members of Business Angel Networks (BANs)/LINC Scotland syndicates.

In the USA, the Center of Venture Research at the University of New Hampshire conducts an annual study of the scale of business angel investment. The last available study estimated that in 2013, the scale of business angel investment in the USA was $24.8 billion, representing investments in 70,730 companies. When compared with previous estimates, it appears that investment activity has grown steadily over recent years: $22.9 billion was estimated to have been invested in 2012, $22.5 billion in 2011, $20.1 billion in 2010 and $17.6 billion in 2009. Thus, the investment volumes seem to be steadily recovering toward the pre-crisis level ($26 billion invested in 2007).[1] The estimates are made by extrapolating data from an annual survey of individuals known to be making business angel investments, both independently and as members of angel groups/networks. However, the exact definition used is not provided, nor the methodology for making the extrapolation.

The Center for Strategy and Evaluation Services (CSES, 2012) has estimated the volume of business angel investments in France at €157 million annually (2010 data). The estimate is based on extrapolation from investment data reported by 81 BANs in France representing more than 3000 active angels, on the basis of a presumed degree of business angels' participation in BANs and adjusted for non-respondents. Like the

*Table 3.2 Contemporary estimates of business angel activity*

| Country | Estimate of business angel investment (amount) | Source |
|---|---|---|
| UK (2010 data) | £317.7 million | Mason and Harrison (2011) |
| USA (2010 data) | $20.1 billion | CVR (2014) |
| France (2010 data) | €157 million | CSES (2012) |
| Norway (2009 data) | €295 million[a] | Menon (2010) |

*Note:* [a] The study does not provide data on the amount invested, only the number of business angels. If we assume that the financial activity of an individual angel in Norway is on the same level as in the late 1990s, the average yearly amount invested by a business angel would be approximately €122,874 in 2009 monetary value (€100,000 according to Reitan and Sörheim, 2000 estimates, adjusted for approximately ten years of inflation, https://www.ssb.no/en/kpi), giving a total annual investment amount of €295 million.

studies mentioned above, this study does not apply a specific definition of business angels but relies on a self-defined population – investors who are members of BANs.

In 2010 Menon Business Economics conducted a study of business angel activity in Norway on behalf of the Ministry of Enterprise and Trade. The study, which was based on tax authority data from 2009, found that there were about 2400 active business angels in Norway who held equity stakes in around 4500 unquoted businesses. The study does not provide an estimate of the size of the market, but based on previous evidence of the average annual investment by business angels in Norway (Reitan and Sörheim, 2000), the market can be estimated at €295 million annually. The definitional alternatives are discussed in detail in the report and the definition chosen by the authors was private investor who owns an equity stake of less than 50% in an unquoted company, who receives less than 800,000 NOK (about €100,000) per year in salary from that company, who has equity stakes in at least two firms worth at least 500,000 NOK (about €60,000), is on the board of at least one of these firms and is not an ordinary manager/CEO of these firms.[2]

Table 3.2 summarizes these estimates of business angel investment in France (2010), the UK (2010), the USA (2010) and Norway (2009).[3, 4]

### 3.2.4 Summary

We have argued that in the last 30 years, the research field has progressed from providing no answers to presenting a plethora of answers about the scale of business angel investment. However, most of the studies remain methodologically weak, drawing upon self-selection samples, in addition to using unclear definitions and methodologies. While some advanced approaches to estimating the scope of the market have been successfully tested, for example, using large surveys to randomly select a sample of individuals in a country (Avdeitchikova, 2008) or employing information contained in tax and firm register databases (Menon, 2011), they have not been widely adopted, probably due to high costs and data access problems.

With regard to suggestions for future research, we reiterate the recommendations of Avdeitchikova et al. (2008) and Mason and Harrison (2008), who called for increased use of registry-based data that would give us almost full coverage of the population, an opportunity to work with accurate definitions and align data collection practices between countries. It also appears to be more accurate and fruitful to focus on the investments made by business angels (and thus work with investment-based data), as opposed to business angel investors as individuals (that is, using individual-related data), which has implications for the choice of data sources.

## 3.3 THE SIGNIFICANCE OF BUSINESS ANGEL INVESTMENT

So far in this chapter we have discussed the scope of business angel investment by means of estimates of business angel investment activity. However, the significance of this financing source is a more complex but potentially more relevant concept. It goes beyond measuring the scope of the market and refers to the relative (actual or potential) importance of this source of finance for businesses.

Earlier studies based on relative measures of venture capital activity (institutional and informal) have mainly used a country's gross domestic product (GDP), one of the common measures of the size of the economy, as the denominator (Avdeitchikova, 2008; OECD, 2013). While having some obvious strengths, for example, simplicity, stability over time, good data access and comparability, such an indicator is inherently problematic as it does not reflect the structure of the economy, nor the size and composition of the SME sector that receives the financing. Thus, we argue, such indicators are not a particularly meaningful ground for cross-national comparisons or tool for policy-making. Moreover, given the problems in calculating gross regional product (GRP), it is likely that they provide even less opportunity for regional comparisons.

Instead, we suggest two alternative sets of indicators of the significance of business angel finance: one that focuses on the supply perspective (the relative importance of business angels as a source of finance to firms compared to other financing sources) and another that highlights the demand perspective (the extent to which business angel finance is available in relation to the structure of the SME sector). Below, we discuss these indicators' strengths and weaknesses in terms of (1) information value and pose the questions: Does the indicator advance our understanding of the importance of business angels? Can the indicator potentially serve as a basis for more informed policy-making? and (2) methodological issues, asking: Is the underlying data available, comparable and of sufficient quality?

### 3.3.1 Indicators of Business Angel Significance from the Supply Perspective

As a first step, we look at the significance of business angels from the supply perspective. One possible way of determining the significance of business angels as financiers is by relating business angel investment volumes to the total supply of external equity in the early stages, thus addressing the question of how important business angels are as providers of external equity finance. Another possible way to increase our understanding of business angels' significance is by relating business angel finance to the total amount of external finance that flows to SMEs, that is, addressing the question of their overall significance as providers of external finance.

In order to illustrate our argumentation, we bring together the data provided by the studies of the scope of business angel activity in the UK, France, the USA and Norway presented in Subsection 3.2.2, as well as data on the scope of other external financial flows to SMEs (European Venture Capital Association (EVCA) and the National Venture Capital Association (NVCA) for data on venture capital investing, and Organisation for Economic Co-operation and Development (OECD) Financing SMEs and Entrepreneurs Scoreboard for loan financing). The following conclusions can be made:

- In the UK, out of £1.1 billion early-stage external equity finance invested in 2010, £318 million, or 28.4 percent, was provided by business angels. Business angels' share of total external financing, including bank loans and government guaranteed loans, that went to SMEs in the UK that year was 0.28 percent.
- In the USA, out of $27.9 billion early-stage external equity finance that was invested in SMEs in 2010, $20.1 billion, or 72.0 percent, was provided by business angels. Business angels' share of total

external financing to SMEs in the USA that year was 2.57 percent. Thus, the significance of business angels as providers of external equity finance in 2010 was about 2.5 times larger in the USA than in the UK, while their overall significance as a supplier of finance to SMEs was about nine times larger in the USA compared to the UK.

- In France, out of €1.0 billion early-stage external equity finance that was invested in 2010, €157 million, or 15.7 percent, was provided by business angels. Business angels' share of total external financing, including bank loans and government guaranteed loans, that went to SMEs in France that year was 0.09 percent. Compared to the USA, this would mean that in 2010 business angels in France were four to five times less significant as providers of external equity finance to firms, while their overall significance as a supplier of finance to SMEs was almost 30 times lower than in the USA. Measured in this way, business angel activity in France would also be almost two times less significant than that in the UK in terms of a source of external equity finance and about three times less significant as an overall source of external finance.
- In Norway, out of €429 million early-stage external equity finance that was invested in SMEs in 2009, approximately €295 million, or 69.0 percent, was provided by business angels. Business angels' share of total external financing that went to Norwegian SMEs that year was 0.59 percent. This means that business angels as players on the external equity market for unquoted SMEs were considerably more important in Norway than in the UK during the same period, and relatively speaking almost as significant as they were in the USA. Nevertheless, if business angel activity is compared to the total flow of finance to these firms, the significance of business angels in Norway, while more than twice as high as in the UK and almost seven times higher than in France, was about four times lower than in the USA.[5]

Table 3.3 summarizes the data on external early-stage equity/total external capital flow to SMEs (including bank loans) in the UK, USA, France and Norway, and presents both indicators per country, expressed as percentages.

### 3.3.2 Strengths and Weaknesses of the Indicators

In this section we have suggested two indicators of the significance of business angel investment from the supply perspective: (1) business angels' share of total early-stage external equity investment in SMEs and

*Table 3.3 Business angel investments versus external equity/capital flow to SMEs*

| Country | Estimate of scope of business angel investment (amount) | Total equity flow to SMEs (business angel and venture capital)[a] | Business angel's share of total equity flow to SMEs | Total capital flow to SMEs (including bank loans)[b] | Business angel's share of total capital flow to SMEs |
|---|---|---|---|---|---|
| UK (2010 data) | £318 million | £1.1 billion | 28.4% | £114.0 billion | 0.28% |
| USA (2010 data) | $20.1 billion | $27.9 billion | 72.0% | $783.0 billion | 2.57% |
| France (2010) | €157 million | €1.0 billion | 15.6% | €173.9 billion | 0.09% |
| Norway (2009 data) | €295 million | €429 million | 69.0% | €50.4 billion[c] | 0.59% |

*Notes:*

[a] The sum of venture capital in early stages according to EVCA and NVCA estimates and business angel investments according to the sources stated above. The data for comparison is derived for the same year as the observation data.

[b] The sum of bank loans to SMEs (OECD, 2014), venture capital in early stages according to EVCA and NVCA estimates and business angel investments according to the sources stated above. The data for comparison is derived from the same year as the observation data.

[c] Conversion rate as per 2009, €1 = 8.33 NOK.

(2) business angels' share of total external financing that flows to SMEs. Below, we discuss the strengths and weaknesses of these indicators.

**Information value**

The two indicators provide different and potentially valuable information about the state of the business angel market. The first demonstrates how well positioned business angels are as a source of external equity funding, while the second highlights their overall significance for financing SMEs. If the first indicator has a relatively low value, the attention of policy-makers should probably turn to understanding what hinders business angel investment, while if the second indicator has a relatively low value, the attention of policy-makers should probably focus on understanding the barriers to external (unquoted) equity investment as a whole. There can also be combinations when one of the indicators is high and the other low, which would signal the area of the potential problem.

Nevertheless, both indicators should be interpreted with caution. Here, it is important to keep the relativity aspect of the measure in mind, because of the complementarity and substitutability of different capital sources. A high proportion of firms financed by business angels does not in itself indicate a well-functioning business angel market, nor does the opposite necessarily imply a poorly functioning market. The financing eco-system is complex, as different sources of finance (loans, angel investments, venture capital investments, grants, customer credits and so on) can be both complementary to each other and act as substitutes.

One possible scenario is that certain sources of financing grow increasingly important, primarily due to others being unavailable. An example is the business angel market in Scotland, where business angels organized themselves in syndicates and grew increasingly strong financially, to the extent that they can play in a niche normally occupied by venture capital firms, mainly due to the fact that Scotland does not have a functioning institutional venture capital market ('supplementary role,' cf. Gregson et al., 2013). In the same way, some business angels found themselves increasing their investment activity during the last financial crisis, because their portfolio companies lost sales, were not paid by their customers and were unable to obtain bank loans. Thus, what might look like an increasingly well-functioning business angel market may in reality be a sign of a poorly functioning bank sector and a depressed economy. We can also find more general signs of such a supplementary relationship. In countries that traditionally have bank-centered financial systems (Black and Gilson, 1998; Jeng and Wells, 2000) such as Germany and Austria, banks have been more important in financing new, high-risk ventures than in market-centered economies, where this role is played by external equity financiers to a larger degree. The role of banks, business angels, government agencies and so on is also likely to differ between regions, depending on the relative availability of other financial sources.

Equally important is the 'complementary role' of different sources of finance, where business angel financing can trigger other forms of capital inflow. For instance, banks are more likely to lend to firms that have received an equity investment, while a condition of many government funding programs is co-financing from a private source. Thus, an active and well-functioning business angel market can contribute to a better overall financing system for SMEs, which in turn can lower the relative significance of business angels when measured in this way.

Finally, relating business angel financing to external equity or total capital provided to SMEs disregards the specificity of business angel financing, which most SMEs never attract or even consider. Thus, a more nuanced view of the demand side would contribute to a better understanding of the significance of business angels. Therefore, in the next subsection we discuss some suggestions for demand side indicators.

**Methodological issues**

The availability of internationally comparable data has increased substantially over recent years. The NVCA in the USA and the EVCA provide yearly data on venture capital investment and the OECD intends to collect data on a variety of financing sources on a yearly basis, gradually increasing the number of countries involved (now 32 countries). However, a great deal remains to be done in terms of streamlining methodologies and definitions, as well as increasing the quality of data.

Based on existing data, both indicators of the relative significance of business angel activity are likely to overestimate it. At present, the measure of the total external capital flows to SMEs does not incorporate government grants, tax subsidies and types of state support other than loans, which means that the total pool of finance to SMEs is larger than that indicated by the data used here. Furthermore, the external equity measure does not include corporate venture capital and crowdinvesting, which means that the total external equity flow is also larger than indicated by the figures presented here. Enhancing the quality of the data and incorporating other data sources will increase the quality of this set of indicators.

### 3.3.3 Indicators of Business Angel Significance from the Demand Perspective

Addressing the significance of business angel funding from the demand perspective necessarily requires a discussion about who receives it and how significant this source of finance is for the recipients. In the literature, the 'target group' for business angel funding is usually only vaguely described. Most studies indicate that business angels target young, innovative, often technology-based SMEs; however, there is no agreement about what companies fall under this definition. It may also be the case that the target population for business angel investment changes over time, as a result of general technological developments, the emergence of other financing mechanisms (public sector venture capital, crowdfunding and so on) and the decreasing cost of starting a business, shifting the first round of financing for most firms toward the post-seed stage. While technology-based firms were considered to be the main attractor of business angel financing during the IT boom of the late 1990s, a significant share of start-ups in the mid 2010s has a technological component in their business model. For that reason, we did not investigate start-ups, nor did we attempt to identify technology-based firms. Instead, we propose a set of demand-based indicators that relate business angel activity to (a) the total stock of small and middle-sized firms and (b) the stock of growth-oriented early-stage firms. While the former is a way of relating business angel investment to the total business activity, the latter provides a more nuanced view of potential users of business angel finance, and also, as demonstrated here, presents a somewhat unexpected picture of the financing situation in the countries that we have looked at.

To illustrate this, we brought together the estimates of business angel activity presented in Subsection 3.2.2 (Table 3.2) with the OECD Scoreboard data on the SME sector and the Global Entrepreneurship Monitor (GEM) data on growth-oriented early-stage entrepreneurship,[6] which yielded the following estimates:

- In the UK, with an SME stock of approximately 1.6 million (2010), total business angel investment in relation to the number of SMEs is £267.4 per year. If we instead relate the angel activity to the number of growth-oriented new ventures, the annual investment per firm would be approximately £411.
- In the USA, with an SME stock of approximately 5.0 million (2010), business angel investment divided by the number of firms is $4021.4, approximately ten[7] times larger than in the UK. Furthermore, if only growth-oriented new ventures are considered, the annual investment per firm is $2421, approximately four times higher than in the UK.
- In France, with an SME stock of approximately 2.5 million (2010), total business angel investment in relation to the number of SMEs is around €62.6 per year, approximately 50 times lower that in the USA and five times lower than in the UK. If we instead relate the angel activity to the number of growth-oriented new ventures, the annual investment per firm would be approximately €214, which is about one-eighth of the US level and half of the UK level.
- In Norway, with an SME stock of approximately 142,400 enterprises (2009), total business angel investment in relation to the number of SMEs is €2071, which is about 30 percent lower than in the USA.[8] However, if only growth-oriented new ventures are considered, the annual investment per firm in Norway would be €3829, almost twice as high as in the USA, nine times higher than in the UK and 18 times higher than in France.

The results are presented in Table 3.4.

*Table 3.4 Business angel investments in SMEs*

| Country | Estimate of scope of business angel investment (amount) | Size of SME stock* | Business angel investment per number of SMEs | Number of growth-oriented new ventures[a] | Business angel investment per number of growth-oriented new ventures |
|---|---|---|---|---|---|
| UK (2010 data) | £318 million | 1,188,025 | £267.4 | 77,750 | £411 |
| USA (2010 data) | $20.1 billion | 4,998,243 | $4021.4 | 8,302,310 | $2421 |
| France (2010 data) | €157 million | 2,509,345 | €62.6 | 733,284 | €214 |
| Norway (2009 data) | €295 million | 142,442 | €2071.0 | 76,839 | €3839 |

*Note:* [a] Calculated on the basis of the country's adult population (OECD Statistics) and Medium-High Job Expectation TEA (MHEA), averages 2009–11 (Bosma et al., 2012).

*Source:* * OECD SME Financing Scoreboard, 2010 data (UK, USA, France) and http://ec.europa.eu/enterprise/policies/ sme/facts-figures-analysis/performance-review/files/countries-sheets/2010-2011/norway_en.pdf, 2009 data (Norway).

It can be concluded that considerable differences seem to exist between the four countries in the way in which the SME sector is supplied by business angel finance. When business angel activity is calculated in this way, France lags behind the other three countries, both when it comes to relating angel activity to the total SME stock and to the group of growth-oriented new ventures. Norway seems to be best off, significantly outperforming the UK in terms of angel investment per number of SMEs and outperforming both the UK and the USA with regard to the relative availability of business angel finance per number of growth-oriented new ventures.[9]

The results are in line with an earlier study by Avdeitchikova (2009) that explored the variations in the supply of business angel finance between different regions of Sweden and found that differences in demand had high explanatory power. Our results are also in line with the more general discussion that venture finance activity clusters around dynamic entrepreneurial systems, while the opposite is far less obvious.

### 3.3.4 Strengths and Weaknesses of the Indicators

In this section we have suggested two indicators of the significance of business angel activity from the demand perspective: (1) the amount of business angel investment in relation to the total stock of SMEs and (2) the amount of business angel investment in relation to the stock of growth-oriented early-stage firms. Their strengths and weaknesses are discussed below.

**Information value**

Depending on whether the focus of entrepreneurship policy in a country is on SMEs or on growth-oriented new ventures, both indicators are potentially of considerable relevance for policy-makers. Instead of looking at the supply of business angel finance, the indicators answer the question: 'Are the SMEs/growth-oriented start-ups disadvantaged in terms of access to business angel finance?' This provides concrete tools for determining whether there is a 'problem' to be 'fixed' and can be more easily translated into policy standpoints and action.

One weakness of the proposed indicators is that they are based on an assumption about who receives business angel funding. However, this can vary between (and within) countries, as well as over time, and we still have very little systematic knowledge about what companies business angels invest in. Thus, the potential relevance of the indicator is affected by the choice of 'denominator.'

Another weakness is that these indicators assume that supply and demand can be separated in a meaningful way. However, the actual level of investment is better described as equilibrium, the quantities being determined by both the supply of and demand for different types of capital (cf. Robb and Robinson, 2012; see also the discussion under Subsection 3.3.1). In addition, this equilibrium may change over time, as greater availability of finance could contribute to increased entrepreneurial activity and especially ambitious entrepreneurship. Finally, it is important to note that these indicators do not measure the extent to which business angel finance is actually used by SMEs/growth-oriented new ventures; they only reflect the amount of finance available to the firms. Naturally, there can be considerable differences between countries when it comes to which firms receive the finance, but understanding this would require a different type of analysis.

**Methodological issues**

Methodologically, one of the major strengths of the indicators is data availability. Data on the size of the SME sector is available for most

OECD countries and is accessible through OECD Statistics. Data on growth-oriented new ventures is also easily accessible through GEM reports, which are collected annually and made available within less than a year (aggregated data).

A potential weakness of the data on growth-oriented new ventures is that an entrepreneur's growth aspiration is inherently subjective. It can also be assumed that systematic differences between countries influence this variable, for instance, related to culture and societal norms, which would mean that the data is not entirely comparable between countries. However, this is a common weakness of self-reported data, rather than of this specific variable.

### 3.3.5 Summary

We have argued that the significance of business angels as a source of finance is a more relevant concept than the volume of business angel investment. While there is no straightforward answer to how this significance can and should be measured, we propose two sets of indicators (demand and supply-oriented) and discuss their informational value and challenges in terms of measurement and interpretation.

When relating business angel activity to the nature of the financial flows to enterprises, on the one hand, and the structure of the SME sector, on the other, we find some significant differences between the countries included in the analysis. In particular, an unexpected finding was that Norway seems to be better off than the USA when business angel investment is related to the number of new growth-oriented firms, while France lags considerably behind. From the supply perspective, the USA seems to be far 'superior' in terms of business angel activity to the other three countries in the comparison.

## 3.4 CONCLUSIONS: TOWARD COMPARABLE INDICATORS AND RELEVANCE FOR POLICY

In this chapter, we have briefly reviewed the studies of business angel activity in different countries and summarized recent estimates of the scope of business angel activity in countries where post-2008/09 crisis estimates were available (the USA, the UK, France and Norway). We have also discussed the need for understanding the significance of business angel finance in a particular national context (rather than merely measuring the scope), and suggested two sets of indicators for measuring the significance of business angel activity. In this concluding section we summarize the findings and discuss how they can be of value for policy-makers. We also suggest some paths for further knowledge development.

### 3.4.1 From Data to Information: Constructing Meaningful Indicators

In the early phases of knowledge development on business angels, research and policy analysis focused on exploratory studies of the phenomenon – how prevalent is the phenomenon and how does it function? However, the information value of such data for policy-makers remains low unless they have tools to understand it. Moreover, as the amount of empirical evidence grows, the plethora of evidence may become increasingly difficult to deal with, due to conflicting evidence, uncertainty about whether and how the data can be compared and overall confusion regarding what the data actually says. Nevertheless, most policy-making in the area of business angel financing has, at best, been based on fragmented data on business angel activity.

Indicators, as opposed to data, say something about the situation in a way that is relevant to the context of the phenomenon. In the present case, we have suggested measuring the relative significance of business angels by relating business angel activity to the prevalence of other sources of funding as well as the number of firms that are potential users of business angel financing. Thus, instead of discussing 'How prevalent is business angel investment (in a particular country)?' we suggest moving the focus to the following questions: 'How important are business angels as providers of finance to firms?' and 'How well supplied are firms with business angel finance?'

Describing business angel activity using meaningful indicators allows comparison between countries (benchmarking). It also enables the tracking of business angel activity over time, which can be useful as a base for evaluating policy effectiveness when a government is pursuing policies to increase business angel investment. However, having indicators of business angel activity does not automatically imply having tools for policy-making. For the latter, the key is intelligent interpretation of the indicator values.

### 3.4.2 From Information to Knowledge: Using Indicators to Guide Policy

While low business angel activity values probably deserve the attention of policy-makers, they do not automatically require a policy response. As discussed earlier, even well-functioning financial eco-systems can have relatively low levels of business angel activity due to substitutability and complementarity between different financial sources. Therefore, it is not necessarily a 'problem,' even if the indicators suggest that it is.

Moreover, there is always an alternative cost to be considered from a policy perspective; thus, can public money be used more productively elsewhere? Creating policies to promote business angel investment is not necessarily the right 'solution,' given the cost-effect tradeoff of the policy.

Finally, SME access to finance, as well as the need for external finance, is affected by a considerable number of factors in different spheres of the economy, such as taxation, administrative burdens, financial market regulations and other framework conditions. The formulation of business angel policies must be driven by a holistic understanding of these conditions (and developments), in combination with information about the current state of business angel activity that the indicators suggested here can provide.

### 3.4.3 Future Research

In this chapter we have focused on national level indicators and comparisons as opposed to the regional perspective, although we are aware that business angel activity is highly concentrated in certain regions (for example, Avdeitchikova, 2009). Thus, even if a country 'comes out well' in an international comparison, there may still be an under-supply at a regional level. Therefore, one potentially fruitful path for further studies would be to explore regional business angel activity/indicators of angel finance.

In this chapter, we have focused on business angels and discussed their economic significance. As new ways of providing finance emerge, for example, crowdfunding (and specifically crowdinvesting, which comprises the equity part of crowdfunding), a broader perspective on informal venture capital investment becomes increasingly useful in order to capture these new developments. Therefore, another potentially fruitful path for future studies would be investigating and benchmarking the significance of informal venture capital investment in broader terms. Given the recent introduction of the use of registry-based data (for example, tax data) in studies of venture finance, there is good potential for finding ways to capture the informal venture capital market as a whole in countries where such data is systematically gathered and available. Crowdinvesting platforms are also a potential source of data on these particular investments, although the quality and reliability of such data has not been tested.

Finally, to reiterate our earlier argument, as the quality of indicators is only as good as the quality of the underlying data, future research must focus on aligning definitions and data collection practices across countries, in addition to producing periodic, reliable estimates.

## NOTES

1. http://paulcollege.unh.edu/research/center-venture-research/cvr-analysis-reports.
2. The sensitivity of estimates to the criteria used is also discussed. For instance, if the cut-off point for the value of the portfolio is raised from 500,000 to 1 million NOK, the estimate of the number of business angels would drop by over 50 percent.
3. The years 2009 and 2010 were chosen (instead of the most recent available estimate for each country) to increase comparability and ensure availability of secondary data for the construction of indicators.
4. In addition to this review, fairly detailed recent data on business angel investment is available in Canada, derived from a database of all incoming external financing at firm level. However, as this database only covers British Columbia, we chose not to present it here. For more information about the dataset, see http://www.tinbergen.nl/wp-content/uploads/2013/11/Angels-and-Venture-Capitalists-Complements-or-Substitutes.pdf.
5. The example of the USA and Norway is particularly interesting for illustrating that supply and demand side analysis can give a very different picture of the state of the business angel market. Having a traditionally bank-based financial system (Demirgüç-Kunt and Levine, 2001), Norway did not develop an active venture capital market. At the same time, the level of personal wealth is very high in Norway compared to the rest of the OECD countries, which may have triggered the formation of a relatively active business angel market. Thus, what we seem to be seeing here is business angels being a significant player in a moderately developed external equity finance market. This differs from the situation in the USA, where business angels appear to be important players in a well-developed and highly active external equity market (Gambacorta et al., 2014).
6. According to the Global Entrepreneurship Monitor, newly started firms or firms in the start-up process that intend to employ at least five people in the next five years (that is, medium or high growth aspirations according to the GEM definition, Bosma et al., 2012).
7. Exchange rate on 31 December 2010, $1 = £0.64.
8. Exchange rate on 31 December 2009, $1 = €0.70; on 31 December 2010, $1 = €0.75.
9. It is important to consider the following factors when comparing Norway to the other countries. First, the general cost level is significantly higher in Norway than in the countries used for comparison (https://stats.oecd.org/Index.aspx?DataSetCode=CPL), which means that the (absolute) cost of creating and growing a firm is also likely to be higher. Second, Norway is by far the smallest country in this comparison, which means that the domestic market for goods and services is small and that expansion often requires internationalization, which is more expensive than domestic growth. Third, the Norwegian economy is dominated by traditional industries, such as oil, gas, forestry and fishing, and the number of growth-oriented new ventures is low (Bosma et al., 2012). Thus, the lower demand for venture financing in Norway rather than better supply explains the difference between Norway and the USA when it comes to the final indicator.

## REFERENCES

Avdeitchikova, S. (2008), 'Close-ups from afar: the nature of the informal venture capital market in a spatial context', PhD thesis, Department of Business Administration, Lund University, Sweden.

Avdeitchikova, S. (2009), 'False expectations: reconsidering the role of informal venture capital in closing the regional equity gap', *Entrepreneurship and Regional Development*, **21**(2), 99–130.

Avdeitchikova, S., H. Landström and N. Månsson (2008), 'What do we mean when we talk about business angels? Some definition and sampling reflections', *Venture Capital: An International Journal of Entrepreneurial Finance*, **10**(4), 371–94.

Black R.J. and B.S. Gilson (1998), 'Venture capital and the structure of capital markets: banks versus stock markets', *Journal of Financial Economics*, **47**, 243–77.
Bosma, N.S., S. Wennekers and J.E. Amorós (2012), *Global Entrepreneurship Monitor 2011 Executive Report*, Babson Park, MA, Santiago, Kuala Lumpur and London: Babson College, Universidad del Desarollo, Universiti Tun Abdul Razak and Global Entrepreneurship Research Association.
Conti, A., M.C. Thursby and F. Rothaermel (2011), 'Show me the right stuff: signals for high tech startups', NBER Working Paper 17050, Cambridge, MA.
CSES (2012), *Evaluation of EU Member States' Business Angel Markets and Policies*, Final report, October, available at http://ec.europa.eu/enterprise/dg/files/ba-rep_en.pdf (accessed 1 November 2015).
CVR (2014), *Full Year 2013 Angel Market Analysis Report*, available at https://paulcollege.unh.edu/sites/paulcollege.unh.edu/files/2013%20Analysis%20Report%20FINAL.pdf (accessed 1 June 2016).
Demirgüç-Kunt, A. and R. Levine (2001), *Financial Structures and Economic Growth: A Cross-country Comparison of Banks, Markets and Development*, Cambridge, MA: MIT Press.
Elitzur, R. and A. Gavious (2003), 'Contracting, signaling and moral hazard: a model for entrepreneurs, angels and venture capitalists', *Journal of Business Venturing*, **18**(6), 709–25.
Farrell, E. (1998), *Informal Venture Capital Investment in Atlantic Canada: A Representative View of Angels*, Moncton, New Brunswick: Atlantic Canada Opportunity Agency.
Gambacorta, L., J. Yang and K. Tsatsaronis (2014), 'Financial structure and growth', *BIS Quarterly*, March, 21–35.
Gaston, R. (1989), 'The scale of informal venture capital markets', *Small Business Economics*, **1**, 223–30.
Gregson, G., S. Mann and R.T. Harrison (2013), 'Business angel syndication and the evolution of risk capital in a small market economy: evidence from Scotland', *Managerial and Decision Economics*, **34**, 95–107.
Jeng, L.A. and P.C. Wells (2000), 'The determinants of venture capital funding: evidence across countries', *Journal of Corporate Finance*, **6**(3), 241–89.
Landström, H. (ed.) (2007), *Handbook of Research on Venture Capital*, Cheltenham, UK and Northampton, MA, USA: Edward Elgar.
Landström, H. and C. Mason (eds) (2012), *Handbook of Research on Venture Capital: Volume 2*, Cheltenham, UK and Northampton, MA, USA: Edward Elgar.
Månsson, N. and H. Landström (2006), 'Business angels in a changing economy: the case of Sweden', *Venture Capital*, **8**(4), 281–301.
Mason, C.M. (2009), 'Public policy support for the informal venture capital market', *International Small Business Journal*, **27**(5), 536–56.
Mason, C.M. and R.T. Harrison (2000), 'The size of the informal venture capital market in the United Kingdom', *Small Business Economics*, **15**, 137–48.
Mason, C.M. and R.T. Harrison (2008), 'Measuring business angel investment activity in the United Kingdom: a review of potential data sources', *Venture Capital*, **10**(4), 309–30.
Mason, C.M. and R.T. Harrison (2011), *Annual Report on the Business Angel Market in the United Kingdom: 2009/10*, available at http://www.bvca.co.uk/Portals/0/library/Files/News/2011/2011_0041_business_angel_report.pdf (accessed 30 March 2015).
Mason, C.M. and R.T. Harrison (2015), 'Business angel investment activity in the financial crisis: UK evidence and policy implications', *Environment and Planning C: Government and Policy*, **33**, 43–60.
Menon (2010), *Forretningsengler i Norge: Omfang, betydning og behov for offentlig Involvering*, Report 15/2010, Oslo: Menon.
Menon (2011), *The Need for Government Supported Capital Measures in the Market for Early Stage Risk Capital in Norway*, Report 18/2011, Oslo: Menon.
OECD (2011), *Financing High-growth Firms: The Role of Angel Investors*, Paris: OECD Publishing. doi: 10.1787/9789264118782-en.

OECD (2013), *Entrepreneurship at a Glance 2013*, Paris: OECD Publishing. doi: 10.1787/entrepreneur_aag-2013-en.
OECD (2014), *Financing SMEs and Entrepreneurs 2014: An OECD Scoreboard*, Paris: OECD Publishing, available at http://dx.doi.org/10.1787/fin_sme_ent-2014-en (accessed 1 June 2016).
Ou, C. (1987), *Holdings of Privately-held Business Assets by American Families*, Washington, DC: Small Business Administration.
Reitan, B. and R. Sørheim (2000), 'The informal venture capital market in Norway: investor characteristics, behavior and investment preferences', *Venture Capital*, **2**, 129–49.
Riding, A.L. (2005), 'On the size and structure of the informal market', Working Paper, School of Business, Carleton University, Canada.
Riding, A.L. (2008), 'Business angels and love money investors: segments of the informal market for risk capital', *Venture Capital*, **10**(4), 355–69.
Robb, A.M. and D.T. Robinson (2012), 'The capital structure decisions of new firms', NBER Working Paper No. 16272, Cambridge, MA.
Shane, S. (2009), *Fool's Gold: The Truth Behind Angel Investing in America*, New York: Oxford University Press.
Short, D.M. and A.L. Riding (1988), 'On the estimation of the investment potential of informal investors', *Journal of Small Business and Entrepreneurship*, **5**, 26–40.
Sohl, J.E. (2003), 'The private equity market in the USA: lessons from volatility', *Venture Capital*, **5**, 29–46.
Sohl, J. (2012), 'The changing nature of the angel market', in H. Landström and C. Mason (eds), *Handbook of Research on Venture Capital: Volume 2*, Cheltenham, UK and Northampton, MA, USA: Edward Elgar, pp. 17–41.
Wetzel Jr, W.E. (1983), 'Angels and informal risk capital', *Sloan Management Review*, **24**(4), 23–34.
Wetzel Jr, W.E. (1987), 'The informal risk capital market: aspects of scale and efficiency', *Journal of Business Venturing*, **2**, 299–313.
Wetzel Jr, W.E. (1994), 'Venture capital', in W.D. Bygrave (ed.), *The Portable MBA in Entrepreneurship*, New York: Wiley, pp. 172–94.
Zacharakis, A.L., D.A. Shepherd and J.E. Coombs (2003), 'The development of venture capital backed internet companies: an ecosystem perspective', *Journal of Business Venturing*, **18**, 217–31.

# 4 Categorisations of business angels: an overview

*Roger Sørheim and Tiago Botelho*

## 4.1 INTRODUCTION

Pioneering studies of business angels were based on a rather narrow sample of investors. In the 1990s, however, research on business angels became more sophisticated as researchers sought to widen the research agenda; that is, they conducted studies inspired by research on entrepreneurship and institutional venture capital (Mason and Harrison, 2000). Although pioneering studies indicate that business angels share many common traits, the investor population has been shown to be heterogeneous (Mason and Harrison, 2000). Thus, to achieve a better understanding of this heterogeneity and the informal venture capital market overall, it has been suggested that informal investors should be profiled and categorised. Over the last three decades, a number of studies have attempted to categorise business angels. In this chapter, we provide an overview of previous research on angel categorisations and explore the contributions and shortcomings of previous research. Thus, the main aims of this chapter are as follows: (1) to provide an overview and discuss the contribution of previous categorisations of business angels and (2) to provide an agenda for future research.

The overview provided in this chapter shows that different studies have categorised business angels or their investments using a wide range of variables. The majority of studies focus on grouping investors according to investor characteristics (for example, investment activity, competence, entrepreneurial background). These studies have, with a few exceptions, been 'data driven'. The main contribution from these studies has been a more sophisticated view of the 'definition' of a business angel, angel investment patterns and behaviour, and business angels' contributions to their portfolio firms. Studies of this type have clearly been important in breaking free of the oversimplified stereotypical view of what a business angel is and what contributions a start-up firm might gain from involvement with this type of investor.

Previous studies have indicated that investors by and large exhibit static investment patterns; however, there are a number of exceptions.

The most novel attempt was made by Avdeithchikova (2008), who used a representative sample of Swedish investors to challenge the view of the investor in only one type of investor role, taking into account the fact that investor behaviour varies from case to case. In general, however, the existing research on business angel categorisations is fragmented, lacking in a theoretical anchor, supply side driven, and fails to capture insight from the investment process over time.

In this chapter, we first give an overview of the pioneering studies of categorisations, followed by a discussion of developments since the year 2000. We then discuss whether policymakers should take into account the differences among angels. Finally, we summarise what we know and provide an agenda for future research.

## 4.2 CATEGORISATION OF INVESTORS: PIONEERING STUDIES

The first study that sought to develop a categorisation of business angels was presented in Gaston's seminal work (1989). Since then, various studies have examined business angels' categorisation using different units of analysis and clustering variables. All of these studies reinforce the idea that scholars cannot assume that business angels are a single population without any discrepancies between them. Gaston (1989) presents his classification of ten different 'groups' of informal investors (that is, Business Devils, The Godfather, Peers, Cousin Randy, Dr Kildare, Corporate Achievers, Daddy Warbucks, High-tech Angels, The Stockholder and Very Hungry Angels). This classification was based on the author's empirical perceptions of what he encountered in his meetings with angel investors. The segmentation was empirically driven, based on what the author assumed to be relevant for each particular type of angel (for example, investor background, investment goals, investment activity, levels of wealth, entrepreneurial experience and so on) without assigning a specific clustering variable. As a result of this lack of objective measures, the segmentation did not generate mutually exclusive groups; that is, an angel investor in this analysis could belong to more than one group. Another limitation that can be highlighted is the lack of theoretical implications derived by this classification. However, the importance of this research should not go unappreciated. This research sought to 'put boundaries on our ignorance', following Wetzel's tradition to angel research. Hence, the main contribution of this exploratory research is the fact that it was the first attempt to segment the business angel population.

The second study to present a segmentation of the angel population was conducted by Landström (1992), who tested the fit of Ouchi's model (Ouchi, 1977) of angel behaviour. The author interrogates agency theory (Jensen and Meckling, 1976), seeking to determine whether it could be used in the informal investment context. Hence, the entrepreneur has the capacity and incentive to affect wealth transfers between different parties and to behave in his own interest. The most important contribution of this research was to highlight the need for a strong theoretical framework in categorisation studies. Nonetheless, the study concludes that the framework suggested therein does not present acceptable evidence with which to elucidate the relationship between the entrepreneur and angel investor. In comparison with Gaston (1989), this research uses a narrower set of investor characteristics, which can be seen as an improvement upon the previous study.

The following categorisation study (Freear et al., 1994) developed a clustering variable to gauge levels of investment activity in entrepreneurial ventures. Three clusters emerge from this study: business angels, interested potential investors and non-interested potential investors. Chronologically, this is the first of several classification studies that have used the level of investment experience as a clustering variable. Although this research is not based on a strong theoretical framework, it endows insights as to the relationship between groups and their investment preferences (for example, stage of investment, location, amount invested and so on). Another contribution of this research lies in its substantial improvement of the statistical procedures used to conduct classification studies.

Sullivan and Miller (1996) present an analysis supported by investment motivations that identifies three 'groups': Economics, Hedonism and Altruism. Economics motivations are based on conventional economic and financial theories supporting wealth maximisation and individual rationality. Informal investors categorised in this cluster are focused on the financial return resulting from the investments they make. Hedonistic motivations are related to non-financial factors, that is, factors that are not easily measured, such as a 'psychic income' (Simon, 1959, p. 253). This type of angel investor could easily be described as 'man tries to maximize his pleasure and minimize his pain'. Finally, investors with altruistic motivations are encouraged to accept entrepreneurs' proposals based on what Etzioni (1988) calls a 'moral dimension'. The investors of this group seek to give back to society something that they themselves received years ago. The key contribution of this research is to be the first to examine whether informal investors should be distinguished based on their investment preferences and, in particular, the reasons they chose to invest. The biggest critique that can be made of this research is the fact that its unit of analysis is the business angel. Hence, it does not allow for variance in investment motivations across the same informal investor.

A study dating from the same year (Kelly and Hay, 1996) analyses the serial investor segment of the angel population. This particular segment of the angel market is defined by investors who have made three or more investments. Referencing informal investor preferences for investing at an individual or collective level, the authors identified two sub-segments: solo serial investors and syndicate serial investors. The main limitation of this research is that it only analyses a subset (that is, serial angels) of the whole population; consequently, it lacks completeness. However, this study also provides additional insights into investment activity, returns and the investment behaviour of serial angels. In his doctoral dissertation, Kelly (2000) follows this approach of using investment activity as a clustering variable. The author divides his sample into three sub-groups: investors with three or fewer investments; investors that made between four and nine investments; and investors with ten or more investments. Among other factors, the study contributed to our understanding of the contractual relationship between entrepreneurs and informal investors and elucidated the ways in which the number of investments made can affect this relationship. This approach is highly suitable for providing a comprehensive overview of the different types of investors and identifying factors that influence their decisions. Kelly and Hay (2000) continued their research on this topic by dividing Kelly's middle group (that is, investors with four to nine investments) into two separate subsets. The study thus clustered the angel population into four types of investors based on investment activity (that is, fewer than three investments, three to five, six to nine and more than ten). The focus of this research was to test the impact of investment activity on the type of suppliers of leads used and on the quality of opportunity deal flow. Their findings reinforce the idea that investment procedures will vary across the angel population, as well as the argument that investors have different networks that influence the deal flow of investment opportunities. In terms of understanding the diversity of informal investors, however, this study fails to include in its analysis the effect of investing in groups (that is, angel networks, angel groups, angel syndicates).

Stevenson and Coveney (1994) present a cluster analysis sustained on two main criteria: investment activity and the entrepreneurial experience of the angel investor. Entrepreneurial experience was measured by financial and business background, while investment activity was measured by the number of investments made and the total funds invested. These two criteria allowed the authors to create and profile four 'groups' of active angels (that is, wealth-maximising angels; entrepreneur angels;

income-seeking angels; and corporate angels). Two groups of inactive investors were also identified and profiled: those who are not currently investing (latent angels) and those that have not yet made an investment (virgin angels). The limitations of this study are associated with its failure to provide information as to how these groups were categorised and the absence of a clear justification for this classification.

Sørheim and Landström (2001) maintain that investment activity should be one of the units of analysis in cluster analysis; however, instead of using entrepreneurial background, they utilise competence as a second unit of analysis. The authors measure investor competence through a set of experiences: Professional, Self-employed, Education, Business Background and Entrepreneurial Background. To measure investment activity a set of future and past investment questions, the authors identified each angel investor's amount of investment activity. These two criteria enabled the researchers to create four 'types' (that is, Lotto Investors, Analytical Investors, Traders and Business Angels). This study made both methodological and empirical contributions to the field. Regarding the former, this research presents a more robust method of categorisation using a set of angel characteristics as the unit of analysis. Additionally, this article refines the way investment activity was measured and emphasised the importance of wider criteria in terms of research robustness. The results draw attention to differences within the four groups of informal investors in regard to investment preferences and investment procedures, among others.

### 4.2.1 The Main Contributions of the Pioneering Studies

The pioneering categorisations (Table 4.1) were important in creating a more sophisticated view of the informal venture capital market. Several of these categorisations were easily communicated and drew attention from both academics and non-academics, thus reaching a wider audience. These categorisations should be particularly important for policymakers, who could use them to understand how different types of investors could be stimulated. These categorisations can assist policymakers in being more precise when introducing means to stimulate the informal venture capital market. However, even if we note outreach to non-academics in official government reports, private initiatives to support business angels, it is still difficult to see how these studies have affected policies in stimulating different categories of business angels. Finally, it should also be noted that these pioneering studies opened avenues for future research and could be considered an explicit call for more in-depth studies of informal investors.

*Table 4.1 Pioneering studies categorising informal investors*

| Author(s) | Methodology | Dimensions explored | Investor profiles |
|---|---|---|---|
| Gaston (1989) | • A series of survey studies comprising a total of 425 informal investors/ business angels<br>• Convenience sample<br>• Unclear how the data are analysed | • Unclear<br>• Godfather | • Business devils<br>• Godfather<br>• Peers<br>• Dr Kildare<br>• Corporate Achievers<br>• The Stockholder<br>• High-tech Angels<br>• Daddy Warbucks<br>• Cousin Randy<br>• Very Hungry Angels |
| Landström (1992) | • Survey of 62 business angels in Sweden<br>• Convenience sample<br>• Statistical analysis | • Investors' attitude towards the portfolio firm<br>• Interaction between informal investors and portfolio firm | • Individuals in business environment<br>• Individuals making few investments and small amounts of capital per deal<br>• Individuals who make few investments but larger amounts per deal<br>• Professional informal investors, frequent investments and large amounts per deal |
| Sullivan and Miller (1996) | • Survey of 217 potential and active investors in four states in the USA<br>• Convenience sample<br>• Statistical analysis | • Investor motivation<br>• Perceived risk | • Economic investors<br>• Hedonistic investors<br>• Altruistic investors |
| Kelly and Hay (1996) | • Semi-structured interviews of a small number of serial investors in the UK | • Risk management<br>• Investment activity<br>• Investment behaviour | • Solo serial investors<br>• Syndicated serial investors |
| Stevenson and Coveney (1994) | • Survey of 262 informal investors in the UK<br>• Convenience sample<br>• Unclear how the data are analysed | • Number of businesses founded<br>• Total amounts of funds invested | • Virgin investor<br>• Latent investor<br>• Wealth maximising<br>• Entrepreneurial<br>• Income seeker<br>• Corporate |

*Table 4.1* (continued)

| Author(s) | Methodology | Dimensions explored | Investor profiles |
|---|---|---|---|
| Sørheim and Landström (2001) | • Survey of 425 active informal investors in Norway<br>• Convenience sample<br>• Statistical analysis using cluster analysis | • Investor activity and investor competence | • Lotto investors<br>• Traders<br>• Analytical investors<br>• 'Pure' business angels |

## 4.3 FURTHER DEVELOPMENT: REPRESENTATIVENESS AND IN-DEPTH STUDIES

Although it is easy to recognise the importance of pioneering studies of informal investor categorisations, previous studies have suffered from a number of shortcomings. (1) They were all based on convenience samples (and several of them were narrow, that is, based on data from business angel networks or the number of investors covered were few); thus, we question the studies' generalisability and whether they actually cover different categories of angels. (2) Several of the studies suffer from a lack of statistical rigour (see Table 4.1) that should be expected in robust empirical studies. (3) These pioneering studies are to a large extent 'data driven' and thus suffer from the lack of theoretical development needed in order to make further progress within the field. (4) Investors are considered to exhibit static investment patterns; thus, none of these pioneering studies captures how investors develop in their careers as investors. In that vein, another criticism is related to the fact that investors could play different roles in different investments.

### 4.3.1 Towards Representativeness

In a novel study of informal investors, Avdeithchikova (2008) used a representative sample of Swedish investors to create a typology of investors based on levels of contribution related to financial and human resources. Her research draws attention to the limitations of previous typology studies while also suggesting an alternative way in which to classify the angel population. Avdeithchikova (2008) reviews the deficiencies of previous studies by pointing out three crucial points. The first issue raised concerns about the reasoning behind the choice of the clustering rules. The author defends three justifications for this choice: first, scholars have failed to explain their reasoning for past categorisations. The second is the lack of a strong theoretical background pertaining to clustering rules. The last is the idea of using investor-related variables and investment-related variables simultaneously. According to the author, this approach creates ambiguity in regard to the classification's unit of analysis; the reader does not know whether clusters characterise investors or investment. The second concern raised by this study is the static nature of previous categorisation studies. Previous studies did not allow investors to adapt, evolve or take on different roles. Hence, the author makes a case for setting investments as the unit of analysis. The lack of theoretical frameworks in previous classification studies is regarded by the author as a third key deficiency. The identification of these limitations had a direct impact on the classification system suggested in this research. This classification builds upon the two different types of contributions an angel investor can provide (that is, financial and non-financial). The use of the investment rather than the investor as the unit of analysis was one of the key contributions of this study; this approach opened a new line of research within classification studies. Additionally, this research shows that investor behaviour (investor contributions) may change depending on firm requirements.

Avdeithchikova found that informal investors' roles are, to a large extent, explained by the availability of financial and human capital resources and the willingness to use these resources. However, an intriguing finding was that the resource requirements of entrepreneurial firms were less important in explaining the roles adopted by investors. This outcome can be explained by a high degree of conservatism and lack of flexibility among the investors involved in this study. Avdeithchikova's novel study, however, may also have some shortcomings. The author did not take into account the possibility of business angels investing with others. This cooperative investment has a direct impact on the type and level of contributions that an informal investor can provide. Additionally, the choice of contribution might be investor dependent, that is, contributions might depend on investors' personal preferences. This dependence might result in measurement problems because investors' characteristics might provide better justification for this categorisation than do different types of investments.

### 4.3.2 In-depth Studies of Specific Categories of Informal Investors

A number of studies focus on specific categories of informal investors. Erikson et al. (2003) compared angel investors who invest mainly in opportunities to which they have family ties with all other types of informal investors. The authors investigate four areas of angel investing (that is, investing stages, number of investments, degree of involvement and exit preferences), concluding that the contrast between 'family angels' and other types of angels is significant. Erikson and Sørheim (2005) studied the differences between angel investors who invest in technology-driven opportunities and all other informal investors. The analysis looked at the different dimensions of angel investing (that is, deal origin, selection, monitoring and exit preferences) and concluded that 'technology angels' are atypical in comparison to other types of business angels.

One common factor shared by most investor categorisation studies is the lack of explanation as to how scholars have chosen clustering variables for their study. Erikson (2007) breaks this tradition in typology studies by suggesting a classification of investors based on the two dominant schools of entrepreneurship (that is, Schumpeterian and Austrian). The author operationalised this classification by assessing the investment history (that is, the past three years) of each investor. Schumpeterian classification required that the majority of investment be made in new technology-driven firms with an international market potential. The prerequisites of qualification as an Austrian investor involve having a majority of one's investments in firms equipped to reach the international market. This study breaks the dominant paradigm in categorisation studies by presenting a theoretical base for classification. However, some questions are raised by this study. First, group classification seems to be too simplistic; there are no references to different levels of technology orientation in the Schumpeterian typology. Second, the length of the analysis is too short, that is, three years. The number of group members could be biased by market trends. Third, the scope of the study only includes the investment, not the investor. Hence, a majority rule does not reflect the dynamics of angel investing. A possible solution would be to use a 100 per cent rule to define the two groups and all of the other cases would be hybrids. In a categorisation study conducted by Lahti ( 2011), the author advocates that investments can be segmented into sub-groups using the time spent by the informal investor in pre-investment (that is, due diligence) and post-investment involvement in the invested companies (that is, value-added activities). This analysis creates four different 'groups' (that is, Gambles, Conventional Angel Investments, Due Diligence Driven Investments and Professionally Safeguarded Investments). The theoretical background of this research is based on the means by which informal investors can reduce both pre- and post-investment risks. This risk reduction is done via a principal agent approach and contract theory. The first theory is the same as that used previously by Landström (1992), which emphasises that the principal (angel investor) will try to align the incentives of the agent (entrepreneur) with his own. Alignment can be achieved through complete contracts; however, contracts are not complete because it is impossible to contract all states of nature. Therefore, pre- and post-investment risk reduction will be a function of the time spent in due diligence (pre-investment) and time spent in active involvement (post-investment).

Some recent studies focus on the investor as a founding angel, that is, an investor is involved from the very start (or even before the founding; Festel and De Cleyn, 2013). In a case study of 16 new technology-based firms (NTBFs), Festel and De Cleyn (2013) found that these founding angels play a key role in providing support on a day-to-day basis and provide operational resources to the company. Thus, the investment role is defined by both the investment stage and management resources provided in addition to the financial capital. Festel and De Cleyn (2013) suggested that founding angels help fill the gap that has been demonstrated by previous literature in the pre-seed funding of technology-based firms in general and academic spin-offs in particular. Furthermore, the category 'founding angel' can be considered a form of parallel or portfolio entrepreneur (for example, entrepreneurs holding a position as a minority shareholder in at least two companies). The literature on portfolio entrepreneurs contends that firms with this type of minority shareholder on board have access to more resources and networks than do other firms (Alsos and Kolvereid, 1998; Alsos, 2007). Moreover, Festel and De Clyn (2013) can be viewed as an extension of the Landström (1998) study that focused on the relationship between investor and entrepreneur and used the concepts 'business creator' and 'co-creator'; these creators want to participate in the creation process. It can also be argued that earlier studies of very experienced investors conducted by Sørheim (2003, 2005), who further examined the role of 'pure business angels', are a part of the same research string. Through a qualitative study of five experienced angel investors using an integrated social capital framework, he found that for these investors, one of the main investment criteria was the creation of a common platform enabling the investor and entrepreneur to work closely together, often on a day-to-day basis. In a later study using the same data, Sørheim (2005) found that these highly involved investors played a key role in facilitating further financing for their portfolio firms by providing access to equity investors and debt financiers, as well as acting as referrers by capitalising on their own positive track records and good reputation.

There are very few studies focusing on decision-making among different categories of investors, that is, asking whether experience matters in regard to investment decisions. In a study of Scottish investors, Smith et al. (2010) used verbal protocol analysis while studying three groups (each of four investors). Group 1 consisted of experienced/super angels who had each made at least five investments, and Group 2 consisted of novice angels who had each made only one investment. Group 3 consisted of nascent angels who were very interested in making their first investment, despite not yet having done so. The most experienced investors made quicker investment decisions and put more emphasis on investor fit than did the two other groups. This finding is very much in line with the findings in the Sørheim (2003) study. Novice and nascent angels put more emphases on financial issues than did experienced angels, thus indicating that experienced angels know from the start that initial finances must be reworked before they give meaning to the investor. Both experienced and novice angels recognised that previous investment experience affected their investment behaviour. This effect is especially evident when it comes to the due diligence of an entrepreneurial team (that is, the experienced ones focusing more on the team). This study also indicates that nascent angels are overconfident and rely too much on experience accumulated through their corporate careers. Though the Smith et al. (2010) study provides some insight as to decision-making among different categories of investors, there are very view studies taking into account the dynamics of the ways in which business angels develop their careers or the reasons why they become business angels. An exception here is a study by Politis and Landström (2002) wherein the authors discuss an in-depth case study of the careers of four business angels. Based on empirical results, they identify a career path whereby investors go through three career phases: (1) a period as an employee in a corporate firm; (2) a phase of entrepreneurial learning; and (3) the investment career phase. In each career phase, investors develop experience and competencies that prepare them to act as 'classical' business angels in the later stages of their careers. During the corporate career period, investors develop an understanding of managerial logic, establish networks and build their reputations. In the following entrepreneurial learning phase, investors break out of the corporate sphere and involve themselves in entrepreneurial projects, often as consultants. As such, they learn the basic logic of entrepreneurial processes. During the investment career phase, business angels combine their managerial and entrepreneurial competencies to act as entrepreneurs and investors, that is, providing their portfolio firms with 'smart capital'.

## 4.4 SHOULD POLICYMAKERS TAKE INTO ACCOUNT DIFFERENCES BETWEEN BUSINESS ANGELS?

Overall, previous studies have shown that business angels are heterogeneous. Though we find traces of recognition of the differentiation in governmental reports, white papers and so on, it is difficult to actually see that differentiation has influenced the way policymakers attempt to stimulate the angel market. Governmental and private efforts to stimulate the angel market could broadly be separated into two measurement categories (Sørheim and Landström, 2001): (1) to reduce 'search costs' (for example, making it easier for entrepreneurs and investors to meet virtually or physically through organised business angel networks) or (2) to reduce the risk and increase the rewards related to these types of investments (for example, as with varying types of front or back end tax incentives). Overall, it is likely that policymakers think that one size fits all. This is especially problematic when it is claimed that new policies will infuse an amount of 'smart capital' in the angel market. The resource constraints (related to capital, management resources and networks) for a potential high-growth firm are highest in the earliest stages of a venture's life cycle. Potential contributions from very experienced angels could be of vital importance to ensuring that they reach their full potential. As such, if the aim of measurement is to stimulate the inflow of 'smart capital', this factor must be taken into account when developing new mechanisms. The stimulation of venture accelerator programmes (for example, high growth-oriented incubators) seems to be a good place to start. Examples of such measures include efforts by the Scottish co-investment fund, which has been vital in engaging Scottish angel investors, and the even more specialised Finnish VIGO scheme whereby companies affiliated with a new venture accelerator get on the 'fast track' to public funding (Lithander et al., 2011). However, the development of such measures must adapt to a context wherein business angels operate.

## 4.5 CATEGORISATIONS OF BUSINESS ANGELS: WHAT DO WE KNOW AND WHAT DO WE NOT KNOW?

Over the last 25 years, there have been numerous attempts to categorise business angels. The main contribution from these studies has been a more sophisticated view of what a business angel is, what his or her investment patterns and behaviours are and what contributions he or she makes to portfolio firms.

However, there are still challenges to overcome. Small heterogeneous samples have made it very difficult to establish robust categorisations of investors. The most novel attempt is made by Avdeithchikova (2008), who uses a representative sample of Swedish investors. Avdeithchikova also makes a contribution in breaking out from the view of an investor in one investor role, taking into account the fact that investor behaviour varies from case to case. However, even this type of approach has challenges, including the fact that studies demand very large 'base' samples to obtain a sufficient number of investors to create robust categorisations and that, even with large samples, we struggle to capture the most active and experienced investors (that is, they are considered 'outliers', or investors praise the anonymity and refuse to participate in surveys).

Another issue related to research design is that previous studies have, to a large extent, adopted a supply-side view of the issue using cross-sectional data. There are, in general, surprisingly few longitudinal qualitative studies that have attempted to follow different categories of investors over time. Longitudinal studies could help in developing insights related to investor roles (that is, roles' parallel cases and also how this changes over time). The scarcity of longitudinal and qualitative studies may be related to the fact that this type of data collection is very time-consuming. Similarly, business angels are reluctant to cooperate closely with researchers. Furthermore, there is clearly a need to examine different investors' roles from the entrepreneur's side (supply side). Another important issue is the fragmented nature of previous research, which is perhaps best illustrated by the lack of 'dialogue' between the field of entrepreneurial finance related to founding angels and the research on portfolio entrepreneurship. Such studies ultimately use different labels to research the same thing. Overall, there is much to gain in aligning research designs among actors within both 'paradigms'.

## 4.6 CATEGORISATIONS OF BUSINESS ANGELS: THE ROAD AHEAD

The aim of this chapter has been to give an overview of the previous categorisations of business angels. This review has introduced a number of interesting avenues for further research, the most promising of which are outlined here:

- Research on categorisations is largely empirically driven; theoretical development and robust theoretical concepts are scarce. Thus, the accumulation of knowledge and the rigorous development of this research stream are more challenging. The concept of 'proximity' has been used to develop a fine-grained framework for understanding the different advantages that might arise from similarities between collaborative actors who influence interaction and knowledge accumulation among partners (Boschma, 2005; Steinmo, 2015). The proximity concept refers to being close to something measured on a certain dimension. These dimensions could, for example, include social proximity, technological proximity, cognitive proximity and cultural proximity. We recommend that this concept be adapted and further developed in future studies of business angel categorisation.

- The existing literature is yet dominated by studies that adopt an investor view. There is a need for more studies with a demand-side view that would address the manner in which entrepreneurial ventures experience the processes and contributions of different categories of investors. A longitudinal research design including insight from entrepreneurs and investors could potentially give unique insight into the process of involving different categories of business angels in entrepreneurial ventures (furthermore, a study with a solely supply-side approach could potentially make a nice contribution to this field of research).
- A study by Avdeithchikova (2008) suggested that experienced investors are more limited than expected in their ability to adapt 'smart' contributions to their portfolio firms. Does this mean that experienced investors use a 'one size fits all' strategy? In line with this notion, future categorisations should develop a design whereby the dynamic development of investor roles is taken into account. This longitudinal approach should also imply the introduction of a learning perspective to the development of different investor roles.
- There is a need for longitudinal studies in which various research designs are aligned. A more holistic research design that examines the investment process from inception to exit is also needed. Research should be conducted from both the supply side and the demand side. This research could also include other investor types, such as venture capitalists and corporate venture capitalists.
- Studies that categorise business angels have previously been conducted only in a US or European setting. There is a need for research on different types of business angels in other geographic regions as well. This could be done by establishing a broad international research consortium labelled the 'Global Business Angel Monitor'. International cooperation could serve to address the sample and representativeness issues raised in this chapter.

- The question of investor exit needs to be further explored. How will different categories of investors influence the exit (in terms of both process and outcome)? To what extent could failure or success be related to the categories of investors involved? What are the exit vehicles, and what roles do different categories of investors play in preparation for exit?
- Another under-researched issue is the question of whether business angels are always beneficial to entrepreneurial ventures. Could some types of investors actually be harmful to long-term venture development?
- A rapidly growing phenomenon is equity crowdfunding. How can these investors be categorised, and how do they fit into the big picture?

## REFERENCES

Alsos, G.A. (2007), *Portfolio Entrepreneurship, General and Farm Contexts*, Norway: Bodø Graduate School of Business.

Alsos, G.A. and L. Kolvereid (1998), 'The business gestation process of novice, serial and parallel business founders', *Entrepreneurship Theory and Practice*, **22**, 101–14.

Avdeitchikova, S. (2008), 'On the structure of the informal venture capital market in Sweden: developing investment roles', *Venture Capital*, **10**(1), 55–85.

Avdeitchikova, S., H. Landström and N. Månsson (2008), 'What do we mean when we talk about business angels? Some reflections on definitions and sampling', *Venture Capital*, **10**(4), 371–94.

Boschma, R. (2005), 'Proximity and innovation: a critical assessment', *Regional Studies*, **39**, 61–74.

Erikson, T. (2007), 'Discriminating "Schumpeterian" from "Austrian" informal investors – an empirical assessment', *Journal of International Entrepreneurship*, **5**(1), 1–10.

Erikson, T. and R. Sørheim (2005), 'Technology investors vs. other investors', *Technovation*, **25**(5), 489–96.

Erikson, T., R. Sørheim and B. Reitan Reston (2003), 'Family angels vs. other informal investors', *Family Business Review*, **16**, 163–171.

Etzioni, A. (1988), *The Moral Dimension: Toward a New Economics*, New York: The Free Press.

Festel, G.W. and S.H. De Cleyn (2013), 'Founding angels as an emerging subtype of the angel investment model in high-tech businesses', *Venture Capital*, **15**(3), 261–82.

Freear, J.E., J. Sohl and W.E. Wetzel (1994), 'Angels and non-angels: are there differences?', *Journal of Business Venturing*, **9**(2), 109–23.

Gaston, R. (1989), *Finding Private Venture Capital for Your Firm: A Complete Guide*, New York: John Wiley & Sons.

Jensen, M. and M. Meckling (1976), 'Theory of the firm: managerial behavior, agency costs, and ownership structure', *Journal of Financial Economics*, **3**, 305–60.

Kelly, P. (2000), 'Private investors and entrepreneurs: how context shapes their relationship', PhD thesis, London Business School.

Kelly, P. and M. Hay (1996), 'Serial investors and early stage finance', *Journal of Entrepreneurial and Small Business Finance*, **5**(2), 159–74.

Kelly, P. and M. Hay (2000), '"Deal-makers": reputation attracts quality', *Venture Capital*, **2**(3), 183–202.

Lahti, T. (2011), 'Categorization of angel investments: an explorative analysis of risk reduction strategies in Finland', *Venture Capital*, **13**(1), 49–74.
Landström, H. (1992), 'The relationship between private investors and small firms: an agency theory approach', *Entrepreneurship and Regional Development*, **4**, 199–223.
Landström, H. (1998), 'Informal investors as entrepreneurs', *Technovation*, **18**, 321–33.
Lithander, J., R. Sørheim and E. Rasmussen (2011), *Competent Capital? Three Countries, Three Attempts*, Report 2011:05, Östersund, Sweden: Tillväxtanalys.
Mason, C. and R. Harrison (2000), 'Informal venture capital and the financing of emergent growth businesses', in D. Sexton and H. Landström (eds), *Handbook of Entrepreneurship*, Oxford: Blackwell Publishers, pp. 221–39.
Politis, D. and H. Landström (2002), 'Informal investors as entrepreneurs – the development of an entrepreneurial career', *Venture Capital*, **4**(2), 78–101.
Ouchi, W.G. (1977), 'The relationship between organizational structure and organizational control', *Administrative Science Quarterly*, **22**(1), 95–11
Simon, H.A. (1959), 'Theories of decision-making in economics and behavioral science', *American Economic Review*, **49**(3), 253–83.
Smith, D.J., R.T. Harrison and C.M. Mason (2010), 'Experience, heuristics and learning: the angel investment process', *Frontiers of Entrepreneurship Research*, Wellesley, MA: Babson College.
Sørheim, R. (2003), 'The pre-investment behaviour of business angels: a social capital approach', *Venture Capital*, **5**(4), 337–64.
Sørheim, R. (2005), 'Business angels as facilitators for further finance: an exploratory study', *Journal of Small Business and Enterprise Development*, **12**(2), 178–92.
Sørheim, R. and H. Landström (2001), 'Informal investors – a categorization with policy implications', *Entrepreneurship and Regional Development*, **13**, 351–70.
Steinmo, M. (2015), 'Collaboration for innovation: a case study on how social capital mitigates collaborative challenges in university–industry research alliances', *Industry and Innovation*, **22**(7), 597–624.
Stevenson, H. and P. Coveney (1994), *Fallacies Corrected and Six Distinct Types of Angel Identified*, Oxford: Venture Capital Report.
Sullivan, M.K. and A. Miller (1996), 'Segmenting the informal venture capital market: economic, hedonistic, and altruistic investors', *Journal of Business Research*, **36**(1), 25–35.

# 5 Women business angels: theory and practice

*Frances M. Amatucci*

## 5.1 INTRODUCTION

Business angel investing has traditionally been a male-dominated activity. However, there has been significant progress in terms of addressing the low representation of women as a proportion of the total number of business angels worldwide (Elder, 2012; Casserly, 2013). Despite the dearth of academic research examining women business angels (WBA), this subject is being discussed extensively in business trade magazines and journals worldwide. Advocates for greater representation of women in the angel investor community argue that male investors may overlook lucrative investment opportunities in non-traditional sectors. Therefore, increased diversity evidenced by larger numbers of female angel investors can increase deal flow. Early stage funding is critical for start-ups and women entrepreneurs may receive disproportionately less giving them an unfair handicap. In this chapter, a review of extant research on women business angels is presented. This topic has not been explored significantly in academic research but what little research that currently exists is examined. Additionally, the author reviews business media, websites and blogs to obtain the most current information in the field. As a primary source of data, several women business angels are profiled and narratives of their opinions on key subjects of debate are provided.

In the first section of the chapter, I describe where women angel investors are and the relatively low representation of women business angels in the global investment community. This is further explained by identifying several causes and effects of the low numbers despite growing numbers of female entrepreneurs. The second section examines who current women business angels are, the types of investment sectors that interest them and how their investment behavior might differ from those of men. This corresponds to the initial attitudes, behaviors and characteristics (ABC) research conducted on business angels in the early stages of its historical development; however, now the focus is on women business angels, in particular. Next, trends, challenges and opportunities for women business angels are presented. Trends such as the increases in numbers of high net wealth women, numbers of women-led angel groups and training programs for women business angels suggest progress is being made in narrowing the gap, although a great deal more progress is warranted. Finally, a future research agenda for expanding existing knowledge about women business angels is discussed with several recommendations regarding public policy implications.

## 5.2 A NOTE ON METHODOLOGY

Although the purpose of this chapter is to explain the current status of women angel investing and investigate future trends as they impact both women investors and women entrepreneurs, relatively little academic research exists on the topic. Therefore, the author conducted an extensive content analysis of research center and professional organization publications, web-based blogs, business media, webinars and social media, in addition to academic journals. These secondary sources of data collection proved to be very informative and provided timely information that may not be possible in traditional forms of a literature review.

The methodology also included primary source data collection in the form of a web-based survey that was sent out to numerous female angel investors identified in the media and on websites. The author used LinkedIn to contact potential respondents, in addition to leveraging professional relationships to obtain introductions and support (Swartz et al., 2016a). The survey contained 14 questions with a Likert-type scale and a comment section to explain the response. Two demographic questions, including the respondent's name, were included. Five high profile female angel investors provided responses. Although anonymity was an option, all five of the respondents gave permission for their names and the names of their firms to be published in the research.

## 5.3 WOMEN BUSINESS ANGELS: WHERE ARE THEY?

The notion that investing is primarily a male activity that excludes women can be traced back to the Victorian era. However, research by Maltby and Rutterford (2006) and Rutterford and Maltby (2005) on investors in the UK from the mid-nineteenth to early twentieth century proposes that the role of women investors has been significantly under-reported. Although women were not directly linked to the male investor network, they were 'peripherally linked' to these networks as well as to the family and friends of businessmen. Moreover, to compensate for the lack of direct personal contacts, women had access to information about investing due to growth in financial publications and the increasing availability of financial professionals. In the twenty-first century, while the role of women investors is no longer ignored, participation is still in the minority.

Statistics about the presence and activities of women angel investors in the USA have been reported by the Center for Venture Research in its quarterly and annual reports since 2004. At that time women angels represented a mere 5 percent of the angel market and, of that group, only a quarter actually made an investment (Sohl, 2006). More recent reports show a significant increase with approximately 26.1 percent representation in 2014 and 25.3 percent in 2015 (Sohl, 2015, 2016). The *2014 Halo Report* of business angel investing in the USA published by the Angel Resource Institute and PitchBook does not provide information about female angel investors (ARI, 2015).

Although statistics in the 2015 Center for Venture Research report (Sohl, 2015) show a slight decline, they are significantly higher than representation of women business angels in other countries (Harrison and Mason, 2007). Research published on business angel activity in the UK does not report female participation (Deloitte and UK Business Angel Association, 2013), although Mason and Harrison (2011) reported 8 percent of the sample of 147 business angels in their 2009/10 study were female. Most estimates report the percentage of women business angels in the UK to be approximately 5 percent (Williams, 2013). In the 2012 report by the Center for Strategy and Evaluation Services, which provides an extensive review of research conducted on business angel markets and policies in the European Union, women business angel numbers and investment amounts were obtained from the 2010 European Business Angel Network (EBAN) survey report. The countries, number of business angel networks, number of female angels and percentage of women angel investors are provided in Table 5.1. All countries in the European Union exhibited representation under 10 percent. Yet, as discussed later, in the UK women hold 48 percent of Britain's personal wealth and this is expected to grow. A 2010 EBAN report recommends a number of public policy initiatives directed toward achieving the objective of 20 percent of female business angel representation by 2015 (EBAN, 2010).

In 2013 the Women's Angel Investor Network (WAIN) was founded as the first women angel investor group in the United Arab Emirates; 30–40 percent of all start-ups in the Middle East are owned by women entrepreneurs and WAIN plans to provide training to these women-led businesses (http://www.changemakers.com/project/womens-angel-investment-network-wain).

With an increasing number of women entrepreneurs who need access

*Table 5.1 Representation of female business angels in the European Union*

| Country | Number of business angel networks | Number of female business angels | Percentage of women angel investors |
|---|---|---|---|
| France | 66 | 375 | 9.3 |
| Italy | 10 | 7 | 2.3 |
| Germany | 13 | 20 | 4.9 |
| Netherlands | 11 | 30 | 1.3 |
| Poland | 3 | 12 | 9 |
| Spain | 13 | 18 | 2.2 |
| Sweden | 5 | 10 | 7.4 |
| UK | 22 | 30 | 5.6 |

*Source:* Center for Strategy and Evaluation Services (2012).

to financial resources, is this low representation of female angel investors problematic? There are arguments that increased female presence in the angel investment community can provide benefits in many ways (Hudson et al., 2006; EBAN, 2010). The EBAN published a white paper in 2010 entitled, 'Women and European early stage investing,' which portends the low representation of women business angels as problematic because of the important role this type of funding plays in accessing financial capital for early stage and start-up ventures. Based on a study by research sponsored by the Kauffman Foundation in 2006 involving in-depth interviews with 12 US women angel investors, the shortage of women business angels is described 'as a missed opportunity for women, for the entrepreneurial community, and for the US economy' (Hudson et al., 2006, p. 3).

These studies and others describe the following potential barriers that can prevent larger numbers of women from becoming angel investors:

1. Women underestimate themselves regarding risk propensity.
2. Women tend to be more conservative, less experienced investors.
3. Women are in different social networks than men and don't have similar social capital in the form of access to key relationships and information.
4. Women have different schedules due to family responsibilities.
5. Women are less likely to be 'cashed-out' entrepreneurs and more likely to have inherited wealth.
6. Business angel activity is male-dominated and primarily marketed to men.

7. Business angel networks focus primarily on the technology sector while women investors may be more likely to consider health care, retail, consumer products and/or green/social businesses.

In a survey distributed to several prominent women angel investors, the following comments were made when asked about the problems associated with low participation of women in the angel investment community.

> In our culture [US], women tend to expect to be invited to be an angel investor, or invited to participate in an angel investor group. Men invite themselves to be part of angel investor activity. They typically don't wait for an invitation. Women need to learn to invite themselves to the party. Also, women tend to believe that they need to learn every detail about angel investing before they engage in the activity. On the contrary, men will jump into the activity knowing that they will learn as they invest, and will confidently act like they know what they are doing. (Catherine V. Mott, CEO and Founder, BlueTree Allied Angels, Blue Tree Venture Fund I and BlueTree Capital Group)

> People need role models to identify themselves with and think they can do it as well. Seeing more examples of women investors will open the way. In my opinion, a woman investor would be seen as far more accessible than a man investor. The glass ceiling is still not completely broken. In France, entrepreneurs, and even more investors, are often viewed as rich capitalists. The opinion is stronger for women as the traditional view that a woman's place is at home is still alive in many places. I had to 'lower my voice' when expressing my enthusiasm to become an angel investor. My mother tried to persuade me not to prepare for an MBA. 'A woman's place is to start a family, not to manage companies.' (Morgane Rollando, Femmes Business Angels, Paris, France)

> I think women are less aware of the angel investing opportunity. We don't talk about our investments with friends like men do. We may be missing out on some of the benefits that can bring such as access to new networks, information, etc. Low numbers of women angels makes it more difficult for women entrepreneurs to raise funding, especially in the tech space. However, well intentioned, gender-blindness is not possible. (Sarah Turner, Founder, Angel Academe)

> I don't think the low number of women angels is a bad thing in an absolute sense. But if women want to become angel investors and are not because they don't have access to resources and networks, that is when the problem arises. The barriers come more from social pressures. We know from one Harvard study that men are 40 to 50 per cent more likely to apply for a job for which they are under qualified. By definition, every angel investor is under qualified when they start investing, and even throughout their investing career when they are investing in 'disruptive technologies.' (Angel Lee, Founder, 37 Angels)

> Women-led companies are constrained by a lack of access to capital. Women are much more likely to fund their new ventures with credit cards or savings

> than male-led ventures which are more successful in obtaining equity and debt instruments to fuel growth. It's definitely mostly a white boy's club in the angel/VC [venture capital] world. Women VCs are scarce, yet are more likely to fund firms with women founders or senior leadership. (Lauren Flanagan, Belle Capital USA LP)

While the barriers may present challenges for increased representation of women business angels, they can also present opportunities for increased deal flow and benefits for the economy, in general. An increase in the number of angel investors can increase the number of deals being funded. Moreover, it can increase the diversity of angel investments because women may be inclined to invest in a broader range of under-represented sectors in addition to technology and software. Women are often thought to be more collaborative and bring new perspectives to the investment decision-making process. They may express a stronger commitment to funding women-owned businesses and may involve angel education in fund activities.

The Kauffman Foundation report (Hudson et al., 2006) found that the 12 women angel investors who were interviewed benefited from: obtaining financial returns; being provided an opportunity to serve as role models or mentors to other women; entrepreneurial enterprises and other potential women angel investors; creating new social and professional networks; and engaging in high-passion work that is challenging and can diversify their prior activities (Hudson et al., 2006). The EBAN white paper projected numerous benefits at the sector, angel network and individual levels so that the goal for female representation in the business angel community in the European Union by 2015 is 20 percent (EBAN, 2010). Similar to the debate about women serving on male-dominated boards, there are myriad projected benefits of increased diversity in a business angel network or investment community (Milne, 2009).

## 5.4 WHO ARE WOMEN BUSINESS ANGELS? WHAT TYPES OF INVESTMENTS DO THEY MAKE? HOW ARE THEY DIFFERENT FROM MALE ANGEL INVESTORS?

Kelly's (2007) research on attitudes, behaviors and characteristics profiling business angels in the USA, UK, Sweden, Finland, Norway, Canada, Germany, Australia, Singapore and Japan reveal the following common traits: (1) they are middle-aged males; (2) their decision is based on both financial and non-financial motivations; (3) they rely on personal and professional networks for referrals; (4) deals are made in close proximity to the investor's home; (5) they are attracted to deals that can benefit from their experience; and (6) many have yet to make their first investment. Sohl and Hill (2007) likewise profile a business angel as a male who is a cashed-out entrepreneur with a moderately high-risk tolerance, an extensive professional network and business experience. These profiles suggest entrepreneurial experience is a prerequisite for angel investing activity. Most researchers agree that typically an angel investor is an experienced entrepreneur who can apply prior experience and social capital in addition to financial resources. But is it really necessary to have business experience to be an angel investor?

Sarah Turner, founder of Angel Academe, an angel investment syndicate that invests in female-led start-ups, considered the 'chicken or the egg' issue of whether one has to be an entrepreneur in order to be an angel (Turner, 2013). Turner proposes that 'being entrepreneurial is much more important than being an entrepreneur' and quotes Professor Rob Wiltbank in stating that 'angel investing IS entrepreneurship, rather than a financial class.' Of course, both entrepreneurs and women business angels are necessary to satisfy the need women entrepreneurs have for financial resources. But if one needs to be 'only' a high net worth individual, this opens the floodgates for many women with inherited wealth, or corporate backgrounds, and is the catalyst for the business angel training programs that are discussed later.

In an effort to eradicate the stereotype of angel investors as being male and increase the pipeline for women angel investors, Angie Chang, co-founder and editor-in-chief of Women 2.0, published a weekly series that profiles women angel investors called 'This is what an angel investor looks like.' The series promotes women business angels with the underlying assumptions that women investors are more likely to understand women-led businesses, they are better able to attract women-led ventures and they can provide the capital needed to take women-led ventures to the next level (Chang, 2013). The list shows that most of the women who become angel investors had prior professional experience. They invested in a variety of sectors, although many were focused on the high-tech sector in the Silicon Valley in the USA. Several stated that they prefer not to be sector-focused but are willing to invest in any sector, as long as it is a good deal. Another extensive list of women angel investors and angel networks can be found in a weblog on the Belle Capital USA homepage (Burnett, 2015).

Table 5.2 profiles several women angel investors who have been very active in the angel investing community, either on their own or through angel networks. While the research of nineteenth-century investing in the UK showed women investors to be primarily 'spinsters and widows', twenty-first-century women business angels have accumulated wealth from

*Table 5.2 Profiles of female angel investors*

| Angel investor | Profile |
|---|---|
| Catherine Mott, Blue Tree Allied Angels, Pittsburgh, PA USA | Founder and CEO, Blue Tree Allied Angels since 2003. Former Chairman of the Board, Angel Capital Association. Education: MBA (Finance), Youngstown State University, Ohio. |
| Morgane Rollando, Synerfia, Paris, France | CEO and Founder at SYNERFIA. Board Member/ Advisor at YUMP France, Babyloan and RED CARPET Paris. Treasurer, Femmes Business Angels. Invests in digital industry (software, web 2.0, telecom industry) and innovation that is supported or directed to women in general. Education: Rotterdam School of Management. |
| Anna-Carin Månssom, Theia Investment AB, Stockholm, Sweden | CEO, 1080 Motion AB. Founder and partner of Theia Investment AB. Partner, Wasted Space AB. Board member, Maxtruck AB. Member of Nominating Committee of Swedish Venture Capital Association. Education: Degree in International Economy, Linköping University. |
| Angela Lee, Founder, 37 Angels, New York City, USA | Founder, 37 Angels. Executive Director and adjunct faculty Columbia Business School. Consultant Delphinity, McKinsey & Co. and Teach for America. Completed Pipeline Fellowship. Education: MBA, Columbia University. Advice: 'Look at at least 50 deals before you invest in one.' |
| Sherri Coutu, London, UK | Founded Interactive Investor (1995) with subsequent initial public offering (IPO) and sale (2001). Voted into TechCrunch Industry 'Hall of Fame' 2014. Education: MBA, Harvard Business School, MSc, London School of Economics, BA, University of British Colombia. Quote: 'If you are good, you are good, no matter what gender you are' (Loizou, 2014). |
| Sarah Turner, Turner Hopkins, UK | Founder, Angel Academe. Founder and Director, Turner Hopkins. Expertise in media, digital media, arts and entertainment. Dealmaker, Global Entrepreneur Programme. Education: MSc, University of Brighton, Information Systems. Advice: 'Target investors who are a good fit for what you are doing.' |
| Lauren Flanagan, Belle Capital USA | Founder and CEO, SCIO. Managing Partner, Bell Capital USA LP. Founded companies in SaaS platform, enterprise and consumer software. Voted in *Business Week* 'Top 25 Angels in Tech' in 2010. Board Member Springboard Enterprises. Education: University of California at Berkeley. |

a variety of sources including past entrepreneurial experience, corporate affiliations and/or inheritance. Susan Preston, founder of Seraph Capital Forum, the first women-focused angel group in the USA, posed several questions a potential investor may ask herself before becoming an angel. One set of questions was related to financial resources including annual income and having enough money to do multiple deals. The second set dealt with the commitment an angel investor needs in terms of the amount of time it takes to do due diligence per deal. The third set asked the investor to consider her motivation for angel investing. These could include a variety of both extrinsic (financial returns) and intrinsic (mentoring, giving back to the community and so on) rewards (Stengel, 2013).

While any individual can become an angel investor, most funds and syndicates have a minimal criterion that potential investors are 'accredited' or a 'high net worth' individual. To recruit women who are eligible to become angel investors in the USA, many adopt the Security Exchange Commission (SEC) definition of an 'accredited investor' as an individual 'with a high net worth of at least one million, or earned income of at least $200000 per year individually or $300,000 on a household basis.' This is often the minimum criterion for choosing who might qualify to be an angel investor. In the UK the Financial Services and Markets Act 2000 (Financial Promotion) Order 2005 provides the guidelines for certified high net worth individuals and self-certified sophisticated investors (http://www.legislation.gov.uk/uksi/2005/1529/schedule/5/made).

As stated earlier, women angel investors may consider investing in sectors that have been traditionally overlooked by men. Golden Seeds, one of the largest early stage investment firms in the USA that is focused on women-led firms, has a portfolio of investments including: 30 percent in consumer goods; 30 percent in life sciences; 30 percent in technology; and 10 percent in media and hardware. In a recent interview with Peggy Wallace, co-founder of Golden Seeds, she commented that this portfolio models the degrees women are earning that are more highly represented in hard sciences, or life sciences, such as biology, over computer science (Wallace, 2014). There is also evidence to suggest women are more interested in health care, retail, consumer products and green/social enterprises.

The final issue in this section relates to how women investors may be different than men. Do women entrepreneurs seek women angels? Do women angels give preference to women entrepreneurs? Are there gender-related differences? The presence of 'homophily' or the 'tendency of individuals to seek others who are the same' has been examined in academic research on women business angels. In this study four of the five angel investors expressed opinions supportive of homophily – that women entrepreneurs may seek or be more comfortable with women business angels.

Companies with women in senior leadership or on the board generally perform better than all male teams. Women investors are generally more aware of these statistics than male investors are. Women express confidence differently than men do. Women investors don't 'penalize' female leaders for expressing growth prospects more cautiously while a male investor may interpret this as lack of confidence or ability of the CEO. (Lauren Flanagan, Belle Capital USA LP)

We tend to be drawn to people like ourselves. When a woman walks into a room of strangers, she will seek out other women in the room with whom to connect. When a man walks into a room of strangers, he will seek out other men in the room. There is a subliminal comfort to connect with others that we perceive are like ourselves. This also transcends beyond gender. Younger men have less of an issue with this because they have seen some good female success stories and live role models. (Catherine V. Mott, Blue Tree Allied Angels)

I think entrepreneurs are drawn to people who are writing checks! (Angela Lee, 37 Angels)

Women entrepreneurs, in particular, find it a more comfortable experience even if they are very experienced technology entrepreneurs. (Sarah Turner, Angel Academe)

When asked about whether women angels show a preference toward women-led firms, given similar financial projects with males, both Angel Academe and Pipeline Fellowship specifically focus on women-led companies and do not invest in male-led firms. Although Femmes Business Angels invests in male companies, the priority is promoting women-led firms.

Of course! That is the aim of our group. We want to invest in either gender when potential success is there. As we are ambassadors for women, we like to encourage women entrepreneurs with ambition. France Angels shows that the angel community invests in about 10 percent of women driven projects when FBA shows 33 percent. A problem we saw is that the women tended to be 'softer negotiators' than men and showed lower company valuations. (Morgane Rollando, Femmes Business Angels)

This is certainly not true for the women investors in our network. We want to invest in the best startups and entrepreneurs, regardless of gender. (Angela Lee, 37 Angels)

Gender-related differences have been discussed earlier in the chapter in terms of some of the benefits of having increased investor diversity in the angel community. Women may exhibit more collaborative interpersonal styles, choose sectors that male investors may overlook, are not in the same professional networks, may show increased risk adversity and may have wealth from sources other than prior entrepreneurial experience.

Four of the five survey respondents strongly agreed that there are gender-related differences between male and female angel investors.

> Female investors like to see more detailed due diligence and often have lower tolerance for investment losses. According to the Angel Capital Association, there is a high correlation between more diligence and higher portfolio returns. (Lauren Flanagan, Belle Capital USA LP)

> I have attended lots of angel investment and VC pitch events. The behavior at male dominated events can be very combative, with one or two men dominating the event and no attempt to seek the opinions of others. At our majority women events, we try to be more constructive and collaborative. In my experience questioning and due diligence by women is deeper and more thorough. (Sara Turner, Angel Academe)

Early research conducted by the Diana Project found no evidence that gender was a factor in investment decision-making in the venture capital industry (Brush et al., 2004). However, women in the venture capital industry may be in networks that lead to more deals with women-led ventures. In a follow-up study to the original Diana Project, researchers found that venture capital firms with women partners were twice as likely to invest in companies with women in the management team and three times more likely to invest in a firm with a woman CEO (Brush et al., 2014). In a study of differences between male and female angel investors, Harrison and Mason (2007) found that women were marginally more likely to be motivated to help the next generation of entrepreneurs and support socially beneficial products, but in general investment motivation is similar to male counterparts. Becker-Blease and Sohl (2007) found evidence of homophily, that is, men (women) are more likely to receive funding requests and fund proposals from men (women). However, the relationship was stronger in seeking funding than in awarding funding.

In a subsequent study on gender diversity and angel group investment, these authors found evidence that did not suggest that women investors favor women entrepreneurs. However,

> when women angels have a sizeable representation within an angel group, their investment tendency will mirror that of men. As a result, if women entrepreneurs, due to homophily, are more likely to know about and seek funding from groups with more women, and these groups invest at rates similar to groups that receive high proportions of proposals from men, then this will help to insure equality of access for women entrepreneurs to vital early stage capital. (Becker-Blease and Sohl, 2010, p. 725)

This finding encourages greater participation of women in predominant or all women angel investor groups.

## 5.5 TRENDS, CHALLENGES AND OPPORTUNITIES

It is apparent that in many countries female participation in the business angel market is increasing. There are several favorable trends that may serve as catalysts for this growth: an increase in the number of high net worth women; an increase in the number of women-led angel investment funds; and the proliferation of programs to train female business angels.

### 5.5.1 Increase in the Number of High Net Worth Women

Although it is US-centric and critics dispute some of Liza Mundy's predictions in *The Richer Sex*, there is ample evidence that women are becoming a forceful economic power (Mundy, 2013). Women control more than 48 percent of estates worth more than $5 million in the USA, 45 percent of all American millionaires are women and 60 percent of high net wealth women earned their own fortunes (Stanny, 2012; Pax World, 2014; Stengel, 2014). The number of wealthy women is growing twice as fast as the number of wealthy men (Quist-Newins, 2009). Outside the USA, women are predicted to inherit nearly three-quarters of wealth globally over the next 40 years. The number of UK female millionaires has increased approximately 11 percent a year and in 2011, about 46 percent of UK millionaires were women. India has over 1200 ultra-high net worth women with assets of $30 million or more. At 16 percent, this may be the highest proportion of high net wealth women in the world (Chadha, 2013).

### 5.5.2 Increase in Women-led Angel Groups

Concerns about the low amount of equity investment that goes to women entrepreneurs despite increases in the number of high net wealth women have led to the proliferation of predominantly women or women only angel groups (Moules, 2009). Incito Ventures and Addidi Business Angels are examples of such clubs in the UK (Addidi Business Angels, 2014; Incito Ventures, 2014). In 2013, the first angel investor networks for women and funded by women were launched in Scotland (The Investing Women) and New Zealand (ArcAngels) (Askeland, 2013; Springall, 2013). A French female business angel group, Femmes Business Angels, was founded in 2003 (Weverbergh, 2013). See Table 5.3 for a selective list of women angel groups worldwide. The table includes investor diversity, investee diversity, role of angel education and the year the group was founded.

The first women angel fund in the USA was Seraph Capital launched in 1998. In the USA there are approximately nine women-focused groups of angel investors. One of the largest is Golden Seeds, founded in 2004, and

*Table 5.3 A sample of women angel investor groups (2015)*

| Firm | Country | Women investors | Male investors | Women entrepreneurs | Male entrepreneurs | Angel education | Year founded |
|---|---|---|---|---|---|---|---|
| 37 Angels | USA | Yes | Advisors | Yes | Yes | Yes | 2012 |
| Addidi Business Angels | UK | Yes | No | Yes | Yes | Yes | 2009 |
| Angel Academe | UK | Yes | Some | Yes | No | Some | 2013 |
| ArcAngels | New Zealand | Yes | No | Yes | No | | 2013 |
| Astia Angels | USA, UK | Yes | Yes | Yes | No | No | 2013 |
| Belle Capital USA | USA | Yes | No | Yes | No | No | 2012 |
| Broadway Angels | USA | Yes | No | Yes | Yes | No | 2010 |
| Femmes Business Angels | France | Yes | Some indirectly | Yes | Yes | Yes | 2003 |
| Golden Seeds | USA | Yes | Yes | Yes | No | Yes | 2005 |
| Incito Ventures (FSE Angel Group) | UK | Yes | Some | Yes | No | Yes (FSE) | 2005 (FSE) |
| Investing Women | Scotland | Yes | No | Yes | No | No | Not launched |
| Pipeline Fellowship | USA | Yes | No | Yes | No | Yes | 2011 |
| Scale | Australia | Yes | Yes | Yes | No | Yes | 2013 |
| Seraph Capital Forum | USA | Yes | No | Yes | Yes | No | 1998 |
| Theia AB | Sweden | Yes | Yes | Yes | Yes | No | 2006[a] |
| Women's Angel Investor Network | United Arab Emirates | Yes | No | Yes | No | Yes | 2013 |

*Note:* [a] Liquidated 2014.

involving about 275 angel investors. Since 2005, it has invested approximately $60 million in 60 companies (Leondis, 2011; Golden Seeds, 2013; Klein, 2014). Other US women-focused angel groups are Belle Capital USA and the Pipeline Fellowship. Wallace (2014) emphasized the importance of a potential angel investor in becoming part of a group or network. In 2010 a group of female venture capitalists, corporate executives and company founders created Broadway Angels, an angel investment network based in San Francisco (Novellino, 2014). Co-founder Sonja Hoel Perkins stated that 40 percent of all angel investments made by the group went to women entrepreneurs, a rate higher than the average for venture capital. Other female-dominated firms and angel networks in the USA include Cowboy Ventures, Aspect Ventures, Illuminate Ventures, Forerunner Ventures and Aligned Partners (Miller, 2015).

### 5.5.3 Training Programs for Women Business Angels

In order to fill the gap between the number of women entrepreneurs seeking equity and the number of women business angels in the industry, numerous training programs have been developed to assist high net worth women in developing technical expertise and confidence for angel investing. Two noteworthy programs are the Pipeline Fellowship and 37 Angels, both in the USA. Since its first angel investing boot camp in 2011, the Pipeline Fellowship has trained 70 women and invested approximately $350,000 (Pipeline Fellowship, 2014). Founder Natalia Oberti Noguera comments, 'The Pipeline Fellowship is committed to increasing diversity in the angel investing community and training a new generation of angels to invest for good' (Elder, 2012). A graduate of the Pipeline Fellowship, Angela Lee, went on to launch 37 Angels, which is also a training program and fund for women angel investors (37 Angels, 2013). In the UK, Addidi and Incito, likewise, provide support to their members although they are considered to be more funds than training programs. Table 5.3 identifies the women angel funds that are also involved in angel education.

## 5.6 FUTURE OPPORTUNITIES FOR RESEARCH

In the first volume in this series both Kelly (2007) and Sohl (2007) called for more research on female angel investors. Since then, although some progress has been made, there are still many unanswered questions. A summary of most of the existing research on women angels is provided in Table 5.4. Despite the difficulty associated with collecting data on the business angels, there are ample research opportunities. As the landscape

*Table 5.4 Women business angels: a literature review*

| Citation | Research design | Findings |
|---|---|---|
| Becker-Blease and Sohl (2010) | Annual survey, 183 angel groups, 2-limit Tobit analysis, male/female comparisons | Confidence, risk tolerance and social capital |
| EBAN (2010) | Qualitative, interviews | Policy paper identifies problems, causes and recommendations. Gender-based homophily |
| Sohl and Hill (2007) | Postal survey, 11 angel groups, male/female comparisons, descriptive statistics | Gender-based homophily |
| Becker-Blease and Sohl (2007) | Comprehensive survey to 174 angel portals | Women seek less angel funding. Gender-based homophily |
| Harrison and Mason (2007) | Survey, 15 angel groups, 21 women, 19 men, Chi-square | Gender-based homophily |
| O'Gorman and Terjesen (2006) | GEM survey data, 131 informal investors, male/female, Chi-square, t-tests | No difference in financial capitalization between male and female informal investors |
| Hudson et al. (2006) | Qualitative, interviews with 12 women angel investors | Gender-based homophily. Discusses reasons women invest, problems, benefits to the economy of increased participation |
| Brush et al. (2014) | Update of venture capital industry and women entrepreneurs 2011–13 | Number of women VCs declining. Presence of gender bias. VC firms with women partners three times more likely to invest in firms with women CEOs |
| Brush et al. (2004) | Qualitative, interviews, comprehensive review of venture capital industry 1995–2000 | Women venture capitalists more likely to be connected to and attract female-led ventures |
| Brush et al. (2002) | Examined demand and supply sides of venture capital industry, analysis of data from multiple databases | Call for research on women angels and their participation in the seed funding process |

is changing in today's modern world, many women are stepping up as activists to address the perceived gender-related inequities in demand and supply of equity investment. Traditional views about the typical attributes of a business angel are being challenged.

The increase in the number of high net worth women worldwide, and the commensurate economic power they possess, creates interesting possibilities for addressing the problem. There is not a great deal of research on whether the source of net wealth (inherited or self-generated) influences angel investment behavior.

The surge in training programs to provide women with the technical, negotiating and analytic skills needed for making effective investment decisions provides another creative solution to fill the gap.

Although there are challenges associated with obtaining the data required for large sample statistical analysis, there are opportunities for case studies and qualitative, ethnographic studies of smaller sample sizes. Case studies to share the journeys of successful women business angels can serve as role models for both potential women investors and women entrepreneurs. Social media and web-based secondary data collection sources can be leveraged extensively to obtain larger sample sizes.

More research on gender blindness, or the lack thereof, can shed light on the barriers women entrepreneurs and investors encounter. A recent study involving two controlled experiments where male and female entrepreneurs gave exactly the same pitch to investors showed evidence that the investors preferred pitches presented by male entrepreneurs. Moreover, the effect was moderated by physical attractiveness since attractive males were particularly successful whereas physical attractiveness did not matter among female entrepreneurs (Brooks et al., 2014). Evidence of 'second generation gender bias' was found in a study of women entrepreneurs in the private equity negotiation process (Nelson et al., 2009; Ibarra et al., 2013; Swartz et al., 2016b). An earlier study involving Goldberg-type experimental procedures found that women experienced gender discrimination when seeking start-up capital (Fay and Williams, 1993). Verbal protocol analysis with subsamples of male and female investors evaluating business opportunities pitched by male and female presenters can provide interesting insights into the role gender plays in investor–investee relationships.

As mentioned in Sohl (2007), the emergence of women angel investor groups provides another research opportunity. Questions related to women angel group dynamics, the effects they may have on the gender gap with regard to sourcing external equity, the relative importance of investor diversity and the financial performance of these portfolios need to be addressed.

### 5.6.1 Public Policy Implications

Data from the Kauffman firm survey shows that male entrepreneurs raised 27 times more external equity than women in their first year of operation (Coleman and Robb, 2012). Public policy initiatives related to increasing the number of women angel investors may help narrow the gender gap. These may involve promoting the inclusion of women in investor networks that were previously male-dominated, and providing information and support to potential female angel investors. Tax incentives may be provided for first time female investors. Government support for training programs that facilitate learning about angel investment can be helpful. Policies involving partnerships with the media could address negative social pressures to portray positive role models of women and reduce stereotype threat. Public policy can and must play an important role in promoting further economic development and job creation by providing the appropriate incentives to support women investors and investees so that all entrepreneurs are on a level playing ground with regard to access to growth capital.

The purpose of this chapter has been to review the changes occurring in the business angel market related to gender. The gap between the increasing number of women seeking equity investment and relatively small numbers of women business angels is slowly being addressed – in some countries faster than others. But global trends suggest that women are becoming a powerful economic force on both the demand and supply side, and that these trends are most likely irreversible. In particular, the increase in high net wealth women globally, the increase of women-focused angel groups and the creation of programs dedicated to training women business angels are significant developments.

The positive effect of increased diversity in the investment community mirrors the movement toward increased diversity of corporate boards (Milne, 2009; Catalyst, 2014; Soares et al., 2015). The advantages of gender diversity in decision-making, opportunity recognition and problem solving have fostered a global effort to change male-dominated boards. The paucity of academic research on diversity in the angel investment community is problematic but not surprising due to the difficulty in data collection. Qualitative methodologies or mixed mode research designs can offer opportunities to extend our knowledge about this emerging phenomenon.

# REFERENCES

37 Angels (2013), http://37angels.com (accessed 30 December 2013).
Addidi Business Angels (2014), http://www.addidi.com (accessed 10 January 2014).
ARI (2015), *2014 Halo Report*, Angel Resource Institute and PitchBook, 15 April.
Askeland, E. (2013), 'First women's Scottish angel investor network launch', *The Scotsman*, 18 August.
Becker-Blease, J.R. and J.E. Sohl (2007), 'Do women-owned businesses have equal access to angel capital?', *Journal of Business Venturing*, **22**, 503–21.
Becker-Blease, J.R. and J.E. Sohl (2010), 'The effect of gender diversity on angel group investment', *Entrepreneurship Theory and Practice*, **34**(4), 709–33.
Brooks, A.W., L. Huang, S.W. Kearney and F.E. Murray (2014), 'Investors prefer entrepreneurial ventures by attractive men', *Proceedings of the National Academy of Sciences of the United States of America*, **111**(12), 4427–31.
Brush, C.G., N.M. Carter, P.G. Greene, M.M. Hart and E. Gatewood (2002), 'The role of social capital and gender in linking financial suppliers and entrepreneurial firms: a framework for future research', *Venture Capital*, **4**(4), 305–23.
Brush, C., N. Carter, E. Gatewood, P. Greene and M. Hart (2004), *Clearing the Hurdles: Women Building High-growth Businesses*, Upper Saddle River, NJ: FT Prentice Hall.
Brush, C.G., P.G. Greene, L. Balachandra and A.E. Davis (2014), *Diana Report Women Entrepreneurs 2014: Bridging the Gender Gap in Venture Capital*, Babson College, available at http://www.babson.edu/Academics/centers/blank-center/global-research/diana/Documents/diana-project-executive-summary-2014.pdf (accessed 25 October 2015).
Burnett, M. (2015), 'List of female angel and early-stage investors in tech', 8 June weblog, available at https://medium.com/ladies-storm-hackathons/finding-female-angel-and-early-stage-investors-in-tech-a67c998e2e9f#.27j0yn7oa (accessed 25 October 2015).
Casserly, M. (2013), 'Tipping the scales: women angel investing reaches all-time high', *Forbes*, 25 April.
Catalyst (2014), *Increasing Gender Diversity on Boards: Current Index of Formal Approaches*, August, New York: Catalyst.
Center for Strategy and Evaluation Services (2012), *Evaluation of EU Member States' Business Angel Markets and Policies Final Report*, October, available at http://www.eban.org/evaluation-of-eu-member-states-business-angel-markets-and-policies-final-report/#.V1CWN1f4OFI (accessed 20 January 2014).
Chadha, S. (2013), 'Wealth report: India has more super-rich women than other BRICS', FirstBiz, available at http://www.firstbiz.com/corporate/wealth-report-india-has-more-super-rich-women-than-other-brics-45638.html (accessed 17 February 2014).
Chang, A. (2013), 'This is what an angel investor looks like', Weekly series published by Women 2.0, available at http://women2.com/tag/this-is-what-an-angel-investor-looks-like/ (accessed 21 January 2014).
Coleman, S. and A.M. Robb (2012), *A Rising Tide: Financing Strategies for Women-owned Businesses*, Stanford, CA: Stanford University Press.
Deloitte and the UK Business Angel Association (2013), *Taking the Pulse of the Angel Market*, available at https://www2.deloitte.com/content/dam/Deloitte/uk/Documents/about-deloitte/deloitte-uk-taking-the-pulse-of-the-angel-market.pdf (accessed 20 July 2014).
EBAN (European Business Angel Network) (2010), 'Women & European early state investing: strengthening European entrepreneurship by enrolling more women in early stage investing', White paper, November.
Elder, J. (2012), 'Women investors on the rise', available at http://www.triplepundit.com/2012/women-angel-investors-rise (accessed 16 July 2014).
Fay, M. and L. Williams (1993), 'Gender bias and the availability of business loans', *Journal of Business Venturing*, **8**, 363–76.
Golden Seeds (2013), http://www.goldenseeds.com/About.aspx (accessed 26 November 2013).

Harrison, R.T. and C.M. Mason (2007), 'Does gender matter? Women business angels and the supply of entrepreneurial finance', *Entrepreneurship Theory and Practice*, **31**(3), 445–72.
Hudson, M., M. Kenefake and M.J. Grinstead (2006), *Women and Angel Investing: An Untapped Pool of Equity for Entrepreneurs*, Research report, Kansas City, MI: Ewing Marion Kauffman Foundation.
Ibarra, H., R. Ely and D. Kolb (2013), 'Women rising: the unseen barriers', *Harvard Business Review*, September, 61–6.
Incito Ventures (2014), http://www.thefsegroup.com/investors-landing/incito-ventures (accessed 10 January 2014).
Kelly, P. (2007), 'Business angel research: the road traveled and the journal ahead', in H. Landström (ed.), *Handbook of Research on Venture Capital*, Cheltenham, UK and Northampton, MA, USA: Edward Elgar, pp. 315–31.
Klein, K.E. (2014), 'Rise of female investors fuels women run companies', *Business Week*, 10 September.
Leondis, A. (2011), 'Angels lend a hand to startups: group hopes to add to ranks of female investors', *Ottawa Citizen*, 16 April.
Loizou, K. (2014), 'Secret angel paves the way for our first trillion-dollar company', *The Sunday Times*, London, 22 June.
Maltby, J. and J. Rutterford (2006), 'She possessed her own fortune: women investors from the late nineteenth century to the early twentieth century', *Business History*, **48**(2), 220–53.
Mason, C.M. and R.T. Harrison (2011), *Annual Report on the Business Angel Market in the United Kingdom: 2009/10*, UK Business Angel Association, available at http://www.ukbusinessangelsassociation.org.uk (accessed 17 February 2014).
Miller, C.C. (2015), 'Female-run venture funds alter the status quo', *New York Times*, 2 April
Milne, R. (2009), 'Skirting the boards', *Financial Times*, 15 June.
Moules, J. (2009), 'Too few angels are women', *Financial Times*, 1 August.
Mundy, L. (2013), *The Richer Sex: How the New Majority of Female Breadwinners is Transforming Our Culture*, New York: Free Press.
Nelson, T., S. Maxfield and D. Kolb (2009), 'Women entrepreneurs and venture capital: managing the shadow negotiation', *International Journal of Gender and Entrepreneurship*, **1**(1), 57–76.
Novellino, T. (2014), 'Alpha females of Broadway Angels pull out purses for startups', *Upstart*, 25 June.
O'Gorman, C. and S. Terjesen (2006), 'Financing the Celtic tigress: venture financing and informal investment in Ireland', *Venture Capital*, **8**(2), 69–88.
Pax World (2014), http://www.paxworld.com/advisors/investment-advisors/women-and-wealth (accessed 17 February 2014).
Pipeline Fellowship (2014), http://www.pipelinefellowship.com/ (accessed 15 January 2014).
Quist-Newins, M. (2009), *Women and Money: Matters of Trust*, Mawr, PA: American College Press.
Rutterford, J. and J. Maltby (2005), 'The widow, the clergyman and the reckless: women investors in England 1830–1914', *Feminist Economics*, **12**(1/2), 111–38.
Soares, R., H. Foust-Cummings, C. Francoeur and R. Labelle (2015), *Companies Behaving Responsibly: Gender Diversity on Boards*, New York: Catalyst.
Sohl, J.E. (2006), *The Angel Investor Market in 2005: The Angel Market Exhibits Moderate Growth*, April, Center for Venture Research, University of New Hampshire.
Sohl, J.E. (2007), 'The organization of the informal venture capital market', in H. Landström (ed.), *Handbook of Research on Venture Capital*, Cheltenham, UK and Northampton, MA, USA: Edward Elgar, pp. 347–68.
Sohl, J.E. (2015), *The Angel Investor Market in 2014: A Market Correction in Deal Size*, 15 May, Center for Venture Research, University of New Hampshire.
Sohl, J.E. (2016), *The Angel Investor Market in 2015: A Buyers' Market*, 25 May, Center for Venture Research, University of New Hampshire.

Sohl, J.E. and L. Hill (2007), 'Women business angels: insights from angel groups', *Venture Capital*, **9**(3), 207–22.

Springall, L. (2013), 'Angels to take women under their wings', *The New Zealand Herald*, 11 October.

Stanny, B. (2012), 'Women, wealth, and power: the emerging paradigm', *Forbes*, 12 March.

Stengel, G. (2013), 'Is investing in women entrepreneurs for you? 9 questions to ask if you want to find out', *Forbes*, 20 March.

Swartz, E., F. Amatucci and S. Coleman (2016a), 'Using a multiple method and mixed mode approach to examine women entrepreneur negotiating styles', *International Journal of Gender and Entrepreneurship*, **8**(1).

Swartz, E., F. Amatucci and S. Coleman (2016b), 'Still a man's world? Second generation gender bias in external equity term sheet negotiations', *Proceedings of the United States Association for Small Business and Entrepreneurship (USASBE) Annual Conference*, San Diego, California, 10–12 January, 2016.

Turner, S. (2013), 'What comes first: chicken or egg? Some thoughts on women investors and women entrepreneurs', 8 July blog on Angel Academe website, available at http://angelacade.me/2013/07/08/what-comes-first-chicken-or-egg-some-thoughts-on-women-investors-and-women-entrepreneurs/ (accessed 21 January 2014).

Wallace, P. (2014), 'How to become an angel investor', Interview on Bloomberg TV, available at http://www.bloomberg.com/video/how-to-become-a-successful-angel-investor (accessed 16 July 2014).

Weverbergh, R. (2013), 'Female business angels invest 12k per round on average (France)', Whiteboard, available at http://www.whiteboardmag.com/female-business-angels-invest-12k-per-round-on-average-france/ (accessed 26 November 2013).

Williams, M. (2013), 'What angel investors can do for your business', *Guardian*, 13 November.

# PART II

# THE BUSINESS ANGEL INVESTMENT PROCESS

# 6 Investment decision-making by business angels

*Andrew Maxwell*

## 6.1 THE IMPORTANCE OF UNDERSTANDING THE BA INVESTMENT DECISION PROCESS

Most high growth early stage companies need to attract equity finance to fund growth in advance of their ability to earn revenue. Although family and colleagues are still the most common source of early stage funding (Morissette, 2007) business angels (BAs) are increasingly recognized as an important source of equity finance for such companies (Kelly, 2007). Given that less than 5 percent of fund-seeking entrepreneurs are able to attract this type of equity investment (Riding et al., 1997), entrepreneurs and BAs are both interested in better understanding why obtaining this type of funding is so difficult. Governments, too, are interested in how to increase the number of ventures that attract funding, given the economic impact that BA-funded companies can have on regional economies (Harrison et al., 2010). Current low success rates in attracting funding creates a negative cycle as this acts as a disincentive for entrepreneurs to seek funds, and for BAs to actively look for early stage equity investment opportunities (Freear and Wetzel, 1990), raising questions about the need for, and effectiveness of, government support (Mason, 2009).

Maxwell (2011) suggests three fundamentally different causes that contribute to the low success rates that result from fund-seeking entrepreneurs 'pitching' their venture opportunities to high net worth BAs. First, he identifies essential shortcomings in the entrepreneur/business that limit the potential for a successful long-term investment outcome (Feeney et al., 1999). Second, he suggests that entrepreneurs are not 'investment ready' because they are either unwilling to surrender equity/control as part of the equity investment or unable to provide essential information to enable the BA to make an investment decision (Mason and Harrison, 1996). Third, he points out that most entrepreneurs do not understand BAs' motivations, or how they make investment decisions, and as a result provide inappropriate information or behave inappropriately during the investment interaction behaviors being manifest (Feeney et al., 1999).

In this chapter, we focus on this third cause of low success rates, and discuss research undertaken to better understand the BA investment decision process. Such research will help entrepreneurs better prepare their ventures for investment (Mason and Harrison, 2001), improve how entrepreneurs present their investment opportunity (Mason and Rogers, 1997) and increase the quality of responses entrepreneurs make to specific BA questions (Mason and Harrison, 1996). BAs will also benefit from a better understanding of their own investment decision processes, as improved understanding of how they make investment decisions will allow them to improve the quality of their decisions, resulting in making investments that lead to better investment outcomes (San José et al., 2007). It will also enable BAs to improve the efficiency of their decision-making, by minimizing the decision-making effort and resources required (Jeffrey et al., 2016). Better understanding of the BA investment decision process will also enable governments to develop policies and deploy resources that are more likely to achieve the intended outcomes: catalyzing more BA investment in successful ventures (Freear et al., 1995).

To date, much of the research into the BA investment decision process has been constrained by the inherently confidential nature of the interaction between BA and entrepreneur (Harrison et al., 2002). This has led researchers to either ask BAs how they anticipate they will make a future investment decision or rely on their post-decision recollections of how they made a previous decision. Unfortunately, these approaches raise validity concerns that limit insights that can be drawn, causing Alan Riding and his colleagues to comment that 'there remains considerable room for research on the nature of the investment process itself' (Riding et al., 2007, p. 336).

In this chapter, we provide a summary of research into the BA investment decision, and emphasize research that has attempted to address some of these validity concerns. We deliberately focus attention on the more recent research that has explored the previously inaccessible, critical stage of the investment decision process, when entrepreneur and investor first meet (May and Simmons, 2001). Improved understanding of the investment decision process has been facilitated through observing how experienced BAs use an adaptive decision-making approach that involves using decision shortcuts (heuristics) to reject opportunities through a multistage sequential elimination process (Payne et al., 1988).

Increased interest in this research area, and the BA investment decision process, has been stimulated by the global success of the reality TV show *Dragons' Den/Shark Tank*, now seen in 22 countries. The format of the show allows viewers to have a 'fly-on-the wall' view of multiple entrepreneurs pitching to five investors in return for equity investment. Not only has this show glamorized the idea of entrepreneurship, but it has also exposed the concept of equity investment to a much wider audience allowing us to better understand the differences between opportunities that receive investment and those that are rejected. In addition, the rise of new online forums that match investors and entrepreneurs (together with some changes in legislation) has encouraged more entrepreneurs (and investors) to consider crowdfunding as an alternative source of third party equity funding (Harrison and Baldock, 2015). Lessons learned from the BA investment decision process might be applied to help better understand the equity crowdfunding investment decision.

We conclude this chapter by discussing the implications of current research and suggesting directions for future research. We consider the practical implications for entrepreneurs anticipating an investment interaction with a BA, enabling them to better prepare in advance of the interaction, and guiding their behavior during the interaction, in order to increase their likelihood of attracting funding. We also consider the implications of our research for BAs, especially as the context in which they are operating is changing, for example, increasingly they are making funding decisions in groups, and through co-investing, and learning about how to enhance their ability to add value and achieve successful exits. We hope that this research can help BAs improve the quality of their decision – so that more investments result in long-term venture success, and reduce the decision effort required – so that BA's waste less time on poor opportunities. Governments, too, can use this research to inform their development of new policies and BA/entrepreneur support programs, in order to stimulate more funding in successful companies, rather than just in more companies. Our suggestions for future research are informed by the opportunity to both overcome the constraints of current research and extend research to a broader spectrum of BA decision-making participants and contexts. Future research can be undertaken leveraging new insights from the research outlined in this chapter. Indeed, BAs and entrepreneurs are becoming increasingly aware of how BAs make their investment decisions, enabling entrepreneurs to modify the ways in which they pitch to them. Investigating the impact of the changes in how entrepreneurs approach BAs will be a fruitful area for future research.

## 6.2 EVOLUTION OF RESEARCH INTO BUSINESS ANGEL INVESTMENT DECISIONS

There has been a growing body of research on the topic of BAs, from only three papers between 1990 and 1994, to 138 between 2010 and 2015 (Google Scholar). Harrison and Mason (1999) categorized Business Angel research as being either first generation: investigating the impact of BA investment on regional economies, and the characteristics and motivations of BAs (for example, Wetzel, 1981, 1983; Haar et al., 1988; Riding and Short, 1989; Harrison and Mason, 1992), or second generation: examining the BA investment process, who makes decisions at each stage of the process, and how the decision process evolves (for example, Riding et al., 1993; Mason and Harrison, 1996; Mason and Stark, 2004). While this research focused attention on the role and importance of BAs, it offered limited insights in how to improve the percentage of BA–fund-seeking entrepreneur interactions that resulted in an investment being made. This is a substantive concern given that less than 5 percent of entrepreneurs seeking funds from BAs are able to attract it (Riding et al., 1993).

### 6.2.1 The BA Investment Decision Process

As we have noted, research into the BA investment decision process was constrained by the inherently confidential nature of the interaction (Harrison et al., 2002). Early research (that is, Riding et al., 1993; Cressy and Olofsson, 1997) used surveys to investigate previous BA decisions. Validity concerns about this approach encouraged Landström (1998) to capture the actual decision factors deployed by BAs using conjoint analysis to compare BAs' assessment of the relative importance of each factor while making an investment decision. An alternate research approach, taken by Mason and Stark (2004), used verbal protocol analysis to capture insights based on BAs talking aloud about an investment opportunity while reviewing it.

Unfortunately, these research approaches raise validity concerns. Most investors don't really understand how they make decisions (Zacharakis and Meyer, 1998), use decision techniques that are different from those they espouse (Shepherd, 1999), exhibit hindsight or confirmation bias that reflects how they think they made a decision rather than how they actually make a decision (Mynatt et al., 1977) and/or believe that they consider more investment factors than they actually use in practice (Zacharakis and Meyer, 1998). Further, generalizability concerns arise because decision outcomes reported by the BA during a hypothetical exercise are likely to differ from those decisions made under conditions of actual risk (Rabin, 2000). In addition, gathering insights at the end of the decision process reduces our ability to examine details of interim stages of the process, which can be critical when trying to understand the complete decision (Svenson, 1979). These concerns led Hans Landström (1998) to note, '[t]here are few studies which have attempted to bring out the nuances in informal investors' decision making criteria' and suggests the development of studies that consider 'investment as a process in which decision making criteria may vary in the course of time' (p. 322).

### 6.2.2 Third Generation Studies

We now define a third generation of research studies where we 'explore the deal as the unit of analysis' (Kelly, 2007, p. 327). A number of researchers have examined the progress of real investment interactions in an attempt to untangle the complex relationship between specific factors and rejection at specific stages of the decision process (for example, Mason and Harrison, 1996; Sudek, 2006; Maxwell, 2011; Pollack et al., 2012). Third generation studies are built on a growing body of evidence of a staged decision process (Mason and Harrison, 1996), where different factors contribute to opportunities being rejected for different reasons at each stage of the multi-stage decision process (for example, Landström, 1998; Jeffrey et al., 2016).

Third generation studies are designed to address some of the nuances in BA investment decision research. For example, Mason and Harrison (2003) noted that factors that cause an opportunity to be rejected at one stage are not just the opposite of factors that helped an opportunity progress to the subsequent stage. They also noted that some factors are compensatory (that is, a shortcoming in one factor can be compensated for by an abundance in another) and other factors are non-compensatory. Untangling complex relationships between factors requires a research approach that gathers data based on real time collection of data, and examines the factors considered, and the likelihood of rejection, at each stage of the investment decision process.

One of the first to investigate actual BA decisions being made was Richard Sudek (2006), a successful entrepreneur and member of Tech Coast Angels in Silicon Valley, who gathered real-time information from his colleagues. His research involved gathering data from members of his BA group, while they were listening to pitches from fund-seeking entrepreneurs. This allowed him to better understand the relationships between factors considered, when in the multi-stage process they were assessed, and how the consideration of one factor earlier in the interaction influenced the subsequent assessment of other factors. This enabled him to address important questions about the relationship between the horse (venture) and the jockey (entrepreneur), making the observation that the assessment of the entrepreneur could only take place once the key characteristics of the venture are understood (Harrison and Mason, 2002; Mitteness et al., 2012b).

Maxwell (2011) continued this research approach, based on his direct involvement and access to unedited recordings of interactions in the reality TV show *Dragons' Den,* where the fund-seeking entrepreneur pitches to five BAs or '*Dragons*'. He coded each information exchange and the entrepreneur's behaviors, in order to understand the influence of each on the investment decision outcome. He was able to break down the investment interaction into four sub-stages based on the rejection reason given by each BA (with those not rejected eventually receiving an investment offer). Andrew Maxwell explains the sequential approach in which different factors were retrieved/assessed based on his observation that the BAs use heuristics to reduce the overall decision effort required. Experienced BAs look for reasons to reject opportunities using a sequential elimination process that minimizes the overall decision effort required (Payne et al., 1988; Jeffrey et al., 2016). Observations that BAs use heuristics confirm the earlier findings of Mason and Rogers (1997) and Mason and Harrison (2003) that BAs, operating under time constraints, enter the interaction with a negative mindset and follow a multi-stage rejection process to rapidly reject opportunities. Interestingly, the use of heuristics explains why BAs frequently make decisions that deviate from normative assumptions, for example, rejecting a promising opportunity because they did not want to put time into reducing some of the perceived risks when there were other, less risky opportunities to be considered. In the next section we discuss aspects of the BA decision process.

## 6.3 ASPECTS OF THE BUSINESS ANGEL INVESTMENT DECISION

Understanding the BA investment decision process requires an understanding of the characteristics and motivations of BAs (Subsection 6.3.1), the impact of critical venture, entrepreneur and investment factors (Subsection 6.3.2) and the nature of the multi-stage decision process (Subsection 6.3.3). Importantly, the BA's anticipation about his or her long-term relationship with the entrepreneur (Subsection 6.3.4), and his or her expectations about the long-term exit plan (Subsection 6.3.5) also influence the investment decision process.

### 6.3.1 Business Angel Motivations, Characteristics and the Investment Decision Context

Much early research on BAs focused on their characteristics and motivations, for example, Wetzel (1981, 1983) noted that beyond expectations about the financial return resulting from the investment, BAs look to also derive psychic income from their investment by helping the entrepreneur achieve his or her goals (Maddill et al., 2005), making a contribution to their community (Benjamin and Margulis, 1996) and fostering new venture creation and entrepreneurial activity (Freear et al., 1995). Riding et al. (1993) attempted to better understand BAs' psychological motivations, noting the influence on their behaviors of the fact that most BAs seem to have a high internal locus of control as well as a strong need for achievement. Further, although not all BAs are active in the venture post-investment, most consider their role contribution post-investment to be critical. Their ability to play such a role is frequently influenced by their industry experience (Benjamin and Margulis, 1996) and/or access to complementary operational or market-based resources (Smith et al., 2010). Interestingly, Mason and Botelho (2016) observe that BAs seem to pay less attention to possible exit strategies than one might expect, given that the ultimate goal of a BA investment includes realizing a successful exit.

BA experience plays an important role in how they make investment decisions, with relevant knowledge of the industry, or market, enabling them to feel better able to evaluate venture potential (Mason and Stark, 2004). BAs with more investment experience tend to make faster decisions (Smith et al., 2010), and pay less attention to financial projections (Van Osnabrugge and Robinson, 2000) than those with less experience. More experienced BAs also tend to focus on a limited number of critical factors (Maxwell et al., 2011), spend less time on due diligence (Benjamin and Margulis, 1996) and more time examining the entrepreneur's previous partnerships (Madill et al., 2005; Sørheim, 2005). BA experience can also influence their perspectives on the relationships between different factors; some BAs might view two of the factors they assess during the process as compensatory, while other BAs, viewing the same factors, may consider them to be non-compensatory (Feeney et al., 1999).

One important issue that emerges from this research is that BAs are not a homogeneous group; rather, each BA has an individual personality, unique experiences and personal motivations that influence the way he or she makes investment decisions. Further, BAs are not even consistent in how they make decisions when faced with the same opportunity on subsequent occasions, as they can be influenced by circumstances and how previous investments played out. Mason (2008) attempted to identify BA characteristics that might indicate common approaches to the investment decision, noting that BAs with similar motivations or investment experience could be grouped together, as can those with common expectations about their post-investment role, or how they will manage their longer-term relationships with the entrepreneur. BAs with common perspectives, backgrounds, ethnicity and shared institutional experiences are more likely to follow similar decision processes and to co-invest. Such commonalities between the BA and the entrepreneur can also have an impact on the investment decision (Maxwell and Levésque, 2014).

The external market environment and the context in which the investment decision is made can also influence the manner in which the decision is made as well as the decision outcome. BAs are often more willing to invest in a specific industry sector if they have seen recent successful ventures in that same sector, while economic trends also influence their investment appetite for certain sectors or types of venture (Mason, 2006). Investment decisions are also influenced by direct government financial support (Baldock and Mason, 2015), indirect government support for BA activities (Mason, 2009) and access to government funded education and/or critical infrastructure (San José et al., 2007).

Cultural factors also affect how BAs make their decisions, for example, German BAs tend to be more interested in technology ventures with high growth potential than their counterparts in the UK or USA (Stedler and Peters, 2003). While Ding et al. (2014) note that BAs in China tend to rely more on prior entrepreneur relationships than do BAs in Denmark, and to depend less on the objective assessment of risk. There are a multitude of studies that highlight the differences between BAs in different regions, for example Silicon Valley BAs tend to behave differently from those in other parts of the USA (Sohl, 2003). These differences highlight the importance of considering the environment and culture in which BAs make their decisions, and the impact these factors have on the decision-making process.

Investment decisions are also influenced by the context in which the interaction occurs: the location/audience, the nature of the decision process, the number of BAs simultaneously involved and the structure of the interaction. Traditionally, BAs have made individual investment decisions in a private setting. While such interactions are still common, there has been an increase in the number of BAs making investment decisions in group-based semi-public meetings. The growth of BA groups, where entrepreneurs present to several BAs simultaneously, is having an increasing impact on the investment decision process (Mason et al., 2013). The structure of the BA group can also impact both the decision process and the outcome. BA groups, with formal membership, better informed investors and structured screening/diligence processes, have more impact on the decision process than less formal Business Angel Networks (BANs) that act more as introduction services (Gregson et al., 2013).

The manner in which the investment interaction occurs also influences the way in which the investment decision is made. Brush et al. (2012) note a facilitated interaction between an entrepreneur and a group of BAs has an impact on the decision process due to the selection bias (those chosen to present may not represent the best opportunities, but be chosen because they are of interest to most of the group) and to the interaction effect (BAs can seek input from each other, influence each other's decisions and even co-invest). In the extreme case, where BA investment interactions are seen globally on the reality TV shows, *Dragons' Den* and *Shark Tank*, there are additional factors that influence the investment decision process as well as the outcome. Selection bias influences the entrepreneurs chosen to pitch (with a bias to more outrageous individuals, as well as those who have a consumer product or service that is easier to explain on national television). Further, the fact that the interaction is seen on national television encourages entrepreneurs to participate for product exposure rather than to attract investment. This national exposure also influences the behaviors and decisions of BAs and entrepreneurs, who are conscious of the impact of each on their reputations (Maxwell, 2011). These decision process influences must be considered when generalizing outcomes from such data sets.

### 6.3.2 Investment Factors Considered by Business Angels

In Table 6.1 we summarize various investment factors considered by BAs looking at investment opportunities. Based on Maxwell (2011) we categorize these as: (a) BA-venture-entrepreneur fit factors (Duxbury et al., 1997); (b) venture-market factors (Bachher and Guild, 1996); (c) entrepreneur capability factors (Haines et al., 2003); (d) factors linked to the BA's anticipated relationship with the entrepreneur (Maxwell and Levésque, 2014); and (e) the factors inherent in the investment proposal itself (Mason and Harrison, 2003).

However, analyzing these factors individually can over-simplify the relationship between these factors and the investment decision outcome. This is because each factor is weighted differently and has a different impact on the decision to reject or select an opportunity for investment (Mason and Harrison, 2003). It is also unlikely that all of these factors are considered during a time-constrained interaction (Zacharakis and Meyer, 1998), rather different factors are considered at each stage of the decision process (Van Osnabrugge, 2000). Further, the relationship between individual factors is complex, with some being compensatory (a weakness is compensated by a strength in another) while others are non-compensatory (Mason and Harrison, 1996). In addition, the way in which specific factors are presented can have either a positive or negative impact on the assessment of the venture and the entrepreneur (Mason and Harrison, 2003; Clark, 2008; Pollack et al., 2012).

*Table 6.1 Positive and negative factors considered by business angels*

| Criteria (+++ indicate positive effect) (– – – indicate negative effect) | | Mason & Harrison (1996a) | Bachher & Guild (1996) | Haar et al. (1988) | Landström (1998) | Feeney et al. (1999) | Van Osnabrugge (2000) |
|---|---|---|---|---|---|---|---|
| Product | Interest/benefits | – | ++ | +++ | ++ | – – – | ++ |
| | Status | – – – | ++ | | | | |
| | Protectability | – – – | +++ | ++ | ++ | | + |
| | Innovation/ quality | – | +++ | | | | +++ |
| Market | Market size | – | + | +++ | + | | +++ |
| | Growth potential | | +++ | | ++ | + | +++ |
| | Supply/ distribution | – | | | + | | |
| | Market dynamics | – | ++ | + | + | – – – | +++ |
| Entrepreneur | Industry experience | – – – | +++ | +++ | +++ | +/– – – | |
| | Track record | – | + | | +++ | +++/– | ++ |
| | Passion, commitment | | +++ | | | +/– – – | +++ |
| | Integrity, trustworthy | | | | | +++/– – – | +++ |
| | Tech. knowledge | | +++ | | ++ | | +++ |
| Financial | Profitable/ realistic | – – – | | | | +++/– – – | ++ |
| | Capitalization, cash flow | – | | | | – – – | ++ |
| | Size of investment | | | | | +++ | + |
| | Plan/presentation | – | + | + | +++ | +/– – – | |
| | ROI /valuation | – | | | ++ | +/– | +++ |
| | Liquidity | | | | ++ | +++/– | + |
| Investment (Deal) | Team characteristics | – – – | | +++ | +++ | – – – | |
| | Entrepreneur fit | | ++ | | | +/– – – | +++ |
| | Business fit | – | | ++ | ++ | – | + |
| | Location | | ++ | + | + | | + |
| | Referral source | – | +++ | | | | |
| | Co-investment | | + | | + | | + |
| | Exit | | | | | | |
| | Investor role | | +++ | | ++ | +++ | +++ |
| Sample size | | 1 | 20 | 121 | 73 | 153 | 143 |
| Country | | UK | Canada | US | Sweden | Canada | UK |
| Methodology | | Interview | Survey/ interview | Question-naire | Question-naire | Interview | Interview/ question-naire |

| Haines et al. (2003) | Mason & Harrison (2003) | Stedler & Peters (2003) | Mason & Stark (2004) | Sudek (2006) | Paul et al. (2007) | Clark (2008) | Maxwell (2011) | Mitteness et al. (2012b) |
|---|---|---|---|---|---|---|---|---|
| | – – – | ++ | ++ | ++ | | | – – – | |
| | | | | | | | – – – | +++ |
| | | + | | +++ | | | – – – | |
| | – | | ++ | | | ++ | | |
| | | | | | | | | |
| + | – – – | | ++ | +++ | | ++ | – – – | ++ |
| +++ | – | ++ | | ++ | ++ | ++ | – – – | +++ |
| | – | + | | | | | – – – | |
| | | | | | | | | |
| | – | + | | ++ | | + | | |
| + | – – – | | ++ | +++ | +++ | ++/– – | – – – | +++ |
| | | | | | | | | |
| + | | | ++ | ++ | | ++/– – | – – – | +++ |
| + | | ++ | ++ | +++ | | ++/– – | – – – | +++ |
| | | | | | | | | |
| + | | | | +++ | | | – – – | +++ |
| | | | | | | | | |
| | | | ++ | | ++ | | – – | ++ |
| | – – | + | | ++ | | ++/– – | – – – | |
| | | | | | | | | |
| | | + | | ++ | | | – – | |
| | | | | | | | | |
| | | | | + | | | | |
| | | | | | | | | |
| | – – | ++ | ++ | | | ++/– – | | |
| + | – – | ++ | ++ | ++ | | ++/– – | – – – | |
| + | – – | | | +++ | + | | | |
| | | | | +++ | +++ | ++ | | +++ |
| | | | | | | | | |
| +++ | | + | | ++ | ++ | – – | – – | |
| | – – | | ++ | + | +++ | – – | – – | ++ |
| | | | | | +++ | +++ | | |
| + | | ++ | | | | | | |
| | | + | | + | | | | + |
| | | ++ | | | | | | ++ |
| +++ | | | | | | | – – – | |
| 51 | 30 | 232 | 10 | 72 | 30 | 3 | 602 | 57 |
| Canada | UK | Germany | UK | US | US | UK | Canada | USA |
| Focus groups | Question-naire | Question-naire | Video obser-vation | Verbal protocol | Obser-vation | Interview | Live/video observation | Real time question-naire |

### 6.3.3 Stages of the Investment Decision Process

Tyebjee and Bruno (1984) and Fried and Hisrich (1994) developed an initial model of the multi-stage investment decision process based on observations of how venture capital (VC) investors made their decisions. Duxbury et al. (1997) challenged the assumption that BAs followed this same process based on interviews with almost 300 Canadian BAs. They developed Model 1 (in Figure 6.1), which has substantive differences from the VC decision process. Van Osnabrugge (2000) and others attribute these differences, in part, to differences in the agency relationships between the two types of investor. VCs who have to be accountable to their investors for their decisions, need to embed more formal process than BAs who only have to justify their decisions to themselves. There are other differences between the way BA and VC investors make their investment decisions. BAs look to work alongside the entrepreneur, not to replace them (Bruton et al., 2000) and therefore consider their own role post-investment (Wetzel, 1981; Haines et al., 2003). BAs spend less time on due diligence than VCs (Benjamin and Margulis, 1996) and therefore rely more on trusted referrals as a source of opportunities, and focus more than VCs on the relationship risk rather than the market risk because they see the investment as the start of a long-term relationship (Fiet, 1995).

Model 1 offers a multi-stage model of the BA decision process that includes: 'Deal Origination' – when opportunities are sourced and 'Initial Screening and Business Plan Review' – where opportunities are rejected without the BA and entrepreneur meeting. The next stage, 'Evaluation/ Selection', is the time when entrepreneur and BA first meet, while 'Due Diligence' occurs after an initial decision to make an investment offer has been made, and confirms the accuracy of the information provided by the entrepreneur. If all these stages are successfully passed, the next stage is 'Negotiation and Consummation', which includes negotiating the investment amount and the various terms of the shareholder agreement that includes not only the amount of equity but also the role of the BA post-investment as well as control clauses imposed by the BA on the entrepreneur.

In 2007, Riding, Maddil and Haines extended this model (Model 2) to include subsequent stages, after the investment decision has been made, because they observe that the BAs anticipation about subsequent activities fundamentally influence the decision process itself. The post-investment factors that influence the interaction include both the BA's anticipation of the nature of the long-term relationship with the entrepreneur (Maxwell and Lévesque, 2014) as well as the BA's expectations about his or her role post-investment (Haines et al., 2003). The BA will also consider exit plans

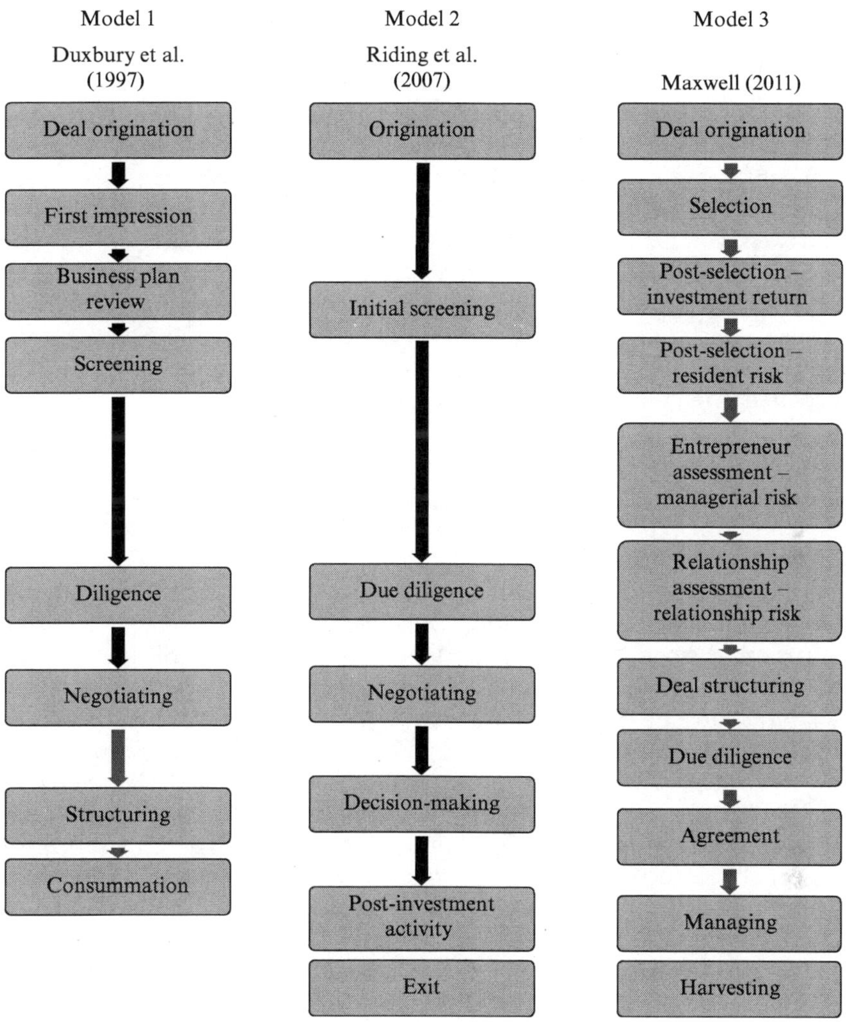


*Figure 6.1 Stages of the business angel investment process*

and the long-term financial goals of the venture, such as subsequent VC funding (Maddil et al., 2005) or a trade sale or initial public offering (IPO) (Carpentier and Suret, 2015), although perhaps exit considerations have less impact on the decision than might be expected (Mason et al., 2015).

Maxwell and his colleagues (2011) further enhance this multi-stage model (Model 3), investigating in detail the selection stage when the BA and entrepreneur first meet. This is often viewed as the most vital part of the whole investment process (May and Simmons, 2001). Based on observations of nearly 500 interactions between entrepreneurs and BAs on the TV show *Dragon's Den*, Maxwell et al. (2011) broke down the interaction between BA and entrepreneur into four sub-stages based on different rejection reasons. They observe that different factors about the entrepreneur, venture and anticipated relationship are considered at each stage, confirming earlier observations of Mason and Rogers (1997) that the nature of the interaction changes though a multi-stage process. They explain their observation arguing that experienced investors, faced with numerous investment opportunities, use heuristics to minimize the decision effort required (Jeffrey et al., 2016). We now discuss each of the stages in Model 3 in detail.

**Deal origination**

Experienced BAs wish to review multiple opportunities in order to identify those that combine good potential returns with the opportunity for them contribute to venture success (Mason and Rogers, 1997). Most BAs operate under severe time constraints, splitting their time between identifying and selecting new investment opportunities, managing their current investment portfolio and pursuing other activities (Shepherd et al., 2005). As a consequence of this time pressure, most experienced investors tend to source investment opportunities from informal personal contacts (business associates, friends and directly from entrepreneurs) rather than accountants, lawyers and banks and informal BA groups (Kelly and Hay, 2003). Sourcing opportunities from personal networks, including formal BA groups, or trusted referrals both filters out less promising opportunities (Harrison et al., 1997) and increases the likelihood that a referred opportunity will meet the BA's specific investment expectations (Harrison and Mason, 1999). Referrals from trusted sources are also seen as proxies for quality (Riding et al., 1997; Sørheim, 2005), which can reduce subsequent due diligence requirements (Van Osnabrugge, 2000).

**Initial screening and business plan review**

Initial screening takes place when the BA first receives the opportunity, and he or she assesses its fit with their personal investment criteria. Common factors considered at this stage include: location, industry knowledge and the BA's ability to contribute post-investment (Mason and Rogers, 1997). At this stage, BAs undertake a quick review of the opportunity, but are unlikely to review the business plan in too much detail (Mason, 2008). Riding et al. (1993) observe that more than 70 percent of opportunities offered are rejected at this stage, even before any formal meeting or conversation between the BA and entrepreneur takes place. Common causes of the high rejection rate at this stage are linked to issues with the venture itself (Bachher and Guild, 1996), concerns about the entrepreneur (Feeney et al., 1999) and fit with the BA's personal investment preferences (Mason and Kwok, 2012). Another reason why the BAs might reject an opportunity at this stage is if they are unable to see a role for themselves post-investment (Van Osnabrugge, 2000).

**Selection (evaluation) stage**

Maxwell et al. (2011) focus attention on the selection stage, when BA and entrepreneur meet and interact to determine whether or not an investment offer will be made (Mason and Rogers, 1997). This stage continues until either the BA rejects the opportunity or makes an investment offer. Given the high failure rate during this stage, Maxwell and his colleagues observe fundamentally different rejection reasons that allow them to identify four distinct sub-stages of the selection stage. Identifying why opportunities are rejected offers important lessons for entrepreneurs who can learn by observing others' shortcomings and the importance of being prepared to deal with failure (Shepherd, 2003).

Maxwell et al. (2011) develop a heuristics framework to explain the sequential elimination process observed based on the BA's desire to minimize the retrieval and assessment effort required. The four sub-stages include: selection – rejection due to presence of a single fatal flaw; venture assessment – rejection due to insufficient return or excessive venture risk; managerial assessment – rejection due to concern about the entrepreneur's ability; and relationship risk – rejection due to concern that the entrepreneur will not manage the venture in the BA's best interests. In Table 6.1, we organize the various individual factors identified in line with the sequence stages herein described. We now explain each of these sub-stages in more detail.

**Rejection due to the presence of a fatal flaw**

At the initial stage of the interaction between BA and entrepreneur, the BA looks to rapidly reject opportunities using an 'Elimination by Aspects' heuristic (Tversky, 1972). The BA eliminates from further consideration any opportunity with a fatal flaw in any one of eight critical venture factors identified (Maxwell et al., 2011). Decision effort is reduced because there is no need to retrieve additional information about other factors, once a critical flaw has been identified, and because there is no need to integrate the assessment of one factor with another. The eight critical venture factors considered as potential fatal flaws and thus reasons for rejection include: low market potential (Feeney et al., 1999), limited evidence of product adoption (Bachher and Guild, 1996), lack of protectability (Mason and Harrison, 1996; Landström, 1998), and limited entrepreneur experience (Cassar, 2014), as well as excessive time to market (MacMillan et al., 1986; Mason and Harrison, 2002), lack of a viable route to market (Mason and Stark, 2004), limited customer engagement (Mason and Harrison, 1996; Wiltbank et al., 2009) and financial forecasts that imply the venture will run out of money (Mason and Stark, 2004; Collewaert, 2012).

**Rejection due to insufficient investment return or excessive venture risk**

Scott Jeffrey and his colleagues (Jeffrey et al., 2016) identify how the eight venture factors assessed in the previous stage are linked to two underlying factors: investment return and investment risk, which influence the investment decision at the nest stage. It is interesting to note that at this stage the BA pays limited attention to the entrepreneur's characteristics because assessing the impact of the entrepreneur on the investment can only be determined once details of the venture are understood (Mitteness et al., 2012b). This explains some of the horse (venture) versus jockey (entrepreneur) debate in the literature (Harrison and Mason, 2002). It is not that one is more important than the other, rather that the assessment of the entrepreneur involves assessing their ability to manage venture specifics and the assessment of the entrepreneur takes more time and effort than the assessment of the venture. The assessment of the entrepreneur is therefore undertaken subsequent to the assessment of the venture (Mitteness et al., 2012b).

Opportunities that reach the subsequent stage of the interaction are assessed (and sometimes rejected) due to the BA's concerns that the investment might not produce the desired investment return (Haines et al., 2003) or where the BA perceives that there is an excessive level of inherent venture risk (Yazdipour, 2010). In the case of BA investing, the investment risk is the likelihood of a complete loss rather than a distribution of negative outcomes (Benjamin and Margulis, 2000) and is a combination of the venture risk, the managerial risk and the relationship risk. At this stage of the interaction, BAs focus on the venture risk component of the investment risk, as factors linked to the venture risk are easy to retrieve and assess than the assessment of the managerial or relationship risk, which are in part based on the BA auditing the behaviors of the entrepreneur. The BA minimizes the decision effort required at this stage by integrating the assessment of the venture factors examined during the previous stage of the interaction, rather than retrieving additional information (Jeffrey et al., 2016).

Jeffrey et al. (2016) note that concerns about the investment return require that the BA integrate their previous assessment of four of the critical factors linked to revenue and profitability (which predict long-term venture value). These four venture factors are: insufficient market potential, lack of product adoption, unclear protectability that enables competition and limited entrepreneur experience. A combination of low ratings in these venture factors raise concerns about the venture's ability to create adequate return on investment – usually between 30–40 percent per annum (Feeney et al., 1999).

The BA's assessment that the venture will fail is based on their assessment of the inherent risk in the venture, which Das and Teng (2001) suggest includes technology risk, operational risk, market risk and financial risk. Concerns about the venture risk require that the BA integrate their previous assessment of the other four critical venture factors: excessive lead time to market (implying high level of technology risk), supply chain issues (suggesting operational risk), limited evidence of customer need (linked to market risk) and poor cash flow projections linked to financial viability (indicating financial risk). The BA's integrates the assessment of these factors to allow him or her to determine if the inherent risk in the venture exceeds his or her investment risk threshold (Freear et al., 2002).

Given that at this stage of the process BAs are integrating factors to inform their assessment of return and risk, Mason and Harrison (1996) note the importance of understanding the relationships between the factors, when they are compensatory and when they are not. Interestingly, in assessing opportunities that are rejected at this stage, Jeffrey et al. (2016) find that BAs integrate the assessment of factors that predict investment return as well as factors that inform the assessment of venture risk, suggesting that within these fundament factors, individual venture factors are compensatory. However, they observe that BAs don't integrate the assessment of the two fundamental factors: investments return and venture risk. As a consequence, insufficient return cannot be compensated for by low levels of venture risk (and vice versa), indicating the non-compensatory nature of the relationship between investment return and investment (venture) risk. Jeffrey and his colleagues note that in addition to using a non-compensatory heuristic to reduce the effort otherwise required to make trade-offs between fundamentally different factors (fear of a loss versus calculation of a gain), BAs also use a satisficing heuristic to reject opportunities that fail to either reach a minimum level of investment return or exceed a threshold level of venture risk.

**Rejection due to excessive managerial risk**

At the subsequent stage, BAs consider opportunities not previously rejected, and now look to reject those perceived as having excessive managerial risk. The managerial risk is the risk that the entrepreneur will not be able to deliver on the venture's potential (Feeney et al., 1999). The assessment of the managerial risk can only be undertaken subsequent to the assessment of the venture risk, as it is based on the entrepreneur's ability to mitigate these risks (Mitteness et al., 2012b). Maxwell (2011) observes that this assessment is based on the BA's observations of the entrepreneur's behaviors and responses to questions during the interaction (Ouellete and Wood, 1998) that help the BA determine the entrepreneur's capabilities: technical expertise (Sandberg et al., 1988), social skills (Baron and Markman, 2003), capacity to identify new opportunities (Baron, 2007), management capability (Reuber and Fischer, 1994), ability to manage risk (Baron and Markman, 2003), and leadership skill (Mitteness et al., 2010). The BA also assesses the entrepreneur's experience, that is, industry knowledge (Cassar, 2014), track record as a founder (Feeney et al., 1999; Haines et al., 2003; Gompers et al., 2006), educational background (Franke et al., 2008) as well as the entrepreneur's traits: commitment (Feeney et al., 1999), passion (Mitteness et al., 2012a), confidence (Brush et al., 2012), enthusiasm (Sudek, 2006), and action-orientation (Ciavarella et al., 2004). Interestingly, Maxwell (2011) finds some evidence that excessive levels of some of these traits can be seen by the BA as negative, such as over-confidence (Åstebro et al., 2007).

Auditing the behaviors and responses of the entrepreneur allows the BA to assess the managerial risk, for example, the manner in which the entrepreneur presents essential information impacts the BA's assessment of capability (Clark, 2008), while the provision of relevant technical expertise informs the BA's assessment of the entrepreneur's ability to manage the venture's technology risks. Similarly, the entrepreneur's response to feedback and criticisms is an indicator of his or her coachability (Mitteness et al., 2012b), while setting an unrealistic venture valuation creates concerns about the entrepreneur's pragmatism, as well as his or her willingness to collaborate (Maxwell, 2011).

Other entrepreneur behaviors also influence the BA's assessment of the managerial risk, for example, an entrepreneur who makes a poor investment pitch is unlikely to be able to sell to customers (Mason and Harrison, 2001). Similarly, the quality of the presentation (Mason and Harrison, 2003; Clark, 2008), the entrepreneur's preparedness (Pollack et al., 2012) and physical appearance (Grégoire et al., 2008) influence the BA's assessment of the entrepreneur, which can cause an opportunity to be rejected at this stage due to excessive managerial risk.

### Rejection due to excessive relationship risk

At the final stage of the interaction, before an investment offer is made, BAs focus on the relationship risk (Fiet, 1995). The relationship risk is the risk that the entrepreneur may take actions, or make decisions, that are not in the long-term interests of the BA. These actions or decisions can either be due to the entrepreneur's lack of knowledge/experience or because the entrepreneur puts his or her own interests ahead of the BA's (Harrison et al., 1997). BAs inform their assessment of the likely future relationship based on a combination of auditing the trust behaviors of the entrepreneur during the interaction (Sudek, 2006) and the entrepreneur's recollections of previous relationships (Kelly and Hay, 2003).

Maxwell and Lévesque (2014) argue that assessing the entrepreneur's trustworthiness requires more cognitive effort than the assessment of the venture or the managerial risk, and therefore only takes place with opportunities not rejected for other reasons, earlier in the process. This is because trust building and trust damaging behaviors only emerge after an extended interaction between entrepreneur and BA (Boon and Holmes, 1999). Excessive displays of trust damaging behaviors lead to the interaction being terminated at this stage, while an investment offer is only made if the entrepreneur displays sufficient trust building behaviors to overcome the BA's concerns about the relationship risk (Maxwell and Lévesque, 2014). BAs audit the entrepreneur's trust behaviors (willingness to trust, trustworthiness, capability and communications), noting certain behaviors damage trust (which can be repaired) while other behaviors violate trust, making an investment impossible. The difference between behaviors that damage trust and those that violate trust is one of intent, often discernable by the reaction of the person who has experienced the negative trust behavior.

The development of trust in the relationship complements the deployment of formal controls in the shareholder agreement (Harrison et al., 1997; Kelly and Hay, 2003). Trust in the relationship is required because the contract cannot foresee all of the eventualities that might occur during the life of the agreement, and because trust is an essential part of the long-term partnership that develops between BA and entrepreneur (Arthurs and Busenitz, 2003).

**Due diligence**

In the Canadian setting, Haines et al. (2003) report that BAs use a wide range of informal due diligence approaches to confirm that information provided, in the business plan or during the interaction, is accurate. Diligence patterns vary depending on the BA. There is evidence that more experienced BAs look for different things when completing due diligence than BAs with less experience, for example, paying less attention to the financial projections and more to the characteristics of the entrepreneur (Harrison et al., 2015). This is because they are more concerned with the relationship risk than the market risk (Fiet, 1995). As we have already noted, BAs conduct less due diligence when the entrepreneur is referred through a trusted source, or can rely on a BA group manager who completes some diligence before the entrepreneur and BA meet. In addition, operating in BA groups may allow individual BAs to share aspects of the due diligence process. BAs also perform less due diligence than VCs, in part because their decisions only have to meet their own needs, and they don't need to justify to a third party that they have investigated every aspect of the venture/entrepreneur in detail (Van Osnabrugge and Robinson, 2000).

The most common reasons for rejection at the due diligence stage are material inaccuracies in the entrepreneur's claims or because the BA discovers aspects of the business that may limit the venture's success, such as the company's contractual obligations, intellectual property agreements or onerous clauses in the shareholder agreement (Mason et al., 2015).

**Negotiation and consummation**

Subsequent to confirmation of the veracity of information provided, and the absence of any fundamental concerns, BAs look to conclude an investment agreement that is fair to both sides. During this negotiation, the BA will offer an investment amount, in return for a certain equity percentage, subject to a broad array of clauses in the shareholder agreement (Haines et al., 2003; Kelly and Hay, 2003). Unfortunately, even at this point, in about 50 percent of cases, potential investments are not consummated because founders and BAs disagree about the firm valuation (Riding et al., 1993), the relative values of their respective contributions to the firm (Mason and Harrison, 1996) and/or terms in the shareholder agreement (for example, the investor's role post-investment – Haines et al., 2003). Each of these issues can cause either party to withdraw from the negotiation.

Valuation is the issue usually cited as the reason investment offers fail at this stage, because the entrepreneur tends to overvalue the venture (pre-money), often because they ignore the value created by the BA's involvement – providing advice and signaling credibility (Maxwell, 2011). Negotiation is often viewed by each party as a win-lose situation, despite the fact that lower valuations can help in attracting subsequent rounds of investment (Mason et al., 2015), and that the behaviors of each party during the negotiation are seen as indicators of likely future behaviors subsequent to the investment.

In fact behaviors manifest during the interaction and negotiation often influence the structure of clauses in the shareholder agreement (Kaplan and Strömberg, 2004). These clauses are also influenced by the experience of the entrepreneurs. Kelly and Hay (2003) find that in these cases

BAs tend to insert tighter contract clauses that specify roles and responsibilities of entrepreneur and BA, and the need for mutual agreement on strategically important issues such as making acquisitions, formulating budgets and issuing share options. In contrast, when entrepreneurs are referred through a trusted third party, or a strong bond develops between entrepreneur and BA during the interaction, Kelly and Hay note that control clauses are more relaxed and the relationship between BA and entrepreneur is characterized as trusted. In many cases the BA sees their direct participation in the venture post-investment as an alternate way of controlling the entrepreneur to the introduction of control clauses in the agreement itself. Kelly and Hay also find that certain clauses (such veto rights over acquisitions) are non-negotiable, while others, such as hiring management, establish initial controls that are often relaxed as the relationship develops.

### 6.3.4 Post-investment Management of the Venture

Once an offer has been made and accepted, the due diligence complete and the final terms of the shareholder agreement finalized, money flows from the BA to the venture (usually in tranches against milestones negotiated in the agreement) and the BA and entrepreneur start to work together. As we have noted, the behaviors and negotiations during the interaction influence both the roles of BA and entrepreneur subsequent to investment, and the relationship between them. In contrast to VCs, BAs are often found to be more involved in the venture, not for the purpose of monitoring the performance of the entrepreneur, but rather to help the entrepreneur achieve success. As a consequence, BA's anticipation about their anticipated role influences their investment decision and the way they negotiate an investment agreement. Further, passing on their experiences to a less experienced entrepreneur is often seen by the BA as a continuation of their entrepreneurial career (Politis and Landström, 2002). BAs can play a variety of formal and informal roles subsequent to the investment that include providing general management advice, making introductions, joining the advisory board and helping the venture source subsequent rounds of funding (Madill et al., 2005). As a result, most BAs and entrepreneurs view their ongoing relationship favorably, and the contribution played by the BA to the venture's success as positive (Mason and Harrison, 1996).

### 6.3.5 Exit

Colin Mason and his colleagues (Mason et al., 2015) point out that there has been limited research on how potential exit options influence the investment decision process, despite the fact that BA investing requires successful exits to justify future investment and the recycling of funds from these exits into new ventures (Mason and Harrison, 2006). Interestingly, discussing or establishing an exit strategy during the interaction does not seem to be a priority for the BA, despite the fact that BAs only achieve a financial return if there is an exit. In fact, it would seem that even after the investment many BAs don't seem to have an exit plan (Lumme et al., 1998). It is possible that exit plans are not discussed during the investment interaction because discussing the exit options prematurely with early stage entrepreneurs who are attached to their venture may reduce the likelihood that the entrepreneur will accept the investment (Cardon et al., 2005).

Another reason why available exit options are not discussed is because of both parties limited awareness of the link between the likely exit route, the structure of the investment opportunity and subsequent business strategy followed (Mason et al., 2015). Exits that are likely to achieve the BA's required return on investment are those in which the value of the company is likely to rise, because the business represents a substantive opportunity to the acquirer, for either financial or strategic reasons (McKaskill, 2009). Financial acquisitions are attractive for the acquirer if they feel they can operate the business more effectively than the BA. Strategic acquisitions occur when the acquisition of the business significantly enhances the value of the acquirer, for example, by complementing the acquirer's product line or giving them access to new markets. In general, as McKaskill notes, strategic acquirers pay a premium over financial acquirers because they are in a better position to leverage their existing resources. Consequently, entrepreneurs and BAs should be motivated to develop a strategy that either makes them more valuable or more visible to a strategic acquirer. The likelihood of exiting by going public or through a management buyout is so rare, that is should not influence the investment decision (Freear and Wetzel, 1990). Failure as an exit option should also be considered, encouraging the entrepreneur to rapidly test market demand, as rapid failure (rather than prolonged) can increase the likelihood of obtaining investment when the BA's views investment as part of his or her investment portfolio (Mason et al., 2015).

Finally, it is worth noting that many in the angel community are concerned about the lack of successful exits (NACO, 2014). It appears that too many of the investments made by BAs fail, or at least fail to attain a successful exit within the anticipated time horizon. Limited successful exits have a profound impact on the BA investment process, both reducing the number of BAs investing and the number of interactions between BAs and fund-seeking entrepreneurs. Low investment success rates will also impact how BAs make decisions: the type of venture they fund, the role they play post-investment and how they negotiate shareholder agreements. A better understanding of exit options and exit strategies and a focus on current low percentage of investments achieving adequate returns should therefore be the subject of future research (Wennberg and DeTienne, 2014).

## 6.4 IMPLICATIONS FOR PRACTICE AND POLICY

Understanding the BA decision process has many practical consequences. For the entrepreneur, a better understanding of the motivations and characteristics of the BA will help him or her choose to pitch to a BA who is most likely to be a fit with the opportunity, and with whom the entrepreneur can develop a long-term relationship. Understanding the BA's motivations will help the entrepreneur identify a role for the BA that will increase the likelihood of venture success and provide the right level of psychic income. An entrepreneur's better understanding of the decision process itself will help him or her better prepare for the investment pitch, emphasize factors considered as important by the BA and provide an appropriate response to the BA's questions or concerns (Brush et al., 2012). Further, a better understanding of the critical issues for venture success will help the entrepreneur address and overcome critical business flaws prior to presenting to the BA, as well as preparing to be 'investment ready' – willing to surrender certain aspects of control and equity to the BA in return for investment.

Better understanding of how the BA's view aspects of risk in the venture, especially the entrepreneur's ability to manage the venture and establish a trusted relationship with the BA, will help the entrepreneur understand the importance of his or her responses and behaviors during the interaction with the BA. In addition, an entrepreneur who understands the BA's perceptions of the investment return and risk is more likely to surrender higher equity levels or agree with the introduction of control clauses in the shareholder agreement, as they will appreciate the positive impact these have on receiving investment through increasing the likelihood of achieving a successful exit or attracting subsequent rounds of finance.

BAs' limited understanding of their own decision-making contributes to inefficiencies in the current process, evidenced by the confusing replies they offer when asked how they make investment decisions (De Noble, 2001). Recognition that the decision process is more consistent will help them better understand the sequential elimination nature of the process, and the impact of specific venture factors and entrepreneur behaviors on their assessment of the investment opportunity. Conscious of how specific factors influence the assessment of investment return and risk, BAs will be able to improve their decision-making processes, increase their confidence in interpreting specific information, and consequently increase both decision efficiency and quality.

Understanding how risks identified earlier in the decision process are, or are not, mitigated later in the process, help the BA compensate for negative aspects of the venture (through their own expertise) or entrepreneur (through their own direct involvement), or make it clearer that an opportunity, however promising, should be rejected. Further, an improved understanding of the factors considered at each stage of the process, can allow the BA to focus attention on the most relevant questions at each stage. Increased understanding of the decision process is even more important when BAs invest in groups, as a shared understanding of how risks can be mitigated can facilitate co-investing, and enable BAs and entrepreneurs to overcome differences in valuation or about concerns with critical control clauses in the shareholder agreement that might otherwise prevent a promising deal from being consummated.

From a policy point of view, given the acknowledged impact of BA investments on regional economic activity, government's increased knowledge of how BAs make investment decisions can help them to better deploy resources and develop programs that address the causes of the high rejection rate. As Alan Riding and his colleagues (Riding et al., 2007, p. 332) note, 'the design of any such incentives should be grounded in a thorough understanding of Business Angels' motivations, decision-making processes and criteria.' Improved knowledge can encourage governments to focus on educating BAs, fostering BA group activity and providing direct incentives to help more opportunities move to subsequent stages of the investment decision process and achieve higher exit rates. Governments can also look to fund resources that will help mitigate some of the risks that currently cause investment opportunities to be rejected or funded ventures to fail to achieve a successful exit. In combination, better informed policy decisions will ensure that government resources are more efficiently deployed, leading to the funding of higher quality opportunities rather than simply funding more ventures (Carpentier and Suret, 2007), with the result that a higher percentage of them will achieve long-term success (Mason and Harrison, 2001).

## 6.5 FUTURE RESEARCH

Given the importance of BA investing to the development of high growth firms, the launch of new technologies in the market, and the regional economic multiplier effect, research designed to help understand how to increase the number of high potential ventures able to attract funding is important. Unfortunately, to date there are many apparent failings in the investment decision process, from the paucity of entrepreneurs able to attract funding and the lack of successful exits for funded ventures, to the limited impact of government policies on increasing the long-term success rates of funded ventures. Any future research into the BA decision-making process needs to seek evidence about how to help entrepreneurs attract funding, and BAs make more successful investments, as well as how governments can develop policies that increase the longer-term impact of BA funded ventures. An appreciation of what we know about the BA investment decision process and the limitations of current research, help inform specific areas for future research.

First, we suggest that more attention can be paid to better understanding the various stages of the investment decision process, by finding alternate ways to observe and code real investment interactions that provide 'fertile untapped resource(s) for future entrepreneurship research' (Sarasvathy and Venkataraman, 2011, p. 127). Specific factors that are worthy of investigation in examining the multi-stage sequential elimination process are the impact of additional venture factors and entrepreneur behaviors during each stage of the interaction, the relationship between these factors and how these combine to influence both the investment decision itself, as well as the impact of these factors on the investment terms and specific clauses in the shareholder agreement.

Second, there is a need to look in more detail at the characteristics of individual BAs, and how his or her individual industry and investment experiences, personalities and motivations influence the decision. For example, there is some evidence that women BAs invest smaller amounts and more frequently in syndicates than men (Ahtila, 2014), or that BAs with the same ethnic or educational background as the entrepreneur are more likely to invest in their ventures (Maxwell, 2011). One important area for research is the impact of female BAs, both in how they make investment decisions and how they respond to pitches by female entrepreneurs (Brush et al., 2002). Also of interest is the observation that BAs from different cultural backgrounds, or operating in different contexts, use several decision processes, and consider the relative importance of specific factors differently. While there is evidence that more objective venture factors are viewed similarly in different environments, Maxwell (2011) notes, in the context of *Dragons' Den* interaction in 22 countries, that similar entrepreneur and BA behaviors can have different impacts on the decision outcome.

Third, a further area of interest is the impact of learning on the investment decision process, both for the entrepreneur and the BA (Harrison and Leitch, 2008). We know that more experienced BAs tend to use different processes than those with less experience, indicating that there might be benefits in better educating BAs about the investment decision process, for example, through BA academies (San José et al., 2007). It is likely that the same is true when educating entrepreneurs.

Fourth, the long-term relationship between BA and entrepreneur is a critical component for long-term venture success. Behavioral patterns manifest during the interaction have a profound effect on the subsequent evolution of the relationship between entrepreneur and BA. Given our ability to observe how capability and trust behaviors manifest during the interaction influence the investment decision, it would be interesting to undertake longitudinal studies that link these behaviors to the longer-term development of the dyadic relationship as well as to longer-term venture success (Madill et al., 2005; Kerr et al., 2014).

Fifth, recently there have been substantive changes in the way BAs make decisions, from confidential interactions between a single BA and an entrepreneur, to entrepreneurs presenting to BA groups (Carpentier and Suret, 2015) or even in the public forum of national TV (Maxwell, 2011). It will be interesting to see the impact of these changes on the decision process: filtering, group decision-making (sometimes operating in the public domain) influence the investment interactions, the long-term success of funded ventures, and the number of entrepreneurs seeking BA investment (Gregson et al., 2013).

Sixth, entrepreneurs seeking to grow their companies are faced with a variety of financing options, of which BA funding is only one. A better understanding of each of these options and the relationship between them, as well as differences and similarities between the investment decision processes, will help entrepreneurs better understand their funding options. For example, Mollick (2014) identifies the positive signaling effect of obtaining customer pre-orders on KickStarter in subsequently raising investment funding. While KickStarter is often used to raise non-equity funds for startups, it is likely that increasing use of crowdfunding platforms will transform the equity financing of early stage ventures, in part by allowing many more individuals to be involved in funding early stage ventures (Harrison, 2013). Complementarities between equity crowdfunding (where there are limited interactions between the investors and the entrepreneur) and BA investing (where the BA plays an important role in guiding the venture, and often in attracting subsequent rounds of funding) need to be investigated to better understand the role of each, how the decision processes differ and how early crowdfunding can increase the likelihood of subsequent BA funding.

Seventh, Mason et al. (2015) identify fundamental issues with BA exits: that they do not seem to be a priority during the investment interaction itself, and that the number of BA investments which lead to a successful exit is small (Wennberg and DeTienne, 2014). This is a critical issue for the long-term sustainability of BAs as a source of equity financing. Future research should investigate the relationship between the investment decision process, and exit strategies. Further, given that successful exits for BA-funded ventures usually involve being acquired through a strategic acquisition, the impact of possible exits on the funding decision, as well as on venture strategy post-investment, needs to be better understood.

Finally, this research has many implications for governments, and others developing policies. The goal of most government funding programs is to increase the number of ventures that succeed in the long term, although there is some evidence that current policies may not achieve this outcome (Aernoudt, 1999; Mason, 2006). Of greater concern is evidence that some government programs distort the market for early stage equity funding, which results in excessive funding of poor performing ventures. This can have the negative effect of limiting follow-on support for high potential ventures. Government policy-makers who wish to encourage BA investment activity, must develop a thorough understanding of the business angel decision process, in order to have better understanding of how to increase the percentage of BA funded ventures that achieve success in order to deploy appropriate resources at each stage of the investment decision process.

## REFERENCES

Aernoudt, R. (1999), 'Business angels: should they fly on their own wings?', *Venture Capital: An International Journal of Entrepreneurial Finance*, **1**(2), 187–95.

Ahtila, O.P. (2014), 'Business angel investment decision-making criteria', Master's thesis, available at http://urn.fi/URN:NBN:fi:aalto-201412043148 (accessed 30 May 2016).

Arthurs, J.D. and L.W. Busenitz (2003), 'The boundaries and limitations of agency theory and stewardship theory in the venture capitalist/entrepreneur relationship', *Entrepreneurship Theory and Practice*, **27**, 145–62.

Åstebro, T., S.A.Jeffrey and G.K.Adomdza (2007), 'Inventor perseverance after being told to quit: the role of cognitive biases', *Journal of Behavioral Decision Making*, **20**(3), 253–72.

Bachher, J.S. and P.D. Guild (1996), 'Financing early stage technology based companies: investment criteria used by investors', *Frontiers of Entrepreneurship Research*, Babson College, 363–76.

Baldock, R. and C. Mason (2015), 'Establishing a new UK finance escalator for innovative SMEs: the roles of the Enterprise Capital Funds and Angel Co-Investment Fund', *Venture Capital*, **17**(1), 59–86.

Baron, R.A. (2007), 'Behavioral and cognitive factors in entrepreneurship: entrepreneurs as the active element in new venture creation', *Strategic Entrepreneurship Journal*, **1**, 167–82.

Baron, R.A. and G.D. Markman (2003), 'Beyond social capital: the role of entrepreneurs' social competence in their financial success', *Journal of Business Venturing*, **18**(1), 41–60.
Benjamin, G.A. and J.B. Margulis (1996), *Finding Your Wings: How to Locate Private Investors to Fund Your Business*, New York: Wiley.
Benjamin, G.A. and J.B. Margulis (2000), *Angel Financing: How to Find and Invest in Private Equity*, New York: Wiley.
Boon, S.D. and J.G. Holmes (1999), 'Interpersonal risk and the evaluation of transgressions in close relationships', *Personal Relationships*, **6**(2), 151–68.
Brush, C.G., N.M. Carter, P.G. Greene, M.M. Hart and E. Gatewood (2002), 'The role of social capital and gender in linking financial suppliers and entrepreneurial firms: a framework for future research', *Venture Capital*, **4**(4), 305–23.
Brush, C., L.F. Edelman and T.S. Manolova (2012), 'Ready for funding? Entrepreneurial ventures and the pursuit of angel financing', *Venture Capital*, **14**(2–3), 111–29.
Bruton, G., V.H. Fried and R.D. Hisrich (2000), 'CEO dismissal in venture capital backed firms: further evidence from an agency perspective', *Entrepreneurship Theory and Practice*, **24**, 69–78.
Cardon, M.S., C. Zietsma, P. Saparito, B.P. Matherne and C. Davis (2005), 'A tale of passion: new insights into entrepreneurship from a parenthood metaphor', *Journal of Business Venturing*, **20**(1), 23–45.
Carpentier, C. and J.-M. Suret (2007), 'On the usefulness of tax incentives for informal investors', *Venture Capital*, **9**(1), 1–22.
Carpentier, C. and J.-M. Suret (2015), 'Canadian business angel perspectives on exit: a research note', *International Small Business Journal*, **33**, 582–93.
Cassar, G. (2014), 'Industry and startup experience on entrepreneur forecast performance in new firms', *Journal of Business Venturing*, **29**(1), 137–51.
Ciavarella, M.A., A.K. Buchholtz, C.M. Riordan, R.D. Gatewood and G.S. Stokes (2004), 'The big five and venture survival: is there a linkage?', *Journal of Business Venturing*, **19**, 465–83.
Clark, C. (2008), 'The impact of entrepreneurs' oral "pitch" presentation skills on business angels' initial screening investment decisions', *Venture Capital*, **10**, 257–79.
Collewaert, V. (2012), 'Angel investors' and entrepreneurs' intentions to exit their ventures: a conflict perspective', *Entrepreneurship Theory and Practice*, **36**(4), 753–79.
Cressy, R. and C. Olofsson (1997), 'The financial conditions for Swedish SMEs: survey and research agenda', *Small Business Economics*, **9**, 179–94.
Das, T.K. and B.S. Teng (2001), 'Trust, control, and risk in strategic alliances: an integrated framework', *Organization Studies*, **22**(2), 251–83.
De Noble, A.F. (2001), 'Raising finance from business angels', *Venture Capital*, **3**(4), 359–67.
Ding, Z., S.L. Sun and K. Au (2014), 'Angel investors' selection criteria: a comparative institutional perspective', *Asia Pacific Journal of Management*, **31**(3), 705–31.
Duxbury, L., G. Haines Jr and A. Riding (1997), 'Financing enterprise development: decision-making by Canadian angels', in S.L. Tracy and E.M. Tracy (eds), *Proceedings of the Association of Management and International Association of Management*, Montreal, pp. 17–22.
Feeney, L., G.H. Haines and A.L. Riding (1999), 'Private investors' investment criteria: insights from qualitative data', *Venture Capital*, **1**, 121–45.
Fiet, J.O. (1995), 'Risk avoidance strategies in venture capital markets', *Journal of Management Studies*, **32**, 551–74.
Franke, N., M. Gruber, D. Harhoff and J. Henkel (2008), 'Venture capitalists' evaluations of start-up teams: trade-offs, knock-cut criteria, and the impact of VC experience', *Entrepreneurship Theory and Practice*, **32**, 459–83.
Freear, J. and W.E. Wetzel (1990), 'Who bankrolls high-tech entrepreneurs?', *Journal of Business Venturing*, **5**, 77–89.
Freear, J., J.E. Sohl and W.E. Wetzel Jr (1995), 'Angels: personal investors in the venture capital market', *Entrepreneurship and Regional Development*, **7**, 85–94.

Freear, J., J.E. Sohl and W.E. Wetzel Jr (2002), 'Angles on angels: financing technology-based ventures: a historical perspective', *Venture Capital*, **4**(4), 275–87.
Fried, V.H. and R.D. Hisrich (1994), 'Toward a model of venture capital investment decision making', *Financial Management*, **23**(3), 28–37.
Gompers, P., A. Kovner, J. Lerner and D. Scharfstein (2006), *Skill vs. Luck in Entrepreneurship and Venture Capital: Evidence from Serial Entrepreneurs*, Report No. w12592, Washington, DC: National Bureau of Economic Research.
Grégoire, D.A., A.J. de Koning and B.M. Oviatt (2008), 'Do VCs evaluate "live" presentations like they evaluate business plans?', in A. Zacharakis, S. Alvarez, G. George et al. (eds), *Frontiers of Entrepreneurship Research*, Babson College, **28**(3), 1–13.
Gregson, G., S. Mann and R. Harrison (2013), 'Business angel syndicisation and the evolution of risk capital in a small market economy: evidence from Scotland', *Management and Decision Economics*, **34**(2), 95–107.
Haar, N.E., J. Starr and I.C. MacMillan (1988), 'Informal risk capital investors: investment patterns on the East Coast of the USA', *Journal of Business Venturing*, **3**, 11–29.
Haines Jr, G.H., J.J. Madill and A.L. Riding (2003), 'Informal investment in Canada: financing small business growth', *Journal of Small Business and Entrepreneurship*, **16**(3/4), 13–40.
Harrison, R. (2013), 'Crowdfunding and the revitalisation of the early stage risk capital market: catalyst or chimera?', *Venture Capital*, **15**(4), 283–7.
Harrison, R.T. and R. Baldock (2015), 'Financing SME growth in the UK: meeting the challenges after the global financial crisis', *Venture Capital*, **17**(1–2), 1–6.
Harrison, R.T. and C.M. Leitch (eds) (2008), *Entrepreneurial Learning: Conceptual Frameworks and Applications*, London: Routledge.
Harrison, R.T. and C.M. Mason (1992), 'International perspectives on the supply of informal venture capital', *Journal of Business Venturing*, **7**(6), 459–75.
Harrison, R.T. and C.M. Mason (1999), 'An overview of informal venture capital research', *Venture Capital*, **1**, 95–100.
Harrison, R.T. and C.M. Mason (2002), 'Backing the horse or the jockey? Agency costs, information and the evaluation of risk by business angels', *Frontiers of Entrepreneurship Research*, Babson College, available at http://fusionmx.babson.edu/entrep/fer/Babson2002/XII/XII_P3/XII_P3.htm (accessed June 2016).
Harrison, R.T., M. Dibben and C.M. Mason (1997), 'The role of trust in the business angel's investment decision: an exploratory analysis', *Entrepreneurship Theory and Practice*, **21**(4), 63–81.
Harrison, R., C.M. Mason and P. Robson (2002), 'Determinants of long-distance investing by business angels,' Babson College, Babson Kauffman Entrepreneurship Research Conference (BKERC), Vol. 2006.
Harrison, R.T., C.M. Mason and P. Robson (2010), 'Determinants of long-distance investing by business angels in the UK', *Entrepreneurship and Regional Development*, **22**(2), 113–37.
Harrison, R.T., C. Mason and D. Smith (2015), 'Heuristics, learning and the business angel investment decision-making process', *Entrepreneurship and Regional Development*, 1–28.
Jeffrey, S.A., M. Lévesque and A.L. Maxwell (2016), 'The non-compensatory relationship between risk and return in business angel investment decision making', *Venture Capital*, forthcoming.
Kaplan, S.N. and P.E. Strömberg (2004), 'Characteristics, contracts, and actions: evidence from venture capitalist analyses', *Journal of Finance*, **59**(5), 2177–210.
Kelly, P. (2007), 'Business angel research: the road travelled and the journey ahead', in H. Landström (ed.), *Handbook of Research on Venture Capital*, Cheltenham, UK and Northampton, MA, USA: Edward Elgar, pp. 315–31.
Kelly, P. and M. Hay (2003), 'Business angel contracts: the influence of context', *Venture Capital*, **5**(4), 287–312.
Kerr, W.R., J. Lerner and A. Schoar (2014), 'The consequences of entrepreneurial finance: evidence from angel financings', *Review of Financial Studies*, **27**(1), 20–55.
Landström, H. (1998), 'Informal investors as entrepreneurs', *Technovation*, **18**(5), 321–33.

Lumme, A., C. Mason and M. Suomi (1998), *Informal Venture Capital: Investors, Investments and Policy Issues in Finland*, Dordrecht: Kluwer Academic Publishers.
MacMillan, I.C., R. Siegel and P.S. Narasimha (1986), 'Criteria used by venture capitalists to evaluate new venture proposals', *Journal of Business Venturing*, **1**(1), 119–28.
Madill, J.J., G.H. Haines Jr and A.L. Riding (2005), 'The role of angels in technology SMEs: a link to venture capital', *Venture Capital*, **7**, 107–29.
Mason, C.M. (2006), 'The informal venture capital market in the United Kingdom: adding the time dimension', in J. Butler (ed.), *Research on Entrepreneurship and Management, Volume 5, Venture Capital and Entrepreneurship*, Greenwich, CT: Information Age Publishing, pp. 137–71.
Mason, C.M. (2008), 'The real venture capitalists: a review of research on business angels', available at https://wwwstrath.ac.uk/rnediafdepartmentslhuntercentrelresearch/worldng-papers/IJMdef (accessed June 2016).
Mason, C.M. (2009), 'Public policy support for the informal venture capital market in Europe: a critical review', *International Small Business Journal*, **27**(5), 536–56.
Mason, C. and T. Botelho (2016), 'The role of the exit in the initial screening of investment opportunities: the case of business angel syndicate gatekeepers', *International Small Business Journal*, **34**, 157–75.
Mason, C.M. and R.T. Harrison (1996), 'Why business angels say no: a case study of opportunities rejected by an informal investor syndicate', *International Small Business Journal*, **14**(2), 35–51.
Mason, C.M. and R.T. Harrison (2001), 'Investment readiness: a critique of government proposals to increase the demand for venture capital', *Regional Studies*, **34**, 663–8.
Mason, C.M. and R.T. Harrison (2002), 'Is it worth it? The rates of return from informal venture capital investments', *Journal of Business Venturing*, **17**, 211–36.
Mason, C.M. and R.T. Harrison (2003), '"Auditioning for money" What do technology investors look for at the initial screening stage?', *Journal of Private Equity*, **6**(2), 29–42.
Mason, C.M. and R.T. Harrison (2006a), 'After the exit: acquisitions, entrepreneurial recycling and regional economic development', *Regional Studies*, **40**, 55–73.
Mason, C.M. and R.T. Harrison (2006b), 'Informal sources of venture finance', in S.C. Parker (ed.), *The Life Cycle of Entrepreneurial Ventures*, New York: Springer, pp. 259–99.
Mason, C. and J. Kwok (2010), 'Investment readiness programmes and access to finance: a critical review of design issues', *Local Economy*, **25**(4), 269–92.
Mason, C. and A. Rogers (1997), 'The business angel's investment decision: an exploratory analysis', in D. Deakins, P. Jennings and C. Mason (eds), *Entrepreneurship in the 1990s*, London: Paul Chapman Publishing, pp. 29–46.
Mason, C. and M. Stark (2004), 'What do investors look for in a business plan? A comparison of the investment criteria of bankers, venture capitalists and venture capitalists', *International Small Business Journal*, **22**, 227–48.
Mason, C.M., T. Botelho and R. Harrison (2013), 'The transformation of the business angel market: evidence from Scotland'. doi: SSRN 2306653.
Mason, C.M., R.T. Harrison and T. Botelho (2015), 'Business angel exits: strategies and processes', in J.G. Hussain and J.M. Scott (eds), *Research Handbook on Entrepreneurial Finance*, Cheltenham, UK and Northampton, MA, USA: Edward Elgar, pp. 102–24.
Maxwell, A.L. (2011), 'Business angel decision making', PhD thesis, University of Waterloo, available at https://uwspace.uwaterloo.ca/handle/10012/6484.
Maxwell, A.L. and M. Lévesque (2014), 'Trustworthiness: a critical ingredient for entrepreneurs seeking investors', *Entrepreneurship Theory and Practice*, **38**(5), 1057–80.
Maxwell, A., S.A. Jeffrey and M. Lévesque (2011), 'Business angel early stage decision making', *Journal of Business Venturing*, **26**, 212–25.
Maxwell, A.L., M. Lévesque and S. Jeffrey (2014), 'The non-compensatory relationship between risk and return in business angel investment decisions', *Academy of Management Proceedings*, **1**, 10463.
May, J. and C. Simmons (2001), *Every Business Needs an Angel: Getting the Money You Need to Make Your Business Grow*, New York: Crown Business.

McKaskill, T. (2009), *Invest to Exit*, Australia: Breakthrough Publications.
Mitteness, C.R., R. Sudek and M.S. Baucus (2010), 'Entrepreneurs as authentic transformational leaders: critical behaviors for gaining angel capital', *Frontiers of Entrepreneurship Research*, Babson College, **30**(5), 3.
Mitteness, C., R. Sudek and M.S. Cardon (2012a), 'Angel investor characteristics that determine whether perceived passion leads to higher evaluations of funding potential', *Journal of Business Venturing*, **27**(5), 592–606.
Mitteness, C.R., M.S. Baucus and R. Sudek (2012b), 'Horse vs. jockey? How stage of funding process and industry experience affect the evaluations of angel investors', *Venture Capital*, **14**(4), 241–67.
Mollick, E. (2014), 'The dynamics of crowdfunding: an exploratory study', *Journal of Business Venturing*, **29**(1), 1–16.
Morrissette, S.G. (2007), 'A profile of angel investors', *Journal of Private Equity*, **10**, 52–66.
NACO (2014), *Report on Angel Investing Activity in Canada: Accelerating the Asset Class*, Toronto: National Angel Capital Association.
Mynatt, C.R., M.E. Doherty and R.D. Tweney (1977), 'Confirmation bias in a simulated research environment: an experimental study of scientific inference', *Quarterly Journal of Experimental Psychology*, **29**(1), 85–95.
Ouellette, J.A. and W. Wood (1998), 'Habit and intention in everyday life: the multiple processes by which past behavior predicts future behavior', *Psychological Bulletin*, **124**(1), 54–74.
Paul, S., G. Whittam and J. Wyper (2007), 'Towards a model of the business angel investment process', *Venture Capital*, **9**(2), 107–25.
Payne, J.W., J.R. Bettman and E.J. Johnson (1988), 'Adaptive strategy selection in decision making', *Journal of Experimental Psychology*, **14**(3), 534–52.
Pollack, J.M., M.W. Rutherford and B.M. Nagy (2012), 'Preparedness and cognitive legitimacy as antecedents of new venture funding in televised business pitches', *Entrepreneurship Theory and Practice*, **36**(5), 915–39.
Politis, D. and H. Landström (2002), 'Informal investors as entrepreneurs – the development of an entrepreneurial career', *Venture Capital: An International Journal of Entrepreneurial Finance*, **4**(2), 78–101.
Rabin, M. (2000), 'Risk aversion and expected utility theory: a calibration theorem', *Econometrica*, **68**(5), 1281–92.
Riding, A.L. and D.M. Short (1989), 'Some investor and entrepreneur perspectives on the informal market for risk capital', *Journal of Small Business and Entrepreneurship*, **5**(2), 19–30.
Riding, A.L., P. Dal Cin, L. Duxbury, G. Haines and R. Safrata (1993), *Informal Investors in Canada: The Identification of Salient Characteristics*, Ottawa: Carleton University.
Riding, A.L., L. Duxbury and G. Haines Jr (1997), 'Financing enterprise development: decision-making by Canadian angels', in *Conference Proceedings for Entrepreneurship Division of the Association of Management and International Association of Management*, 17–22 August.
Riding, A., J. Madill and G. Haines (2007), 'Investment decision making by business angels', in H. Landström (ed.), *Handbook of Research on Venture Capital*, Cheltenham, UK and Northampton, MA, USA: Edward Elgar, pp. 332–46.
Reuber, A.R. and E.M. Fischer (1994), 'Entrepreneurs' experience, expertise, and the performance of technology-based firms', *IEEE Transactions on Engineering Management*, **41**, 365–74.
San José, A., J. Roure and R. Aernoudt (2007), 'Business angel academies: unleashing the potential for business angel investment', *Venture Capital*, **7**(2), 149–65.
Sandberg, W.R., D.M. Schweiger and C.W. Hofer (1988), 'The use of verbal protocols in determining venture capitalists' decision processes', *Entrepreneurship Theory and Practice*, **13**(1), 8–20.
Sarasvathy, S.D. and S. Venkataraman (2011), 'Entrepreneurship as method: open questions for an entrepreneurial future', *Entrepreneurship Theory and Practice*, **35**(1), 113–35.

Shepherd, D.A. (1999), 'Venture capitalists' introspection: a comparison on "in use" and "espoused" decision policies', *Journal of Small Business Management*, **37**(2), 76–87.
Shepherd, D.A. (2003), 'Learning from business failure: propositions of grief recovery for the self-employed', *Academy of Management Review*, **28**(2), 318–28.
Shepherd, D.A., M.J. Armstrong and M. Lévesque (2005), 'Allocation of attention within venture capital firms', *European Journal of Operational Research*, **163**(2), 545–64.
Smith, D.J., C.M. Mason and R.T. Harrison (2010), 'Angel investment decision making as a learning process', *Frontiers of Entrepreneurship Research*, Babson College, **30**(2), 3.
Sohl, J.E. (2003), 'The US angel and venture capital market', *Journal of Private Equity*, **6**(2), 7–17.
Sørheim, R. (2005), 'Business angels as facilitators for further finance: an exploratory study', *Journal of Small Business and Enterprise Development*, **12**, 178–91.
Stedler, H.R. and H.H. Peters (2003), 'Business angels in Germany: an empirical study', *Venture Capital*, **5**, 269–76.
Sudek, R. (2006), 'Angel investment criteria', *Journal of Small Business Strategy*, **17**(2), 89–103.
Svenson, O. (1979), 'Process descriptions of decision making', *Organizational Behavior and Human Performance*, **23**, 86–112.
Tversky, A. (1972), 'Elimination by aspects', *Psychological Review*, **79**(4), 281–301.
Tyebjee, T. and A. Bruno (1984), 'A model of venture capitalist investment activity', *Management Science*, **30**(9), 1051–66.
Van Osnabrugge, M. (2000), 'A comparison of business angel and venture capitalist investment procedures: an agency theory-based analysis', *Venture Capital*, **2**(2), 91–109.
Van Osnabrugge, M. and R.J. Robinson (2000), *Angel Investing: Matching Startup Funds with Startup Companies. The Guide for Entrepreneurs and Individual Investors*, New York: Jossey-Bass.
Wennberg, K. and D.R. DeTienne (2014), 'What do we really mean when we talk about "exit"? A critical review of research on entrepreneurial exit', *International Small Business Journal*, **32**(1), 4–16.
Wetzel, W.E. (1981), 'Informal risk capital in New England', *Frontiers of Entrepreneurship Research*, Babson College, 217–45.
Wetzel Jr, W.E. (1983), 'Angels and informal risk capital', *Sloan Management Review*, **24**(4), 23–34.
Wiltbank, R., S. Read, N. Dew and S.D. Sarasvathy (2009), 'Prediction and control under uncertainty: outcomes in angel investing', *Journal of Business Venturing*, **24**, 116–33.
Yazdipour, R. (2010), 'A behavioral finance approach to decision making in entrepreneurial finance', in R. Yazdipour (ed.), *Advances in Entrepreneurial Finance: With Applications from Behavioral Finance and Economics*, New York: Springer, pp. 11–30.
Zacharakis, A.L. and G.D. Meyer (1998), 'A lack of insight: do venture capitalists really understand their own decision processes?', *Journal of Business Venturing*, **13**, 57–76.

# 7 Business angels as smart investors: a systematic review of the evidence

*Diamanto Politis*

## 7.1 INTRODUCTION

Business angels are individuals who, alone or in a formal or informal syndicate, invests their own money directly in an unquoted business in which there is no family connection, and who, after making the investment, takes an active involvement in the business, in the hope of financial gain. This group of investors are attractive partners for start-up entrepreneurs for at least two main reasons. First, business angels offer financial capital that fills the gap between the initial seed funding from the pockets of the entrepreneurial team and investors who operate in much later stages of firm development, such as professional venture capital firms. Thus, business angels can be considered as a critical source of seed and start-up finance for many growth-oriented ventures (Lindström and Olofsson, 2001; Ben-Ari and Vonortas, 2007), not least as this investment may enable developing the business model, scaling up venture activities and professionalizing business operations (Politis et al., 2012).

Second, business angels are widely recognized as 'smart' investors who contribute with added value beyond their financial investment through active hands-on involvement (Wetzel, 1986; Ehrlich et al., 1994; Politis, 2008). Several studies point out that business angels have a background as practising businessmen or entrepreneurs (Sørheim and Landström, 2001; Politis and Landström, 2002), where many of them prefer to take an active role in the start-up to develop the business (Ehrlich et al., 1994; Mason and Harrison, 1996; Sørheim, 2003). This enables them to provide valuable business skills and access to personal networks with regard to the portfolio firm, the technology employed and the market environment. Besides the financial capital provided, entrepreneurs may hence also benefit from the experientially acquired expertise business angels provide to the fledging venture (Mason, 2006; Kelly, 2007).

However, despite the widespread recognition that business angels are 'smart investors' who can add value both to entrepreneurs and their ventures it is problematic to get a comprehensive and detailed theoretical overview of this process. The available research evidence is heavily weighted towards studies that provide empirical descriptions of the hands-on support provided by business angels. In contrast, studies that provide more detailed empirical and theoretical insights about the process and impact of their hands-on involvement on business performance is much more scarce. The research is also scattered across different disciplinary approaches and reported in a range of different scholarly outlets (Politis, 2008). As a result, few studies relate to each other and theoretical progress remains slow. Research on business angels and value added provided by business angels consequently seems to suffer from a set of shortcomings that call for systematic efforts to collect and accumulate the available research evidence as a focusing device and guide for future scholarly studies.

In this chapter, the aim is to contribute to the scholarly understanding of business angels as 'smart' investors by identifying, reviewing and synthesizing available research evidence reporting on the hands-on involvement provided by business angels. This aim will be achieved by undertaking a systematic literature review of research evidence that has focused on this particular phenomenon in peer-reviewed scholarly journals. Based on these theoretical and empirical insights, the chapter will also provide guidance for future scholarly research addressing the process where business angels contribute with value added to their portfolio ventures.

The chapter is structured as follows. The next section presents a brief synopsis of prior research that has identified business angels as value adding investors, followed by the development of an analytical framework that will be used in the subsequent thematic analysis. The framework emphasizes four interrelated dimensions in the process of value added resulting from the hands-on involvement of business angels: behaviour, context, reception and impact. Thereafter follows a section with details about the systematic literature review used for identifying and analysing available research on business angels and value added. This is followed by a descriptive analysis with respect to main journals, theories used, methodologies and empirical context studied. After this, the outcome of the thematic analysis is presented where the research evidence is reviewed and discussed and suggestions for future research are identified. The chapter ends with a concluding discussion.

## 7.2 BUSINESS ANGELS AND VALUE ADDED: AN ANALYTICAL FRAMEWORK

Business angels have always been a very hard-researched topic since these investors are a largely hidden and very private group of people

(Farrell et al., 2008). Despite their important role in funding venture activities throughout modern corporate history (Kelly, 2007), for decades there was little general knowledge available about the business angel market and its actors. However, a growing interest in business angels from the early 1980s and onwards resulted in increasingly better understanding of the attitudes, behaviour and characteristics of these investors (for example, Wetzel, 1986; Haar et al., 1988; Gaston, 1989; Landström, 1993, 1998; Mason and Harrison, 1994, 1996; Freear et al., 1995; Van Osnabrugge, 1998; Aernoudt, 1999; Mason and Stark, 2004; Kelly, 2007).

The most distinct and well-known feature of business angels that has come out of this stream of research is perhaps that they offer *more* than just money. This feature is linked to the fact that many business angels have made their fortunes through a cash-in of their own ventures (Landström, 1993; Mason and Harrison, 1996). Scholars examining business angels have reported that 67–95 per cent have previous business ownership experience (Wetzel, 1981; Gaston, 1989; Short and Riding, 1989; Mason et al., 1991; Landström, 1993; Sørheim and Landström, 2001) and also that practising entrepreneurs are four times as likely as non-entrepreneurs to be a business angel in another entrepreneur's venture (Bygrave and Hunt, 2005). Many business angels thus have a track record as entrepreneurs, with personal experience of owning and running a small business. In addition, while business angels seldom become directly involved in daily operations they can nevertheless be characterized as fairly active investors (Freear et al., 1995; Van Osnabrugge, 1998), most often through active board work and by providing consultancy services when required (Landström, 1993; Mason and Harrison, 1996; Gabrielsson and Huse, 2002; Politis and Landström, 2002). As a result, business angels can be depicted as 'smart investors' with high likelihood of providing added value beyond their financial investment (Politis, 2008).

However, while the value added feature of business angels is widely acknowledged there is surprisingly little scholarly work that approaches this phenomenon in any systematic sense. Rather, available research reporting on business angels and value added has been scattered across different disciplines and research traditions, often providing empirical descriptions rather than systemizing these observations into analytical generalizations (Politis, 2008). Hence, while past empirical research has contributed to the accumulation of knowledge about business angels and value added, this chapter builds on the belief that there is a need to continue scholarly efforts by developing an analytical framework with a distinct and well-defined set of concepts to enable further theoretical development.

The remainder of this section presents and develops the initial building

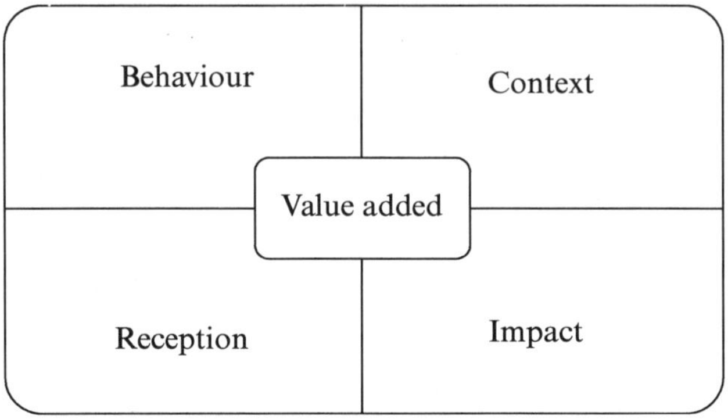


*Figure 7.1 Analytical framework*

blocks of such an analytical framework embedded and building on the recommendations for future research provided in Politis (2008, pp. 140–42). By doing this, the framework recognizes the value of theoretical pluralism to advance research in the field while at the same time emphasizing the need for developing a set of core concepts and dimensions to embark on future research efforts with clarity and consistency. *Value* in the analytical framework is defined as the relative worth, utility or importance of a business entity, and *value added* is from this definition understood as a process coming from the hands-on involvement of a business angel and resulting in a potential enhancement of value in a business. Recognizing vale added as a process further emphasizes the need to conceptualize the hands-on involvement of business angels as consisting of a sequence of interdependent and linked procedures or activities, where inputs may be processed and subsequently translated into outputs that generate value (Politis, 2008).

Based on these premises and assumptions, the analytical framework conceptualizes the process of value added as a multifaceted phenomenon that centres around four distinct but interrelated dimensions: behaviour, context, reception and impact. An illustration of the analytical framework is depicted in Figure 7.1. Each dimension is discussed below.

Behaviour refers to the hands-on involvement of business angels (Landström, 1993; Stedler and Peters, 2003) as well as potential variations that may exist among different groups of investors due to their personal motives, characteristics and competence profiles (Sørheim and Landström, 2001; Politis and Landström, 2002). Serving as the key input for all subsequent occurrences and outcomes in the process of value added, this dimension captures the way business angels behave in relation to their portfolio ventures, which may produce a set of potential value adding benefits that a new venture can receive from the investor (for example, Politis, 2008, p. 142).

Impact refers to the effect or influence resulting from the hands-on involvement of business angels on the behaviour and performance of entrepreneurial ventures. This dimension thus recognizes the crucial and important question of whether, and to what extent, the hands-on involvement of business angels translates into significant and measurable outputs (Politis, 2008, p. 140) by capturing value as a firm-level quantity that can be assigned or determined by assessment or calculation.

Reception refers to how the hands-on involvement of business angels are received and valued, as well as used and implemented by entrepreneurs. This dimension recognizes the need to question value added as a simple transferring process, where its value and use is captured from the perspective of the receiver. This dimension emphasizes that entrepreneurs can vary significantly both in their ability to appreciate and understand, as well effectively implement and utilize the potential value adding benefits that business angels may provide to the portfolio venture (Politis, 2008, p. 142).

The final dimension in the framework, context, refers to situational circumstances, as well as temporal and spatial conditions, that may influence the hands-on involvement of business angels. This dimension captures the critical role of environmental circumstances and conditions in the ongoing process of venture development (Politis, 2008, p. 141), thus recognizing the need to acknowledge and take into account the wide range of internal or external contingencies that can influence the value adding process.

Taken together, the analytical framework provides a sorting logic to examine the process of value added by showing it to be a multidimensional phenomenon, where each component only conceptualizes and captures a single dimension. While much past research has been largely one-dimensional, foreseeing only single aspects of value added (for example, Politis, 2008), the proposed framework might in this respect contribute with a more solid theoretical footing in the attempt to study and conceptualize the complex process of value added.

## 7.3 SEARCH METHODOLOGY: A SYSTEMATIC LITERATURE REVIEW

The search methodology used in this chapter has followed the principles of a systematic literature review (Gough et al., 2012). To enable and support both accountability and repeatability of research reviews this approach emphasizes the importance of describing the various steps involved in the

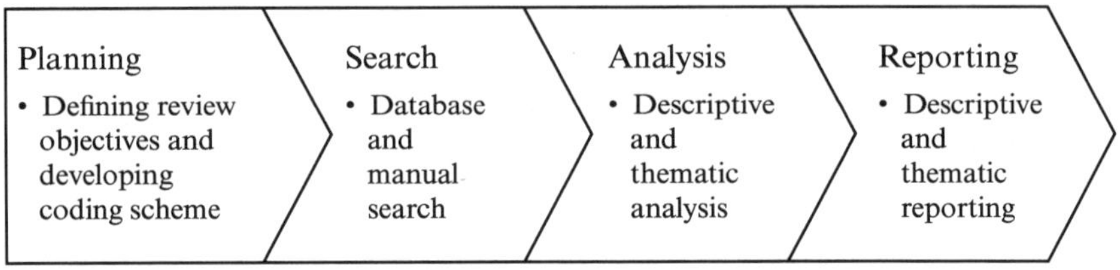


*Figure 7.2 Action steps in the systematic literature review*

review process based on detailed criteria from citation indexes. Inspired by previous entrepreneurship and small business management research that has followed the methodological principles underlying a systematic literature review (for example, Thorpe et al., 2005; Pittaway and Cope, 2007; Yar Hamidi and Gabrielsson, 2014) the review in this chapter was structured in four stages, as illustrated in Figure 7.2.

Figure 7.2 depicts each stage in the review as a set of action steps. The first step represents the planning stage where one or several review objectives are defined. This is followed by the development of a coding scheme that serves as a tool to assemble and synthesize relevant data. The review objective for this specific study was set in accordance with the overall aim of the chapter and it was decided to include empirical studies reporting on the hands-on involvement of business angels in peer-review journals. The variables in the coding scheme were linked to the review objective and enabled systematic collection of data about the number of publications per year, target journals, theoretical approaches, geographical contexts studied, data collection methods and methods of analysis.

The second step represents the search stage of a number of bibliographical electronic databases using the root search string 'business angel* AND value added*'. In this process it was found that ABI/INFORM Complete, Business Source Elite and Scopus provided greatest coverage when it comes to full-article access. Combinations of the following keywords focused the electronic search: Business Angel (or) Private Investor (or) Personal Investor (or) Informal Investor (or) Informal Risk Capital (or) Informal Venture Capital (and) Contribution (or) Involvement (or) Value Added (or) Support (or) Impact. Search terms were separated when consisting of multiple words.

First, all multiple entries were deleted as they substantially increased the number of observed hits. To be consistent with the review objectives the search was then limited to include only empirical studies reported in peer-reviewed journals. The search was thereafter aligned with our working definition of business angels (see introduction), where studies that clearly lacked relevance were deleted. The electronic search was then supplemented with a narrative cross-referencing method, where a manual search of the bibliographies of all identified entries was performed. Then all titles and abstracts were examined with respect to the review objective. In this step articles that acknowledged the value added provided by business angels but that did not empirically investigate and report about it in any detail were excluded. After this screening a sample of 27 academic articles were identified. All identified articles were then downloaded for further reading and analysis.

In the analysis stage the 27 identified articles were first coded in accordance with the pre-made coding scheme, which enabled data about the number of publications per year, target journals, theoretical approaches, geographical contexts studied, data collection methods and methods of analysis. After a first round of coding a colleague was consulted to identify and correct coding errors. This dataset was used as an input in the descriptive analysis of the articles.

The subsequent thematic analysis was initiated and structured with reference to the analytical framework developed in Section 7.2. Following this analytical logic, the following basic questions were asked when reading through the available research evidence: What types of hands-on support do business angels provide, and what is the nature of the value added that they contribute (behaviour)? Is there much variation between angels, and how does involvement and support vary depending on situational contingencies (context)? Do entrepreneurs value and act upon the active involvement and hands-on support received from business angels (reception)? And, crucially, what evidence is there on the effectiveness of their hands-on involvement on business performance (impact)? The underlying methodological principle in this process was based on content analysis due to its flexibility in analysing textual data (Cavanagh, 1997) combined with its applicability to areas where the knowledge of a phenomenon is relatively limited (Hsieh and Shannon, 2005). This analysis resulted in the identification of three main themes that were seen as helpful for advancing theory and research on business angels and value added.

In the final reporting stage six tables were created to illustrate the outcomes of the descriptive analysis and the use of the three main themes as a point of departure for summarizing and organizing the findings. In the next section, a descriptive overview is provided of the findings from the review, while the outcomes of thematic analysis are reported in Section 7.5.

## 7.4 THE HANDS-ON INVOLVEMENT OF BUSINESS ANGELS: A DESCRIPTIVE OVERVIEW

The systematic literature review identified a total of 27 empirical articles reported in peer-reviewed academic journals. Eight of these articles (29.6 per cent) can be classified as core studies, as they are directly addressing the hands-on involvement and value added of business angels, either in their problem discussion and research questions, or in their overall approach and research design (Ehrlich et al., 1994; Ardichvili et al., 2002; Saetre, 2003; Madill et al., 2005; Sørheim, 2005; Macht and Robinson, 2009; Macht, 2011a, 2011b). The remaining 19 articles (70.4 per cent) can be classified as periphery studies, as they report on the value added involvement or value added contribution of business angels as a smaller issue among several other issues (for a full overview of all articles, see Appendix 7A.1). However, as all identified studies provide some empirical details about the phenomenon of interest the analysis that follows will not distinguish between them if it is not absolutely necessary.

### 7.4.1 Number of Publications Per Year and Target Journals

When going through the identified articles with respect to the year of publication the observed pattern suggests a steady development over the past three decades, with a growing interest among scholars in the 1990s, and with increasing attention in the research reported from 2000 and onwards. Notable is that seven out of the eight articles that can be classified as core studies were published after 2000. The overall pattern of development in the identified articles is reported in Figure 7.3.

The identified articles were reported in nine different academic journals. Over half of these articles (55.6 per cent) were published in *Venture Capital: An International Journal of Entrepreneurial Finance*. This is unsurprising, given its role as the premier outlet for research on venture capital and small business finance. The total distribution of articles per academic journal is reported in Table 7.1.

### 7.4.2 Theories Used and Geographical Contexts Studied

The identified articles were also categorized based on their use of theories when addressing the issue of value added and in what geographical contexts they were studying the phenomena. When it comes to the use of theories, it was found that the large majority of all identified studies, about 59.3 per cent, were providing empirical descriptions without any theoretical embeddedness. A smaller proportion, about 22.2 per cent, were using

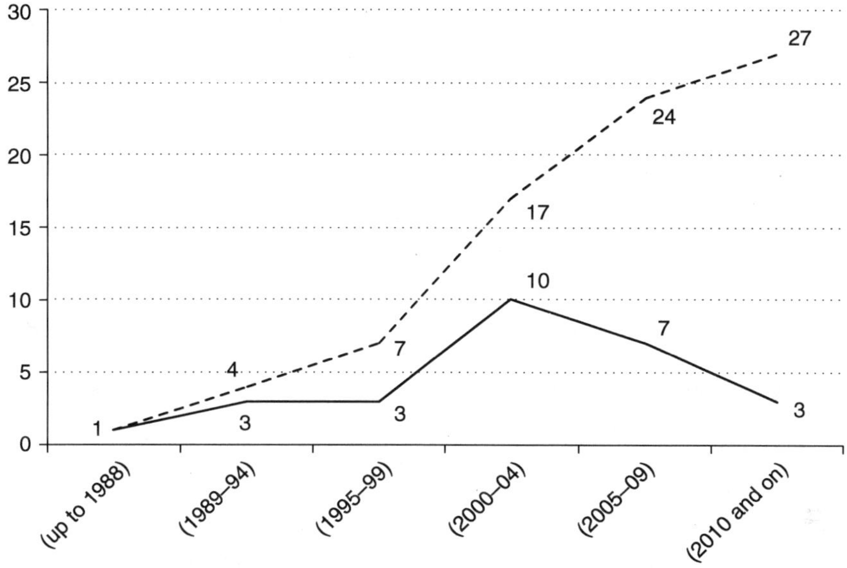


*Figure 7.3* *Number of publications per period and accumulated over time*

*Table 7.1* *Target journals*

| | Number | Per cent (%) |
|---|---|---|
| *Venture Capital: An International Journal of Entrepreneurial Finance* | 15 | 55.6 |
| *Entrepreneurship & Regional Development* | 3 | 11.1 |
| *Journal of Business Venturing* | 2 | 7.4 |
| *Strategic Change* | 2 | 7.4 |
| *International Journal of Entrepreneurial Behaviour and Research* | 1 | 3.7 |
| *Journal of Enterprising Culture* | 1 | 3.7 |
| *Journal of Small Business and Enterprise Development* | 1 | 3.7 |
| *Sloan Management Review* | 1 | 3.7 |
| *Technovation* | 1 | 3.7 |
| | 27 | 100 |

*Table 7.2 Theoretical approach*

| | Number | Per cent (%) |
|---|---|---|
| Theory driven | 5 | 18.5 |
| Theoretical concepts | 6 | 22.2 |
| No theory | 16 | 59.3 |
| | 27 | 100 |

or relating to theoretical concepts in their reasoning but without the use of explicit theories. The remaining 18.5 per cent were studies driven by one or several explicit theories. In the latter category, theories like agency theory, evolutionary theory, network theory, portfolio theory, resource-based theory and resource dependence theory were used and applied, often in various combinations. The use of theories in the identified articles is reported in Table 7.2.

Even if not explicitly addressed, most research on business angels has an underlying spatial dimension where scholars have tried to map and report about the size, behaviour and impact of the market in different geographical contexts. When it comes to the geographical contexts where the hands-on involvement of business angels have been studied the available evidence comes from eight different countries. The majority of these studies are from the UK, closely followed by the USA, and together these two countries cover close to half of all studies available. After this follows a cluster of studies from Scandinavian countries (including Finland, Norway and Sweden) and together they cover one-third of all identified studies. Another country where a series of empirical studies has been conducted is Germany, while Canada and Japan (together with Finland) each has been covered in a single study. The different geographical contexts studied in the identified articles are reported in Table 7.3.

### 7.4.3 Data Collection Procedures and Methods of Analysis

When it comes to data collection, there was a near-balance between pre-structured (deductive) and semi- or loosely structured (inductive) procedures. Just above half of the studies, 51.9 per cent, have used questionnaire surveys, while an almost equal share, 44.4 per cent, used interviews. The one remaining study relied solely on secondary data. The distribution of different procedures for data collection is reported in Table 7.4.

The average number of respondents in the studies using questionnaire surveys is 132.6 individuals, compared to an average of 23.2 respondents in the studies using interviews. However, it is notable that over half of the

*Table 7.3 Geographical contexts studied*

| | Number | Per cent (%) |
|---|---|---|
| UK | 7 | 25.9 |
| USA | 6 | 22.2 |
| Norway | 4 | 14.8 |
| Sweden | 4 | 14.8 |
| Germany | 3 | 11.1 |
| Canada | 1 | 3.7 |
| Finland | 1 | 3.7 |
| Japan | 1 | 3.7 |
| | 27 | 100 |

*Table 7.4 Data collection methods*

| | Number | Per cent (%) |
|---|---|---|
| Questionnaire survey | 14 | 51.9 |
| Interviews | 12 | 44.4 |
| Secondary data | 1 | 3.7 |
| | 27 | 100 |

studies using questionnaire surveys have relatively small samples with less than 50 respondents. A closer look reveals that the average number of respondents across these studies is heavily inflated by two studies reporting from the same questionnaire survey with responses from 425 business angels in Norway. Most studies collecting and using interview data rely on four to five interviews, while there is one outlier study that collects data from 124 interviews. The single study relying on secondary data includes two samples, with 215 and 143 cases/observations respectively.

As previously indicated, research on business angels has for a long time been driven by an interest in exploring and describing the market and its actors. Thus, it is not surprising to find that most studies reporting on business angels and value added follow this tradition when analysing the data collected. In this respect, about 40.7 per cent of the identified studies rely on descriptive analyses when reporting their findings. About one-third, or 33.3 per cent, use qualitative analysis, while just above one-fifth, about 22.5 per cent, uses statistical (quantitative) analysis. One other study has used a mixed method approach with both qualitative and statistical (quantitative) analysis. The distribution of different methods of analysis is reported in Table 7.5.

*Table 7.5 Methods of analysis*

| | Number | Per cent (%) |
|---|---|---|
| Descriptive analysis | 11 | 40.7 |
| Qualitative analysis | 9 | 33.3 |
| Statistical analysis | 6 | 22.2 |
| Mixed analysis | 1 | 3.7 |
| | 27 | 100 |

## 7.5 BUSINESS ANGELS AS SMART INVESTORS: A THEMATIC ANALYSIS

In this section the outcome of the thematic analysis of research addressing business angels in relation to the value adding process is reported. The following three themes emerged from the analysis and they were subsequently used when structuring the discussion: (1) business angel involvement and value added; (2) the translation and impact of value added benefits provided by business angels; and (3) situational contingencies influencing the process of value added.

### 7.5.1 Business Angel Involvement and Value Added

The first theme that emerged from the analysis address the involvement of business angels in the ventures in which they invest and how this involvement translates into a set of potential value adding benefits. Overall, a review of the available research evidence provides robust support for the view that business angels – on the aggregate – are actively involved in the post-investment period by providing hands-on support to the portfolio ventures in which they invest. Following the pioneering study of Wetzel (1986), where business angels are characterized as a fairly active group of investors, this pattern is something that seems to hold across temporal and spatial contexts. For example, in one of the earliest studies of business angels outside the USA, Landström (1993) reports that the relationships between business angels and their portfolio ventures in Sweden can be characterized as active. In a similar vein, Freear et al. (1995) report from a study of new technology-based firms in the USA that the vast majority (80 per cent) of business angels maintain an active working relationship with their portfolio ventures. The generality of this overall pattern continues in subsequent studies from the UK (Mason and Harrison, 1996; Harrison and Mason, 2000; Paul et al., 2007), the USA (Wong et al., 2009), Canada (Madill et al.,

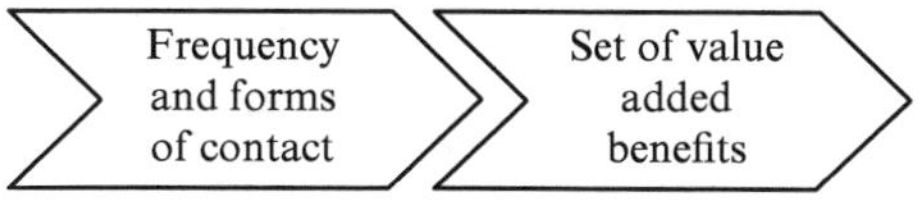


*Figure 7.4 Critical steps in the process of involvement and value added*

2005), Germany (Brettel, 2003; Stedler and Peters, 2003), Sweden (Politis and Landström, 2002), Norway (Reitan and Sørheim, 2000; Saetre, 2003), Finland (Lahti, 2011) and Japan (Tashiro, 1999).

However, despite the accumulated empirical evidence that support and corroborate the general conception that business angels are active investors providing hands-on support there is little scholarly work that conceptualizes how this process occurs in a more systematic and analytically detailed way, from the initial involvement of business angels to their ongoing provision of value adding benefits. By reviewing the available empirical evidence with respect to the process of value added at least two critical and conceptually distinct steps could be identified. Figure 7.4 illustrates the two critical steps identified in the analysis.

The first critical step illustrated in Figure 7.4 is the business angel's contact with a specific portfolio venture. This refers to both the frequency and forms of contacts with the portfolio ventures, that is, how the business angel chooses to structure and organize his or her involvement. A higher frequency of contacts can in this respect be expected to provide greater opportunity for a business angel to add value to the portfolio venture, while lower frequency of contacts will provide less opportunity. While the available research evidence typically characterizes business angels as a fairly active group of investors there is, however, little information about their frequency of contacts, with two notable exceptions. Landström (1993) reports in his study that business angels in Sweden have a rather high frequency of contact with the portfolio ventures, where over three-quarters indicated contacts every day (35 per cent) or every week (43 per cent). In addition, Stedler and Peters (2003) report in their study of business angels in Germany that most of them (54 per cent) are found to commit several days a month to the investment, while some (32 per cent) are actively involved in the venture more than one day per week. Thus, the available research evidence suggests that frequency of contact with the portfolio ventures overall is high, but at the same time varied between investors.

Compared to the level of involvement the available research evidence provides a much wider range of empirical insights when it comes to how the business angel organizes different *forms* of contacts. Common forms of contact reported in the studies include serving as board members

(Wetzel, 1986; Landström, 1992, 1993; Freear et al., 1995; Tashiro, 1999; Harrison and Mason, 2000; Reitan and Sørheim, 2000; Brettel, 2003; Macht and Robinson, 2009; Lahti, 2011), working in a full or part-time capacity (Wetzel, 1986; Ehrlich et al., 1994; Freear et al., 1995), providing ongoing consulting and advisory help (Wetzel, 1986; Freear et al., 1995; Tashiro, 1999; Harrison and Mason, 2000; Reitan and Sørheim, 2000; Brettel, 2003), receiving and following periodic economic reports (Wetzel, 1986; Landström, 1992, 1993; Ehrlich et al., 1994; Reitan and Sørheim, 2000; Stedler and Peters, 2003), participating in stockholder meetings (Wetzel, 1986; Reitan and Sørheim, 2000; Brettel, 2003) and serving on advisory councils (Brettel, 2003).

While there are some common forms of involvement across the various studies there seems to be a need to further systematize and aggregate these observations in some way. Following this idea, the different forms of involvement can be distinguished and sorted both in the degree to which they can be categorized as more active or passive forms of involvement (Wetzel, 1986), as well as in whether they involve a high or low degree of formality. While the full usefulness of such a categorization in explaining different outcomes in the value adding process remains to be explored a tentative illustration that can be used for further assessment and development is presented in Table 7.6.

The second critical step illustrated in Figure 7.4 is the set of value added benefits provided by business angels via the frequency and forms of contacts with portfolio ventures. In a previous review Politis (2008) summarized and aggregated the available empirical evidence into a set of four distinct but complementary value adding roles that business angels may perform when dealing with their portfolio ventures: sounding board/strategic role; supervision and monitoring role; resource acquisition role; and mentoring role. Being key inputs in the process of value added, these complementary roles could be described as the set of potential benefits that a portfolio venture can receive from a business angel, which – if successfully channelled and implemented – can be subsequently utilized and translated into valuable or helpful results or effects in the process of venture development. In line with

*Table 7.6 A categorization of different forms of involvement by business angels*

| | Formal | Informal |
|---|---|---|
| Active | Board membership<br>Full- or part-time employment | Providing consulting and advisory help |
| Passive | Attending shareholder meetings | Following periodic reports |

*Table 7.7 Value added benefits by business angels*

| Value adding roles | Empirical studies acknowledging the role |
|---|---|
| *Sounding board/strategic role* Providing strategic advice based on extensive business know-how and management experience | Ehrlich et al., 1994; Mason and Harrison, 1996; Tashiro, 1999; Ardichvili et al., 2002; Politis and Landström, 2002; Brettel, 2003; Paul et al., 2003; Amatucci and Sohl, 2004; Madill et al., 2005; Macht and Robinson, 2009; Schäfer and Schilder, 2009; Wong et al., 2009. |
| *Supervision and monitoring role* Shielding the investment from potential managerial misbehaviour | Ehrlich et al., 1994; Saetre, 2003; Madill et al., 2005. |
| *Resource acquisition role* Channelling timely resources through their personal networks | Ehrlich et al., 1994; Mason and Harrison, 1996; Ardichvili et al., 2002; Brettel, 2003; Paul et al., 2003; Saetre, 2003; Amatucci and Sohl, 2004; Madill et al., 2005; Sørheim, 2005; Macht and Robinson, 2009; Wong et al., 2009. |
| *Mentoring role* Being a helpful, open and trustful partner | Freear et al., 1995; Mason and Harrison, 1996; Politis and Landström, 2002; Brettel, 2003; Saetre, 2003; Macht and Robinson, 2009. |

the overall intention of this chapter to enable the accumulation of knowledge in this field of research the complementary roles identified in Politis (2008) were used as a point of departure in the analysis of value added benefits provided by business angels. The outcome is presented in Table 7.7.

To conclude this theme, the available research evidence reporting on the hands-on involvement of business angels provides a basis for systemizing and conceptualizing the initial process of value added via two critical steps: the frequency and forms of contacts with the portfolio venture, and the set of value added benefits provided by business angels. This conceptualization provides theoretical insights into the value adding process, where the hands-on involvement of business angels can be seen as consisting of a sequence of interdependent and linked procedures or activities. However, the primary contribution of this conceptualization is the guidance it provides for future scholarly research. The following questions can initially be raised for this purpose:

- How do frequency of contact relate to various forms of involvement in portfolio ventures? Does active involvement automatically correspond to certain forms of involvement, as suggested by Wetzel (1986), or can we see other patterns?

- To what extent do various forms of involvement serves as complements or substitutes to each other? For example, do close informal relationships between business angels and portfolio ventures make intensive reporting unnecessary (for example, Schäfer and Schilder, 2009)?
- How do various forms of involvement cluster together? Is there any interrelation of reciprocity between various forms of involvement, where one form of involvement may supplement or depend on some other form of involvement (for example, Wong et al., 2009)?
- To what extent do various forms of involvement produce different kinds of potential value added benefits? Do less formal forms of involvement, like provision of consulting and advisory help, lead to different sets of potential benefits compared to more formal forms of involvement, such as board memberships?

### 7.5.2 The Translation and Impact of Value Added Benefits Provided by Business Angels

The second theme that emerged in the analysis addresses how and to what extent the set of potential benefits that a portfolio venture may receive from a business angel may translate into valuable or helpful results or effects in the process of venture development. This theme has two dimensions. The first dimension is the subjective value that entrepreneurs may perceive when being exposed to business angels who are involved in their venture. The second dimension is the successful implementation of the set of potential benefits that business angels offer into venture operations, thereby impacting venture performance. While these two dimensions may correlate they are nevertheless two conceptually distinct and empirically different phenomena.

The available research evidence provides some insights into the subjective value perceived by entrepreneurs when they are exposed to business angels who are involved in their venture. Overall, the studies suggest that a majority of entrepreneurs consider their relationships with business angels to be productive (Freear et al., 1995; Mason and Harrison, 1996; Lindström and Olofsson, 2001; Ardichvili et al., 2002; Amatucci and Sohl, 2004). For example, Lindström and Olofsson (2001) find that business angels are the most valued partner when studying how entrepreneurs in new technology-based firms in Sweden compare and assess the involvement of business angels, venture capitalists and other governmental bodies providing funding to the venture. Adding to this, Mason and Harrison (1996) report in their study of the post-investment experience of entrepreneurs in the UK that respondents value a wide range of specific task-centred contributions such as accounting, project planning and guidance on marketing and financial control. However, they find no consensus among the entrepreneurs of the single most important contribution, and many responses highlight intangible and more people-centred contributions such as 'lifting the spirits', enthusiasm, sharing the burden and providing a broader view. In contrast, Ehrlich et al. (1994) report from a study of entrepreneurs in the USA that, while being satisfied overall, they express a desire for increased investor involvement in formal task-centred activities such as developing professional support groups, soliciting customers and distributors, monitoring financial performance, serving as a sounding board and managing crises and problems. Thus, the available research evidence suggests that entrepreneurs value the involvement of business angels in both task-centred and people-centred activities.

The available research evidence also suggests that the perception of value from the perspective of the entrepreneur depends on whether the business angels possess relevant experience and expertise in the area where he or she becomes involved in (Saetre, 2003; Macht, 2011a). Interestingly, Macht (2011a) finds that the perception of value from the perspective of the entrepreneur can still be high, even when business angels are involved in activities clearly outside their lack of experience. This happens if their involvement comes in the form of 'soft' (people-centred) activities instead of 'hard' (task-centred) activities. The findings thus suggest that the perceived value by entrepreneurs is not only influenced by active involvement in areas where the business angel possesses relevant experience, but also by coaching the entrepreneur and serving as mentor. Again, it emphasizes the intangible and 'soft' contributions of business angels in the process of value added highlighted above in the study by Mason and Harrison (1996).

The available research evidence is, on the other hand, surprisingly limited when it comes to the second dimension addressing how the set of potential benefits that a business angel may offer becomes implemented into the operations of the portfolio venture, thereby impacting business performance. The only contribution found in the review is Landström (1992), who in his study of manufacturing and technology-based firms in Sweden examines how the hands-on involvement of business angels impacts the working relationship between the business angel and the entrepreneur (relationship performance) as well as its impact on the venture (business performance). He reports that a higher frequency of contacts between the business angel and the entrepreneur and a high involvement of the business angel in operational work in the portfolio venture contribute to better relationship performance. However, there is no evidence that a high frequency of contacts and higher involvement in operational work lead to better business performance. Neither does Landström's (1992) study find any support that business angels' higher experience/knowledge of the portfolio firm's market or technology lead to better business performance. Thus, while the study provides some evidence that higher levels of involvement of business angels lead to a more productive working relationship between the investor and the entrepreneur, the evidence does not support that higher levels of involvement influence the business performance of the portfolio venture.

While insightful, the study by Landström (1992) does not address the process where the hands-on involvement of business angels translates into realized value added benefits. However, Macht (2011b) provides interesting empirical evidence about this issue when she suggests that the hands-on involvement of business angels is not only an investor-centred concept but also includes active involvement of the chief executive officer (CEO) of the portfolio venture. Rather than being a 'passive' receiver her study finds that CEOs play a critical role in enabling the contribution of business angels. This is processed through their working relationship via responsiveness to the involvement, the CEOs' communication of feedback on their response to involvement, the CEOs' reaction to queries from the business angels and the CEOs' role in initiating involvement activities. The CEO thus plays a critical gatekeeper role where active responsiveness is required from their side if continued involvement from the business angel is to occur, and for the business angel to realize his or her value adding potential. Macht's (2011b) study reminds us in the words of the well-known idiom that 'it takes two to tango', thus suggesting a potential theoretical foundation for linking the set of potential value adding benefits that a new venture can receive from the business angel and the effective implementation and utilization of these value adding benefits in venture operations, thereby increasing the likelihood of impacting venture performance.

To conclude this theme, the available research evidence reporting on the hands-on involvement of business angels provides a basis for systemizing and conceptualizing the reception and impact of business angel involvement in two dimensions. The first dimension is the subjective value that entrepreneurs perceive when being exposed to business angels (Freear et al., 1995; Mason and Harrison, 1996; Lindström and Olofsson, 2001; Ardichvili et al., 2002; Amatucci and Sohl, 2004) and the second dimension is how potential benefits that business angels offer may impact business performance (Landström, 1992). While there are some studies that have addressed issues related to the first dimension there is an almost complete void of studies that have addressed issues related to the second dimension. This is surprising since it is the impact on business performance that many regard as being the *sine qua non* of a business angel investment and what typically motivates entrepreneurs to highly rate and seek this source of finance. The limited number of studies addressing how the set of potential benefits offered by business angels are subjectively valued by entrepreneurs as well as impacting business performance calls for intensified scholarly inquiry. The following immediate questions can be raised for this purpose:

- How do the frequency and forms of contacts by business angels impact business performance? What is the relationship between their provisions of value adding roles (see Table 7.7) and business performance? Is the impact of the frequency and forms of contacts of business angels on business performance mediated via their provisions of value adding roles? Do different roles have different impacts on different performance indicators?
- Do different group of entrepreneurs assess and value 'soft' (people-centred) versus 'hard' (task-centred) activities (Macht, 2011a) differently? What is the relative impact of the involvement by business angels in 'soft' versus 'hard' activities on business performance?
- To what extent is the active involvement of the CEO in responsive activities (Macht, 2011b) a necessary condition for realizing and implementing the potential value added provided by business angels? Are there other conditions in and around the portfolio venture necessary for this to happen?

### 7.5.3 Situational Contingencies Influencing the Process of Value Added

The third and final theme that emerged in the analysis addresses how situational contingencies may influence the process of value added. In this respect, the available research evidence not only suggests that the hands-on involvement of business angels consists of a sequence of interdependent and linked procedures or activities, as has been discussed above, but also that this process can vary with respect to situational contingencies in and around the portfolio venture. The remainder of this section reports on this issue.

The most immediate question addressed in the research has been how the active involvement and hands-on support provided by business angels may vary with respect to different contingencies. Landström (1992) reports in his study that business angels' frequency of contacts with their portfolio ventures and levels of involvement in these ventures vary with individual and firm-level contingencies such as the experience of the business angel, the novelty of the product and geographical proximity. Interestingly, and contrary to prediction, Landström (1992) reports lower levels of involvement when the offered product is new on the market. As could be expected, however, greater geographical distance leads to fewer contacts and lower levels of involvement while business angels who have experience from venture operations (technology and market) have more contacts and show higher levels of involvement.

Much in line with the findings reported in Landström (1992), Wong et al. (2009) report that geographical closeness (or proximity) is a critical contingency influencing venture development activities. In their study they show that entrepreneurs were more likely to receive help from business angels if the investor resided less than 50 miles from their firm. They also show that local business angels have a higher frequency of contacts, which make them more involved and thereby providing more help to the portfolio venture. Hence, even if more local investors may not be as sophisticated as more professional investors who invest larger amounts of equity capital, they tend to provide better assistance. In addition, their findings suggest that the need for formal forms of involvement, for example, monitoring via board membership, may be reduced because of this geographical proximity. However, relying on local business angels may delay subsequent equity investment since they may not possess a well-developed contact network connecting them to more professional investors. Thus, close geographical proximity may both influence levels and forms of involvement, and lead to both advantages and disadvantages when it comes to how this involvement will impact venture performance.

Mason and Harrison (1996) provide empirical evidence of how the involvement of business angels in their portfolio ventures varies during the post-involvement process. Their findings suggest that in the majority of cases (63 per cent) the involvement is relatively stable over time. In the cases where there has been a change this mainly reflects the changing needs of the business, as it has progressed from the early start-up phase into a phase where the ventures are producing and selling products. Interestingly, this relative stability in terms of their overall level of involvement can be contrasted with the amount of time that business angels devote to their portfolio venture. About one-quarter of the responding business angels in the study report that they have increased their time input, while another one-third report that the amount of time that they devote has declined. The increased time input has generally occurred in situations where the portfolio venture experienced difficulties. However, there is no evidence suggesting that the reduced time input from investors leads to increased dissatisfaction in the relationship with the entrepreneurs. Overall, the findings suggest that the value added contribution of business angels primarily is a function of qualitative (expertise-based) elements rather than quantitative (time-based).

Another contingency that may influence the value adding process is when business angels make co-investments together with venture capital (VC) firms. Based on responses from VCs, Harrison and Mason (2000) report that such co-investments can be associated with both advantages and disadvantages. The main advantages lie in the complementarities that are created with respect to wider access to knowledge, management expertise, contacts and networking opportunities that aid venture development. The main disadvantages include the potential diversity in objectives, personality and interests, which may slow down decision-making and thus hamper the ongoing value adding process.

The technology level of the firms is another contingency reported as influencing the process of value added. In this vein, Erikson and Sørheim (2005) find that business angels who make technology investments are more actively involved compared to other business angels when it comes to activities such as reading financial reports, attending shareholder meetings and board meetings, and providing consultancy services. These technology-oriented business angels were also found to be more actively involved in their portfolio firms at both strategic and operational levels.

Landström (1993) suggests that the active involvement and hands-on support provided by business angels also can be attributable to institutional country-level differences, which is embedded in cultural and legal traditions such as investment climate, entrepreneurial traditions, fiscal regimes, regulatory environments and wealth distribution. Comparing Sweden, the USA and the UK,[1] he reports that business angels in Sweden are different in their post-investment behaviour compared to business angels in the UK and the USA. In the UK the relationship is in relative terms more passive, with lower involvement in daily operations and where they to a higher extent review periodic reports and attend stockholder meetings. In contrast, business angels in the USA are characterized as much more active and highly involved in daily operations. Business angels in Sweden are placed 'in between' these two, not typically involved in daily operation but working actively via the board of directors and by providing consulting help when needed. Adding to this, Reitan and Sørheim (2000) show that business angels in Norway are much less involved compared to the UK and Sweden. They explain this by the high importance of working in syndicates in the Norwegian market where a lead investor performs a 'hands-on' role in the portfolio venture while the remaining investors in the syndicate play little or no role.

To conclude this theme, the available body of research evidence suggests a range of critical contingencies that seems to provide a non-trivial influence on the hands-on involvement of business angels in the value added process. Table 7.8 summarizes the available research evidence

*Table 7.8 Critical contingencies influencing the process of value added*

| Contingencies and findings | Studies reporting on the issue |
|---|---|
| Institutional (country-level) differences may explain higher or lower levels of involvement by business angels | Landström (1993), Reitan and Sørheim (2000) |
| Business angels with experience from venture operations show higher involvement | Landström (1992) |
| Product novelty is associated with lower levels of involvement by business angels | Landström (1992) |
| Close geographical distance is associated with higher levels and less formal forms of involvement by business angels, but may also delay subsequent equity investments for the portfolio venture | Landström (1992), Wong et al. (2009) |
| The involvement by business angels is relatively stable over time, where changes are primarily reflecting changing needs of the portfolio venture | Mason and Harrison (1996) |
| Co-investment with a VC firm is associated with advantages for the portfolio venture, such as complementarities in expertise, but also disadvantages, such as diverse goals and personalities in the process of venture development | Harrison and Mason (2000) |
| The technology level of the portfolio venture is associated with higher involvement at both strategic and operational levels | Erikson and Sørheim (2005) |

reviewed above. Overall, this summary provides insights that are important to consider both in terms of micro- and macro-level contingencies that surround specific business angel investments. In addition, the review may serve as a useful point of departure for future scholarly studies of how variations in the active involvement and hands-on support provided by business angels can be referenced to contingencies in and around the portfolio venture. Some immediate questions that can be raised for this purpose are as follows:

- What is the relative influence of macro- (country and regional) versus micro-(individual or firm) level contingencies on the hands-on involvement of business angels? Which level(s) plays more significant roles in explaining various outcomes, such as business angels' frequency and forms of contacts, their provision of value adding roles or the value assessed by entrepreneurs receiving angel investments?

- Are there any differences in business angels' frequency and forms of contacts with portfolio ventures across different regions or countries across the world? Can we find any systematic differences depending on industry? How about their provision of value adding roles? To what extent does national/regional culture and industry play a role in how entrepreneurs perceive and value different sets of potential value adding roles/benefits?
- What are the complementary effects of different micro- (individual and firm) level contingencies on the value adding process? To what extent are they independent of each other, and do certain contingencies improve each other's qualities? For example, do co-investments with VCs (for example, Harrison and Mason, 2000) increase (or decrease) the value added impact from business angel involvement? Do the potential value added of business angels with experience from venture operations (for example, Landström, 1992) increase (or decrease) when dealing with experienced serial entrepreneurs?
- To what extent do business angels use modern information and communications technologies (ICT) in their interactions with their portfolio ventures and what impact does ICT have on the value adding process? How does ICT impact the frequency and forms of contacts that business angels have with their portfolio ventures? Does ICT decrease (or increase) the value and importance of geographical closeness for influencing venture development activities?

## 7.6 CONCLUSIONS

This chapter has contributed to the accumulation and development of scholarly knowledge on business angels as 'smart' investors by identifying, reviewing and synthesizing available research evidence reporting on the hands-on involvement of business angels in the post-investment period in scholarly peer-reviewed journals. The articles have been reviewed and described with respect to the number of publications per year, target journals, theoretical approaches, geographical contexts studied, data collection methods and methods of analysis. The chapter also develops and uses a multidimensional analytical framework to analyse the articles with respect to the process where business angels contribute with value added to their portfolio ventures.

Overall, the analysis of the available research evidence reported in the identified scholarly articles resulted in three main themes providing insights into the process of value added. The first theme addresses the involvement of business angels in the ventures in which they invest and how this involvement translates into a set of potential value adding benefits. The available research evidence provides a basis for systemizing and conceptualizing the initial process of value added via two critical steps: the frequency and forms of contacts with the portfolio venture and the set of value added benefits provided by business angels. This conceptualization provides theoretical insights into the value adding process as a sequence of interdependent and linked procedures or activities.

Following the process-oriented conceptualization in the first theme, the second theme that emerged in the analysis addresses how and to what extent the set of potential benefits that portfolio ventures may receive from business angels may translate into valuable or helpful results or effects in the process of venture development. Two theoretically distinct dimensions were identified in this theme. The first is the subjective value that entrepreneurs may perceive when being exposed to business angels who are involved in their venture. The second is the successful implementation of the set of potential benefits that business angels offer into venture operations, thereby impacting venture performance.

The third and final theme that emerged in the analysis addresses how situational contingencies may influence and thus strengthen or interfere in the process of value added of business angels. The review identified both micro- and macro-level contingencies as playing a significant role in the process where business angels contribute with value added to their portfolio ventures. In this respect, the available research evidence suggests that the hands-on involvement of business angels can vary with a range of situational contingencies in and around the portfolio venture.

Rather than being reductive, the review and synthesis of theoretical and empirical findings under each theme provide valuable insights into the process where business angels contribute with value added to their portfolio ventures. Together, these insights contribute to the observed need to support and promote the accumulation of knowledge within the field of business angel and value added by conceptualizing it as a complex, interdependent and multidimensional phenomenon. By recognizing the variety and complexity in the process of value added the synthesis and analysis of the available research evidence also provide ample guidance for future scholarly research that seeks a better understanding of the hands-on involvement of business angels.

## ACKNOWLEDGEMENTS

This research has been conducted within the research project Entrepreneurial Systems – A Condition for Growth, financed by the Swedish Research

Council. The author is grateful for the valuable comments and feedback from Jonas Gabrielsson in the course of developing this work.

## NOTE

1. The Swedish sample is compared to findings reported in Aram (1987), Gaston (1989), Mason et al. (1991) and Harrison and Mason (1992).

## REFERENCES

Aernoudt, R. (1999), 'Business angels: should they fly on their own wings?', *Venture Capital*, **1**(2), 187–95.

Amatucci, F.M. and J.E. Sohl (2004), 'Women entrepreneurs securing business angel financing: tales from the field', *Venture Capital*, **6**(2/3), 181–96.

Aram, J.D. (1987), *Informal Risk Capital in the Eastern Great Lakes Region*, Washington, DC: US Small Business Administration.

Ardichvili, A., R.N. Cardozo, K. Tune and J. Reinach (2002), 'The role of angel investors in the assembly of non-financial resources of new ventures: conceptual framework and empirical evidence', *Journal of Enterprising Culture*, **10**(1), 39–65.

Ben-Ari, G. and N.S. Vonortas (2007), 'Risk financing for knowledge based enterprises: mechanism and policy options', *Science and Public Policy*, **34**(7), 475–88.

Brettel, M. (2003), 'Business angels in Germany: a research note', *Venture Capital*, **5**(3), 251–68.

Bygrave, W. and S. Hunt (2005), *Global Entrepreneurship Monitor 2004 Financing Report*, Wellesley, MA and London: Babson College and London Business School.

Cavanagh, S. (1997), 'Content analysis: concepts, methods and applications', *Nurse Researcher*, **4**(3), 5–16.

Ehrlich, S.B., A.F. Noble, T. Moore and R.R. Weaver (1994), 'After the cash arrives: a comparative study of venture capital and private investor involvement in entrepreneurial firms', *Journal of Business Venturing*, **9**(1), 67–82.

Erikson, T. and R. Sørheim (2005), 'Technology angles and others informal investors', *Technovation*, **25**(5), 489–96.

Farrell, E., C. Howorth and M. Wright (2008), 'A review of sampling and definitional issues in informal venture capital research', *Venture Capital*, **10**(4), 331–53.

Freear, J.F., J.E. Sohl and W.E. Wetzel (1995), 'Angels: personal investors in the venture capital market', *Entrepreneurship and Regional Development*, **7**(1), 85–94.

Gabrielsson, J. and M. Huse (2002), 'The venture capitalist and the board of directors in SMEs: roles and processes', *Venture Capital*, **4**(2), 125–46.

Gaston, R.J. (1989), *Finding Private Venture Capital for Your Firm: A Complete Guide*, New York: Wiley.

Gough, D., S. Oliver and J. Thomas (2012), *An Introduction to Systematic Reviews*, London: Sage.

Harr, N.E., J. Starr and I.C. MacMillan (1988), 'Informal risk capital investors: investment patterns on the East coast of the USA', *Journal of Business Venturing*, **3**(1), 11–29.

Harrison, R.T. and C.M. Mason (1992), 'International perspectives on the supply of informal venture capital', *Journal of Business Venturing*, **7**(6), 459–75.

Harrison, R.T. and C.M. Mason (2000), 'Venture capital market complementarities: the links between business angels and venture capital funds in the United Kingdom', *Venture Capital*, **2**(3), 223–42.

Hsieh, H. and S.E. Shannon (2005), 'Three approaches to qualitative content analysis', *Qualitative Health Research*, **15**(9), 1277–88.
Kelly, P. (2007), 'Business angel research: the road travelled and the journey ahead', in H. Landström (ed.), *Handbook of Research on Venture Capital*, Cheltenham, UK and Northampton, MA, USA: Edward Elgar, pp. 315–31.
Lahti, T. (2011), 'Categorization of angel investments: an explorative analysis of risk reduction strategies in Finland', *Venture Capital*, **13**(1), 49–74.
Landström, H. (1992), 'The relationship between private investors and small firms: an agency theory approach', *Entrepreneurship and Regional Development*, **4**(3), 199–223.
Landström, H. (1993), 'Informal risk capital in Sweden and some international comparisons', *Journal of Business Venturing*, **8**(6), 525–40.
Landström, H. (1998), 'Informal investors as entrepreneurs', *Technovation*, **18**(5), 321–33.
Lindström, G. and C. Olofsson (2001), 'Early stage financing of NTBFs: an analysis of contributions from support actors', *Venture Capital*, **3**(2), 151–68.
Macht, S.A. (2011a), 'Inexpert business angels: how even investors with "nothing to add" can add value', *Strategic Change*, **20**(7–8), 269–78.
Macht, S.A. (2011b), 'The role of investee company managers in business angels' involvement: empirical insights from dyadic data', *Venture Capital*, **13**(3), 267–93.
Macht, S.A. and J. Robinson (2009), 'Do business angels benefit their investee companies?', *International Journal of Entrepreneurial Behaviour and Research*, **15**(2), 187–208.
Madill, J.J., G.H. Haines Jr and A.L. Riding (2005), 'The role of angels in technology SMEs: a link to venture capital', *Venture Capital*, **7**(2), 107–29.
Mason, C.M. (2006), 'Informal sources of venture finance', in S. Parker (ed.), *The Lifecycle of Entrepreneurial Ventures*, Berlin: Springer, pp. 259–99.
Mason, C.M. and R.T. Harrison (1994), 'The informal venture capital market in the UK', in A. Hughes and D.J. Storey (eds), *Financing Small Firms*, London: Routledge, pp. 64–111.
Mason, C.M. and R.T. Harrison (1996), 'Informal venture capital: a study of the investment process, the post-investment experience and investment performance', *Entrepreneurship and Regional Development*, **8**(2), 105–26.
Mason, C.M. and M. Stark (2004), 'What do investors look for in a business plan?', *International Small Business Journal*, **22**(3), 227–48.
Mason, C.M., R.T. Harrison and J. Chaloner (1991), 'Informal risk capital in the UK: a study of investor characteristics, investment preferences and investment decision making', Venture Finance Research Project Working Paper No. 2, Southampton University, Southampton.
Paul, S., G. Whittam and J.B. Johnston (2003), 'The operation of the informal venture capital market in Scotland', *Venture Capital*, **5**(4), 313–35.
Paul, S., G. Whittam and J. Wyper (2007), 'Towards a model of the business angel investment process', *Venture Capital*, **9**(2), 107–25.
Pittaway, L. and J. Cope (2007), 'Entrepreneurship education. A systematic review of the evidence', *International Small Business Journal*, **25**(5), 479–510.
Politis, D. (2008), 'Business angels and value added: what do we know and where do we go?', *Venture Capital*, **10**(2), 127–47.
Politis, D. and H. Landström (2002), 'Informal investors as entrepreneurs – the development of an entrepreneurial career', *Venture Capital*, **4**(2), 78–101.
Politis, D., J. Gabrielsson and O. Shveykina (2012), 'Early stage finance and the role of external entrepreneurs in the commercialization of university-generated knowledge', *Venture Capital*, **14**(2/3), 175–98.
Reitan, B. and R. Sørheim (2000), 'The informal venture capital market in Norway – investor characteristics, behaviour and investment preferences', *Venture Capital*, **2**(2), 129–41.
Saetre, A.S. (2003), 'Entrepreneurial perspectives on informal venture capital', *Venture Capital*, **5**(1), 71–94.
Schäfer, D. and D. Schilder (2009), 'Smart capital in German start-ups – an empirical analysis', *Venture Capital*, **11**(2), 163–83.

Short, D.M. and A.L. Riding (1989), 'Informal investors in the Ottawa-Carleton region: experiences and expectations', *Entrepreneurship and Regional Development*, **1**(1), 99–112.
Sørheim, R. (2003), 'The pre-investment behaviour of business angels: a social capital approach', *Venture Capital*, **5**(4), 337–64.
Sørheim, R. (2005), 'Business angels as facilitators for further finance: an exploratory study', *Journal of Small Business and Enterprise Development*, **12**(2), 178–91.
Sørheim, R. and H. Landström (2001), 'Informal investors – a categorization, with policy implications', *Entrepreneurship and Regional Development*, **13**(4), 351–70.
Stedler, H.R. and H.H. Peters (2003), 'Business angels in Germany: an empirical study', *Venture Capital*, **5**(3), 269–76.
Tashiro, Y. (1999), 'Business angels in Japan', *Venture Capital*, **1**(3), 259–73.
Thorpe, R., R. Holt, A. Macpherson and L. Pittaway (2005), 'Using knowledge within small and medium-sized firms: a systematic review of the evidence', *International Journal of Management Reviews*, **7**(4), 257–81.
Van Osnabrugge, M. (1998), 'Do serial and non-serial investors behave differently? An empirical and theoretical analysis', *Entrepreneurship Theory and Practice*, **22**(4), 23–42.
Wetzel Jr, W.E. (1981), 'Informal risk capital in New England', in K. Vesper (ed.), *Frontiers of Entrepreneurship Research*, Wellesley, MA: Babson College, pp. 217–45.
Wetzel Jr, W.E. (1986), 'Angels and informal risk capital', *Sloan Management Review*, **24**(4), 23–34.
Wong, A., M. Bhatia and Z. Freeman (2009), 'Angel finance: the other venture capital', *Strategic Change*, **18**(7–8), 221–30.
Yar Hamidi, D. and J. Gabrielsson (2014), 'Developments and trends in research on board leadership: a systematic literature review', *International Journal of Business Governance and Ethics*, **9**(3), 243–68.

# APPENDIX 7A.1 LIST OF ALL ARTICLES IN THE LITERATURE REVIEW


Amatucci, F.M. and J.E. Sohl (2004), 'Women entrepreneurs securing business angel financing: tales from the field', *Venture Capital*, **6**(2/3), 181–96.

Ardichvili, A., R.N. Cardozo, K. Tune and J. Reinach (2002), 'The role of angel investors in the assembly of non-financial resources of new ventures: conceptual framework and empirical evidence', *Journal of Enterprising Culture*, **10**(1), 39–65.

Brettel, M. (2003), 'Business angels in Germany: a research note', *Venture Capital*, **5**(3), 251–68.

Ehrlich, S.B., A.F. Noble, T. Moore and R.R. Weaver (1994), 'After the cash arrives: a comparative study of venture capital and private investor involvement in entrepreneurial firms', *Journal of Business Venturing*, **9**(1), 67–82.

Erikson, T. and R. Sørheim (2005), 'Technology angles and others informal investors', *Technovation*, **25**(5), 489–96.

Freear, J.F., J.E. Sohl and W.E. Wetzel (1995), 'Angels: personal investors in the venture capital market', *Entrepreneurship and Regional Development*, **7**(1), 85–94.

Harrison, R.T. and C.M. Mason (2000), 'Venture capital market complementarities: the links between business angels and venture capital funds in the United Kingdom', *Venture Capital*, **2**(3), 223–42.

Lahti, T. (2011), 'Categorization of angel investments: an explorative analysis of risk reduction strategies in Finland', *Venture Capital*, **13**(1), 49–74.

Landström, H. (1992), 'The relationship between private investors and small firms: an agency theory approach', *Entrepreneurship and Regional Development*, **4**(3), 199–223.

Landström, H. (1993), 'Informal risk capital in Sweden and some international comparisons', *Journal of Business Venturing*, **8**(6), 525–40.

Lindström, G. and C. Olofsson (2001), 'Early stage financing of NTBFs: an analysis of contributions from support actors', *Venture Capital*, **3**(2), 151–68.

Macht, S.A. (2011a), 'Inexpert business angels: how even investors with "nothing to add" can add value', *Strategic Change*, **20**(7–8), 269–78.

Macht, S.A. (2011b), 'The role of investee company managers in business angels' involvement: empirical insights from dyadic data', *Venture Capital*, **13**(3), 267–93.

Macht, S.A. and J. Robinson (2009), 'Do business angels benefit their investee companies?', *International Journal of Entrepreneurial Behaviour and Research*, **15**(2), 187–208.

Madill, J.J., G.H. Haines Jr and A.L. Riding (2005), 'The role of angels in technology SMEs: a link to venture capital', *Venture Capital*, **7**(2), 107–29.

Mason, C.M. and R.T. Harrison (1996), 'Informal venture capital: a study of the investment process, the post-investment experience and investment performance', *Entrepreneurship and Regional Development*, **8**, 105–26.

Paul, S., G. Whittam and J.B. Johnston (2003), 'The operation of the informal venture capital market in Scotland', *Venture Capital*, **5**(4), 313–35.

Paul, S., G. Whittam and J. Wyper (2007), 'Towards a model of the business angel investment process', *Venture Capital*, **9**(2), 107–25.

Politis, D. and H. Landström (2002), 'Informal investors as entrepreneurs – the development of an entrepreneurial career', *Venture Capital*, **4**(2), 78–101.

Reitan, B. and R. Sørheim (2000), 'The informal venture capital market in Norway – investor characteristics, behaviour and investment preferences', *Venture Capital*, **2**(2), 129–41.

Saetre, A.S. (2003), 'Entrepreneurial perspectives on informal venture capital', *Venture Capital*, **5**(1), 71–94.

Schäfer, D. and D. Schilder (2009), 'Smart capital in German start-ups – an empirical analysis', *Venture Capital*, **11**(2), 163–83.

Stedler, H.R. and H.H. Peters (2003), 'Business angels in Germany: an empirical study', *Venture Capital*, **5**(3), 269–76.

Sørheim, R. (2005), 'Business angels as facilitators for further finance: an exploratory study', *Journal of Small Business and Enterprise Development*, **12**(2), 178–91.

Tashiro, Y. (1999), 'Business angels in Japan', *Venture Capital*, **1**(3), 259–73.
Wetzel Jr, W.E. (1986), 'Angels and informal risk capital', *Sloan Management Review*, **24**(4), 23–34.
Wong, A., M. Bhatia and Z. Freeman (2009), 'Angel finance: the other venture capital', *Strategic Change*, **18**(7–8), 221–30.

# 8 Angel–entrepreneur relationships: demystifying their conflicts

*Veroniek Collewaert*

## 8.1 INTRODUCTION

As Maxwell revealed in Chapter 6, a vast amount of angel research has focused on the pre-investment stage examining angels' investment decision-making process. Amongst others, this research showed that angels do not solely invest for financial reasons, but also non-financial ones such as personal satisfaction, opportunities to influence the development of a new venture and job creation (for example, Harrison and Mason, 1992; Hindle and Wenban, 1999; Landström, 1993). This non-financial motive for investing explains why angels tend to be rather patient investors; their general anticipated time-to-exit ranges from four to seven years (for example, Wetzel, 1981; Freear et al., 2002; Mason and Harrison, 2002). Some angels even indicate not having a clear preference as to when they want to exit or indicate not wanting to exit at all (for example, Landström, 1993; Collewaert, 2012). Yet, despite the relatively long-term working relationship angels develop with their entrepreneurs, we know very little about this relationship and the dynamics inherent to them.

Specifically, most research on the post-investment relationship between angels and entrepreneurs has focused on angels' degree of involvement in their portfolio ventures and the roles angels take on in those ventures. As discussed by Politis in Chapter 7, these studies have shown that angels have more to bring to the table than just their financial means – they also bring their skills, experience – either managerial or entrepreneurial – and contacts (for example, Ehrlich et al., 1994; Freear et al., 2002; Paul et al., 2003). Angels' emphasis on post-investment involvement is also reflected in their contracts, which tend to be more entrepreneur-friendly, have weaker control rights and include less contractual provisions than their venture capital counterparts (Kelly and Hay, 2003; Goldfarb et al., 2008; Wong, 2010). Also, angels take on different roles in their portfolio companies such as taking on a seat on the board of directors, providing consulting help or even working part or full time with the venture, each of which implies quite varying degrees of active participation (for example, Harrison and Mason, 1992; Landström, 1993; Prowse, 1998).

What is lacking from this literature overview, however, is insight into how angels and entrepreneurs work together to create an effective investment relationship and to foster venture performance and innovation. To shed light on this question, I draw on prior angel research that has argued that conflicts are critical to the day-to-day functioning of angel–entrepreneur teams (for example, Mason and Harrison, 1996; Collewaert, 2009, 2012; Collewaert and Fassin, 2013). For instance, angel–entrepreneur conflicts have been shown to increase both angels' and entrepreneurs' intentions to exit their ventures (Collewaert, 2012) and to, under certain circumstances, severely affect the venture's innovativeness (Collewaert and Sapienza, 2016).

Given the important ramifications of angel–entrepreneur conflicts for both the individuals and ventures involved, the goal of this chapter is to provide a comprehensive review of this concept, including its definition, antecedents and consequences. To this end, I combine insights from the organizational behaviour literature on intragroup conflicts with insights from the angel literature to depict angel–entrepreneur conflict as a process that unfolds over time and as a concept that requires a contingency perspective to study it. Adopting a dynamic view on conflict allows one to explore the conditions that may lead up to angel–entrepreneur conflicts, but also recognize the possibility that not all angel–entrepreneur teams characterized by similar conditions will experience similar levels of overt conflict. Specifically, it may require some sort of conflict-triggering event to facilitate this transformation from latent to overt conflict. In this chapter, I explore both latent conditions that create the context for angel–entrepreneur conflicts to occur and an example of a conflict-triggering event. Further, the conflict contingency framework recognizes that not all conflict is equally good or bad – it may depend on the type of conflict that occurs, the outcome studied and moderating influences such as team and task characteristics (De Dreu and Weingart, 2003; Jehn and Bendersky, 2003). I will explore some of the implications of this contingency framework for effects of angel–entrepreneur conflicts.

In so doing, I aim to contribute to the angel literature by enhancing our practical and theoretical understanding of conflicts between angels and entrepreneurs. More broadly, this chapter also seeks to contribute to the literature on angel involvement. Whereas many have argued that the relationship angels develop with their entrepreneurs is the primary means through which angels add value (for example, Politis, 2008), we know very little about the nature of that relationship. By exploring angel–entrepreneur conflicts, their causes and consequences, I aim to provide a more thorough understanding of how angels and entrepreneurs can work together to nurture a fruitful investment partnership.

The chapter starts by providing an overview of what conflicts between angels and entrepreneurs embody. In other words, when angels and entrepreneurs argue, what do they argue about? Next, I provide some statistics based on prior research to indicate how frequently angel–entrepreneur conflicts occur. This will address the question of to what extent their relationship is consensual versus conflictual. To wrap this section up, I also discuss to what extent angels and entrepreneurs tend to share the same view on how much conflict they have. In the next section, I detail how such conflicts may arise. Specifically, I explain how scarce resources, interdependent relations, goal incompatibilities, interference to reach these goals, personal differences, inefficient communication and unethical behaviour all have a role to play in explaining angel–entrepreneur conflicts and I shall illustrate these with real-life examples where possible. Then, I try to shed some light on the question as to whether conflict matters. To this end, I review existing research on effects of angel–entrepreneur conflicts on performance-, affect- and attitude-related outcomes. Finally, based on this review of past research on angel–entrepreneur conflicts I provide some suggestions for future research.

## 8.2 ANGELS AND ENTREPRENEURS: A MATCH MADE IN HEAVEN?

Past empirical research has indicated that the angel investor–entrepreneur relationship is not always so rosy. Among the first to notice this were Mason and Harrison (1996). Out of their sample of 33 British angels, five considered their relationship with their entrepreneurs to be less than neutral, leaning towards adversarial. Five out of the 27 respondent entrepreneurs had a similar opinion. Whereas this early research suggests that extreme or strong conflicts only occur sporadically, more recent research by Brettel (2003) revealed that 77 per cent of the respondent (German) angels had experienced some problems with their entrepreneurs.

Before delving into the results of my own studies on angel–entrepreneur conflicts, let me start by offering a definition of what I refer to when talking about conflicts. Conflict is generally defined as 'perceived incompatibilities or discrepant views among the parties involved' (Jehn and Bendersky, 2003, p. 189), with a distinction traditionally made between relationship and task conflicts (Jehn, 1995; De Dreu and Weingart, 2003). In the setting of angel-financed ventures, relationship conflicts pertain to perceived interpersonal incompatibilities or personality clashes between angel investors and entrepreneurs. Task conflicts, on the other hand, refer to perceived disagreements between angel investors and entrepreneurs about what should be done. Although task and relationship conflicts often occur together, empirical evidence suggests that both represent distinct dimensions of intragroup conflict (De Dreu and Weingart, 2003; Jehn and Bendersky, 2003). Task and relationship conflicts are commonly used in studies on intragroup conflict (De Dreu and Weingart, 2003; Jehn and Bendersky, 2003) and, as such, have also found their way to the entrepreneurship literature (for example, Ensley et al., 2002; Higashide and Birley, 2002; Forbes et al., 2010).

Based on data collected from both the entrepreneurs' and angel investors' side with a sample of US and Belgian angel-backed companies, I found that average reported conflict levels were relatively low. More specifically, when asked about how much tension, personal friction or anger there had been between angels and entrepreneurs, 10 out of the 54 teams reported 'none'; 89 per cent of the teams gave this more personal, relationship conflict a score between 1 and 3 (on a scale between 1 and 5), indicating low to average levels of conflict. The overall average score in the sample was 1.80 (SD 0.89). Interestingly, levels of task-related disagreements were higher (average overall score of 2.24, SD 0.72). When asked about how many disagreements angels and entrepreneurs had had regarding different ideas or content of decisions and how many differences of opinion there had been, no single team replied that there had been none (overall). Levels still remain low though with 83 per cent of the teams indicating low to average levels of task-related disagreements (score 1–3). Overall, these results are consistent with the pattern depicted by the earlier research on the post-investment relationship between angels and entrepreneurs: whereas most angel–entrepreneur couples will experience some disagreements throughout their partnership, especially task-related ones, relationships that turn truly hostile are relatively rare.

As a point of comparison, average conflict levels in top management teams (task conflict: 2.52; relationship conflict: 1.93 (Amason and Sapienza, 1997)) and new venture boards (task conflict: 2.49; relationship conflict: 2.21 (Forbes et al., 2010)) are higher than the ones reported here. Interestingly, comparisons with average levels of conflict between venture capitalists and entrepreneurs are inconclusive to this date. Some studies have reported lower levels of conflict compared to those between angels and their entrepreneurs (for example, Higashide and Birley, 2002; Brettel et al., 2013). For instance, Higashide and Birley (2002) report venture capitalist–entrepreneur task conflict levels to vary from 1.61 to 1.71 and their relationship conflict levels to vary from 1.40 to 1.43 (depending on whether the disagreements concerned were related to either company policy or goals). In Zacharakis et al. (2010), on the other hand, reported task conflict levels were significantly higher than those between angels and entrepreneurs (average overall score of 2.67). Hence, more research is needed to address the question of whether the angel–entrepreneur relationship is more versus less conflict-prone than the venture capitalist–entrepreneur relationship.

Another interesting observation relates to differences in conflict perception between angels and entrepreneurs. While overall angels and entrepreneurs show high consensus in their individual perceptions of how much conflict they have (for example, Collewaert, 2012), this does not mean that they always perceive the exact same amount of conflict. For instance, when looking into pairs of lead investors and entrepreneurs, we noted that 16 out of 54 pairs have symmetrical (that is, the same) relationship conflict perceptions, 18 have an investor who perceives more conflict than the entrepreneur and 20 have an entrepreneur who perceives more conflict than the investor. For task conflict perceptions, there are fewer pairs who perceive the same amount of conflict (only 7). In 24 pairs, the investor perceives more conflict than the entrepreneur and in 23 pairs it is the other way around. This is important as it should warn against just relying on the high consensus observation to motivate data collection strategies on investor–investee relational dynamics where one gathers data from one side of the investor–investee dyad only. While there may not be huge differences in the individual perceived levels of team-level constructs such as conflict and trust, these individual perceptions (that is, angels' versus entrepreneurs') may, however, have quite significant divergent implications for both individual- and organizational-level outcomes (see, for example, Bammens and Collewaert, 2014).

Taken together, this body of research shows that both having no conflict whatsoever and having extreme levels of conflict is rare among angels and entrepreneurs. In most angel–entrepreneur partnerships there is some degree of disagreement, even though this degree tends to be lower than in other strategic decision-making units such as top management teams. What is even more important to note is that when such disagreement occurs, it tends to most often revolve around task-related issues (rather than personal ones). The latter finding could be related to the fact that angels attach a great deal of importance to interpersonal fit between the angel and the entrepreneur during their investment decision-making process (Mason and Stark, 2004; Mason, 2006). By selecting entrepreneurs with whom they have a good 'click' they may be able to avoid many interpersonal conflicts later on in their relationship. Given that angels and entrepreneurs together decide on the strategic direction of the venture, some degree of more task-related debate, however, seems unavoidable.

## 8.3 HOW DO ANGEL–ENTREPRENEUR CONFLICTS ARISE?

Knowing how common conflicts are within the angel investor–entrepreneur relationship, a next logical step is to explore how they arise. According to process theory, one of the dominant intragroup conflict theories (for example, Pondy, 1967; Thomas, 1992; Korsgaard et al., 2008), conflict is a process that unfolds over time. Conflict originates with latent conditions such as scarce resources, interdependent relations, goal incompatibilities, interference to reach these goals, personal differences and inefficient communication (Kochan et al., 1976; Bartos and Wehr, 2002; Wilmot and Hocker, 2005). These conditions, representing the context in which angel–entrepreneur conflicts occur, evoke events, which in turn trigger a sense-making process. Sense-making, also referred to as naming and blaming, comprises the process whereby individuals perceive an injurious event, label it as such and subsequently attribute the fault to someone or something else (Felstiner et al., 1980). As such, latent conflict is turned into overt conflict. It is critical to note that latent conflict may hence not necessarily transform into overt conflict. It may instead require some kind of event or behaviour to trigger this transformation.

Thus, to examine how angel–entrepreneur conflicts may arise, we first need insight into which of the aforementioned sources of conflict (that is, latent conditions) are present in an angel–entrepreneur setting. In a second step, we need to explore conflict-triggering events. In this chapter, I shall delve into a specific example of a conflict-triggering event that has been shown to be relevant in angel–entrepreneur dyads, namely, unethical behaviour on either or both the entrepreneur or investor side (Collewaert and Fassin, 2013). Figure 8.1 provides a visual overview of this process.

### 8.3.1 Causes of Conflict

Based on the aforementioned list of latent conditions, conflicts may arise as a consequence of individuals competing over the access to and distribution of scarce resources, of them having to work together yet wanting incompatible things (that is, which cannot be attained simultaneously), of some individuals' activities blocking others from attaining their goals, of people differing with regard to aspects such as values and ideologies, and of them communicating disrespectfully or infrequently, for instance. All of these sources of conflict, although to different extents, are also present in the angel investor–entrepreneur relationship.

For example, in the average angel-backed company, angel investors and entrepreneurs are dependent on each other in that they make a deal

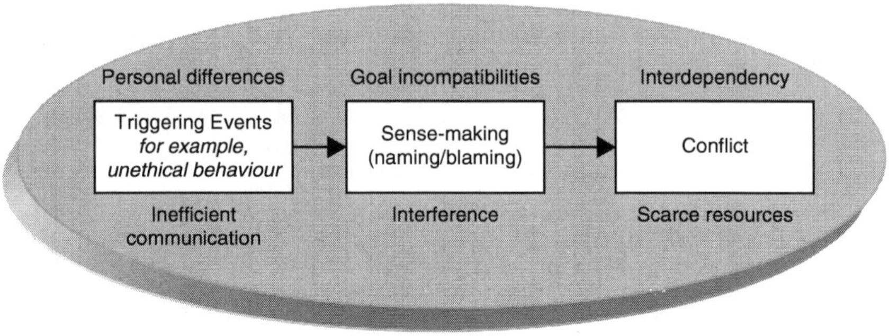


*Source:* Adapted from Collewaert and Fassin (2013).

*Figure 8.1 Potential causes of angel–entrepreneur conflicts*

to exchange the angel's human, social and financial capital for the opportunity or potential to make financial gains (Mason, 2006). In order for the portfolio company to survive and grow, the entrepreneurs need the angel's capital, although the degree can differ from company to company. Similarly, the angels, whose degree of active participation in a portfolio company can also vary, need the entrepreneurs to run and manage the company in a way that will maximize their financial gain. In other words, both parties have their own particular role to play, but both roles are vitally and equally important to the company's final success and growth. It also implies that actions undertaken by one will affect the outcomes of the other. This may become problematic when angels and entrepreneurs have different goals in mind. Regardless of their mutual overarching goal of value creation, angel investors and entrepreneurs could have different and even incompatible sub-goals.[1] For instance, entrepreneurs could see their company as a life-long commitment, whereas investors could only want to maximize their short-term returns (Yitshaki, 2008; DeTienne, 2010). This, in turn, may lead to quite divergent views between angels and entrepreneurs as to the best way to run the company or allocate resources.

Higher interdependency and goal incompatibility may also require more frequent communication between investors and entrepreneurs to monitor entrepreneurs, to avoid misunderstandings or quite simply to coordinate their efforts. With communication taking on such a vital role in this setting, problems in the investor–investee information stream may easily create conflicts. Brettel (2003) also suggested that angels' intense involvement in and interference with their portfolio firms may cause conflicts with entrepreneurs. A similar finding has appeared in the literature on venture capitalist–entrepreneur conflicts. Yitshaki (2008) revealed that a venture capitalist's strategic involvement may increase task-related disagreements with entrepreneurs, whereas their managerial involvement may increase their personal conflicts. That malfunctioning communication between entrepreneurs and angels can cause conflicts was also illustrated in Macht (2011). Based on four case studies, she showed that reactive communication or no communication at all with regard to sensitive issues such as the angel's involvement (and the entrepreneur's opinion thereof) elicited substantially more negative reactions on the angels' part than proactive communication, creating potential for conflict. She recommends explicit and proactive communication to avoid conflicts.

Further fuelling the potential for conflicts between angels and entrepreneurs, there may also be some competition over scarce resources such as power or wealth. For instance, imagine a chief executive officer (CEO)-founder who has invented the intellectual property of a company and who has angel investors on board. When the product is ready for the market, the investors push for a new professional CEO to bring the product to the market. A new CEO is hired and the former CEO is given a new position in the company, let's say VP engineer. More often than not, the original founder is somewhat disgruntled over his loss of power and is frustrated both with the new CEO and the angels who made him relinquish his control. Small squabbles over, for instance, products not selling well can quickly turn into 'I blame you – you blame me' conflicts – resulting in some of the involved participants needing to leave the venture. While in such an example the competition over scarce resources would mostly be between the old and new CEO, the angels – as instigators of the replacement – would be considered partly to blame by the entrepreneur. Another textbook example of this kind of power struggle is entrepreneurs blaming their angels for behaving too much like venture capitalists, focusing too much on the financials and too little on the technology. The angels, however, tend to blame the entrepreneurs for focusing too much on the technology and holding onto their shares too firmly (for example, an entrepreneur with an ownership percentage of 51 per cent that he refuses to give up).

Finally, personal differences between investors and entrepreneurs may cause conflicts. The importance of similarity or fit in values or ideologies between angels and entrepreneurs to avoid conflicts is probably among those most easily understood. Upon investment, angel investors and entrepreneurs enter their partnership with certain expectations and assumptions. One of these is a good fit between investors and entrepreneurs, given that it is one of the most important investment criteria for angel investors (Mason and Stark, 2004; Mason, 2006). This is unsurprising given angel investors' more active involvement in the venture post-investment combined with their desire to help fellow entrepreneurs, which tends to result in a more tight-knit relationship than one would see with venture capitalists, for instance (Landström, 1998). While in some cases a misalignment between investors and entrepreneurs in terms of values and beliefs may already become apparent in the screening phase and, as such, lead to a rejection of the deal (Maxwell et al., 2011), in other instances such differences remain well hidden during the pre-investment phase and then cause conflicts later on. This is what is referred to when scholars speak of strong characters or a clash of egos between investors and entrepreneurs as sources of conflict (for example, Mason and Harrison, 1996; Collewaert and Fassin, 2013).

In conclusion, the root causes of angel–entrepreneur conflicts can be quite diverse ranging from social to more substantive issues. Another important observation is the complexity of angel–entrepreneur conflicts; there can be multiple latent conditions at play simultaneously, which can furthermore be difficult to disentangle. The relative importance of each of these causes is therefore still an open question as is how the conflict process may unfold differently depending on the issue that causes it.

### 8.3.2 Conflict-triggering Events: The Case of Unethical Behaviour

From the subsection above, it is clear that there are several elements present in the average angel–entrepreneur relationship that make it susceptible to conflict. Yet, given – for instance – similar levels of goal incompatibilities, some angel–entrepreneur partnerships will experience overt conflict whereas others will not. This is where conflict-triggering events such as unethical behaviour come into play.

Unethical behaviour may appear in many forms: unfair competition, unfair communication, abuse of power, privileging one's own interests, non-respect of agreement and outright fraud (Crane and Matten, 2004). As illustrated in Collewaert and Fassin (2013), an instance of (perceived) unfair competition occurs when either one party, whether angel or entrepreneur, sidesteps the other one and tries to eliminate them with all means possible. For example, in one of the cases we encountered investors – without the entrepreneur's knowledge – started talking to industrial partners of the venture, who the entrepreneurs were trying to sign a deal with, and proposed a different kind of deal, thereby impeding the entrepreneurs' negotiations with that partner. Angels also often feel unfairly treated by entrepreneurs who provide overoptimistic information to them or who intentionally withhold crucial information from them. Such forms of unfair communication include instances where entrepreneurs present the status of their ventures as being far more advanced than is really the case (resulting in the venture needing substantially more cash than anticipated upon investment) or investors/entrepreneurs presenting their resources, whether financial, human or material, in a more favourable light to their partners.

Further, both entrepreneurs and angels can abuse their power. For instance, entrepreneurs who are unsatisfied with their current angels may go out and search for a new investor who is willing to give them what they want and who has deeper pockets than the initial investors. Such a situation can quickly turn sour when the old investors are only given two options: either sell at a reduced price or stay, but see their investment dilute. Entrepreneurs in need of more financial resources can conversely also be held 'hostage' by unwilling angels. On both angels' and entrepreneurs' side I've encountered stories where either one privileges his or her own interests by billing undue costs. Non-respect of agreements occurs often times; investors refuse to provide follow-on financing without good reason, entrepreneurs do not fulfil promises of bringing in assets or ensuring additional funding.

Finally, in exceptional situations there may also be fraud, for example, when information is deliberately falsified or concealed to mislead the other party. To illustrate the latter, imagine the following story. A former entrepreneur in the automobile industry decides he would rather invest some of his earnings in new companies than on the stock exchange. Through a business angel network, he meets a young man, who had previously owned a wholesaler's business trading product X. Building on his current business, he wants to set up a chain of specialist stores, a plan that seems feasible to the investor. With the guidance of an audit company, they draw up the articles of association and shareholder agreement. All partners agree on the entrepreneur putting in a contribution in kind valued by the auditor at one-third of the total capital, the angel investor putting in the same amount in cash and a third partner putting in about a quarter of their respective amounts. The remainder would be made up by a government institution. Within one month after start-up, the angel investor notices that the entrepreneur brings in office desks, but not the contribution in kind he promised, he buys new supplies of product X using money from the company, sells it as well, but revenues disappear and undue costs are billed. When urging the entrepreneur to rectify the situation, he does not and is fired as the representative of the company. The investor afterwards learned that the assets the entrepreneur had promised to put in the company had basically been non-existent. This company has closed down in the meantime – unsurprisingly, this was this angel's one and only investment.

Despite the great variation in unethical practices, what they all have in common is that they more easily trigger investor–entrepreneur conflicts through increased fault attribution. Perceived unethical behaviour seems to cause partners to look at their interaction and conflicts more negatively and to see them as a bigger hurdle to their partnership compared to when no unethical practices were perceived. Whereas understanding, exoneration and shared responsibility prevail in conflict situations without unethical behaviour, holding the other party accountable prevails in those where unethical behaviour is perceived. In sum, what this should illustrate is that when thinking about how angel–entrepreneur conflicts emerge, it is important to not only delve into what latent conditions are the conflicts' root causes, but also take into account potential conflict-triggering events.

## 8.4 THE CONSEQUENCES OF INVESTOR–ENTREPRENEUR CONFLICTS

Given the investor–entrepreneur relationship's conflict-prone nature, it is somewhat surprising that research into the 'dark side' of the relationship between external investors and entrepreneurs has been lacking (Parhankangas and Landström, 2006, p. 775). Yet, what if these parties do not get along? In other words, if disagreements between angels and entrepreneurs occur, then how do they impact both the performance of their portfolio companies and the attitudes of all individual parties involved? A long tradition of research on conflict in work groups has revealed that conflicts may substantially affect both the well-being of the individuals involved and the performance of their work units (for example, Jehn and Bendersky, 2003). As such, it makes sense to discuss the impact of angel–entrepreneur conflicts along two dimensions: (1) performance-related outcomes and (2) individual affect- and attitude-related outcomes. These outcomes are complementary in that together they provide us with a good overview of how conflicts between angel investors and entrepreneurs affect their combined effectiveness. Moreover, according to the intragroup conflict contingency framework, the impact of conflict may vary depending on the conditions that surround it such as the type of outcome and conflict studied (De Dreu and Weingart, 2003; Jehn and Bendersky, 2003). Where relevant, I shall thus distinguish between the previously discussed conflict types (task and relationship conflict).

### 8.4.1 Angel–Entrepreneur Conflicts and Performance-related Outcomes

When assessing a work unit's performance effectiveness, one essentially examines its quantity and quality of output (Hackman and Richard, 1987;

Cohen and Bailey, 1990). One aspect of this effectiveness, and an essential one to any entrepreneurial company, is innovation. As entrepreneurial companies generally operate in a highly dynamic and volatile environment, innovation and innovativeness are of the utmost importance to their survival, growth and success (for example, Rosenbusch et al., 2011). Not only is innovation essential in an entrepreneurial setting, past literature has also suggested that conflict is one of the key mechanisms affecting both team and organizational innovation (De Dreu, 2006). What is less clear is whether or not conflict is beneficial to innovation.

Task conflicts are generally considered to play a crucial role in the innovation process (De Dreu, 2006; Song et al., 2006), making it the most relevant type of conflict to study in relation to this outcome. Task conflict and its effect on innovation has been the subject of much debate. Some scholars have argued for a generally negative effect of task conflict on decision-making, innovation and team functioning (for example, Walton, 1969; Pelled, 1996; Jehn and Bendersky, 2003). Creativity and innovation namely require cognitive resources or capacity, which are both reduced when conflict is present (De Dreu, 2006). It also produces stress and tension, which could in turn block information handling and processing, and reduce the capacity for creative thinking. Others, however, have argued that task conflicts increase information sharing, critical evaluation and assessment of alternatives, avoid 'groupthink', and result in a greater number of diverse opinions and perspectives (Baron, 1984; Nemeth, 1995; De Dreu and West, 2001), which should lead to more creativity and optimal decision-making (Jehn and Bendersky, 2003). This line of reasoning would lead to hypothesizing a positive relation between task conflict and innovativeness (as in, for example, Jehn and Bendersky, 2003; Matsuo, 2006).

Despite this debate, the central position we put forward in Collewaert and Sapienza (2016) is that task conflicts between angels and entrepreneurs inhibit their portfolio companies' innovativeness. Teams composed of angels and entrepreneurs are not characterized by the same degree of hierarchy as are other work teams; angels and entrepreneurs often tend to consider each other as equal partners. However, this also means that there is no clear director to take up responsibility and to resolve conflicts, which may cause delays in angels and entrepreneurs dealing with and solving their conflicts.

Not only may investor–entrepreneur task conflicts take longer to solve, such delays are also more detrimental compared to in other work teams. Angels and entrepreneurs being key strategic decision agents must work together in an integrated and coordinated fashion to produce high quality solutions rapidly or otherwise face the risk of running out of time and money. When in conflict, however, entrepreneurs' and angels' attention is redirected away from maximizing the innovative potential of the portfolio company and its products to their disagreement at hand. Cognitive capacity otherwise spent on creative thinking is now entirely consumed by these conflicts, thus reducing the final innovativeness of the portfolio companies. In sum, angel–entrepreneur disagreements and delays about what should be done, how it should be done and who should do it necessarily impede not only the functioning of the team and the interim process, but also the production of innovative output.

What we found in Collewaert and Sapienza (2016) is, in fact, a bit more of a nuanced picture. Specifically, we found that task conflict between angels and entrepreneurs was only weakly negatively related to portfolio company innovation. However, this negative association became significant in the presence of several moderating variables. Specifically, the negative association was made significantly stronger when angels and entrepreneurs had less agreement on the venture's strategic priorities, when there was more equality among angels and entrepreneurs in terms of their entrepreneurial experience and when they communicated more frequently.

Compared to task-related disagreements, relationship conflicts have been the subject of much less debate as research has consistently produced negative results (see, for example, Amason, 1996; Jehn, 1997; Jehn and Mannix, 2001; Bayazit and Mannix, 2003). Following this traditional view, one would expect that underlying tensions, personal frictions or anger between angel investors and entrepreneurs are likely to increase feelings of cynicism, avoidance and anxiety, interfere with their ability to handle new or complex information, to decrease cooperation and to absorb time and energy necessary for creativity (Jehn, 1995; Amason, 1996; Pelled, 1996; Matsuo, 2006). If anything, one would thus expect relationship conflicts between angel investors and entrepreneurs to also hamper innovation. In line with this reasoning, we find a significant negative correlation between relationship conflict and innovativeness in Collewaert and Sapienza (2016). However, this relation becomes insignificant in more comprehensive models and hence seems to be quite weak.

### 8.4.2 Angel–Entrepreneur Conflicts and Affect- and Attitude-related Outcomes

In the venture capital literature, scholars have revealed that conflicts tend to negatively affect an entrepreneur's perception of investor value added (Sapienza, 1992) as well as the entrepreneur's confidence in partners' cooperation (Zacharakis et al., 2010). In my own research (Collewaert, 2012),

I set out to examine how angel–entrepreneur conflicts would affect both parties' intentions to exit their venture. In the organizational behaviour literature, intentions to remain or leave have been shown to be important predictors of actual turnover or exit (O'Reilly et al., 1991; Westerman and Cyr, 2004). As the exit of both (or either) the entrepreneur and angel investor could have dramatic consequences for the company involved, gaining an insight into what factors influence their intentions and motivations to voluntarily remain with their businesses is crucial.

Prior non-angel studies on the relationship between task conflict and intentions to exit have suggested that task conflict should have no effect in settings where tasks embody a certain degree of complexity, such as strategic decision-making, because conflict would be inherent to the task and would thus be expected (Jehn, 1995; Jehn et al., 1999; Bayazit and Mannix, 2003). Because angel investors and entrepreneurs are key strategic decision agents, one could expect the same effect for their task conflicts. Although I follow this line of reasoning for the lack of effect of task conflicts on angel investors' intentions to exit, I expect a positive effect on entrepreneurs' intentions to exit.

Entrepreneurs have a strong sense of psychological ownership over and emotional attachment to their ventures (Pierce et al., 2001), even after receiving external equity funding (Arthurs and Busenitz, 2003). They have generally invested substantial amounts of sweat equity into their ventures, have nurtured and developed them from idea inception and have a firm idea of where to take their ventures next (Arthurs and Busenitz, 2003; Forbes et al., 2010). Consequently, they generally prefer investors who they suspect will help them guide their venture towards those ultimate goals (Boot et al., 2006). They tend to welcome and are receptive to investor advice on how to achieve their vision, although the degree of receptivity varies among entrepreneurs (Barney et al., 1996). However, confrontation with many task conflicts may make entrepreneurs think that investors are working against rather than with them. In this case, rather than viewing an investor's input as well-intentioned advice, entrepreneurs may be more likely to perceive conflicts as threatening (Avey et al., 2009). In addition, entrepreneurs may interpret these disagreements as investors questioning their ability, judgement and contributions to the venture. When they feel pressured by external constituents, such as investors, entrepreneurs are likely to become less committed to their ventures (Dobrev and Barnett, 2005). Taken together, this should make entrepreneurs more susceptible to feelings of fear and distrust and make them less satisfied with their investor relationship, thus leading to detachment and withdrawal.

In contrast, angel investors may frame these disagreements differently. Given that they 'suffer' less from emotional bonds to the venture, they will likely see these discussions as part of normal business (Mason and Harrison, 1996; Politis, 2008). Angel investors see it as their job to probe entrepreneurs to help them find and formalize a vision, and they may not be aware of the effects this probing has on the entrepreneur's self-confidence and commitment. To this end, some angel investors have even developed formal planning tools such as questionnaires (see, for example, Berkus, 2006). Debate is thus innate to the task or job of being an advisor and investor, thereby cancelling out task conflict's negative effects (Bayazit and Mannix, 2003). In sum, one would thus expect angel–entrepreneur task conflicts to positively affect entrepreneurs' intentions to exit their ventures, and to not affect angels' intentions to exit. Both hypotheses were supported in Collewaert (2012). Relationship conflicts did not affect either party's intentions to exit.

Taken together, theoretical arguments and empirical evidence would support the assertion that angel–entrepreneur conflicts have a substantial effect on both the individuals and venture concerned. Further, it seems that in both cases the more consequential type of conflict is task conflict – a finding that is quite important given the descriptive evidence presented earlier suggesting that it is also the more frequently occurring type of conflict among angels. Finally, our findings also support adopting a contingency perspective when studying angel–entrepreneur conflicts as aspects such as not only the type of conflict and outcome studied matter, but also the context in which this conflict occurs. Doing so will also allow us to develop more insight as to when angel–entrepreneur conflicts may actually be beneficial.

## 8.5 AGENDA FOR FUTURE RESEARCH

While progress has been made in examining how angels and entrepreneurs work together and get along with one another on a day-to-day basis, many options for future research remain. Below I have listed some of the more promising ones.

1. How does conflict arise? While causes of angel–entrepreneur conflicts have been examined qualitatively (for example, Collewaert, 2009; Collewaert and Fassin, 2013), we need quantitative research to validate these causes. In addition to verifying whether all of the mentioned latent conditions contribute significantly to angel–entrepreneur conflicts, a quantitative large-scale research design would also allow disentangling which of these conditions are the most troublesome in terms of generating conflict. Building on this insight, future studies

could then also examine what angels and entrepreneurs can do to manage these conflict antecedents and hence the potential conflicts resulting from them. For instance, we often advise both entrepreneurs and angels to communicate more openly and honestly with each other about their goals prior to investment. Up to the present, though, we do not know how effective this strategy truly is in terms of lowering goal incompatibilities between angels and entrepreneurs. More research is also needed into what kind of events can trigger latent angel–entrepreneur conflicts to turn into overt ones (that is, similar to perceived unethical behaviour).

2. Consequences of angel–entrepreneur conflicts: more research is also needed into the effects of angel–entrepreneur conflicts. For instance, what impact do these conflicts have on the performance of the portfolio company? Findings from a recent meta-analysis on intragroup conflict would suggest that the effects of a relationship conflict are similar for different types of performance-related outcomes such as innovativeness, decision quality, financial performance and effectiveness (De Wit et al., 2012). For task conflict, however, differences did appear depending on the specific outcome studied. This variation in effects would hence support more studies looking into the effects of angel–entrepreneur conflicts on other performance-related outcomes than innovativeness. When looking into the effects of conflict on affect- and attitude-related outcomes, future research could try to explain the lack of effects of relationship conflicts on angels' and entrepreneurs' intentions to exit. Do angels and entrepreneurs not care whether they get along on a personal level? Or do they just need a minimum amount of personal fit to make it work? Or does relationship conflict only come into play when it concerns more affect-laden outcomes such as satisfaction?
3. How do angels and entrepreneurs deal with their conflicts? In the intragroup conflict literature, conflict management, or the way in which conflicts are handled, has received a lot of attention. In most of these cases, a distinction was made between cooperative and competitive conflict management styles (for example, Lovelace et al., 2001; Jehn and Bendersky, 2003; Song et al., 2006). When a cooperative conflict management approach is used, team members seek a mutually beneficial solution (Lovelace et al., 2001). When a competitive or contending conflict-handling strategy is used, on the other hand, conflicts are approached from a win-lose standpoint (Chen et al., 2005). Research is needed to examine what conflict management strategies angels and entrepreneurs rely on and what effects this has. For instance, one could easily imagine that relying on a more

cooperative approach could contribute to a more constructive atmosphere, an increased team spirit, increased information sharing and thus understanding of each other's opinions. A competitive approach, on the other hand, may lead to a more destructive atmosphere, closed-minded discussions and frustration. In a similar vein to Parhankangas and Landström (2006) who examined venture capitalists' reactions to disappointments caused by their entrepreneurs, future studies could also explore what may explain potential variation in angels' and entrepreneurs' conflict management approaches; why do some teams rely on a constructive approach whereas others adopt a more competitive approach in dealing with their conflicts? What happens when there is an asymmetry between angel and entrepreneur, that is, one behaves cooperatively but the other one behaves competitively? All of these represent intriguing questions for future research.

4. Moderating variables: according to the conflict contingency framework studied (De Dreu and Weingart, 2003; Jehn and Bendersky, 2003), conflict's effects may also vary depending on some moderating influences. In the traditional team literature, such moderating effects have been suggested for group diversity and task type, amongst others (Jehn and Bendersky, 2003). It would be interesting to see what kind of aspects related to angel–entrepreneur teams could moderate its conflicts' effects. For instance, a fascinating question is whether angel–entrepreneur conflicts operate differently depending on contextual factors such as culture, degree of professionalization or maturity of the angel market and stage in the investment relationship.
5. Measurement: most conflict studies to date have relied on Jehn's (1995) intragroup conflict scale or a revised version thereof (for example, Jehn and Mannix, 2001; Pearson et al., 2002). Task and relationship conflict is measured by asking respondents, on a scale from 1 (= none) to 5 (= a great deal), how many disagreements concerning task-related issues and how much personal friction and tension there has been. Even though it is still the most widely used conflict scale worldwide, some scholars have suggested looking into alternative ways of measuring conflicts; for instance, by – rather than asking people – observing their actual interactions and behaviours (Korsgaard et al., 2008).
6. Angels' versus venture capitalists' post-investment relationship: an interesting question for further research is how angel–entrepreneur conflicts compare to venture capitalist–entrepreneur conflicts. As shown earlier in this chapter, current empirical evidence is inconclusive in answering the question which of these two relationships is most conflict-prone. One way of addressing this could to be compare their

antecedents. Theoretically speaking, the relationship between both types of external investors and their entrepreneurs presents many similarities in terms of potential conflict antecedents. For instance, in both cases there is some competition over scarce resources (whether it be money or power), communication is of huge importance and personal differences are something to be avoided rather than sought out. That being said, though, there are some differences between these two groups that could alter the conflict dynamics at play in their relationship. One could argue that venture capitalists and entrepreneurs are somewhat less dependent on each other than angel investors and their entrepreneurs are. This as venture capitalists are more concerned with market risk than they are with agency risk, making them rely more on pre-investment due diligence and contracting rather than post-investment monitoring (Fiet, 1995; Van Osnabrugge, 2000). Hence, both parties' roles will have been clearly outlined prior to investment, making them having to rely less on each other in order to complete these roles successfully. These lower levels of interdependency could result in a reduced probability of conflict presenting itself between venture capitalists and entrepreneurs. However, one could also argue that goal incompatibilities between venture capitalists and entrepreneurs will be higher than those between angels and their entrepreneurs. Consistent with stewardship theory, angels have been shown to treat their entrepreneurs as true partners – more so than do venture capitalists (for example, Collewaert and Manigart, 2016). This more steward-like behaviour is more likely when motives and goals are more closely aligned (Davis et al., 1997). Hence, one could expect lower levels of goal incompatibilities between angels and their entrepreneurs than between venture capitalists and their entrepreneurs. Future research examining and comparing conflict antecedents among venture capitalist–entrepreneur teams versus angel–entrepreneur teams could thus shed more light on the conflict-prone nature of both teams and any differences therein.

7. Going beyond conflict: finally, many more aspects related to angel–entrepreneur post-investment interactions are worth examining. For instance, in Bammens and Collewaert (2014) we looked into the impact of angels' and entrepreneurs' trust perceptions on perceived performance. One of the intriguing questions that came up was the entrepreneur's use of impression management techniques. While impression management has recently made its entry into the study of angel investment decisions (Mason and Harrison, 2003; Parhankangas and Ehrlich, 2014), it would be interesting to see what we can learn about how entrepreneurs deal with and behave themselves towards

their angels once the investment has been made by adopting an impression management lens.

## NOTE

1. As such, the distinction between angel investors and entrepreneurs forms a natural divide between these two parties so one could argue that angels and entrepreneurs are actually subgroups within their overarching teams.

## REFERENCES

Amason, A.C. (1996), 'Distinguishing the effects of functional and dysfunctional conflict on strategic decision making: resolving a paradox for top management teams', *Academy of Management Journal*, **39**(1), 123–48.

Amason, A. and H. Sapienza (1997), 'The effects of top management team size and interaction norms on cognitive and affective conflict', *Journal of Management*, **23**(4), 495–516.

Arthurs, J. and L. Busenitz (2003), 'The boundaries and limitations of agency theory and stewardship theory in the venture capitalist/entrepreneur relationship', *Entrepreneurship Theory and Practice*, **28**(2), 145–62.

Avey, J., B. Avolio, C. Crossley and F. Luthans (2009), 'Psychological ownership: theoretical extensions, measurement, and relation to work outcomes', *Journal of Organizational Behavior*, **30**, 173–91.

Bammens, Y. and V. Collewaert (2014), 'Trust between entrepreneurs and angel investors: exploring positive and negative implications for venture performance assessments', *Journal of Management*, **40**(7), 1980–2008.

Barney, J., L. Busenitz, J. Fiet and D. Moesel (1996), 'New venture teams' assessment of learning assistance from venture capital firms', *Journal of Business Venturing*, **11**, 257–72.

Baron, R. (1984), 'Reducing organizational conflict: an incompatible response approach', *Journal of Applied Psychology*, **69**(2), 272–9.

Bartos, O.J. and P. Wehr (2002), *Using Conflict Theory*, Cambridge: Cambridge University Press.

Bayazit, M. and E. Mannix (2003), 'Should I stay or should I go? Predicting team members' intent to remain in the team', *Small Group Research*, **34**(3), 290–321.

Berkus, D. (2006), *Extending the Runway*, Boston, MA: Aspatore Books.

Boot, A., R. Gopalan and A. Thakor (2006), 'The entrepreneur's choice between public and private ownership', *Journal of Finance*, **61**(2), 803–36.

Brettel, M. (2003), 'Business angels in Germany: a research note', *Venture Capital*, **5**(3), 251–68.

Brettel, M., R. Mauer and D. Appelhoff (2013), 'The entrepreneur's perception in the entrepreneur-VCF relationship: the impact of conflict types on investor value', *Venture Capital*, **15**(3), 173–97.

Chen, G., C. Liu and D. Tjosvold (2005), 'Conflict management for effective top management teams and innovation in China', *Journal of Management Studies*, **42**(2), 277–300.

Cohen, S.G. and D.E. Bailey (1990), 'What makes teams work: group effectiveness research from the shop floor to the executive suite', *Journal of Management*, **23**(3), 239–90.

Collewaert, V. (2009), 'The pre- and post-investment relationship between angel investors and entrepreneurs: the scope and impact of information problems and conflicts', PhD dissertation, Ghent University, Belgium.

Collewaert, V. (2012), 'Angel investors' and entrepreneurs' intentions to exit their ventures: a conflict perspective', *Entrepreneurship Theory and Practice*, **36**(4), 753–79.

Collewaert, V. and Y. Fassin (2013), 'Conflicts between entrepreneurs and investors: the impact of perceived unethical behavior', *Small Business Economics*, **40**(3), 635–49.
Collewaert, V. and S. Manigart (2016), 'Valuation of angel-backed companies: the role of investor human capital', *Journal of Small Business Management*, **54**(1), 356–72.
Collewaert, V. and H. Sapienza (2016), 'How does angel investor-entrepreneur conflict affect venture innovation? It depends', *Entrepreneurship Theory and Practice*, **40**(3), 573–97.
Crane, A. and D. Matten (2004), *Business Ethics: A European Perspective*, Oxford: Oxford University Press.
Davis, J., D. Schoorman and L. Donaldson (1997), 'Toward a stewardship theory of management', *Academy of Management Review*, **22**(1), 20–47.
De Dreu, C. (2006), 'When too little or too much hurts: evidence for a curvilinear relationship between task conflict and innovation in teams', *Journal of Management*, **32**(1), 83–107.
De Dreu, C.K. and L.R. Weingart (2003), 'Task versus relationship conflict, team performance and team member satisfaction: a meta-analysis', *Journal of Applied Psychology*, **88**(4), 741–9.
De Dreu, C. and M. West (2001), 'Minority dissent and team innovation: the importance of participation in decision making', *Journal of Applied Psychology*, **86**(6), 1191–201.
De Wit, F., L. Greer and K. Jehn (2012), 'The paradox of intragroup conflict: a meta-analysis', *Journal of Applied Psychology*, **97**(2), 360–90.
DeTienne, D. (2010), 'Entrepreneurial exit as a critical component of the entrepreneurial process: theoretical development', *Journal of Business Venturing*, **25**(2), 203–15.
Dobrev, S. and W. Barnett (2005), 'Organizational roles and transition to entrepreneurship', *Academy of Management Journal*, **48**(3), 433–49.
Ehrlich, S.B., A.F. De Noble, T. Moore and R. Weaver (1994), 'After the cash arrives: a comparative study of venture capital and private investor involvement in entrepreneurial firms', *Journal of Business Venturing*, **9**(1), 67–82.
Ensley, M., A. Pearson and A. Amason (2002), 'Understanding the dynamics of new venture top management teams – cohesion, conflict, and new venture performance', *Journal of Business Venturing*, **17**(4), 365–86.
Felstiner, W., R. Abel and A. Sarat (1980), 'The emergence and transformation of disputes: naming, blaming, claiming. . .', *Law and Society Review*, **15**(3–4), 631–54.
Fiet, J. (1995), 'Risk avoidance strategies in venture capital markets', *Journal of Management Studies*, **32**(4), 551–74.
Forbes, D., A. Korsgaard and H. Sapienza (2010), 'Financing decisions as a source of conflict in venture boards', *Journal of Business Venturing*, **25**(6), 579–92.
Freear J., J.E. Sohl and W. Wetzel (2002), 'Angles on angels: financing technology-based ventures – a historical perspective', *Venture Capital*, **4**(4), 275–87.
Goldfarb, B., G. Hoberg, D. Kirsch and A. Triantis (2008), 'Does angel participation matter? An analysis of early venture financing', Working Paper 06-072, Robert H. Smith School of Business, University of Maryland.
Hackman, J.R. and J. Richard (1987), 'The design of work teams', in J.W. Lorsch (ed.), *Handbook of Organizational Behavior*, Englewood Cliffs, NJ: Prentice-Hall, pp. 315–42.
Harrison, R.T. and C.M. Mason (1992), 'International perspectives on the supply of informal venture capital', *Journal of Business Venturing*, **7**(6), 459–75.
Higashide, H. and S. Birley (2002), 'The consequences of conflict between the venture capitalist and the entrepreneurial team in the United Kingdom from the perspective of the venture capitalist', *Journal of Business Venturing*, **17**(1), 59–81.
Hindle, K. and R. Wenban (1999), 'Australia's informal venture capitalists: an exploratory profile', *Venture Capital*, **1**(2), 169–86.
Jehn, K.A. (1995), 'A multimethod examination of the benefits and detriments of intragroup conflict', *Administrative Science Quarterly*, **40**(2), 256–82.
Jehn, K.A. (1997), 'A qualitative analysis of conflict types and dimensions in organizational groups', *Administrative Science Quarterly*, **42**(3), 530–57.

Jehn, K.A. and C. Bendersky (2003), 'Intragroup conflict in organizations: a contingency perspective on the conflict-outcome relationship', *Research in Organizational Behavior*, **25**, 187–242.
Jehn, K.A. and E. Mannix (2001), 'The dynamic nature of conflict: a longitudinal study of intragroup conflict and group performance', *Academy of Management Journal*, **44**(2), 238–51.
Jehn, K.A., G. Northcraft and M. Neale (1999), 'Why differences make a difference: a field study of diversity, conflict, and performance in workgroups', *Administrative Science Quarterly*, **44**(4), 741–63.
Kelly, P. and M. Hay (2003), 'Business angel contracts: the influence of context', *Venture Capital*, **5**(4), 287–312.
Kochan, T.A., L.L. Cummings and G.B. Huber (1976), 'Operationalizing the concepts of goals and goal incompatibilities in organizational behavior research', *Human Relations*, **29**(6), 527–44.
Korsgaard, A., S.S. Jeong, D. Mahony and A. Pitariu (2008), 'A multilevel view of intragroup conflict', *Journal of Management*, **34**(6), 1222–52.
Landström, H. (1993), 'Informal risk capital in Sweden and some international comparisons', *Journal of Business Venturing*, **8**(6), 525–40.
Landström, H. (1998), 'Informal investors as entrepreneurs', *Technovation*, **18**(5), 321–33.
Lovelace, K., D. Shapiro and L. Weingart (2001), 'Maximizing cross-functional new product teams' innovativeness and constraint adherence: a conflict communications perspective', *Academy of Management Journal*, **44**(4), 779–93.
Macht, S. (2011), 'The role of investee company managers in business angels' involvement: empirical insights from dyadic data', *Venture Capital*, **13**(3), 267–93.
Mason, C. (2006), 'Informal sources of venture finance', in S. Parker (ed.), *The Life Cycle of Entrepreneurial Ventures*, New York: Springer, pp. 259–99.
Mason, C. and R. Harrison (1996), 'Informal venture capital: a study of the investment process, the post-investment experience and investment performance', *Entrepreneurship and Regional Development*, **8**(2), 105–26.
Mason, C. and R. Harrison (2002), 'Is it worth it? The rates of return from informal venture capital investments', *Journal of Business Venturing*, **17**(3), 211–36.
Mason, C. and R. Harrison (2003), 'Auditioning for money: what do technology investors look for at the initial screening stage?', *Journal of Private Equity*, **6**(2), 29–42.
Mason, C. and M. Stark (2004), 'What do investors look for in a business plan?', *International Small Business Journal*, **22**(3), 227–48.
Matsuo, M. (2006), 'Customer orientation, conflict, and innovativeness in Japanese sales departments', *Journal of Business Research*, **59**(2), 242–50.
Maxwell, A., S.A. Jeffrey and M. Lévesque (2011), 'Business angel early-stage decision making', *Journal of Business Venturing*, **26**(2), 212–25.
Nemeth, C. (1995), 'Dissent as driving cognition, attitudes, and judgments', *Social Cognition*, **13**(3), 273–91.
O'Reilly, C., J. Chatman and D. Caldwell (1991), 'People and organizational culture: a profile comparison approach to assessing person-organization fit', *Academy of Management Journal*, **34**(3), 487–516.
Parhankangas, A. and M. Ehrlich (2014), 'How entrepreneurs seduce business angels: an impression management approach', *Journal of Business Venturing*, **29**(4), 543–64.
Parhankangas, A. and H. Landström (2006), 'How venture capitalists respond to unmet expectations: the role of social environment', *Journal of Business Venturing*, **21**(6), 773–801.
Paul, S., G. Whittam and J.B. Johnston (2003), 'The operation of the informal venture capital market in Scotland', *Venture Capital*, **5**(4), 313–35.
Pearson, A., M. Ensley and A. Amason (2002), 'An assessment and refinement of Jehn's Intragroup Conflict scale', *International Journal of Conflict Management*, **13**(2), 110–26.
Pelled, L. (1996), 'Demographic diversity, conflict, and work group outcomes: an intervening process theory', *Organization Science*, **7**(6), 615–31.

Pierce, J., T. Kostova and K. Dirks (2001), 'Towards a theory of psychological ownership in organizations', *Academy of Management Review*, **26**(2), 298–310.
Politis, D. (2008), 'Business angels and value added: what do we know and where do we go?', *Venture Capital*, **10**(2), 127–47.
Pondy, L.R. (1967), 'Organizational conflict: concepts and models', *Administrative Science Quarterly*, **12**(2), 296–320.
Prowse, S. (1998), 'Angel investors and the market for angel investments', *Journal of Banking and Finance*, **22**(6–8), 785–92.
Rosenbusch, N., J. Brinckmann and A. Rausch (2011), 'Is innovation always beneficial? A meta-analysis of the relationship between innovation and performance in SMEs', *Journal of Business Venturing*, **26**(4), 441–57.
Sapienza, H. (1992), 'When do venture capitalists add value?', *Journal of Business Venturing*, **7**(1), 9–27.
Song, M., B. Dyer and J. Thieme (2006), 'Conflict management and innovation performance: an integrated contingency perspective', *Journal of Academy of Marketing Science*, **34**(3), 341–56.
Thomas, K. (1992), 'Conflict and conflict management: reflections and update', *Journal of Organizational Behaviour*, **13**(3), 265–74.
Van Osnabrugge, M. (2000), 'A comparison of business angel and venture capitalist investment procedures: an agency theory-based analysis', *Venture Capital*, **2**(2), 91–109.
Walton, R. (1969), *Interpersonal Peacemaking: Confrontations and Third Party Consultation*, Reading, MA: Addison-Wesley.
Westerman, J.W. and L.A. Cyr (2004), 'An integrative analysis of person-organization fit theories', *International Journal of Selection and Assessment*, **12**(3), 252–61.
Wetzel Jr, W.E. (1981), 'Informal risk capital in New England', in K.H. Vesper (ed.), *Frontiers of Entrepreneurship Research*, Wellesley, MA: Babson College, pp. 217–45.
Wilmot, W. and J. Hocker (2005), *Interpersonal Conflict*, Blacklick, OH: McGraw-Hill.
Wong, A. (2010), 'Angel finance: the other venture capital', in D. Cumming (ed.), *Venture Capital: Investment Strategies, Structures and Policies*, New York: Wiley, pp. 71–110.
Yitshaki, R. (2008), 'Venture capitalist-entrepreneur conflicts – an exploratory study of determinants and possible resolutions', *International Journal of Conflict Management*, **19**(3), 262–92.
Zacharakis, A., T. Erikson and B. George (2010), 'Conflict between the VC and entrepreneur: the entrepreneur's perspective', *Venture Capital*, **12**(2), 109–26.

# PART III

# INTERNATIONAL DIMENSIONS

# 9 Business angels in China: characteristics, policies and international comparison

*Jiani Wang, Yi Tan and Manhong Liu*

## 9.1 INTRODUCTION

In China, with the development of the Internet and high-tech enterprises at the end of the twentieth century, angel investment emerged. In recent years, more and more successful entrepreneurs, private investors and professionals have started angel investing. Additionally, lots of angel groups such as angel clubs, angel funds and matchmaking services have appeared, systemizing the angel investing process, providing information and other kinds of supports to their members and raising awareness about angel investing. Also, some local governments have issued relevant policies to support the development of angel investing, such as government-led angel funds and risk allowance for angel investors. However, the scale of the current business angels is comparably small because most people invest cautiously, and concentrate more on real estate, stocks and fixed income securities over startups.

There have been a number of studies shedding light on the characteristics of business angels (BAs) and their investment behavior across the world, but BAs in China remain largely unexplored (Li et al., 2014). The pioneering study by Liu and Chen (2007) provided insights into BA investment in the Chinese market, including five types of BAs and their industry focus, the BA club and the limitations on BA investment. They regard government-led funds (so-called 'Angel Fund') as the special investor for the incubation of high-tech firms in China. In Chinese academic circles, most scholars have great interest in venture capital and private equity while fewer researchers are focused on angel investment. Those academic papers on BAs just show simple descriptions and have no statistical basis. Tingchi and Chang (2007) reviewed the history, current situation and trends of the BA investment market in China. Xiao and Ritchie (2011) provided empirical evidence about the characteristics of Chinese informal investors, the effect of institutional changes and the role of networks in investing activities.

Local scholars began to focus on informal investment at the beginning of the twenty-first century. Li et al. (2014) undertook an exploratory study on Chinese BAs through the use of a questionnaire survey. They focused on investors, analyzing their attitude, behavior and characteristics (ABC), particularly regards an international comparison with other countries. There are clearly more differences in ABCs of Chinese angels compared to investors in the market in the west – a possible explanation is that China has its own unique institutional environment that results in different decision behavior of Chinese BAs (Ding et al., 2014, 2015).

The earliest study of informal investment was by Professor Manhong Liu. In 2003, she published a book *Angel Investment and Private Capital* that discussed the concept, origin, development, characteristics and operation mode of angel investment in China. This book first introduced the concept of 'business angel' in China. She published *The Theory and Practice of Angel Investment* in 2009, which analyzed the characteristics and development of BAs based on the Chinese economic background for the first time. In addition, Professor Yaokuang Li and his research team (Li and An, 2009; Li and Wu, 2011; Li and Yang, 2005; Li et al., 2011, 2012a, 2012b) carried out research on angel investment using surveys and statistics. According to the China Knowledge Resource Integrated (CNKI) database,[1] early researchers were mainly focused on international experience of angel investment, the role of angel investment in small and medium-sized enterprise (SMEs) financing, comparative study between angel investment and venture capital. After 2007, exploratory research about BAs in the Chinese context surfaced, and these papers analyzed the development of angel investment in China from the perspectives of the development environment, market characteristic and operation mode.

Searching the CNKI database reveals that the number of papers with 'angel investment' and 'business angel' as keywords in the title is less than 300, and these studies mainly focus on qualitative analysis and normative analysis, with a lack of quantitative research. This chapter intends to provide theoretical and practical reviews on angel activities and government policies in the transitional economy of China. It aims to: (1) outline the development and evolution of the Chinese angel market in terms of investment activities, angel groups and future trends; (2) examine how government policy influences BA development; (3) highlight the distinctive features based on an international comparison; (4) discuss the directions of future research.

The chapter includes six sections. The next section analyzes the economic conditions, legal system and business culture in the Chinese context. The third section covers the methodology, including definitions and data used in this study. The fourth section is concerned with the development and characteristics of the BA market, and elaborates the development of angel investing activities, BAs' characteristics and the formation of special angel groups in China. The next sections discuss public policy support for the

BA market, including central government support for early-stage financing of small businesses and some local policies to help BAs followed by an international comparison whereby Chinese BAs and the Chinese market is compared with investors in other countries. The conclusion to the chapter is given in the final section together with suggestions for future research.

## 9.2 THE CHINESE CONTEXT

The development of BAs requires a supportive external environment, and the Chinese economy now is in a steady growth phase, providing a better external environment.

Firstly, it is recognized that SMEs face considerable difficulties, caused by limitations of existing institutional mechanisms for SMEs in China. Considering the important role that SMEs play in the economy, the Chinese government has made efforts to help SMEs with financing. But with the rapid growth of SMEs, available capital cannot meet the booming needs. So, this gap between the demand and supply of capital gives a large space for angel investment.

Secondly, over the last ten years, entrepreneurship activities have increased and the government has taken great efforts to improve the entrepreneurship ecosystem and provided opportunities to develop the BA market.

Thirdly, there are more and more potential angels in Chinese markets. Rapid development of the economy attracts more top Chinese talent who work in foreign companies and overseas, and they have created a lot of wealth. With rapid economic growth, more people join the millionaire club in China. In April 2012, The Industrial Bank and the Hurun Research Institute jointly issued the *Chinese High Net Worth Individuals Consumer Demand: A White Paper*. This report has shown that the number of high net individuals who have at least 1 million USD (about 6 million RMB) of assets has reached 2.9 million. People are beginning to pay attention to the early-stage investment market, especially successful entrepreneurs, business elites and sophisticated investors. These experienced people enter the angel investment market not only for economic return but also to help other entrepreneurs.

Finally, although the Growth Enterprise Market[2] was established to support SMEs in 2009, initial public offerings (IPOs) are still rare in China. To widen exit channels, some local equity exchanges are encouraged by government and these channels are good exits for angel investors.

However, the Chinese angel investment market is still young many challenges need to be overcome. Investing in early-stage companies is high risk and it is difficult to reshape traditional private investors' ideas grounded on a prudent investment culture. Private investors should therefore be educated and trained to become real BAs. Local governments have made some new policies to support and help angel investment markets. But the legal environment and regulatory policies for the angel market still have some limitations, such as business integrity, intellectual property protection, certification for accredited investors, tax incentives and so on.

## 9.3 METHODOLOGY

The BA market is quite private and fragmented. The limitations of sampling and data collection are common problems in angel investment research. To describe the Chinese angel market, we collected data from mixed resources, including a first-hand survey and other second-hand data collections.

### 9.3.1 Concept Definition

Business angel ('angel investing' or 'angel investment') is a concept from the west. In China, there are few BAs (sometimes we call them individual angels) in the market, but angel groups and angel funds develop fast. Unlike western countries, China tends to emphasize investee and investing behavior in the early stage whether for individual angels or angel groups. 'Angel' is regarded as a special equity investment in the early stage or with a smaller amount. So, there is a broad type of angel investor. In this study, we define angel investor in both a narrow (Landström, 2007) and a broad sense. These two definitions both focus on the early-stage equity investment and some non-financial support for investees. But angel investors in the latter include both individual angels and institutionalized angels. So angel investing in China is used to define a stage and a special behavior of investment rather than a type of investor.

- Narrow definition – business angels: high net worth individuals, acting alone or in a formal or informal syndicate, who invest their own money directly in startups in which there is no family connection, and who, after making the investment, take an active involvement in the business, in the hope of financial gain.
- Broad definition – angel investors: all investors who invest in startups in which there is no family connection, and who, after making the investment, takes an active involvement in the business, in the hope of financial gain. This group include individual angels, angel groups, super angels and other types of angels.

### 9.3.2 Data Collection

There are few quantitative research analyses in BAs in the Chinese context, and the existing data are mainly derived from surveys by research institutions and media. Additionally, invisible market features, opaque data from angel networks and the confidentiality of public departments are real challenges in collecting data and restrict the expansion of academic research. In this chapter, we collected data from mixed resources, including a first-hand survey, which includes questionnaires and interviews, and second-hand data from the literature, research reports, media coverage, business networks and so on.

**Angel investment market information from existing research**

There are eight general reports available to describe the development trend of the Chinese angel investment market, though some differences exist due to the limitations of the methods of analysis and sampling (Table 9.1). The data in these reports are mainly from surveys and business databases. Two databases – PEData and CVSource – have descriptive information about business angels, angel groups and deals, but the lack of detailed data, different standard of classification and definition are key problems.

**Business angels' data from questionnaires, interviews and angel networks**

We visited nine cities in China – Beijing, Shanghai, Suzhou, Guangzhou, Shenzhen, Ningbo, Wuhan, Chengdu, Hong Kong – in order to send out questionnaires and carry out interviews from April to December 2013. By attending angel investment exchange and 'snowball' activities, we identified angel investors and further contacted some informal investors who might be business angels. We sent out 500 questionnaires and received 70 valid responses and carried out 30 face-to-face interviews (Table 9.2).

In China, the opaque information from angel groups and associations and data confidentiality by individuals and government lead to the theoretical research lagging behind its development in practice in the field. Existing data can be used to describe the market trend to some extent. However, the majority of angel investments are done by individuals and that information is private. So, it is extremely difficult to measure its true size, for example, the number of BAs or size of the angel investment market. Lack of a common definition results in poor quality data and also limited data influence the feasibility of studying angels' micro behavior. The biggest challenges are limited data resources, unidentified methodology and difficulty accessing angel investors.

*Table 9.1 Existing research reports and databases*

| Resource | | Overview |
|---|---|---|
| General report about angel investment market | *New Economy Weekly* (2006)[a] | • Samples: deals of nine Internet companies (data are from Capital, Chinalabs, ChinaVenture)<br>• Contents: (1) angel market summary; (2) focusing on Internet startups; (3) hot investment area (Beijing, Shanghai and Shenzhen); (4) angel capital in incubators and special cases |
| | China Venture Capital Research Institute (CVCRI, 2011) | • Samples: business angels (the number of samples is not disclosed)<br>• Survey contents: (1) business angels' ABC; (2) deal data; (3) investing operation; (4) public policies |
| | Zero2IPO (2011, 2012)[b] | • Samples: business angels and angel groups available (the number of samples are not disclosed)<br>• Survey contents: (1) respondents (investing experience, total number and amount of investment); (2) investing operation (deal source, screening, due diligence, shareholding, post-investment); (3) exit (number, method, return, follow-on investment); (4) open questions (market development, third-part service) |
| | CYzone (2012)[c] | • Samples: 309 respondents<br>• Survey contents: (1) business angeld; (2) investment size, shareholding and return; (3) relationship between angel and invested companies; (4) industry and region |
| | ChinaVenture (2013, 2014)[d] | • Samples: angel investments; angel groups; angel funds<br>• Contents: (1) statistics about investment size; (2) industry and region focus; (3) qualitative analysis of market trend and ecosystem |

| | | |
|---|---|---|
| | Li et al. (2014) | • Samples: ad hoc samples (senior management of banking, securities and insurance, as well as EMBA and MBA students); 88 business angels are identified<br>• Contents: (1) demographic characteristics (gender, age and education); (2) investment behavior (investment activities, relationship between angel and invested companies, motivation and investment criteria, hands-on involvement, exit and return); (3) investment preference (regional, stage, strategy) |
| Database | PEData of Zero2IPO | Angel groups, angel fund, business angel, investment activities |
| | CVSource of ChinaVenture[e] | Angel groups, angel fund, business angel, investment activities |

*Notes:*

[a] This report was the first general report that focused on the angel market in China.

[b] Zero2IPO (2011) provided a qualitative description and released survey data in 2012.

[c] Definition of 'angel': (1) investing in more than two startups; (2) the amount of each deal is above 0.1633 million USD (about 1 million RMB).

[d] The report data were from CVSource.

[e] Statistics come from: (1) public information; (2) survey on business angels and angel groups; and (3) include venture capital series A with the investment less than 0.8166 million USD (about 5 million RMB).

*Table 9.2 Questionnaires, interviews and angel networks*

| Survey | Overview |
|---|---|
| Questionnaire targeted at private investors | • Samples: 500 questionnaires were distributed, 85 were returned and 70 valid questionnaires were acquired<br>• Contents: (1) demographic characteristics (gender, age and education); (2) investment behavior (investment activities, motivation and investment criteria, investment preference); (3) investment strategy (co-investment preference, term sheet, post-investment) |
| Interviews with business angels, angel groups, clubs, associations, entrepreneurs, incubators | • Samples: 30 interviewees (30 minutes to around 2 hours) from 9 cities<br>• Questions: definition, data collection, investment preference, investing operation, building angel groups, designing a training plan, ecosystem, opinions on public policies etc. |
| Cases: 4 angel groups/networks | • Samples: China Youth Angel Investor Leader Association, Zhen Fund, Angel Crunch, China Business Angel Association<br>• Contents: strategies and goals, operation structure, venture selection and support, member recruiting and management, angel investing and other activities |

## 9.4 DEVELOPMENT AND CHARACTERISTICS OF ANGEL INVESTOR

In the crucial stage of the transformation of the Chinese economic structure, angel investment should be encouraged and developed to support an increasing number of startups. This section is the key part of this chapter. It mainly discusses development of angel investing activities in China, BAs' characteristics and investing behavior, and types of special angel groups and how they work

### 9.4.1 Origin of Angel Investment Market

Angel investment programs were originally dominated by government and aimed at investing the companies at the seed stage. According to the *Angel Investment Environment Research Report in Z-park* (2007), the earliest angel investment in China originated from the '863 Program' (1986) and the 'Torch Program' (1988).

After 2000, the rapid development of the Internet and other high-tech fields stimulated global entrepreneurial passion, which caused the early-stage investment boom. Some 'Chinese Returnees' who had studied and worked in western developed countries came back to China to start their own businesses and began to do angel investing. Taking advantage of their personal wealth, industrial experience and network of resources, they helped more and more young entrepreneurs to succeed, and motivated more and more successful domestic entrepreneur to engage in angel investment. Over the past five years, the Chinese angel market has grown quickly and particularly super angel funds; additionally, some accelerator-led angel capital is also a popular model.

### 9.4.2 Size of Angel Investment Market

In 2006, the first Chinese angel investment industry research report – *Chinese Angel Investment Research Report* (2006) – was published by a Beijing software and information services promotion center, Internet lab and *New Economy Weekly* magazine. This report showed that Chinese domestic investment in the seed stage accounted for 17 percent of total venture capital in 2006, amounting to 17.22 million USD (about 1.054 billion RMB), and the capital was mainly invested in the technology, media and telecommunications (TMT) industries.

In subsequent years, some organizations like Zero2IPO and ChinaVenture began to research and analyze the Chinese angel investment industry. According to primary research and secondary sources, about 1000 angel investors are shown in public statistics, and half of them are active angels in Z-park; there are 80 angel funds in public disclosure information; there an estimated 50 angel groups and services like angel associations, clubs, leagues and networks. TMT are popular industries. By geographical preference, angel activities mainly occur in Beijing, Shanghai, Shenzhen, Guangzhou and other developed cities in China.

According to the *China Angel Investment Annual Report 2015* issued by Zero2ipo Research, the size of the angel investment market has been increasing since 2008. In 2015, there were 2075 angel round deals with investments of 1635.73 million USD (about 10.188 billion RMB) (Figure 9.1). These deals were made by individual angels and private funds as well as government funds. Because the information about angel investing is sensitive and private, the real number of deals and amounts of angel investment will be higher than these figures.

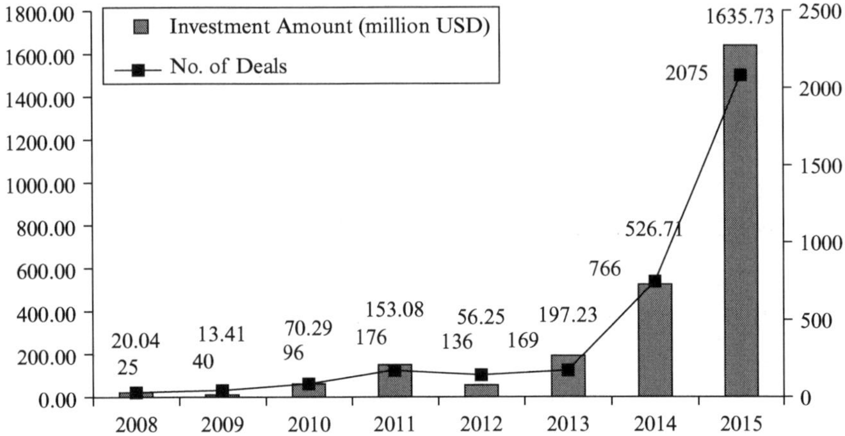


*Source:* Zero2ipo, February 2016.

*Figure 9.1 The size of angel investment in China in 2008–15*

### 9.4.3 Operation Pattern of Angel Investment

Before 2000, Chinese angel investment was mainly done by scattered business angels. From 2001 to 2008, angel investment started in China. Individual investors played a major role but there were also a few super angels like Capital Today and Zhen Fund that appeared in the public view. Since 2009, the angel investment market has entered a stage of rapid development. As well as individuals, different kinds of angel groups, institutions, incubators and crowdfunding were booming. We summarize the existing operation types of angel investment market in China:

- Individuals, few BAs.
- Angel groups based on clubs, non-governmental organizations (NGOs) and other organizations. These organizations provide exchange and communication opportunities for angel investors and entrepreneurs; angel members of these groups usually co-invest in startups for gathering capital and reducing the investment risk.
- Institutional angel investors focus on early-stage companies with formal operation.
- Incubator-based angel investment, which is a special angel investment institution that not only provides financial support, but also gives incubation places and entrepreneur services that can reduce

investment cost and risk. In addition, lots of new incubators provide seeding capital to enterprises.[3]

- Platform-based venture capital, which is mainly provided by the powerful companies[4] and local governments to support entrepreneurship in particular fields, including the Security Venture Fund by Tencent, Cloud Fund by Alibaba, Weibo Development Fund by Sina.
- Internet-based angel investment, which is a new service platform of co-investment and crowdfunding that connects angel investors and startups through the Internet platform.

### 9.4.4 Regional Difference in Angel Investment

There are several factors affecting local angel investment activities, such as industrial foundation, wealth level, the number of universities, entrepreneurs, management talent and so on (Shane, 2008). According to our survey, there are regional differences in the Chinese angel market. Specifically, in the Chinese Silicon Valley, angel deals and investments in Z-park, Beijing led the country. The number of BAs in Beijing accounts for 60 percent of the total number of angels; most angels are successful entrepreneurs and executives that have a certain influence and popularity because of high media exposure. Additionally, angel investment in Shanghai is active; investors are more dispersed and they focus on the TMT industries. Many investors are potential angels in Ningbo, a typical private economy-led city in Zhejiang Province, and they prefer to invest in projects involved with upgrading the traditional industry, which is related to local industry characteristics. Shenzhen is one of the most active cities in south China, and most investors engage in the business and work as part-time angels. Finally, in central and west China, there are more opportunities for local angel investments because of government support, such as the angel investment guiding fund in Wuhan and Chengdu.

## 9.5 BUSINESS ANGELS IN CHINA

### 9.5.1 A Survey on Business Angels

Our survey results show that most BA investors are male (88.5 percent), averaging 41 years of age, highly educated (about 48.6 percent hold Master's and above degrees), work in the financial sector (68.6 percent), have an entrepreneurial background (57.1 percent) and executives experience (54.3 percent). A typical BA in China is 25–50 years old, dealing

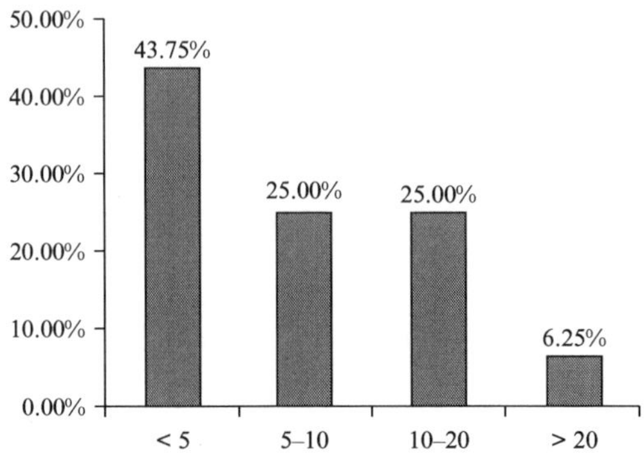


*Figure 9.2 Number of deals*

operationally with business, mentoring and supervising the company being supported, but with no direct involvement in its management. There are high net worth people who invest alone or with others, successful entrepreneurs who love to help others, senior executives who work in large enterprises, experienced professionals like accountants, lawyers, professors and so on, Chinese citizens with overseas experience and foreign investors who live in China.

### 9.5.2 Investment Size

Most investment had finished in recent years (80 percent of respondents have no more than five years' angel investing experience). 43.7 percent of investors invest in less than five deals and investment capital range is roughly equally split between below 163,425 USD (1 million RMB) and above 817,126 USD (about 5 million RMB) (as shown in Figures 9.2 and 9.3). In terms of industry and geography focus, TMT (57.1 percent), energy conservation and environmental protection (34.3 percent) and biological medicine (20 percent) are the most popular investment industries, and Beijing (48.6 percent) and Shanghai (42.9 percent) are active areas.

### 9.5.3 Investment Strategy

In terms of investment strategy, more than 80 percent of investors prefer on-site inspection; over 90 percent of BAs have co-invested investment and the partners are mainly their relatives and friends (54.3 percent) and members from angel groups (51.4 percent). Figure 9.4 shows all investors signed investment agreements, including equity transfer (71.4 percent), anti-dilution (60.0 percent) and valuation adjustment mechanism (54.3

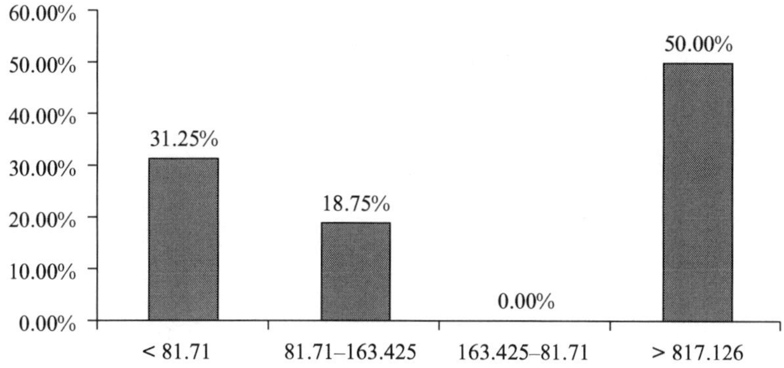


*Figure 9.3 Investment amounts (USD thousand)*

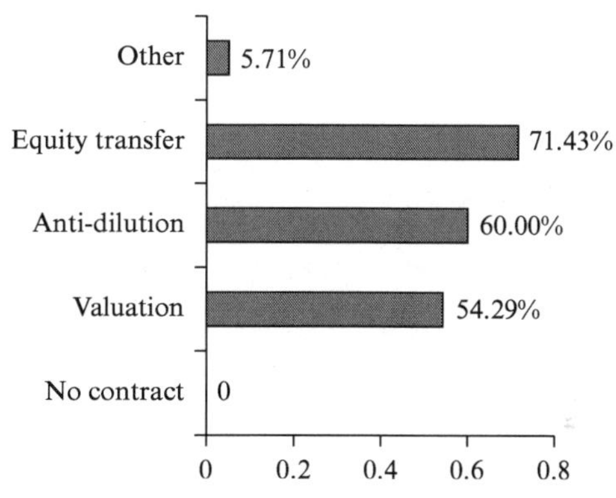


*Figure 9.4 Strategy of term sheet*

percent). Figure 9.5 shows more than 90 percent of investors participate in post-investment management, especially joining the board (88.6 percent).

### 9.5.4 Investment Style

Based on different backgrounds, business skills and characteristics, most active angels vary in investment style. Some successful entrepreneurs, like Mr Jun Lei and Mr Xiaopin Xu, who have entrepreneurial experience, can help startup companies effectively. The results of a survey by Z-park administrative committee show that more than half of the 100 influential BAs have entrepreneurial experience. On the other hand, some corporate

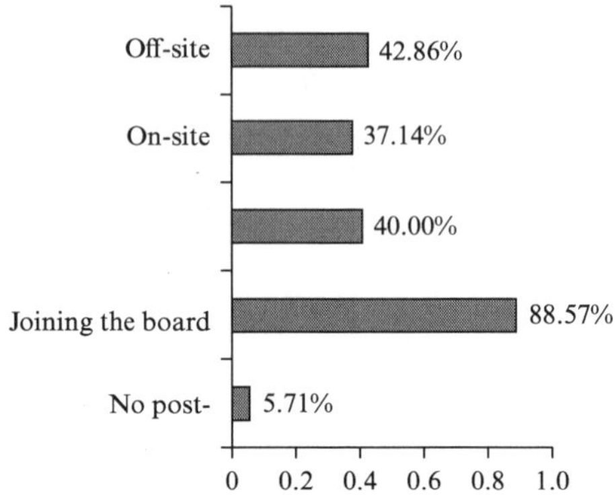


*Figure 9.5 Post-investment activities*

executives, like Mr Kaifu Li, who has financial resources and industrial social networks, are also an important part of angel investors (Table 9.3).

## 9.6 SPECIAL ANGEL GROUPS IN CHINA

### 9.6.1 Member-organized Angel Club

There are two general organizational structure: member-led model (angels run the group themselves) and manager-led model (a professional manager is hired to run the group) (OECD, 2011). At present, the member-led model predominates in China. The reason being that it is difficult to find the right manager to run angel groups and professional angels prefer to make their own decisions or to manage angel funds like venture capital (VC). Chinese angel groups focus on seed and early-stage investment, with less than 1 million USD in series A. In terms of operating model, there is no common fund, and members collaborate on due diligence but make individual investment decisions for each potential deal. In Box 9.1 Case 1 explores how this works in China.

### 9.6.2 Super Angel Fund

Angel investment funds share some characteristics with traditional BA and VC investors. Unlike traditional BAs, super angel funds are formal angel groups and use the typical VC structure. They can be distinguished from VCs in that the angel fund focuses on early-stage companies, involving higher risk, lower capital and the capital of the fund comes from

*Table 9.3 Several well-known Chinese angel investors*

| Investor | Background | Investment style |
|---|---|---|
| Jun Lei | • Founder, chairman and CEO of Xiaomi Tech<br>• Chairman of Duowan.com and Kingsoft | • part-time business angel<br>• focusing on familiar people<br>• investing in earlier stage<br>• entrepreneurial investor<br>• joining post-investment management |
| Xiaoping Xu | • Founder of Zhen Fund and Neworiental Group<br>• Former board member and head of Cultural Research Institute of Neworiental Group | • full-time business angel<br>• focusing on both familiar and strange<br>• supporting<br>• little post-investment management |
| Liqing Zeng | • Chairman of Decent Investment<br>• One of five founders of Tencent | • full-time business angel<br>• focusing on familiar people<br>• investing in earlier stage<br>• entrepreneurial investor<br>• 0.5 million~2 million<br>• joining post-investment management |
| Kaifu Li | • Chairman and CEO of Innovation Work<br>• Former top executive of Apple, SGI, Microsoft, Google etc. | • business angel + incubator<br>• financial support, entrepreneur services<br>• institutionalization mode<br>• focus TMT industry |

*Source:* Li (2012).

wealthy individuals rather than institutional investors. Figure 9.6 shows that the number of new angel investment funds has increased year by year. With VC/private equity markets being weak in 2012, much more new funds were raised to support startups. In 2013, the number of new angel funds continued to increase, but the total amount of capital raised decreased by 60.3 percent compared with the previous year, which means the fund presents a miniaturization development trend. According to founders' with different backgrounds, there are four angel investment funds:

- Angel-led fund, such as Mr Xiaoping Xu's Zhen Fund (see Case 2 in Box 9.2). Such a fund is founded and managed by active BAs.
- VC-led fund, like micro VC focusing on seed and early-stage investments.

## BOX 9.1 CASE 1: CHINA YOUTH ANGEL INVESTOR LEADER ASSOCIATION (CYAILA)

CYAILA was established in January 2013, with the well-known angel Mr Xiaoping Xu as honorary chairman and the active angel Mr Ning Yang as chairman. After more than one year of operation, CYAILA has become the most influential angel group in China.

- Strategies and goals: CYAILA is a group of active business angels, aiming to (1) increase the opportunities for communication, enhance the investment experience and improve the success rate of investment; (2) develop the angel investment market using the health concept and encourage more high net worth individuals to participate in angel investing.
- Operation structure: the group does not get involve in the angel investing business, but provides relevant services to its members. The governing body of the council is the functional committee (membership, trade, finance and activity), which is composed of council members, headed by the elected chair. The secretariat hires several full-time administrative staff to handle matters such as member communications, meeting coordination and database maintenance. The main activities are pitching meeting for angel capital (once a month), pitching meeting for VC funding (non-scheduled) and dialogue between entrepreneurs and their angels (once a month).
- Venture selection and support: there is a strict score system rule for members to recommend deals and maintain investing priority. Each member has an initial 100 points. The group encourages members to recommend high quality deals. If the recommended deal is successfully invested by other members, the referee will obtain new points. Otherwise, the referee will get penalty points. In addition, in the pitching meeting, interested members participate in the bidding by using points, with the maximum amount not exceeding half the total points. Those with high scores will get investing priority. After one month, these members must make an investment decision on whether to invest. If the deal is finally confirmed, the angel member will obtain new points; otherwise, the referee will get penalty points.
- Member recruiting and management: CYAILA has established membership criteria. Applicants must: (1) be honest and enthusiastic individuals, or VC partners and enterprise representatives who focus on seed and early-stage investments; (2) have invested at least two companies with no less than 16,342.53 USD (about 100,000 RMB) in the past three years; (3) agree to pay a lifetime membership fee (about 20,000 USD). By June 2014, there were more than 60 members in the group.
- Angel investing and other activities: to April 2014, CYAILA had organized 11 pitching meetings for angel capital; there were 70 startups participating in road shows; 15 of them had obtained final funding, with total value of 4.56 million USD (about 27.9 million RMB).

*Note:* The case was finished based on an interview with Mr Ning Yang; inside information was provided by the secretariat.

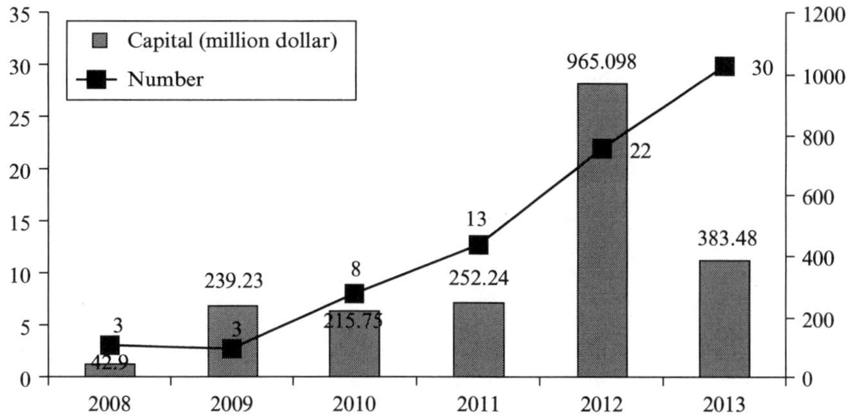


*Source:* Zero2IPO Research, 2014.

*Figure 9.6 The change trend of angel investment fund-raising in China (2000–13)*

- Government-led fund, such as Ningbo angel investment-led fund. Most of the funds work by matching with private capital.
- Incubator-led, such as Innovation Works, which links angel capital with an incubator or accelerator.

### 9.6.3 For-profit Business Angel Networks

Angel networks are platforms for making a good match between angel investors and entrepreneurs. The BA network itself does not make any investments or investment decisions, but provides consulting services such as screening, due diligence, pitching and other charged services. Its profit comes from the charging fee or equity share for successful deals.

In China, BA networks work both online and offline. There are two types: traditional networks (just providing offline services) and e-networks with offline services. E-network is an online platform such as AngelCrunch.com (introduced in Case 3 in Box 9.3) and VC.CN, while offline service is mainly matching and other consulting services. These networks cannot absorb public funds illegally because of a strict regulation environment. Therefore, they operate safely as financial intermediary.

## BOX 9.2 CASE 2: ZHEN FUND

In 2006, Zhen Fund 1.0 was founded by Mr Xiaoping Xu, a famous business angel. In 2012, Zhen Fund 2.0 was co-founded by Mr Xiaoping Xu and Sequoia Capital with 30 million USD capital. The new fund focuses on seed and early-stage companies in the industries of e-commerce, mobiles, Internet, games, education, training, consumer products and medical care.

- Strategies and goals: Zhen Fund aims to encourage young people to start their own enterprises, especially in helping overseas students return home and set up businesses. The overall strategy is to make the judgement to the startup teams. Mr Xu believes that experience of VC investing might not be effective to business angels and the most important issue in angel investing is the entrepreneurial team.
- Operation structure: the organization structure is like VC investors, who have an investing manager group acting as General Partner. Mr Xu plays a very important role in making investment decisions.
- Venture selection and support: deal sourcing is mainly from acquaintances, VC investors, the Internet and finance agencies. Zhen Fund uses a wide net to invest more portfolio companies. Mr Xu gives little post-investment management but provides help, support and advice when needed.
- Member recruiting and management: non-membership system.

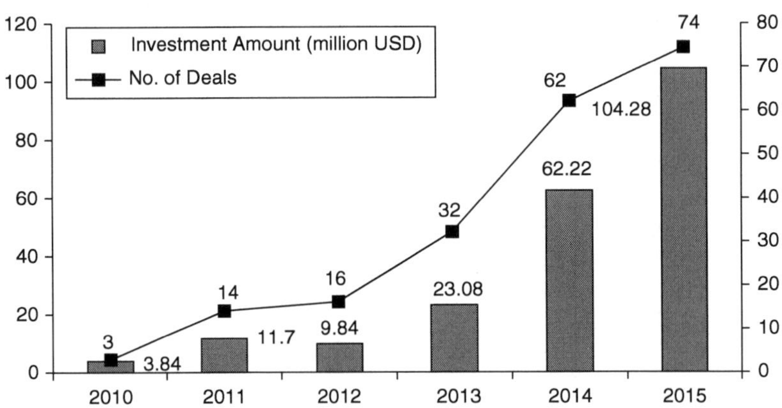


*Source:* CVSource Database.

*Figure 9.7 Angel investment of Zhen Fund (2010–15)*

- Angel investing and other activities: according to incomplete statistics from CVSource database, investment amount and deal numbers of Zhen Fund have been growing since 2010 (Figure 9.7). By the end of 2015, Zhen Fund had invested over 200 deals, focusing on mobiles, Internet, e-commerce and software industry. Furthermore, IPO is the preferred exit method. Jiayuan, Lightinthebox and Jumei that were invested by Zhen Fund have successfully gone public on the American stock market.

*Note:* The case was finished based on public information and statistics in CVSource.

### 9.6.4 Non-profit Angel Associations

Generally, an angel association is a not-for-profit official organization that provides a wide range of services to angel investors, and aims to support the development of the angel capital market in a particular country and region. These organizations are more or less linked to governments. The China Business Angel Association (CBAA) (see Case 4 in Box 9.4) was founded in 2008. It is the only nation-level alliance. In recent years, supported by local government, some regional associations have emerged in the angel investment market, such as Shanghai Angel Investment Club (2008), Tianjin Angel Investment Association (2013), Angel Investment alliance of Jiangsu Province (2013) and so on.

## 9.7 GOVERNMENT POLICIES TO PROMOTE ANGEL INVESTMENT

Since the 1990s, the Chinese government has focused on entrepreneurship and innovation, and has made some polices to promote the development of SMEs and entrepreneurship as well as high-tech business incubators, creating a good external environment for angel investment. With the rapid development of the BA market, government has shifted its efforts to the emerging market. During the past five years, more local governments have made policies to support the development of the angel investment market, such as angel investors' certification, co-investment funds, tax incentive, risk subsidy, angel education, BA network and so on. This section provides an overview of public policies to promote the angel investment market, including supporting SMEs and encouraging innovation and entrepreneurship, targeted angel financing policies and a discussion about the successes and failures of the policies.

### BOX 9.3 CASE 3: ANGELCRUNCH.COM

Most Chinese entrepreneurs don't have enough social networks and finding the right business angel is no easy task. So proper networks are urgently required. AngelCrunch.com, the first business angel e-network in China, was founded in November 2011. It is a platform for startups connecting with business angels and business angels finding investment opportunities.

- Strategies and goals: AngelCrunch.com aims to (1) create the fairest and quickest investment platform; (2) help startups pitch to interested angels; (3) attract the best startups and most valuable investors together. AngelCrunch.com provides free services before finishing the financing, but charges a success fee (typically 5 percent of the investment) for all deals made through their services.
- Operation structure: AngelCrunch.com hires full-time groups (called Deal Flow Team) to perform screening and due diligence, and administrative staff to handle tasks such as member communications, meeting coordination and database maintenance. In addition, there are some free value-added services, such as legal advice, company registration, incubation and so on.
- Venture selection and support: AngelCrunch.com uses unified evaluation criteria for screening, and provides a series of free supporting services for startups (e.g. improving the business plan, media coverage support, road shows).
- Member recruiting and management: you need to sign up online as an entrepreneur or business angel. Only approved startups can be shown on the website, and registrants through authentication can see detailed information about startups. By August 2014, it had about 14,000 entrepreneurship programs and attracted over 1800 investors to register.
- Angel investing and other activities: AngelCrunch.com focuses on three categories of startups: Internet-backed, technology-backed and the transformation and upgrading of traditional industries with technology innovation and business model innovation. By December 2015, AngelCrunch had helped nearly 400 startups to get a total investment of 640 million USD (about 4000 million RMB), including some popular domestic APPs.

*Note:* The case was finished based on public information and statistics in CVSource.

### 9.7.1 Supporting SMEs and Encouraging Entrepreneurship

**Public seed and venture funds**

Several fund policies are implemented at the regional level:

- Technology-based SMEs Innovation Fund
  The Chinese Minister of Science and Technology (MST) has empha-

## BOX 9.4 CASE 4: CHINA BUSINESS ANGEL ASSOCIATION

Professor Mannie Liu is a leading scholar in angel investment in China. Under her advocacy and organization, the China Business Angel Association (CBAA) was founded in 2008. It is currently in charge of the China Association of Technology Entrepreneurs and is the only Chinese member of the World Business Angel Association (WBAA).

- Strategies and goals: CBAA intends to build a platform to promote the development of business angels in China. Specific objectives include: (1) to facilitate information exchanges and cooperation between China and countries worldwide; (2) to promote the research of the business angel and early-stage venture capital from theory to practice; (3) to provide a structured platform for angels and angel groups through cooperation and exchanges, resource sharing and common development. CBAA provides web resources, research, conferences, matching activities, training and entrepreneur services to members.
- Operation structure: CBAA is a non-profit organization, and its council is the highest authority, including 21 members (three honorary chairmen, one chairman, three vice-chairmen and others). There is a secretary-general and three full-time administrative staff in charge of affairs like member communications, meeting coordination, database maintenance and report writing.
- Venture selection and support: CBAA occasionally holds a variety of matching activities. It often screens advanced technology and patents that are consistent with industry development, seeks potential angel investors and builds an exchange platform of technology, startups and capital.
- Member recruiting and management: CBAA recruits BAs, entrepreneurs, experts, professors, policy makers, institutional investors, universities, science parks and other groups. By June 2013, CBAA had 141 members, including 132 individual members and 9 institutional members.
- Angel investing and other activities: this association does not directly invest in startups, but plays a platform role in the angel investment market.

*Note:* The case was finished based on inside information provided by the secretariat.

sized the importance of the development of SMEs, especially the technology-based SMEs. The Technology-based SME Innovation Fund was established in 1999, and is the first central government-led fund aiming to support SME development. This fund supports technology-based SMEs in three ways: soft loans, unpaid subsidy funds and co-investment funds (public money is used to encourage and leverage private investment). At the end of 2012, the Technology-based Innovation Fund had an accumulated investment of 4 billion

USD (about 22 billion RMB), supported more than 40,000 technology SMEs and effectively promoted the growth and development of the technology SMEs group. About 31 percent of the companies listed on the Growth Enterprise Market have received support from the fund (Wang, 2013).

- National SMEs Development Fund
  SMEs are an important part of the national economy. In 2012, influenced by increasing labor costs and the price of raw materials, SMEs suffered from operating pressure and decreasing profits. The Ministry of Finance implemented the *State Council's Decision on Further Support for SME, especially Small and Micro Enterprises Healthy Development*, and issued and implemented a series of policies to support the healthy development of SMEs, especially small and micro enterprises. These included some innovative measures on investment form. In 2012, the central government planned to invest 2.45 billion USD (about 15 billion RMB) to establish the National SMEs Development Fund over five years. This fund will be market-oriented in order to leverage various types of social capital to jointly support the development of SMEs.

**Tax incentives**

Tax incentives in China are widely implemented to promote innovation and entrepreneurship and they are used in industrial restructuring, self-dependent innovation, energy conservation and emission reduction, export rebates, small and micro businesses and so on. Tax policies help to lower costs for small businesses and encourage more people to start their own enterprises. Various measures are used including halving the sales tax rate, value-added tax credit and so on.

**Regional policy for innovation and entrepreneurship**

Some policies are implemented at the regional level.

- Supporting the entrepreneurship incubator

  1. Hubei Province: 3.27 million USD (about 20 million RMB) to support the university students' Entrepreneurship Incubation Demonstration Base.
  2. Shanxi Province: rent subsidies provided for incubated entrepreneurs.
  3. Xiangtan City in Hunan Province: appropriated fund to support university students' projects and incubated entrepreneurs.

- Encouraging university students to venture
  1. Shandong Province: a secured loan, no more than 16,340 USD (about 100,000 RMB), is provided to graduates starting their own business and run low-profit programs.
  2. Zhengzhou in Henan Province: a one-time subsidy, 817.12 USD (about 5000 RMB), is offered to the initial entrepreneurial graduate.
  3. Nanjing in Jiangsu Province: free rent and an award, a maximum of 8171.27 USD (about 50,000 RMB) for students starting up their business.
  4. Xuzhou in Jiangsu Province: government-led fund with 4.9 million USD (about 30 million RMB) for student entrepreneurs.
  5. Chengdu in Sichuan Province: entrepreneurship training subsidy for undergraduates.
  6. Tianjin: housing subsidy for student entrepreneurs.

### 9.7.2 Targeted Angel Financing Policies

International experience shows that there are several forms of angel financing policies including supply-side measures and demand-side interventions. On the supply side, these include fiscal incentive, qualification admittance, BA networks, angel training and education, co-investment funds; the demand-side polices are investment readiness for entrepreneurs and developing the entrepreneurial ecosystem (Lerner, 1998; Mason, 2009; OECD, 2011).

To cultivate more angels, raise awareness of angel investing and address information asymmetry between startups and angel investors, the Chinese government is developing the angel investment market. At present, more than 50 government documents mention supporting or encouraging the development of the angel investment market. Most of these policies are implemented at the regional level, such as angel investors' certification in Shenzhen (2009), co-investment funds in Ningbo (2012), risk subsidy and tax incentive in Jiangsu Province (2011, 2012), investor education in Beijing (2014) and so on. Efforts for entrepreneurs are typically on pitching activities, investor readiness and also supporting the ecosystem. We focus on the efforts for the supply side in this chapter (May and Liu, 2015).

**Investors' certification**

There are specific certification regulations for the 'accredited investor' in the US Securities Law. BAs in China are not certified by law, but several governments have enacted angel investor's certification regulations. These certification regulations match with government-led fund and subsidy policies.

- Angel Investors' Registration System in Shenzhen (2009)
  Individual investors must have net assets of at least 0.82 million USD (about 5 million RMB) and angel investing experience or project resources, and be recommended by a related authorized association. Institutional investors must have registered capital in excess of 4.9 million USD (about 30 million RMB) and angel investing experience or project resources, managed by professionals with two years' experience and be recommended by a related authorized association.
- Angel Investors' Registration System in Ningbo (2013)
  Individual investors must have net assets of at least 0.1634 million USD (about 1 million RMB), and be experienced in angel investing or have the intention to investing in startups. For institutional investors, their single investment should be no less than 0.1634 million USD (about 1 million RMB), and they must have angel investing experience or have the intention to invest in startups with more than three experienced managers.

**Government-led funds**

Government-led funds have been launched to address the seed and early-stage equity financing gap. Some funds are directly invested in startups, while other policies work by matching public money with private investors or early-stage VC. In June 2012, Hi-tech Zone in Chengdu launched the first Chinese government-led funds focusing on seed and early-stage equity investments. After this, more and more local governments became angels. At present, more than ten cities have their own government-led funds, such as Chongqing, Ningbo, Hefei, Wuhan, Qingdao, Yangzhou. Table 9.4 provides an overview of government-led fund programs that target the angel investment market in various areas.

- FOF in Beijing
  Since 2011, the Management Committee of Z-park has made policies targeted at angel investment and created Z-park Angel FOF. By the end of 2013, the FOF established a partnership with 16 angel groups and co-founded five new funds that invested in 22 startups,

*Table 9.4 Cities with government-led funds targeting the angel market*

| Area | Fund | Overview |
|---|---|---|
| Z-park in Beijing | Angel investment government-led fund in Z-park (2011) | • fund of fund (FOF)<br>• cooperate with other angel groups and early-stage fund |
| Hi-tech Zone in Chengdu | Angel investment fund for Hi-tech Zone in Chengdu (2012) | • the first angel fund fully funded by the government (13.07 million USD, about 80 million RMB)<br>• managed by professionals<br>• makes direct investment in local startups |
| Chongqing | Chongqing youth innovation and entrepreneurship angel fund (2012) | • 16.24 million USD (about 100 million RMB) and the 'Angel Project' provided to help young entrepreneurs<br>• loan facility that can give a maximum of 0.82 million USD (about 5 million RMB) to small businesses and 24,497.80 USD (about 150,000 RMB) to micro business |
| Ningbo | Ningbo angel investment government-led fund (2012) | • plan to raise 81.66 million USD (about 500 million RMB) within five years<br>• a co-investment matching a deal made by identified business angels and VC investors<br>• aims to encourage private investors and VC investors to support local startups<br>• expects to exit in five years |
| Hi-tech Zone in Hefei | Angel investment fund for Hi-tech Zone in Hefei City (2013) | • the first angel government-led fund in Anhui Province<br>• on average, 0.49 million USD (about 3 million RMB) is invested in each deal |
| Wuhan | Wuhan technology entrepreneurship and angel fund (2013) | • matches the university students' entrepreneurship support plan<br>• fund size is 8.17 million USD (about 50 million RMB)<br>• gives priority to incubated entrepreneurs and students |
| Qingdao | Qingdao angel investment government-led fund (2013) | • focus on local incubate startups<br>• builds portfolio funds with four private VCs<br>• funds each VC with 5 million RMB<br>• raising 65.32 million USD (about 400 million RMB) in the first phase |

*Table 9.4* (continued)

| Area | Fund | Overview |
|---|---|---|
| Yangzhou | Yangzhou angel investment government-led fund (2013) | • raising 4.9 million USD (about 30 million RMB) in the first phase<br>• gives priority to high-level talents<br>• provides a maximum of 30 percent of the fund's investments, up to a maximum of 1 million USD (about 6 million RMB)<br>• works with risk compensation mechanism |

*Source:* Government documents.

including 17 companies registered in Z-park. These deals focus on the industries of the Internet/mobile Internet, e-commerce, cloud computing, biological medicine and advanced manufacturing.

- Direct investment fund in Chengdu
  The angel investment fund of the Hi-tech Zone in Chengdu was launched in June 2012 and raised 13 million USD (about 80 million RMB) in the first phase. The fund is managed by CDHT Venture Capital to carry out direct investment. During the second half of 2012, total investment was 6.83 million USD (about 41.8 million RMB) with 22 deals, half for mobile Internet companies.
- Co-investment fund in Ningbo
  Unlike the direct investing model, a co-investment fund was founded by Ningbo government in August 2012. It raised 81.71 million USD (about 500 million RMB) to support local innovation startups. This co-investment fund works alongside selected private investors and VC partners. By August 2014, more than 40 startups had obtained funding support of 5.79 million USD (about 35.41 million RMB), 22.88 million USD (about 140 million RMB) was for introducing private angel capital and 67 million USD (about 410 million RMB) for leveraging other capital.

**Risk subsidy**

Risk subsidy is another public policy providing support in two ways: directly funding target startups and subsidizing angel investors.

- Matching funds for startups in Chengdu (2012)
  According to the rules, if angel investment institutions invest more than 81,660 USD (about 500,000 RMB) in the startup, the government will provide risk subsidy funds equal to 20 percent of the

investment to the startups, with a maximum of 65,330 USD (about 400,000 RMB).

- Risks provisions for angel investors in Jiangsu Province (2012)
  The Jiangsu government has set up a special fund as a risk provision to support angel investment institutions that invest in seed and early-stage firms. Provincial governments provide risk provisions that equal 30 percent of the investment to angel investment institutions, up to a maximum of 49,000 USD (about 300,000 RMB). Local governments (city level, county level or national high-tech zone) also match some funds that equal 30 percent of the investment to an angel investment institution. The risk provisions are used to make up for the investors' losses over the three years after the first investment. If there is no loss, the funds should be returned. Otherwise, angel investment institutions withdraw risk provision funds to compensate for 50 percent of the actual loss and the other half is returned to government.

**Tax incentives**

In 2012, Jiangsu government launched *Opinions on Encouraging and Guiding Angel Investors to Support the Development of Hi-tech SMEs.* The policy highlighted tax incentives for angel investment institutions, including: tax credits based on 70 percent of the amount invested for the qualified institutions angel investing for more than two years, solving double taxation issues (pay income tax and business tax) for partnerships, business tax exemption for equity transfer and income tax exemption for high-level angel investment professionals.

**Encouraging construction of angel associations/networks**

There is no funding policy for private angel groups in China. Generally, governments encourage the development of angel associations and networks. In 2012 Jiangsu government clearly emphasized the role of angel investment industry organizations, and encourages the establishment of angel capital associations, angel capital alliances and other social organizations. Also in 2012 Ningbo government proposed building a platform such as angel investment clubs for matching and exchange. To date, there are more than ten angel associations, clubs, alliances and other networks in several Chinese cities, including the Angel Investment Club in Ningbo, Guanggu Angel Investor Club in Wuhan, Tianjin Angel Capital Association, Jiangsu Angel Investment Alliance, Z-park Angel Capital Association.

**Investor education**

As discussed earlier, there are many high net worth individuals in China. But they lack awareness of angel investing. Those new angels need enhanced understanding of the industry, and invest skills such as decision-making in startup teams. There are some informal activities in which angels share their own investing experience in China, while few formal and systematic training plans are made for angels.

The Angel Development Camp (ADC)[5] is the first public training organization co-sponsored by the Angel Association of Z-park and other powerful angel groups in June 2014. This training organization aims to teach ideas about angel investing, share experience and optimizes the angel ecosystem. Lectures, roundtable discussion and analysis of business plans are provided for new angels. ADC has enrolled about 40 new/potential angels including nearly 30 executives of listed companies and about ten heads of businesses. It invites expert and experienced BAs as trainers and offers a one-year curriculum covering the practical skills and theoretical knowledge on angel investing. Every month, students take one and a half days to finish the monthly class. By the end of August 2014, they had completed three training activities.

A mature angel investment industry requires time and does not work without government policy support, such as specialized legislation, tax incentives and so on. Angel investment is an important force for supporting startups, so government should strengthen the angel investment policy and create good external conditions for the angel investing operation. Angel investing is a long process involving many legal problems, and both angel investors and startups need laws and regulations to protect them. In China, at present, there are some local angel investment policies that help to raise awareness about angel investment. However, there is a lack of national legal policies to regulate the market (that is, identify the real angel rather than only financial investors). Also, tax incentives are not enough to encourage more people to become angel investors as well as encourage existing angel investors to invest more.

## 9.8 CONCLUSION AND FUTURE RESEARCH

Generally, Chinese BAs' investing behavior is very similar to that in other countries. However, there are some special market characteristics. Chinese angels are younger, invest infrequently and lack understand of angel investing (that is why angel groups and angel funds are very popular). At present, the Chinese angel investment industry is still in its infancy stage, and its potential to support innovation and entrepreneurship has not been realized. There are three obvious reasons: lack of angel investing awareness; enough incentive policies; and a sound exit mechanism.

According to the various characteristics of the Chinese economic system, we think that it is important to understand the positioning and role of government in the angel investment market. Center government should improve the regulation and guidance of angel investment markets and reduce excessive intervention and administrative monopoly, including: (1) make related laws and regulations to regulate the development of angel investment and build a management system to grow angel investment; (2) improve the angel investment environment, especially by introducing a tax incentive policy for BAs; and (3) establish angel investment funds and strengthen guidance on a national level.

Angel investment activities are flourishing. Over the next five to ten years there will be abundant business and investment opportunities in China during the period of transformation. We predict that: (1) Chinese angel investment is moving through an initial stage to expansion, to more high net worth individuals who prefer investing in traditional finance products like stock, fixed-income securities and real estate, and who will try to invest in startups with increasing recognition of early investment; (2) angel investors, entrepreneurs, intermediary services and other kinds of market subjects will develop toward specialization and standardization, and the startup environment will show a healthy development momentum; and (3) government will strengthen support for innovation entrepreneurship and angel investment, based on the macro-economy trend of the financial industry serving the real economy.

Studying the issues of BAs in the China context is full of challenges. Data collection is not an easy task, and existing data are mainly obtained from surveys in research institutions and the media. Additionally, the invisible market features, opaque data from angel networks and confidentiality of public department make accessing data challenging, and restricting the expansion of academic research. Chinese scholars must therefore continue to improve surveys of the domestic market and establish a necessary database. Future efforts should be made to improve data collection through angel associations and angel networks, identify more BAs and build an effective network for them, and design appropriate topics on which to carry out detailed research.

With the formation of the angel investment culture and strong business atmosphere, the Chinese angel investment market will further develop in the capital size of BAs, institutionalization and government support. Angel investing behavior in China is similar to that in the west to a certain extent. But it is evolving into a special pattern and operation modes because of the unique Chinese cultural and constitutional environment. Future research in the China context should continue and focus on:

- Estimating the angel market size by analysis of informal investment and early-stage investment, and by making a comparison analysis with VC markets (Capizzi and Tirino, 2011).
- Special investing phenomena, for example, some deals with investments too big (Li et al., 2014), some angels preferring to control the company.
- The key factors impacting the angel investing decision process as well as angel performance, such as angels' attributes and social capital, investing strategies and institutional background (Li et al., 2014; Ding et al., 2014, 2015).
- Legal barriers to the angel investment market.
- The optimal operation model of angel groups and angel funds.
- Business angel exits and return of investments (Carpentier and Suret, 2015; Capizzi, 2015).
- The relationship between angels and startups, the relationship between angels and VCs (Capiaai, 2011; Hellman and Thiele, 2013; Ibrahim, 2013).
- Comparing BAs' investing process and performance with those of VCs (Dutta and Folta, 2016).
- Potential angels' attitudes, behavior and characteristics.
- Assessing public policies and designing an effective angel policy system.
- Applicability of methodology about definition and data collection.

## ACKNOWLEDGMENTS

We greatly thank Newhuadu Business School for help and support. We are also grateful for funding from the National Natural Science Foundation of China (71303224, 71573174) and the 2016 Research Project of the Capital University of Economics and Business. Special thanks go to Ms Su Chen for editorial work.

## NOTES

1. The CNKI database is an online publishing platform and includes most journals, dissertations/theses, newspapers, proceedings, yearbooks and so on.
2. The Growth Enterprise Market or second board market is a securities market for those

entrepreneurial firms, SMEs and technology firms that temporarily go public in the main board market.

3. In China, most technology business incubators are operated by public departments, and they play an important role in working space services. Now, some private incubators or accelerators develop and work with angel capital. These new incubators or accelerators highlight entrepreneur mentoring, and help startups to succeed and grow.
4. Some large high-tech companies set up corporate venture capital (CVC), some of which focuses on early-stage investment.
5. We interviewed Mr Yong Xu, one of the co-founders, and got some information.

# REFERENCES


Capizzi, V. (2015), 'The returns of business angel investments and their major determinants', *Venture Capital*, **17**(4), 271–98.

Capizzi, V. and G. Tirino (2011), 'The scale, growth and returns of informal venture capitalists' investments in Italy', SSRN Working Paper, No. 1927878.

Carpentier, C. and J.-M. Suret (2015), ' Canadian business angel perspectives on exit: a research note', *International Small Business Journal*, **33**(5), 582–93.

Ding, Z., L. Sun and K. Au (2014), 'Angel investors' selection criteria: a comparative institutional perspective', *Asia Pacific Journal of Management*, **31**, 705–31.

Ding, Z., K. Au and F. Chiang (2015), 'Social trust and angel investors' decisions: a multilevel analysis across nations', *Journal of Business Venturing*, **30**, 307–21.

Dutta, S. and T.B. Folta (2016), 'A comparison of the effect of angels and venture capitalists on innovation and value creation', *Journal of Business Venturing*, **31**(1), 39–54.

Hellmann, T.F. and V. Thiele (2013), 'Friends or foes? The interrelationship between angel and venture capital markets', SSRN Working Paper, No. 2323553.

Ibrahim, D.M. (2013), 'Should angel-backed start-ups reject venture capital', *Michigan Journal of Private Equity & Venture Capital Law*, **2**, 251–70.

Landström, H. (2007), 'Pioneers in venture capital research', in *Handbook of Research on Venture Capital*, Cheltenham, UK and Northampton, MA, USA: Edward Elgar, Chapter 1.

Lerner, J. (1998), '"Angel" financing and public policy: an overview', *Journal of Banking & Financing*, **22**(6–8), 773–83.

Li, X. (2012), *Why I Invest in Your Relevant Content*, Beijing: China Commercial Publishing House (in Chinese).

Li, Y. and C. An (2009), 'Construction operation model of angel investment in China', *Review of Investment Studies*, **6**, 42–4 (in Chinese).

Li, Y. and J. Wu (2011), 'Review of definition and sampling method of foreign angel investment research', *China Soft Science*, **S1**, 201–9 (in Chinese).

Li, Y. and S. Yang (2005), 'Review of angel investment', *Productivity Research*, **9**, 219–21 (in Chinese).

Li, Y., Q. Yao and Z. Jiang (2011), 'Exploration on operation model of angel investment in China', *Journal of Hefei University of Technology (Social Science)*, **25**(2), 11–15 (in Chinese).

Li, Y., S. Jiang and D. Long (2012a), 'Review on business angel investment in USA', *China Soft Science*, **S1**, 84–92 (in Chinese).

Li, Y., Y. Zhuang and Q. Yang (2012b), 'A value signalling model of business angels under exponential utility function', *Journal of Hefei University of Technology*, **35**(4), 536–40 (in Chinese).

Li, Y., S. Jiang, D. Long, H. Tang and J. Wu (2014), 'An exploratory study of business angels in China: a research note', *Venture Capital*, **16**(1), 69–83.

Liu, T.C. and P.C. Chen (2007), 'Business angel investment in the China market', *Singapore Management Review*, **29**(2), 89–101.

Mason, C.M. (2009), 'Public policy support for the informal venture capital market in Europe: a critical review', *International Small Business Journal*, **27**(5), 536–56.
May, J. and M.M. Liu (2015), *Angels without Borders: Trends and Policies Shaping Angel Investment Worldwide*, Singapore: World Scientific Publishing.
OECD (2011), 'Financing high-growth firms: the role of angel investors', Internal Working Draft, OECD, Paris.
Shane, S. (2008), *Fool's Gold? The Truth Behind Angel Investing in America*, New York: Oxford University Press, 12 November.
Tingchi, M.L. and Chang, B.C.P. (2007), 'Business angel investment in the China market', *Singapore Management Review*, **29**(2), 89–101.
Wang, G. (2013), 'Guiding funds effectively support technology SMEs', *Science and Technology Daily*, 28 February, available at http://www.ebiotrade.com/newsf/2013-2/2013227100651533.htm (in Chinese).
Xiao, L. and B. Ritchie (2011), 'Informal investor investing and networks in China: an exploratory study', *Journal of Private Equity*, **14**(3), 72–85.

# 10 Business angels in emerging economies: Southeast Asia

*William Scheela*

## 10.1 INTRODUCTION

Southeast Asia represents not only one of the top economic growth areas in Asia, but one of the most rapidly growing regions globally. Entrepreneurship is a major factor in this impressive growth cycle according to the most recent Global Entrepreneurship Monitor (GEM) global report (Amoros and Bosma, 2014). Within the Asia Pacific and South Asian region, GEM researchers Amoros and Bosma (2014) report that entrepreneurs in the emerging countries of Indonesia, the Philippines, Thailand and Vietnam have shown above average intentions to become entrepreneurs because of both increasing economic opportunities and the high status of successful entrepreneurs in this region. In spite of impressive economic growth and entrepreneurial activity, there has been minimal research focusing on the impact of business angel (BA) financing entrepreneurial new ventures in this vibrant region of the world. There have been only five scholarly papers published focusing on BA investing in Southeast Asia, along with one book chapter and a small number of conference papers.

There are two major reason for the lack of research. First is the difficulty in finding BA investors in general (described as 'invisible investors' by many Western researchers), especially in emerging markets. Second, because of the lack of developed institutions necessary to support private equity financing, many BAs operate in the informal economy and subsequently prefer a low profile, thus making them even more invisible compared to Western BAs. Do BAs even exist in an environment characterized as an institutional void? In this chapter, I review the limited research to date to answer this question.

The outline or road map for exploring BA investing in Southeast Asia is as follows. I first provide a brief overview of Southeast Asia as the research setting and expand on the economic significance of this region. Then, I summarize the extant BA research published in the key countries of Singapore, the Philippines, Thailand, Vietnam and Indonesia. Finally, I provide suggestions for future research.

## 10.2 SOUTHEAST ASIA

Southeast Asia is comprised of ten countries that are all members of the Association of Southeast Asian Nations (ASEAN), Brunei, Cambodia, Indonesia, Lao PDR, Malaysia, Myanmar, the Philippines, Singapore, Thailand and Vietnam (Asian Development Outlook, 2013). While Singapore is a developed country, most of these ten countries are emerging countries, which are defined as low- or middle-income markets with increasing economic liberalization, but still having significant institutional voids that are caused by absent or underdeveloped institutions (Khanna and Palepu, 2005). Increasing economic liberalization has resulted in recent strong economic growth in spite of high transaction costs caused by institutional voids (Khanna and Palepu, 2010). According to the World Bank, 'Two-thirds of the growth in global investment over the last ten years has originated in developing countries' (World Bank, 2013, p. xi). Asia is projected to collectively hold 55 percent of the world's capital stock (inventory) by 2030, compared to the developed world's current holding of 70 percent (World Bank, 2013). Within Asia, Southeast Asia is the only sub-region to enjoy faster growth in 2012 compared to 2011 (Asian Development Outlook, 2013). More specifically, the five Southeast Asian countries, which are the focus of this chapter (Singapore, Indonesia, the Philippines, Thailand and Vietnam, which I shall refer to collectively as Emerging SEA) have shown impressive gross domestic product (GDP) growth during the past decade in spite of the recent global recession. The Asian Development Bank reports that for 2014 these five countries are projected to experience strong annual GDP growth rates ranging from 3.7 percent for Singapore to 6.6 percent for Indonesia. With the exception of developed Singapore, the projected growth rates for 2014 are all above 5.0 percent (Asian Development Outlook, 2013). As shown in Table 10.1, GDP per capita growth rates for Emerging SEA, to include Singapore, from 2009 to 2011 were even more impressive when compared to the UK and the USA. Table 10.1 clearly shows that Singapore has attained developed country status in terms of GDP per capita exceeding both the UK and USA.

Emerging SEA's financial markets have also been expanding at a relatively rapid rate over the past decade. More specifically, according to a World Bank study (Ghosh, 2006), in comparison to other emerging markets, emerging Asian financial markets are developing at a more rapid pace. While many of Asia's emerging economies' nascent equity markets still rank relatively low, Vietnam, Thailand, the Philippines and Indonesia have successfully reduced some significant challenges facing entrepreneurs when attempting to start and grow new ventures in their respective countries (Doing Business, 2014). However, with the exception

*Table 10.1 Economic indicators*

| Country | GDP per capita, US current dollars 2009[a] | GDP per capita, US current dollars 2011[b] | Percent change | Ease of doing business rank 2010[c] (n = 183) | Ease of doing business rank 2014[d] (n = 189) |
|---|---|---|---|---|---|
| Indonesia | 2329 | 3509 | 50.7 | 122 | 120 |
| Philippines | 1746 | 2223 | 27.3 | 144 | 108 |
| Thailand | 3940 | 5394 | 36.9 | 12 | 18 |
| Vietnam | 1060 | 1374 | 29.6 | 93 | 99 |
| Singapore | 37,293 | 49,271 | 32.1 | 1 | 1 |
| UK | 35,334 | 38,592 | 9.2 | 5 | 10 |
| USA | 46,381 | 48,387 | 4.3 | 4 | 4 |

*Sources:* [a] Schwab (2010); [b] Schwab (2012); [c] Doing Business (2010); [d] Doing Business (2014).

of Singapore, Emerging SEA is still a difficult place to do business as shown in the last two columns of Table 10.1. In comparison to Singapore, the UK and the USA, the four Emerging SEA countries rank considerably lower on the World Bank's Doing Business rankings for both 2010 and 2014. Only the Philippines showed significant improvement in their ranking during the four-year period.

## 10.3 INSTITUTIONAL VOIDS AND BUSINESS ANGEL INVESTING

Emerging SEA, in spite of increasing economic liberalization, still lacks fully developed institutions that are necessary to support BA investing. This 'lack of institutions' has been labeled an institutional void, which is defined as when 'institutions are either absent or under developed in an economy' (Khanna and Palepu, 2005, p. 1). This void represents a lack of legal and financial intermediaries needed to effectively support market efficiencies, which minimize transaction costs, such as the costs of doing business deals in Emerging SEA. Therefore, institutional voids can increase transaction costs for BA investors in emerging countries and have a negative impact on generating investment returns.

As shown in Table 10.1, in four of the five countries of Emerging SEA, doing business is difficult in spite of rapid economic growth. Table 10.2 provides more detail about the institutional voids facing BA investors. Key institutional rankings (1 = highest ranking) for each country were selected

*Table 10.2 Institutional analysis*

| Country (n = 144) | Business corruption[a] (1 = highest rank) | Protect property rights[b] | Protect minority share-holders[c] | Trust of politi-cians[d] | Stock market[e] | Bank sound-ness[f] | Institu-tional score (mean rank) |
|---|---|---|---|---|---|---|---|
| Indonesia | 111 | 81 | 87 | 60 | 30 | 99 | 78.0 |
| Philippines | 108 | 74 | 137 | 95 | 36 | 41 | 81.8 |
| Thailand | 80 | 103 | 29 | 107 | 27 | 45 | 65.2 |
| Vietnam | 118 | 113 | 97 | 42 | 70 | 125 | 94.2 |
| Singapore | 3 | 3 | 8 | 1 | 6 | 8 | 4.8 |
| UK | 17 | 5 | 16 | 31 | 8 | 97 | 29.0 |
| USA | 42 | 42 | 47 | 54 | 18 | 80 | 47.2 |

*Notes:*
[a] Higher rank indicates a low incidence of paying bribes or undocumented extra payments.
[b] Higher rank indicates property rights are clearly delineated and protected by law.
[c] Higher rank indicates minority shareholders are protected by law.
[d] Higher rank indicates higher trust of politicians.
[e] Higher rank indicates companies can easily raise money by issuing shares.
[f] Higher rank indicates that banks are healthy with sound balance sheets.

from the *Global Competitiveness Report 2012–2013* (Schwab, 2012), which is published annually by the World Economic Forum. Institutional scores for each country are calculated by analyzing six institutional rankings from the competitiveness report that can impact BA investing (corruption, property rights, minority shareholder rights, political trust, stock markets and bank soundness). The mean rank for each country from the six institutional variables is calculated to get an Institutional Score for each country (shown in the last column in Table 10.2). Collectively, Emerging SEA countries exhibited lower scores (65.2–94.2) than Singapore (4.8), the UK (29.0) and USA (47.2).

Institutional differences not only exist between Asian and Western countries but also within Southeast Asia. While the USA appears to be struggling with maintaining effective institutions based on Table 10.2, it is still highly ranked for ease of doing business as shown in Table 10.1. Combining Tables 10.1 and 10.2 for analytical purposes shows there are clearly two institutional clusters: a developed institutional cluster (Singapore, UK and USA) and an emerging institutional cluster where Emerging SEA countries face similar problems of corruption, weak property and shareholder rights, lack of trust of politicians, ineffective stock markets and weak banks.

What is the impact of weak institutions or institutional voids on BAs when attempting to do private equity deals in Emerging SEA? To answer this question, I use the *Venture Capital and Private Equity Country Attractiveness Index 2013* for country ranking (Groh et al., 2013) to analyze the seven countries. Countries are ranked based on performances on six measures, which are shown in Table 10.3. The results (private equity rank, column 8) are similar to both Tables 10.1 and 10.2 in that there are again two country clusters: a developed country cluster for Singapore, UK and the USA and an emerging country cluster for Thailand, Indonesia, the Philippines and Vietnam. It appears that private equity investors, to include BAs, investing in Emerging SEA face significantly more obstacles and higher costs to do deals than Singaporean, British and American private equity/BA investors.

So, how do Southeast Asian BAs do deals when investing in the developed market of Singapore that is supported by effective institutions, but primarily investing in Emerging SEA markets in the face of challenging institutional voids? Clearly, the Western or developed country BA investment strategy that is successful in the USA, UK, Western Europe and, as I shall explain, Singapore won't work in Emerging SEA. The next section analyzes the research explaining how BAs do deals in Singapore, the Philippines, Thailand, Vietnam and Indonesia.

## 10.4 BUSINESS ANGEL INVESTING RESEARCH

### 10.4.1 Singapore

Singapore is one of the most developed economies in the world and certainly the most developed country in Southeast Asia. Singapore receives the highest global ranking for ease of doing business (Table 10.1) and also the highest ranking for private equity attractiveness in Southeast Asia (Table 10.3), yet only two published studies have focused on BA investing in Singapore: Hindle and Lee (2002) and Wong and Ho (2007). Hindle and Lee's data were collected via a postal survey focusing on 29 Singaporean BAs who are 90 percent ethnic Chinese. Because of the difficulty of finding BAs, the researchers developed a convenience sample of entrepreneurs who had previously received BA financing. The entrepreneurs responded to a postal survey whereby the investees were requested to provide descriptions of the BAs who invested in their respective businesses. Wong and Ho analyzed 276 Singaporean informal investors (both family and BA investors) based on data from the annual GEM project over a five-year period (2000 to 2004).

*Table 10.3 Private equity attractiveness index*

| Country (n = 118, 1 = highest rank) | Economic activity[a] | Depth of capital market[b] | Taxation[c] | Investor protection and corporate governance[d] | Human and social environment[e] | Entrepreneur culture and deal opportunities[f] | Rank 2013 |
|---|---|---|---|---|---|---|---|
| Indonesia | 2 | 25 | 97 | 95 | 82 | 79 | 47 |
| Philippines | 18 | 38 | 93 | 88 | 88 | 86 | 56 |
| Thailand | 10 | 23 | 51 | 43 | 56 | 45 | 32 |
| Vietnam | 26 | 40 | 112 | 106 | 76 | 81 | 64 |
| Singapore | 40 | 14 | 25 | 2 | 1 | 11 | 5 |
| UK | 33 | 3 | 10 | 5 | 9 | 4 | 3 |
| USA | 3 | 1 | 37 | 8 | 11 | 1 | 1 |

*Notes:*

[a] Size of economy, expected real GDP growth and unemployment.

[b] Size of stock market, stock market trading volume, initial public offerings (IPOs), merger and acquisition (M&A) market activity and bank performance.

[c] Entrepreneurial tax incentives and administrative burdens.

[d] Quality of corporate governance, security of property rights and quality of legal enforcement.

[e] Education and human capital, labor market rigidities and bribing and corruption.

[f] Innovation, scientific and technical journal articles, ease of starting and running/closing a business and corporate R&D.

*Table 10.4 Singapore business angel characteristics*

| Characteristic | Hindle and Lee (2002) (n = 29) | Wong and Ho (2007) (n = 276) |
|---|---|---|
| Median age | 40–49 | 35 |
| Percentage male | 90% | 78% |
| Average investment (USD) | $271,000 | $12,900 |
| Work experience (% managing own business) | Significant 72% | Low 30% |
| Number of deals | 65% of BAs: > 2 deals | Not reported |
| Educational level | Not reported | 53% college graduates |
| Ownership percentage | Minority | Not reported |

Hindle and Lee's stated research objective was 'to provide an initial descriptive profile of Singapore business angels in order to articulate the key attitudes and behavior influencing their provision of informal venture capital to entrepreneurial ventures' (2002, pp. 169–70). According to Wong and Ho (2007), they 'present the first statistical analysis of the characteristics and determinants of informal investment [business angels] in Singapore' (p. 44). I am focusing on Wong and Ho's analysis of BAs, which does not include family investors. Table 10.4 shows the major characteristics of Singaporean BAs summarized from these two studies. Both studies agree that Singaporean BAs are primarily male, relatively young and invest from US$13,000–271,000 per deal. Wong and Ho found that BAs in their sample typically invest less than US$13,000 per deal while BAs in Hindle and Lee's much smaller sample average US$271,000 investment per deal. Similarly, Hindle and Lee's BAs are much more experienced in business, older and invest in multiple deals.

Hindle and Lee determined that networking was very important for BAs to do deals, but focusing exclusively on using family networking and investing in family businesses were both not a priority for the Singaporean-Chinese BAs. This finding is in direct contrast to the 100 percent ethnic Chinese BA sample in Thailand (Scheela and Jittrapanun, 2012) supporting family as being a major factor in sourcing and financing deals (analyzed below). Wong and Ho (2007, p. 64) also found that Singaporean BAs and entrepreneurs are both 'strongly reliant on social networks for identifying opportunities and forming business relationships.' Because of the difficulties of matching good deals with entrepreneurs, Wong and Ho determined there is a critical need for formal BA networks (BANs) in Singapore and Southeast Asia. Also, because of the finding that most BAs in Singapore are relatively inexperienced private equity investors, the authors determined there is a lack of professionalism in BA investing. This combination of matchmaking challenges and lack of professionalism resulted in the founding in 2001 of the first formal BAN in Southeast Asia – the Business Angel Network of Southeast Asia (BANSEA, www.bansea.org) where deals can be facilitated along with providing educational development for BAs to become more effective investors. BANSEA's vision, as stated on their website, is to 'foster a vibrant start-up ecosystem in which angel investors fund entrepreneurs who eventually become angels themselves.' Entrepreneurs can submit their business plans via BANSEA's website. Besides providing funding, BANSEA conducts educational workshops, research, conferences and offers networking sessions with international BA clubs; especially clubs in Malaysia, India, China and Thailand. However, I did not find any other formal BAN that was analyzed in the published BA research in Emerging SEA including Thailand.

The most important investment criteria for the BAs in Hindle and Lee's sample are, in order of priority, the portfolio company's management team, market potential, proven market and financial rate of return. Wong and Ho found a different perspective in their BA sample when doing a deal, whereby the most important investment criterion is knowing the entrepreneur by developing a relationship, which they describe as creating social capital between the BA and the entrepreneur as an integral part of the investment process.

Hindle and Lee identify Singaporean BAs as being more Western than Japanese BAs studied by Professor Yasuhisa Tashiro (1999), which was the first published research of BA investing in Asia. Hindle and Lee posit that 'Singapore has a far more westernized culture than Japan' (2002, p. 180), which is the only reference to the importance of investment environment being a factor in doing deals. Neither study explored the impact (positive or negative) that institutions have on doing deals in Singapore, which, as shown above, is a country with very effective institutions. Both studies strongly support that both entrepreneurs and BAs heavily rely on social networks for identifying deal opportunities and forming business relationships in spite of the existence of fully developed financial and legal institutions. It appears that Singaporean BAs have developed an effective co-investment strategy based on networking (both formal/BAN and informal) to do deals in a relatively small market, where effective legal and financial institutions provide strong support for BA investing.

### 10.4.2 The Philippines

The Philippines is significantly different from Singapore for BA investors, given the low ranking for ease of doing business because of the presence

*Table 10.5 Philippines' BA profile and fund performance*

| Profile | Investing performance |
|---|---|
| Fund size | Number of years investing |
| • range: US$40,000–300 million | • range: 1–35 |
| • mean: not applicable | • mean: 18 |
| • median: US$1.8 million | • median: 19 |
| Investment size/deal | Number of years for exit |
| • range: US$1000–3 million | • median: 5.0 |
| • mean: US$133,000–1.7 million | Investment stage: |
| • median: US$100,000–250,000 | • seed/early: 85% |
| Number of deals | • growth: 8% |
| • total: 238 | • late: 7% |
| • range: 2–30 | • other: 0% |
| • mean: 8.2 | Fund performance: |
| • median: 6 | • below: 14% |
| Number of co-investors/deals | • average: 38% |
| • range: 0–10 | • above: 41% |
| • mean: 3.7 | • too early: 7% |
| • median: 3.0 | |

*Source:* Scheela and Isidro (2009).

of challenging institutional voids, yet BAs are active investors in seed- and early-stage ventures. On the positive side, the Philippines is definitely an emerging market with strong economic growth and significant opportunities for private equity investors. Scheela and Isidro (2008, 2009) provide the only published research focusing on BA investing in the Philippines. They interviewed 29 BAs (26 men and 3 women) who were active investors in primarily seed- and early-stage companies. BAs in this sample were all members of an investment forum that met monthly in Manila and each BA was selected based on their active angel investing performance. These BAs are highly educated as they all have university degrees and 21 have advanced degrees. Table 10.5 shows the descriptive statistics for the 29 investors. All 29 investors have previous work experience and they have been investing in companies/deals for an average of 18 years.

According to Scheela and Isidro, Filipino BAs in their sample have access to sizeable investment funds reporting a median of US$1.8 million available for investing or already invested in portfolio companies. In terms of how much each BA invests per deal, the median investment range is US$100,000–250,000 per deal, which compares favorably with Hindle and Lees's sample of Singaporean BAs.

Most of the BAs invest with partners, resulting in an average of 3.7 co-investors for each investment. In total, the 29 BAs have invested in 238 companies, which are comprised of 203 early-stage companies and 19 growth-stage companies. To date, each investor has made, on average, eight investments. Most BAs are active, hands-on investors, who average five board seats. Investments are typically held for five years (median) with the exit strategy being primarily a trade sale to a third party. IPOs, while technically possible, are not perceived as a viable exit, especially in the Philippines, because of the lack of a fully developed securities market. Investment performance is reported to be very positive as almost 80 percent of the BAs evaluate their overall investment performance as meeting or exceeding expectations.

Scheela and Isidro (2009) asked each BA to identify the challenges of angel investing in the Philippines. The results are summarized in Box 10.1 and basically reflect a poor investment climate. BAs have difficulties in finding the right people (entrepreneurs, co-investors and managers) in order to do deals. This challenge is further exacerbated because it is also difficult to convince foreign investors to enter the Philippines because of the small country market, currency risk of the peso, political instability

## BOX 10.1 PHILIPPINES' BUSINESS ANGEL CHALLENGES

Convince foreigners to invest

- fund raising is difficult
- declining disposable income
- small market size

Finding the right people

- investment partners
- entrepreneurs
- managers

Finding opportunities

- need to educate about private equity
- be patient in doing deals
- accurately estimate market size

Poor economic performance

- weak currency
- political and social risk
- focus on survival

Dealing with red tape/bureaucracy and corruption

- lack of government programs for entrepreneurs
- improve tax collections.

*Source:* Scheela and Isidro (2009).

and government red tape and corruption. Consequently, it is important for BAs to be patient investors, network, co-invest and conduct in-depth due diligence for each potential investment.

In spite of the presence of challenging institutional voids BAs have aggressively co-invested in early-stage companies after conducting in-depth due diligence and subsequently playing an active, hands-on investment strategy. The results have been promising as BAs report positive investment returns in a very challenging investment climate.

### 10.4.3 Thailand

Thailand is similar to the Philippines, especially when also compared to Singapore, possessing a relatively challenging investment climate, while generating impressive macroeconomic results. BAs are active investors, similar to the Philippines, but family plays a much stronger role when doing deals. Scheela and Jittrapanun (2012) interviewed 20 Thai-Chinese BAs (five females and 14 males; one BA requested not to divulge gender) who are all members of the Hainan Association of Thailand and active angel investors. Scheela and Jittrapanun identified association members who were active equity investors in unlisted small and medium-sized enterprises (SMEs). Similar to the Philippines' field study (Scheela and Isidro, 2009), BAs were asked to provide descriptive data about their respective investment strategy, fund performance and investment environment. Table 10.6 summarizes the BA profile and fund performance in this study. All 20 BAs are high school graduates, 18 have earned a Bachelor's degree and 11 have also earned a Master's degree. According to Scheela and Jittrapanun, the high education level is partially explained by the fact that most of the BAs in this study are second and third generation family members who have the resources and family support to pursue higher education. All BAs have significant business experience in a wide variety of industries. The average length of angel investing in companies for the BAs is 16.1 years and each BA, on average, serves on 2.4 boards.

Thai BAs in this sample have access to significant funds to do deals as the median investment fund is US$2.25 million. Similar to Filipino BAs, Thai BAs do not actually create a separate investment fund, but primarily source their investments from personal savings or from fairly liquid assets such as selling a company; so the investment fund represents the amount of accessible capital and capital already invested. Unlike Filipino BAs (Scheela and Isidro, 2009), Scheela and Jittrapanun discovered that Thai BAs also use significant debt (31 percent of the funding) to do deals compared to personal savings (55 percent) and cash flow from existing businesses (10 percent). Most Thai BAs prefer to invest close to home with 43 percent focusing primarily on companies in Bangkok. Only four BAs were open to invest outside Thailand.

Scheela and Jittrapanun calculated the median initial investment range for Thai's BA in a portfolio company is relatively small at US$10,000–125,000, which increases significantly to a median of US$1.0 million–1.25 million for a follow-on investment. This follow-on or two-stage investment strategy is unique in that Singaporean and Filipino BAs did not identify a two-stage investment strategy. Scheela and Jittrapanun posit that an explanation for this difference could be that Thai BAs invest almost exclusively in family businesses in contrast to Singaporean and Filipino BAs making a one-time investment in non-family businesses.

Scheela and Jittrapanun found that Thai BAs invest for the long term (median of 7.5 years), tend to co-invest with 3–4 partners and have collectively invested in 59 companies. As shown in Table 10.6, these portfolio companies were mainly in the seed and early stages at the time of investment, which is similar to the early-stage investment strategy of Filipino BAs. Thai BAs are active, hands-on investors as they report spending

*Table 10.6 Thailand BA profile and fund performance*

| Profile | Investing performance |
|---|---|
| Fund size | Number of years investing |
| • range: US$90,000–15 million | • range: 2–50 |
| • mean: US$3.33 million | • mean: 16.1 |
| • median: US$2.25 million | • median: 10 |
| Investment size | Number of years to exit |
| • mean range: US$2.7 million–4.6 million | • median: 7.5 |
| • median range: US$1.0–1.25 million | Investment stage |
| Number of deals | • seed/early: 47% |
| • total: 74 | • growth: 22% |
| • range: 1–7 | • late: 19% |
| • mean: 3.4 | • other: 12% |
| • median: 3.0 | Fund performance versus expectations |
| Number of co-investors/deals | • below: 25% |
| • range: 0–10 | • average: 40% |
| • mean: 3.6 | • above: 35% |
| • median: 3.0 | • too early: 0% |

*Source:* Scheela and Jittrapanun (2012).

almost 70 percent of their time monitoring and assisting their portfolio companies and 80 percent of these BAs specifically categorize themselves as active investors. This finding is also similar to the active, hands-on strategy of Filipino BAs.

As shown in Table 10.6, the 20 Thai BAs reported generally positive investment performance, with only 25 percent of their investments performing below average and 75 percent of their investments meeting or exceeding expectations, which compares favorably to Filipino BAs reporting 79 percent of their investments meeting/exceeding expectations (see Table 10.5).

Scheela and Jittrapanun asked each Thai BA to identify and explain the major challenges relevant to investing in SMEs in Thailand. Scheela and Jittrapanun categorized BA responses in terms of the frequency that each specific challenge was cited and the top five challenges are summarized in Box 10.2.

Thai BAs report that it is a challenge to operate a business in a highly uncertain and competitive environment where there is high political uncertainty, weak legal support for investors and inefficient government support for SMEs. More specifically, the business landscape in Thailand is a challenge because it is perceived by BAs to be extremely competitive and volatile for both domestic and foreign companies. BAs are concerned

### BOX 10.2 THAILAND BUSINESS ANGELS' CHALLENGES

Very competitive business environment

- results in low profitability
- difficult to obtain reliable data
- high personnel turnover
- volatile market environment

Unstable political environment

- corruption

High financial risks increase costs

- high funding costs
- foreign investors don't understand Thailand
- shortage of key personnel

Weak legal framework

- political connections of big business
- lack of government transparency

Inefficient government

- complicated tax system
- economic development only focuses on big cities.

*Source:* Scheela and Jittrapanun (2012).

about the lack of reliable public data needed for in-depth due diligence to make investments. Other factors that increase the level of competitive rivalry include difficulty in retaining employees, bad work habits, low barriers to entry, limited distribution channels and the lack of a global vision for many SMEs. The outcome of these factors is, on average, high financial risk because of low profitability for both domestic and foreign companies.

Scheela and Jittrapanun summarize that political, financial and legal institutions are perceived to be obstacles for Thai-Chinese BAs operating in Thailand. The researchers further state that these characteristics and challenges collectively indicate a lack of fully developed institutions, which are needed to support an effective BA investing climate in Thailand. Very significantly, similar to Filipino and Singaporean BAs, Thai BAs proactively build social capital by networking (Scheela et al., 2013) to enhance deal making because of the many challenges of investing in an emerging economy weakened by significant institutional voids.

Similar to Filipino BAs, Thai BAs are also co-investing in a challenging business environment requiring in-depth due diligence, but reporting generally positive investment returns based on a very hands-on investment strategy. Thai BAs are very different from their Filipino counterparts because of the predominance of using their family businesses as an investment platform and developing a two-stage investment process when investing in early-stage companies.

### 10.4.4 Vietnam and Indonesia

Vietnam and Indonesia are two of the larger populated countries in ASEAN and have exhibited impressive economic growth over the past decade. But similar to the Philippines and Thailand, their respective business climates are both characterized by significant institutional voids, which have resulted in low rankings for both ease of doing business and private equity attractiveness.

Vietnam and Indonesia are grouped together because, unlike Singapore, the Philippines and Thailand there are no studies published in academic journals focusing on BA investing in these two countries. Pilot studies completed in Vietnam and Indonesia were presented in two conference papers (Gunawan et al., 2011; Scheela et al., 2012) and are expanded in a recent book (Scheela, 2014).

#### Vietnam

Scheela et al. (2012) conducted a pilot study in Vietnam to determine if BA investing is ongoing and whether BAs are receptive to being formally

*Table 10.7 Vietnam BA profile and fund performance*

| Profile | Investing performance |
|---|---|
| Fund size | Number of years investing |
| • range: US$250,000–1.5 million | • range: 2–13 |
| • mean: US$800,000 | • mean: 5.9 |
| • median: US$750,000 | • median: 5 |
| Investment size | Number of years for exit |
| • range: US$5000–200,000 | • median: 4 |
| • mean: US$72,000 | Investment stage |
| • median: US$53,000 | • seed: 51% |
| Number of deals | • early: 33 |
| • total: 61 | • growth: 16% |
| • range: 3–30 | • late: 0% |
| • mean: 7.6 | • other: 0% |
| • median: 4 | Fund performance versus expectations |
| Number of co-investors/deals | • below: 13% |
| • range: 1–12 | • average: 38% |
| • mean: 5.5 | • above: 50% |
| • median: 5 | • too early: 0% |
| Level of education | |
| • Baccalaureate: 2 | |
| • Masters: 5 | |
| • law: 1 | |

*Source:* Scheela (2014).

interviewed. Preliminary results are positive as eight BAs were successfully interviewed. Table 10.7 summarizes the profile and investing performance of the eight BAs, which include seven men and one woman. BAs were selected via word-of-mouth and snowballing whereby each interviewed BA was asked to identify other BAs. Similar to the previously reviewed studies in this chapter, the Vietnamese BAs are both highly educated and experienced investors. All eight are college graduates and six have earned advanced degrees. On average, these BAs have been investing for almost six years ranging from 2 to 13 years.

Similar to the field studies analyzed for the Philippines and Thailand, BAs in Vietnam also have access to significant investment funds as they report a median of US$750,000 available for investing and invest a median of US$53,000 per deal in primarily seed- and early-stage companies. Only one BA invests alone, while the remaining BAs always co-invest with typically four to five other BAs. These BAs are very active investors generating investments in 61 companies with very positive results as 88 percent of

BAs report their respective investments are meeting or exceeding expectations at the time of their investments.

Similar to previous research, Scheela et al. (2012) report that Vietnamese BAs aggressively network to find both attractive deals and quality co-investors. Most BAs prefer to invest 'close to home' in Vietnam or the USA, but four BAs also have a global view (beyond Vietnam and the USA) when investing. All eight BAs indicate they are active, hands-on investors who each average 4.5 board seats. Six BAs report spending at least 25 percent of their time, on a weekly basis, working actively with their portfolio company management teams.

Investments are held for a median of four years. One BA has liquidated two failed investments, another BA has no plans to exit ('I will give the shares to the employees'), four will sell via a trade sale and three BAs anticipate exiting via an IPO in the future. None of the BAs is yet to make a successful exit.

Box 10.3 summarizes the challenges reported by BA investors when investing in private equity deals in Vietnam (Scheela et al., 2012; Scheela, 2014). These challenges primarily focus on weak institutions, especially a lack of protection of minority shareholders, which, of course, is very

### BOX 10.3 VIETNAM BUSINESS ANGELS' CHALLENGES

Private investing is challenging

- no legal protection in general
- minority shareholders not protected
- risk of entrepreneurs cheating
- unprofessional board members
- lack of long-term investors
- lack of business planning
- BA co-investing responsibilities not equally shared
- lack of trust
- weak corporate governance and transparency
- difficult to develop personal relationships

Dealing with the government

- developing the correct legal structure
- takes time to restructure a business
- dealing with government corruption
- difficult exits
- government policies change constantly
- excessive red tape
- unhealthy competition.

*Source:* Scheela (2014).

problematic for BAs who are primarily minority investors. Weak institutions also include weak corporate governance and corrupt entrepreneurs and government officials. Unfortunately, government is perceived by BAs as part of the problem instead of representing the solution to enhance the BA investing process. Government is problematic because of their inability to improve legal institutions to better support minority investors and to streamline the investment process when doing a deal. More specifically, transactions costs for doing business are further increased due to excessive government red tape and continually changing government policies, which increase the time to start or restructure a business and exit an investment.

**Indonesia**

Gunawan et al. (2011) successfully completed a pilot study of five Indonesian BAs with the same goal as the Vietnam pilot study – determine if BAs exist and can they be formally interviewed as part of a research field study. Similar to the Vietnamese field study, BAs were identified via word-of-mouth and snowballing as no formal or informal BANs exist. Gunawan et al. found what appears to be a different type of BA compared to the previously reviewed studies in that these BAs describe themselves as relatively passive investors. BAs report the time spent to help develop their portfolio company is minimal, while the amount of investments vary significantly between the BA investors. In general, Gunawan et al. found there are two types of BAs in this sample. First is the BA with purely economic motives and second, the BA with broader eco-social motives, which is similar to social venture capitalists.

Table 10.8 provides a profile of the Indonesian BA investors. BAs invested a median of US$11,000 in exclusively seed-stage companies. The range of their fund size and investment per deal is somewhat confusing as one BA reports investing up to US$11 million into a seed-stage company, which is highly unusual, but certainly interesting. Yet, this profile is very useful in that it appears BAs exist in Indonesia, they tend to co-invest, have a deal portfolio of 4–5 seed-stage companies and are generally meeting or exceeding their investment goals.

Gunawan et al. asked each BA to identify their major investment challenges and their responses are summarized in Box 10.4. Three major challenges were identified: lack of government leadership in BA investing, a difficult environment to do deals and lack of bank support to do deals. The lack of fully developed institutions necessary for private equity investing is clearly evident in all three challenges; especially government corruption and the lack of ethics in government, investors, entrepreneurs and bankers. Given the difficult investment climate

*Table 10.8 Indonesia BA profile and fund performance*

| Profile | Investing performance |
|---|---|
| Fund size | Number of years investing |
| • range: US$7000–333,000 | • range: 1–36 |
| • mean: US$124,500 | • mean: 9.3 |
| • median: US$75,000 | • median: 2 |
| Investment size | Investment stage |
| • range: US$1500–11 million | • seed: 100% |
| • mean: US$224,000 | • early: 0% |
| • median: US$11,000 | • growth: 0% |
| Number of deals | • mature: 0% |
| • total: 27 | • other: 0% |
| • range: 2–12 | Fund performance versus expectations |
| • mean: 5.4 | • below: 0% |
| • median: 4 | • average: 40% |
| Number of co-investors/deals | • above: 60% |
| • range: 2–4 | • too early: 0% |
| • mean: 2.6 | |
| • median: 3 | |

*Sources:* Gunawan et al. (2011); Scheela (2014).

## BOX 10.4 INDONESIA BUSINESS ANGELS' CHALLENGES

Lack of government leadership

- no clear legal regulations
- significant red tape
- unfair competition due to government favoritism
- government corruption
- need political connections to do business
- lack of ethics in government

Difficult to do a deal

- lack of trust between BA, entrepreneur and co-investors
- difficult to measure risk
- entrepreneurs learn by doing; no training
- difficult to duplicate/grow the business
- inconsistent planning due to short-term focus of entrepreneurs

Lack of support from banks

- difficult for SMEs to get bank financing
- banks are too conservative
- lack of ethics in banking.

*Source:* Gunawan et al. (2011); Scheela (2014).

reported by BAs in this small sample, it is surprising they report positive investment returns.

While the two pilot studies obviously suffer from small sample size, there are interesting similarities between Vietnam and Indonesia that are also comparable to the Philippines and Thailand: access to significant investment funds, co-investing with other BAs, reporting positive returns, investing primarily in seed- and early-stage companies and blaming governments for a lack of leadership. Indonesian BAs appear to be somewhat of an outlier as they are passive investors with both social and economic goals while BAs in the other three countries are very active investors focusing primarily on economic goals.

## 10.5 SUMMARY

The major research issue for BA investing in Southeast Asia is the lack of substantive empirical research, which makes it very problematic to generalize from the published studies. Based on the 'early' research to date, it appears that Southeast Asian BAs exhibit both differences and similarities in terms of investment environments, strategies and performances across countries. Singaporean BAs are unique in that they invest in a business environment supported by well-developed institutions that greatly enhance private equity investing while BAs in Emerging SEA countries face significant investment challenges because of the lack of legal and financial institutions necessary to support minority shareholders. Thai-Chinese and Filipino-Chinese BAs only do deals with family members and some Indonesian BAs appear to be passive investors and may be more socially focused in their investment strategy than their ASEAN counterparts.

Apparent similarities are significant as they are repeatedly reported in all of the studies. Most BAs are both highly educated and experienced, hands-on investors who conduct in-depth due diligence, co-invest with other BAs, actively network to find deals and generally report positive investment returns in spite of the difficult investment environments. Impressively, 62 Emerging SEA BAs report access to significant investment funds that were invested in 400 primarily early-stage ventures.

## 10.6 BUSINESS ANGEL RECOMMENDATIONS

In the field studies conducted in the four Emerging SEA countries, BAs were specifically asked to make recommendations to improve BA

*Table 10.9 Southeast Asian BA recommendations*

| | |
|---|---|
| Singapore<br>• improve BA professionalism<br>• develop BA networks (BANs)<br>  ○ educate BAs<br>  ○ facilitate deal matchmaking | Philippines<br>• form BA club<br>  ○ develop deal database<br>• education of private equity investing<br>  ○ how to do deal<br>• improve institutional development<br>  ○ protection for investors |
| Thailand<br>• government promotion of SMEs/private equity<br>  ○ educate entrepreneurs about BAs<br>• improve the investment climate<br>  ○ support from banks<br>• better political stability & governance<br>  ○ eliminate corruption | Vietnam<br>• provide government leadership<br>  ○ better institutions<br>• education about BA investing<br>  ○ for BAs and entrepreneurs<br>• increase BA investing<br>  ○ need more BAs<br>  ○ form BA clubs |
| Indonesia<br>• government leadership to improve private equity investing<br>  ○ protect minority shareholders<br>• better BA networking to do deals<br>  ○ create BA clubs<br>• bank leadership to support SMEs<br>  ○ easier credit for SMEs | |

financing in their respective countries. Table 10.9 summarizes the top 2–3 recommendations from each study. For Singapore, recommendations were taken from the discussion section of Wong and Ho's (2007) paper.

The most frequently cited recommendations listed in Table 10.9 collectively comprise five areas: formal BA networks, education, institutions, SMEs and the investment climate. BAs want to be able to improve deal flow and reduce risk by developing formal BANs or BA clubs. BAs recommend these clubs can improve deal flow by developing large databases to include BAs and entrepreneurs to facilitate the deal matchmaking process. BA clubs can also educate both entrepreneurs and BAs about private equity financing of SMEs. Not surprisingly, BAs want better political, financial and legal institutions to significantly improve the investment climate. The government needs to play a stronger leadership role in protecting minority shareholders who are investing in countries with challenging institutional voids and to also provide better macroeconomic data so BAs can conduct better due diligence for market opportunity. Finally, banks need to be more proactive in supporting early- and growth-stage SMEs by providing better access to credit.

## 10.7 FUTURE RESEARCH

BA financing is alive and well in Southeast Asia in both developed and emerging countries. BAs are doing deals, adding value to investee companies, looking for more deals and making money. Institutional voids are a serious challenge and impediment for efficient deal making, but not a reason to not invest. BAs need an agenda to improve the business climate for private equity investing to include a much more active role for national governments to improve the legal and financial institutions necessary to support angel investors. BAs strongly believe they must also play a stronger leadership role in creating BANs to improve deal flow and provide the opportunity to develop more professional BAs and knowledgeable entrepreneurs who are seeking private equity.

Clearly, much more BA research is needed in Southeast Asia, especially in Indonesia, which is the largest country and economy in ASEAN. With the exception of Wong and Ho (2007), all of the reviewed studies in this chapter suffer from non-random, small convenience or purposive samples. Only three countries (Singapore, the Philippines and Thailand) of the ten Southeast Asian countries have generated published scholarly research. While it appears that BAs in the larger ASEAN countries are actively involved in private equity investing in seed- and early-stage companies, more research is needed in terms of both including more countries and developing significantly larger databases within each of the ten countries. Basically, more countries and much larger samples are needed. More specifically, both macro and micro studies are needed. For macro research, more large-sample surveys are needed similar to that of Wong and Ho who analyzed GEM data for Singapore to identify characteristics and trends in BA investing. With GEM data now available for most ASEAN countries, this type of research is increasingly possible and very useful for policy development and country comparison purposes. On the micro side, more and larger field studies to ultimately include all ten ASEAN countries are sorely needed to better understand the BA investment process in terms of similarities and differences between these countries and to develop policy recommendations for each country.

Finally, the editors of this book recommend defining BAs as individuals, acting alone or in a formal or informal syndicate, who invest their own money directly in an unquoted business in which there is no family connection, and who, after making the investment, take an active involvement in the business, in the hope of financial gain. This definition fits the BAs in all of the Southeast Asian countries in this chapter except Thailand and a small subset of Chinese-Filipino BAs. Unlike the predominately ethnic Chinese-Singaporean BAs, the Thai- and Filipino-Chinese BAs purposely focus on family investments when doing deals, yet the rest of the above BA definition fits them very well as they are profit-seeking, growth-oriented, active, hands-on investors. This begs the question: how ubiquitous is this family-BA investment model for other ethnic Chinese BAs operating throughout emerging Southeast Asia where ethnic Chinese tend to play a significant and sometimes dominant economic role? I believe this is a potentially significant subset of BA investing in all of Asia and also other emerging countries where family connections is the dominate network when doing deals. As one American, MBA-educated, Filipino BA said in an interview, 'If they [entrepreneurs] are not family, there is no deal.' The impact of family BA investing in emerging Asian countries should be one of the most important research questions for future research on BA investing in emerging countries.

Lastly, a personal note. During our field studies in emerging Asia (Thailand, the Philippines and Vietnam), we were frequently told that family investing in new ventures plays a significant role in job creation, because of very weak institutional support for private equity investing. It could be that family BA investing is more prevalent in the least developed CMLV (Cambodia, Myanmar, Laos and Vietnam) countries in Southeast Asia, a region that has been neglected by BA researchers, which now represents an important research opportunity.

## REFERENCES

Amoros, J.E. and N. Bosma (2014), *Global Entrepreneurship Monitor 2013 Global Report*, Babson Park, MA: Babson College.

Asian Development Outlook (2013), *Asia's Energy Challenge*, Manila, Philippines: Asian Development Bank.

Doing Business (2010), *Reforming Through Difficult Times*, Washington, DC: International Bank for Reconstruction and Development/World Bank.

Doing Business (2014), *Understanding Regulations for Small and Medium-sized Enterprises*, Washington, DC: International Bank for Reconstruction and Development/World Bank.

Ghosh, S.W. (2006), *East Asian Finance*, Washington, DC: International Bank for Reconstruction and Development/World Bank.

Groh, A., H. Liechtenstein and K. Lieser (2013), *The Venture Capital and Private Equity Country Attractiveness Index 2013 Annual*, Barcelona, Spain: IESE Business School, University of Navarra.

Gunawan, J., W. Scheela, N.A. Wessiani and M. Luthfiyah (2011), 'Promoting entrepreneurship research and education about business angels in Indonesia', Paper presented at the UNESCO–APIED International Conference, Jakarta, Indonesia, 6–8 December.

Hindle, K. and L. Lee (2002), 'An exploratory investigation of informal venture capitalists in Singapore', *Venture Capital*, **4**, 169–81.

Khanna, T. and K. Palepu (2005), 'Spotting institutional voids in emerging markets', Teaching Note 9-106-014, Harvard Business School Publishing, Boston, MA.

Khanna, T. and K. Palepu (2010), *Winning in Emerging Markets: A Road Map for Strategy and Execution*, Boston, MA: Harvard Business School Press.

Scheela, W. (2014), *Venture Capital in Asia: Investing in Emerging Countries*, New York: Business Expert Press, available at http://www.businessexpertpress.com (accessed May 2016).

Scheela, W. and E. Isidro (2008), 'Private equity investing in the Philippines: business angels vs. venture capitalists', *Journal of Private Equity*, **11**, 90–99.

Scheela, W. and E. Isidro (2009), 'Business angel investing in an emerging Asian economy', *Journal of Private Equity*, **12**, 44–56.

Scheela, W. and T. Jittrapanun (2012), 'Do institutions matter for business angel investors in emerging Asian markets?', *Venture Capital*, **14**, 289–308.

Scheela, W., E. Isidro, T. Jittrapanun, T.T. Nguyen and J. Gunawan (2012), 'Business angel investing in emerging economies: policy implications for Southeast Asia', Paper presented at the Kauffman Foundation's International Research and Policy Roundtable, Liverpool, UK.

Scheela, W., E. Isidro and T. Jittrapanun (2013), 'Informal venture capital investing in emerging Asian economies', in M. Thai and E. Turkina (eds), *Entrepreneurship in the Informal Economy*, New York: Palgrave Macmillan, pp. 65–82.

Schwab, K. (2012), *The Global Competitiveness Report 2012–2013*, Geneva: World Economic Forum.

Schwab, K. (2010), *The Global Competitiveness Report 2011–2012*, Geneva: World Economic Forum.

Tashiro, Y. (1999), 'Business angels in Japan', *Venture Capital*, **1**, 259–73.

Wong, P.K. and Y.P. Ho (2007), 'Characteristics and determinants of informal investment in Singapore', *Venture Capital*, **9**, 43–70.

World Bank (2013), *Capital for the Future: Saving and Investment in an Interdependent World*, Washington, DC: World Bank.

# 11 Business angels in sub-Saharan Africa

*David Lingelbach*

## 11.1 INTRODUCTION

In 1998 Greg Starke and Damian Conway founded Disa Vascular, a medical stent manufacturer based in Cape Town, South Africa. Early in Disa's development, the firm obtained a Rand 2 million (USD 300,000) investment from two local business angels. Two years later, after differences of opinion between the angel investors and Disa's founders on issues ranging from board composition to Disa's domicile, the angels were bought out at two times their investment cost by a local venture capital fund. Disa subsequently attracted over USD 4 million in funding from both local and foreign investors and continues to develop as an innovative medical devices concern.

Fast forward to 2012, when M-Kazi – a mobile job recruitment app provider – was launched in Nairobi, Kenya. Founded by Nancy Wang, Lino Carcoforo and Mem Maina (Graham, 2012), M-Kazi raised USD 50,000 in equity funding from angel investor Jerome Kisting, who was located in Toronto, Canada and had a background in both Namibia and South Africa. Kisting described his investment as 'blending impact-investing principles with some venture capital principles' (Van Vugt, 2012). Along with Kisting's investment and a follow-on debt investment from him of USD 10,000, M-Kazi had raised USD 100,000 by year end 2012. M-Kazi ceased trading in early 2014.

These two stories illustrate some of the features of business angels in the African[1] context. Business angels have been defined generally as individuals, acting alone or in a formal or informal syndicate, who invest their own money directly in an unquoted business in which there is no family connection, and, who, after making the investment, take an active involvement in the business, in the hope of financial gain (Landström and Mason, Chapter 1 in this volume). The Disa and M-Kazi cases suggest some of the characteristics of both angel investments and business angels in Africa, as well as similarities and differences between these features in the diverse African context and those observed elsewhere.

Three similarities stand out. First, as technology-oriented firms, both Disa and M-Kazi had the capacity to benefit from industry-specific expertise that angel investors can often provide. Second, both firms had investment requirements that far exceeded the capacity of their angels, requiring both to look elsewhere for additional funding. Third, M-Kazi's angel was motivated by a 'double bottom line' investment strategy. This motivation may be similar to 'impact investing' or 'venture philanthropy' (Gordon, 2014) observed in more developed markets.

On the other hand, four important differences with angel practice in the UK or USA can also be observed in these cases:

1. Disa's angel investors were bought out by a domestic venture capital firm, an exit route that is relatively uncommon in either the USA or the UK.
2. Disa's angel investors were bankers by training, while M-Kazi's angel had a background in non-profit management. Consequently, both angels lacked industry-specific knowledge or networks that could have contributed to these firms' growth.
3. One of the Disa's angels sought to gain control of the firm by being appointed as executive chairman of Disa's board and proposed strategies at odds with the founders' vision, leading one founder to refer to these angels as 'delusional.'
4. Unlike much angel activity elsewhere, M-Kazi's angel was located an ocean away, limiting his ability to provide post-investment support.

While these differences may be idiosyncratic to the Disa and M-Kazi cases, they may also suggest differences in the institutional or economic context between sub-Saharan Africa and the UK or USA. For example, industry-specific knowledge may be less important for African angels given that few African startups rely on technological advantages where such knowledge would be important. Broader business knowledge possessed by angel investors may be more relevant in such situations. The less well-developed nature of the local angel market may lead to angels behaving at odds with generally accepted angel investing norms, as Disa's founders discovered.

### 11.1.1 Aims of this Chapter

The purpose of this chapter is twofold. First, it aims to shed some light on the angel investing phenomenon in sub-Saharan Africa. Second, the gaps in our knowledge emerging from a review of what we do know will suggest some possible future research directions.

Business angel investing is increasingly recognized as a significant activity in entrepreneurial finance. When we examine the phenomenon beyond the contexts of developed economies, our knowledge declines precipitously. In this chapter, we consider the phenomenon in a context where we know the least about entrepreneurship and entrepreneurial finance in general: sub-Saharan Africa. This region is comprised of 49 countries with a total population of approximately 970 million and a regional gross domestic product (GDP) in 2013 of approximately USD 1.7 trillion. As many countries in sub-Saharan Africa have experienced significant and increasingly diversified economic growth that is less dependent on commodity prices (*The Economist*, 2015a), angel investing may also experience growth in the years ahead.

However, research on this phenomenon faces two major methodological challenges: a general lack of data and unclear definitions. For example, are the Disa and M-Kazi cases typical of angel investing in Africa? Perhaps, and then again, perhaps not. They are nothing more than case studies drawn by convenience from this author's prior work. They may or may not be representative of angel investing in this context and, in any case, are likely to be a small sample of the population.

However, such case studies may be amongst our best available data at present. Reliable survey data on angel investing does not yet exist, including from the Global Entrepreneurship Monitor (GEM). Academic studies of the phenomenon in the African context do not exist. Thus, this chapter is based largely on data that we recognize upfront as likely to be inaccurate to some degree: anecdotes and small, convenience samples that are likely to be non-representative. These shortcomings are common in much of the extant research on angel investing generally (Mason and Harrison, 2008).

Moreover, observers of this phenomenon have tended to conflate four related activities: angel investing, informal investing, venture capital and private equity. This conflation is typical of angel investing research in general, although the degree of difficulty and definitional fuzziness may be greater when studying the phenomenon in Africa than in the USA and Europe. In the African institutional context, the general definition of business angels – developed to describe the phenomenon in the UK, USA and Europe – faces three challenges. First, given the strong ties that characterize many of the continent's business networks, family connections are likely to be an important factor in angel investing. Second, given these strong ties, it seems possible that local angel investors may trust the startups in which they invest to deploy this capital without active angel involvement after investment. Third, it is not yet clear if the bulk of angel investing in Africa is motivated by financial gain. The presence of 'double bottom line' angel investing such as was the case with M-Kazi requires us to be sensitive to alternative investor and/or investee motivations.

Angel investing is a subset of informal investing. The broader category of informal investors has been defined both narrowly as private individuals who invest risk capital directly in unquoted companies in which they have no family connections (Mason and Harrison, 2000; Landström, 2007) and more broadly as any investments made in startups other than the investors' own businesses, excluding investments in stocks and mutual funds (Reynolds et al., 2003; Landström, 2007). Given the paucity of data on angel activity in sub-Saharan Africa, however, we shall refer in this chapter from time to time to extant academic studies about informal investing, for example, Bygrave (2006).

The chapter is organized as follows. First, we examine the institutional contexts in which angel investing takes place in sub-Saharan Africa. Next, we review the empirical data on this activity. Then, we consider similarities and differences between business angel activity in Africa and elsewhere, focusing on comparisons with UK and US experience. We then review government policy and conclude with a research agenda.

## 11.2 THE INSTITUTIONAL CONTEXT OF AFRICAN ANGEL INVESTING

### 11.2.1 Institutional Influences on Angel Investing in Africa

Institutions have been defined as 'the rules of the game in a society or, more formally, are the humanly devised constraints that shape human interaction' (North, 1990, p. 3). Institutions can be of three types: regulative, normative and cultural-cognitive. Regulative institutions are explicit regulatory processes, such as rule-setting, monitoring and sanctioning. They may be formalized, such as laws and regulations, or relatively informal, such as shaming and shunning. Normative institutions introduce prescription, evaluation and obligation into economic life; they include both values (preferred or desirable outcomes) and norms (how things should be done). Cultural-cognitive institutions constitute shared conceptions of social reality and the ways in which meaning is made (Scott, 2008). Venture capital researchers have classified regulative institutions as formal institutions, while normative and cultural-cognitive institutions have been classified as informal (Li and Zahra, 2012). This chapter adopts that convention.

Institutions have a significant influence on venture capital activity, and therefore this chapter asserts that they may have an influence on angel activity as well. Some scholars have argued that formal institutions are of primary importance to venture capital activity (Lerner and Tåg, 2013). Other researchers have called attention to informal institutions that can substitute for venture capital- (Bruton and Ahlstrom, 2003) or angel-unfriendly (Scheela and Jittrapanun, 2012) formal institutions by filling the institutional voids left by the latter. Still others have found that, while formal institutions are important for venture capital development, their influence is moderated by specific informal institutions such as uncertainty avoidance and collectivism (Li and Zahra, 2012).

The institutional context in which business angels in Africa operate is heterogeneous. Scheela and Jittrapanun (2012) found that business angels in Thailand fill the institutional voids created by weak formal institutions by developing trust-based informal institutions through co-investing with government officials and family members. This finding was echoed and generalized by Li and Zahra (2012), which found that the level of venture capital activity is related to both formal and informal institutional development. Given the similarities between venture capital and angel investing, these findings may suggest the impact of institutional contexts on angel activity.

### 11.2.2 Applying Findings from Venture Capital to African Angel Investing

Li and Zahra (2012) measure the level of formal institutional development using a composite of governance indicators developed in Kauffman et al. (2007). These indicators measure six aspects of formal institutions: voice and accountability; political stability and absence of violence; government effectiveness; regulatory quality; rule of law; and control of corruption. Each measure reflects perceptions measured through multiple surveys over time and across economies. More positive numbers for these measures indicate a relatively higher quality of governance in comparison to other economies. The results for each of these indicators were weighted and summed to create a composite measure of formal institutional development (Li and Zahra, 2012).

These six measures have been defined as follows. Voice and accountability reflects perceptions 'of the extent to which a country's citizens are able to participate in selecting their government, as well as freedom of expression, freedom of association, and a free media'; political stability and absence of violence as 'the likelihood that the government will be destabilized or overthrown by unconstitutional or violent means, including politically-motivated violence and terrorism'; and government effectiveness as 'the quality of public services, the quality of the civil service and the degree of its independence from political pressures, the quality of policy formulation and implementation, and the credibility of the government's commitment to such policies.' The regulatory quality measure reflects perceptions 'of the ability of the government to formulate and implement sound policies and regulations that permit and promote private sector development'; rule of law 'the extent to which agents have confidence in and abide by the rules of society, and in particular the quality of contract enforcement, property rights, the police, and the courts, as well as the likelihood of crime and violence'; and control of corruption 'the extent to which public power is exercised for private gain, including both petty and grand forms of corruption, as well as "capture" of the state by elites and private interests' (Kaufmann et al., 2011). Taken together in a composite, researchers have asserted that these measures are the most robust single indicator of formal institutional development (Li and Zahra, 2012), although other indicators based on different survey databases have also been utilized in related literatures (Hoskisson et al., 2013).

Li and Zahra (2012) identified two informal institutions that influence venture capital activity: uncertainty avoidance and collectivism. These national cultural measures were developed in Hofstede (2001). Uncertainty avoidance is defined as 'the extent to which the members of a culture feel threatened by uncertain or unknown situations' (Hofstede, 2001, p. 113). Li and Zahra (2012) argue that in societies with higher levels of uncertainty avoidance, higher risk premiums are likely to be required by venture capitalists or these actors may seek to make less risky investments. Hofstede (2001) defines collectivism as follows: 'Individualism pertains to societies in which the ties between individuals are loose . . . as its opposite (collectivism) pertains to societies in which people from birth onwards are integrated into strong, cohesive in-groups' (p. 51). Collectivist societies rely more on informal relationships and less on formal institutions to regulate opportunistic behavior, limiting the development of formal institutions, raising transactions costs and restricting access to investment opportunities for investors not part of in-groups (Li and Zahra, 2012). Thus, higher levels of uncertainty avoidance and collectivism are argued to reduce levels of venture capital activity (Li and Zahra, 2012). This chapter argues that the same logic can be applied to angel investing activity.

Li and Zahra (2012) demonstrate that the informal institutions of uncertainty avoidance and collectivism moderate the influence of formal institutions. Uncertainty avoidance and collectivism are measured for a number of African countries by Hofstede (2014).[2] Based on these measures, Table 11.1 suggests the institutional diversity across the continent that may have an impact on angel investing activity.[3]

Several very preliminary conclusions can be reached from studying the data in Table 11.1:

1. Angel activity can exist in economies that have very angel-unfriendly formal institutions. Angola, Ethiopia, Nigeria and Sierra Leone are all examples of economies that have shown evidence of angel investing, but where formal institutions are amongst the weakest

*Table 11.1 Institutional measures and angel activity in sub-Saharan Africa*

| Economy | Informal institutional development | | Formal institutional development[a] (based on Li and Zahra, 2012) | Significant venture capital activity? (Li and Zahra, 2012) | Evidence of angel activity? |
|---|---|---|---|---|---|
| | Uncertainty avoidance | Collectivism (100 – individualism) | | | |
| Angola | 60 | 82 | −3.04 | | X |
| Burkina Faso | 45 | 89 | −0.88 | | X |
| Cape Verde | 40 | 80 | 1.02 | | |
| Ethiopia | 45 | 84 | −2.35 | | X |
| Ghana | 55 | 89 | −0.10 | X | X |
| Kenya | 40 | 78 | −1.76 | X | X |
| Malawi | 40 | 72 | −0.89 | | |
| Mozambique | 44 | 85 | −0.83 | | |
| Namibia | 36 | 72 | 0.74 | | |
| Nigeria | 45 | 72 | −2.78 | X | X |
| Senegal | 45 | 78 | −0.58 | | |
| Sierra Leone | 40 | 84 | −2.32 | X | X |
| South Africa | 39 | 31 | 0.82 | X | X |
| Tanzania | 40 | 78 | −1.10 | X | |
| Zambia | 40 | 66 | −1.07 | X | |

*Note:* [a] These measures have been updated to include data from 1996 to 2012.

*Source:* Hofstede (2014); Kauffman et al. (2007).

in the contemporary world. Angels use a variety of strategies to overcome these environmental challenges. For example, in Nigeria angel investors have formed a club that is backed by the Lagos state governor (*The Economist*, 2012b). In Angola at least one Portugal-domiciled angel investor has been active, suggesting that cross-border angel investment may in some instances mitigate the risks of angel-unfriendly formal institutional environments.

2. Angel investing can also operate in economies with very angel-unfriendly informal institutions. Very high levels of collectivism, such as exist in Ghana, do not seem to deter the formation of formal angel alliances, nor do high levels of uncertainty avoidance, such as found in Angola. This conclusion is consistent with other research showing that significant levels of new business creation can occur in economies with high levels of uncertainty avoidance (Khanna, 2008).

3. Angel investing activity appears to exist in economies where significant venture capital activity has not yet developed. Angola, Burkina Faso and Ethiopia are examples of this outcome. Of course, these conclusions are based on anecdotal evidence and need to be confirmed by more rigorous data collection.

### 11.2.3 A Typology of Institutions and Angel Investing

Li and Zahra (2012) found that higher levels of formal institutional development are associated with higher levels of venture capital activity. However, this relationship is weaker in countries with informal institutional development that is relatively unfriendly to venture capital, specifically those with higher levels of uncertainty avoidance and higher levels of collectivism. To the extent that angel investing in Africa responds to institutional influences in the same manner as venture capital investing does, these findings suggest that angel investing levels can be divided by country into four possible categories (ranked from most to least attractive for angel investing) along two dimensions: (high-low) formal institutional levels and (high-low) informal institutional levels.

Table 11.2 depicts how selected African countries might be classified.

Based on this typology, we would expect the highest levels of angel activity (measured by angel investments/GDP or angel investments/population) in the high formal-high informal quadrant (South Africa),

*Table 11.2 Predicted levels of African angel investing activity based on institutional conditions*

| | High formal institutional levels | Low formal institutional levels |
|---|---|---|
| High informal institutional levels | South Africa | None |
| Low informal institutional levels | Cape Verde<br>Ghana<br>Namibia | Angola<br>Burkina Faso<br>Ethiopia<br>Kenya<br>Malawi<br>Mozambique<br>Nigeria<br>Senegal<br>Sierra Leone<br>Tanzania<br>Zambia |

followed by those in the high formal-low informal quadrant (Cape Verde, Ghana and Namibia), then the low formal-high informal quadrant (none) and finally the low formal-low informal quadrant (Angola, Burkina Faso, Ethiopia, Kenya, Malawi, Mozambique, Nigeria, Senegal, Sierra Leone, Tanzania and Zambia).

This typology assumes that the institutional influence on angel and venture capital investing are similar and that informal institutions moderate the impact of formal institutions. It is possible that these assumptions are incorrect. Institutions may influence angel and venture capital investing differently, in part because angel investing may be less sensitive to formal institutional quality than venture capital investing given its more informal nature. Also, as has been argued in the venture capital literature, it is also possible that: (1) formal institutions may be a dominant influence (Lerner and Tåg, 2013); (2) informal institutions can substitute for unfriendly formal institutions (Bruton and Ahlstrom, 2003; Scheela and Jittrapanun, 2012); or (3) weak institutions may not necessarily be a barrier to economic activity (Allen et al., 2005), such as angel investing.

## 11.3 HAVE ANGELS EMERGED IN AFRICA, HOW LARGE IS THE MARKET AND HOW HAS IT EVOLVED?

Angel investing exists, but it is hard to argue that – with the possible exception of South Africa – an active market has formed yet in most sub-Saharan African economies. Moreover, no formal academic studies have been conducted on this phenomenon to date.

What do we know? First, high levels of informal investing activity across a number of African economies and results from other emerging economies suggest that angel investing – a subset of informal investing – may be more significant than current data suggest. For example, a recent study from North Africa identified significant local business angel investment in local firms that completed initial public offerings (Hearn, 2014), suggesting that angel investing may be significant in sub-Saharan Africa as well. Second, in South Africa an important part of angel investing activity may be represented by 'super angels.' 'Super angels' have been defined in the US context as 'angel investors who have the capacity to invest large sums of their own money (in excess of several hundred thousand dollars U.S. per year, year after year)' (Sudek et al., 2011, p. 2). Third, a wide variety of both regional and economy-specific angel portals are now emerging. Fourth, limited evidence suggests that angel investment contracts are

*Table 11.3 Percentage of 18–64 population who have personally provided funds for a new business, started by someone else, in the past three years*

| Country | 2010 | 2011 | 2012 | 2013 | 2013 improvement-driven opportunity early stage entrepreneurial activity |
|---|---|---|---|---|---|
| Angola | 16.0 | | 24.7 | 24.8 | 8.9 |
| Botswana | | | 7.8 | 10.4 | 10.9 |
| Ethiopia | | | 4.1 | | |
| Ghana | 20.6 | | 17 | 15.4 | 11.4 |
| Malawi | | | 12.7 | 14.1 | 8.3 |
| Namibia | | | 11.0 | | |
| Nigeria | | | 13.5 | 11.6 | 20.9 |
| South Africa | 3.0 | 2.5 | 1.8 | 2.0 | 3.3 |
| Uganda | 26.3 | | 25.9 | 25.6 | 12.0 |
| Zambia | 18.8 | | 13 | 14.8 | 14.8 |

*Source:* Global Entrepreneurship Monitor Consortium (2014).

somewhat different than those observed in the UK or USA. We elaborate on these preliminary findings below.

### 11.3.1 Survey Data on African Informal and Angel Investing

While angel investing is only a subset of informal investing activity, and may have different characteristics than this broader activity, data on informal investing may still give us a general sense of the potential scope of angel activity. Table 11.3 provides background data on African informal investing.

These figures suggest that across sub-Saharan Africa informal investing is composed of different proportions of angel and other types of informal investing. In general, we would expect that angel investors would focus on opportunity-oriented entrepreneurs, as they are more likely to have growth prospects providing adequate investment returns. In some countries informal investing appears to be predominantly directed toward firms that are necessity-oriented (Angola, Malawi and Uganda). At the other extreme, Nigeria has a much higher percentage of opportunity-driven entrepreneurs than available informal investing. A third category of countries (Botswana, South Africa and Zambia) has a relative balance between opportunity-oriented entrepreneurs and informal investing. In comparison to other African countries, South Africa's low level of informal

*Table 11.4 Estimated number of angel investors, selected countries, 2013*

| Country | Estimated number of angel investors (000s) |
|---|---|
| Angola | 84 |
| Botswana | 10 |
| Ethiopia | 360 |
| Ghana | 111 |
| Malawi | 61 |
| Namibia | 10 |
| Nigeria | 657 |
| South Africa | 255 |
| Uganda | 129 |
| Zambia | 53 |

*Source:* For population, http://www.worldbank.org.

investing reflects its relatively low level of early stage entrepreneurial activity (10.6 percent of the labor force in 2013), and its well-developed formal financial sector. Both of these factors are likely to reduce demand for informal financing, including angel investing.

What percentage of informal investing in Africa might be angel investing? Based on GEM data, Aidis et al. (2008) found that approximately 0.8 percent of Brazil's adult population were business angels over a three-year period. While Brazil is a significantly larger emerging economy than those in Africa, a comparison of it to African economies is the only available rough benchmark for the numbers of angel investors. If this percentage were applied in sub-Saharan Africa, Table 11.4 shows estimates of the number of angel investors in selected countries.

These estimates of large numbers of angel investors in sub-Saharan Africa can be contrasted with how little we know about these investors, their activities and characteristics (see Section 11.7 below for a suggested research agenda). Since few African angel investors are reported to be part of an angel group or network, these estimates suggest that much angel activity is conducted by individual investors. The large estimated numbers of angel investors in Nigeria, Ethiopia and South Africa also suggest that these economies may become hubs for angel investing activity in the region.

Studies based on the GEM's databases provide the most rigorous survey to date of informal investing activity. While informal investing is a much broader phenomenon than angel investing, these studies may help give us some general characteristics shaping the business angel landscape. As noted earlier, GEM defines informal investing as any investments made in startups other than the investors' own businesses, excluding investments in stocks and mutual funds (Reynolds et al., 2003). We also have reliable survey data on informal investing from Uganda, which has participated in GEM periodically since 2003. In the most recent GEM study (Namatovu et al., 2010), business angels in the Ugandan context are defined as 'adults who provided funds for new business in the last 3 years' (p. 18). In 2010, 27.2 percent of Ugandan adults (approximately 4.5 million individuals) were identified as angels, a figure that has grown steadily from 13.2 percent of the adult population in 2003;[4] 72.3 percent of these investments were in amounts of USD 88 or less, 24 percent were between USD 88 and USD 438, and 3.7 percent were larger than USD 438; 63 percent of the investors surveyed in this study funded relatives, while 33 percent invested in friends or neighbors, suggesting that the bulk of the identified activity is informal rather than classic business angel investing.

### 11.3.2 Angel Investing in South Africa

Data on angel investing is most developed for South Africa. Using GEM's Adult Population Survey data, Bygrave (2006) measured the scope of this activity across 42 economies, including one African economy – South Africa. Reflecting a relatively low level of startup activity, a little more than 2 percent of South African adults (equal to approximately 620,000 adults in 2006) were identified as active informal investors. This compares to an average of 4 percent of the adult population across the surveyed economies. South African informal investment is estimated at 1 percent of GDP, or USD 2.61 billion in 2006, compared with an average of 1.5 percent across the surveyed countries. South African informal investors invest a little less than USD 5000/investor/per year, typical for an economy with its GDP/capita. Average startup capital requirements in South Africa are a bit more than USD 20,000, again typical for its level of development. A significant early stage funding gap exists, given that approximately 14 percent of nascent South African startups can be funded with available informal investment resources.

These findings are complemented by a more recent – and less rigorous – survey commissioned by the South African Venture Capital and Private Equity Association (Lamprecht and Swart, 2010). In the course of studying the impact of venture capital in South Africa, this study also collected data on angel investing activity over the period 1998–2010; 48 angel investments totaling approximately USD 18.5 million were identified by this survey as having occurred during this period, resulting in an average investment size of approximately USD 384,000 and accounting for 22 percent of venture capital transactions. The large difference between this average angel and informal investment sizes is noteworthy and may reflect the fact that these data were obtained from angel investors that are linked to venture capital funds. The number of angel investments has increased gradually from 1/year in 1998–2000 to 4–8/year in 2008–10, and are much smaller in number than would be expected, given an estimated 255,000 angel investors as noted earlier – 38 percent of the identified angel investments were in technology industries, 11 percent in lifestyle industries and the remainder in other industries. The angels identified in this survey may be 'super angels.'

The South African angels identified in Lamprecht and Swart (2010) had a variety of characteristics – 35 percent were involved with an entrepreneurial startup, 24 percent were engaged in other business activities and 12 percent had an investment background. The largest number (40 percent) were aged 31–44 at the time they were active angel investors, while 30 percent were 45–59, 20 percent were 60 years or older and 10 percent were under 30 years in age; 75 percent of the surveyed angels indicated that return on investment was their primary objective for this activity, while 13 percent were angels primarily to mentor others and 6 percent invested to help out family or friends.

## 11.4 HOW DOES THE AFRICAN ANGEL MARKET OPERATE?

### 11.4.1 The Emergence of African Angel Portals

Beyond the survey findings of informal and angel investing described above, we also have a wide variety of less formal evidence suggesting the scope of angel investing in sub-Saharan Africa. These data are detailed below.

Many of these activities represent different types of angel portals, which represent the bulk of the business angel market. These portals are multifaceted angel organizations that 'represent how entrepreneurs find potential investors, how business angels find and screen deals, how they syndicate into small groups to make an investment and how business angels interact within the larger angel market' (Sohl, 2007, p.348). These portals can be grouped into six types: matching networks (business introduction services); facilitators (event planners); informal angel groups (membership-based where members perform many back office functions); formal angel alliances (larger member groups than informal groups and greater visibility); electronic networks (Internet-based matching); and collections of individual investors (Sohl, 2007). Based on the limited available data, the African angel portals are categorized preliminarily below.

**Regional portals**

VC4Africa (electronic network, www.vc4africa.biz) is a crowdfunding initiative connecting entrepreneurs and investors building innovative new ventures in Africa. Founded in 2007, this website listed 911 new ventures seeking angel financing as of March 2014. This site also identified 26 angel investors domiciled in Africa, including ten in Kenya, six in South Africa, four in Nigeria, three in Ghana and one each in Sierra Leone, Uganda and Zimbabwe. Angel Africa List (formal angel alliance, www.angelafrica.net) was established in May 2013 and seeks to provide a pan-African angel network for early stage firms; according to media reports, approximately 60 individuals are involved in its launch. AngelList (electronic network, https://angel.co) is a similar global platform and reports 50 investors invested in 432 African startups.

VC4Africa has been a useful vehicle for matching some African startups with angel investors, as Nancy Wang, co-founder of M-Kazi, relates:

> I came across VC4Africa on Twitter one day and saw that they connected angel investors with startups in sub-Saharan Africa, which couldn't have been more perfect. After an initial Skype call with one of their founders, Saskia Reus, M-Kazi entered into a contest to enter into a VC4A booster program where we would receive 10 weeks of training on building our investor package and then subsequent media exposure to attract angel interest. We were selected out of 1000 startups to participate in this program. I had no idea how to structure an investor package, construct financial projections, structure the investment (in terms of how much equity to give up for how much money and debt or convertible debt financing options) and produce a written product that would appropriately reflect the ingenuity of our product, its appropriateness for the Kenyan market and the competency of the team. Through a series of 10 weekly Skype calls, VC4A taught me how to do this.

However, such online networks are not for everyone, as Wang describes:

> They [VC4A] charge a 2% success fee, though that may have changed now. They worked very well for us, but not for Penda Health who did not receive a single lead from them. I think they work better for tech startups . . .

In the case of Kenya, M-Kazi's experience in identifying angel investors is related by Nancy Wang:

> We only talked to two investors, one being Jerome Kisting of Baobab Capital and the other eVenture Africa Fund. We successfully received offers from both investors, but ultimately decided to go with Jerome Kisting for USD 50K of equity investment because his terms were much more generous. By the end of the process, I came to realize that I possessed more skills in the way of fund raising than most entrepreneurs in the startup community in Kenya. Most entrepreneurs, especially young techies who were fresh university graduates,

did not know how to structure the deals and often surrendered far more equity than we did to predatory VCs.

Aside from M-Kazi, dozens of Kenyan tech startups have received angel investment. To some extent, angel investing and startup accelerators have blurred together in the region, with 88mph (located in Nairobi and Cape Town) providing both investment via its investor network and a three-month accelerator program.

**Country-specific angel portals: South Africa**

AngelHub (formal angel alliance) has been established as the first angel group in Africa. It is organized into sub-groups based in Cape Town and Johannesburg (OECD, 2011). Formed in September 2011, AngelHub's investors have concluded three investments as of February 2012, including in a cloud-based small and medium-sized enterprise (SME) management system and wine-oriented app. This network's target investment range is USD 132,000–1,320,000 (Carstens, 2012).

AngelHub receives an average of 50 deals/month, of which 20 are selected for initial screening. Of these, AngelHub performs due diligence on ten transactions. AngelHub's goal is to position at least five startups to pitch to their network of 30 angels every 90 days. In collaboration with the University of Cape Town's Graduate School of Business, AngelHub offers a course on early stage investment to some of the startups that approach it for financing. AngelHub receives 25–30 percent of its funding from the Industrial Development Corporation of South Africa and corporate strategic partners. AngelHub also receives an option to acquire up to 5 percent of the equity in startups that it supports (Unsal, 2013).

Other examples of angel investment activity in South Africa include www.investmentnetwork.co.za, Disa's experience (noted above), angel investments reported by media outlets, for example, http://ventureburn.com/2013/06/the-most-comprehensive-guide-to-the-sa-startup-landscape-ever-resource/ and examples provided by the private equity firm Ethos. An Angel Fair was held in Johannesburg in September 2013.

**Other country-specific angel portals**

- Nigeria: the Lagos Angel Network (LAN, formal angel alliance) was established in 2011 and has 15 members (*The Economist*, 2012b). LAN was backed by the Lagos Innovation Advisory Council, which was established by the Lagos state governor. In May 2013 the network held its first pitch competition, in which five startups in the web application development competed for angel investment. The network expects investors to commit USD 6000/year to its investment pool (Okonji, 2013).

- Ghana: the Ghana Angel Investors Network (formal angel alliance) was founded in 2011 by the government's Venture Capital Trust Fund. Abor and Biekpe (2006) report evidence of angel investing activity in Ghanaian export firms.

### 11.4.2 Some Conclusions

The previous two sections have examined what we know about the African angel market and how it operates. Angel investing has emerged as a significant entrepreneurial financing activity in sub-Saharan Africa. The market is large, likely involving at least one million investors across the region, some of whom operate through various portals, groups and networks. Based on North African evidence (Hearn, 2014), it seems likely that relatively wealthy local business angels have invested in firms that have subsequently completed an initial public offering. Cross-border and 'double bottom line' angel investing have been observed, in addition to traditional bilateral angel investment activity between startups and individual local investors. The angel-unfriendly formal institutional environment in many African economies does not seem to be a deterrent to angel investment. However, most of our evidence for these conclusions is either anecdotal or circumstantial. Our conclusions are necessarily speculative, until rigorous academic studies – both cross-sectional and longitudinal – are conducted.

A principal challenge in understanding the African angel market and its operation is to tease out the differences in the African context between angel investing and other forms of informal investment. It may be quite challenging to clearly demarcate arm's length angel investing from informal investment provided by related parties. At least in part, this research will require a clearer understanding of how Africa's informal institutions influence angel investing activity. These influences may include general factors like uncertainty avoidance and collectivism, but the specific elements of Africa's various collectivist traditions and how they affect angel investing seem to be central considerations.

## 11.5 HOW ARE AFRICAN BUSINESS ANGELS SIMILAR TO ANGLO-AMERICAN ANGELS? HOW ARE THEY DIFFERENT?

As described by one observer, African startups seeking angel financing face similar challenges to startups elsewhere, including financial literacy (preparing investor packages and structuring/negotiating deals), finding the right investment partner and limited general business skills. Angel investors also face challenges that are similar to those in the USA or the UK, including the quality of early stage firms (good ideas, but too few good founding teams), an inability of these firms to bring good product ideas to market, startups lacking insufficient business development capacity, few exit opportunities for angel investments (illiquid initial public offering and buyout markets) and the emergence of 'double bottom line' or impact investing as a segment. Angel investors in Africa play a 'spray and pray' game, in which they invest in many startups, provide follow-up investment for a few successful investees and write off the majority of investments.

The largest difference between African and Anglo-American angel investing is likely the institutional environment in which this activity takes place. In general, formal institutions are weaker across sub-Saharan Africa than they are in either the USA or the UK, with the possible exception of South Africa. Consequently, angel investors in Africa cannot rely on investment contracts as heavily as they might in the USA or the UK. Africa's relatively weak formal institutional environment is not compensated for by angel-friendly informal institutions, such as relatively low levels of either uncertainty avoidance or collectivism.

M-Kazi's experience in working with angel investors in Kenya may indicate some of the ways in which angel investing is different from the USA or the UK. Nancy Wang said:

> Angel investors who are interested in investing in Kenyan tech startups have a large risk appetite. This often means that they don't really expect the money back and see the experience as a learning one . . . It seems that when angels invest their personal money, at least in our experience, they do not offer much time or expertise to help the business grow . . . While individual angels aren't very hands-on, they give entrepreneurs more creative sovereignty and the room to make mistakes and learn quickly.

There may also be significant differences across sub-Saharan Africa in terms of the types of startups that are likely to make successful angel investment targets, as Wang described:

> One friend of mine did a consultancy gig where she researched the most successful startups in East and West Africa. In East Africa, the successful ones

are led by expatriates. In West Africa, the successful companies are led by Nigerians.

Angel investment contracts in Africa may also be significantly different than those observed elsewhere. Kelly and Hay (2003) identified five features of investment contracts between business angels and startups in the UK that were considered non-negotiable and very common: (1) veto rights by investors over acquisitions/divestitures; (2) prior approval for strategic plans and budgets; (3) restrictions on management's ability to issue share options; (4) non-compete contracts from founders upon termination of their employment from the startup; and (5) restrictions on the ability to raise additional debt or equity.

While a survey of investment contracts between investors and African startups is not within the scope of this chapter, one contract believed to be typical of such contracts was reviewed and found to be significantly looser in structure than those surveyed by Kelly and Hay. Specifically: (1) the angel investor did not have veto rights over acquisitions or divestitures; (2) the investor did not require prior approval for strategic plans and budgets; (3) management was not restricted from share option issuance; (4) founders were prohibited from being employed by a competitor for three years following employment termination; and (5) no restrictions to limit new debt or equity issuance were in place.

In this example, the angel investor structured its minority investment as a cross-border equity holding in an African startup. In determining the pre-money valuation, the founders prepared projections using industry averages and predicted revenues and costs before the product was launched. These features of the investment contract were not significantly different than angel investments observed in developed economies.

A final significant difference is the relative absence of local or international venture capital to fund African startups after they have received angel investment. Significant venture capital activity has been observed to date in only a handful of African economies, including Ghana, Kenya, Nigeria, Sierra Leone, South Africa, Tanzania and Zambia (Li and Zahra, 2012).

## 11.6 GOVERNMENT POLICY IN SUPPORT OF ANGEL MARKET DEVELOPMENT

Government support for angel investing remains very limited across sub-Saharan Africa. One South African government study of SME access to finance recognized the importance of angel investing and recommended tax incentives for such activity (Falkena et al., 2002). The proposed incentives would allow angel investors to write off any investment losses against their income. To date, no tax credit programs targeted at angels have been established.

M-Kazi in Kenya found that government policy hindered its development, as Wang relates:

> For mobile tech startups the telecom regulatory environment and business environment is a MAJOR issue. Safaricom has a near monopoly in Kenya and largely regulates the prices as well as limits the range of products that private companies can put forth on their network. For example, their bulk premium SMSs are prohibitively expensive for many mobile tech services put forth by startups.

More broadly, government policy in support of angel market development can be related to both formal and informal institutional development. Improvements in formal institutions as measured by improvements in voice and accountability, increases in political stability and reductions in violence, enhanced regulatory quality, strengthened rule of law and better control of corruption are likely to lead to increases in angel investing activity.

Have such improvements taken place? The record is mixed. When using the formal institutional composite as a measure over the period from 1996 to 2012, eight of the economies listed earlier in this chapter experienced improvement (Angola, Burkina Faso, Cape Verde, Ethiopia, Ghana, Sierra Leone, Tanzania and Zambia), four experienced little or no change (Malawi, Mozambique, Nigeria and Senegal) and three saw a decline in formal institutional development (Kenya, Namibia and South Africa). The three largest sub-Saharan African economies – Nigeria, South Africa and Kenya – did not make significant progress. These results occurred despite the general decrease in political violence on the continent over this period. Institutional improvements over which government policy has the most direct control – government effectiveness, regulatory quality and rule of law – have generally improved over this period, albeit modestly.

Improvements in the formal institutional environment across sub-Saharan Africa are likely to lead to increased individualism and hence increased angel activity. Government policy can also improve the informal institutional environment for angel investing through initiatives to reduce uncertainty avoidance. Uncertainty avoidance is a learned trait (Li and Zahra, 2012), hence government policy that promotes education about how to embrace uncertainty and ambiguity in economic life could have a significant effect on angel investing – and new venture creation – over time. This author is not aware of any such initiatives at present.

## 11.7 RESEARCH AGENDA

We have found in this chapter that business angel activity in sub-Saharan Africa may be significant, but it is not well understood. To date, little academic attention has been directed to the study of this phenomenon. As in other domains where angel investing exists, there is an urgent need for more – and more accurate – data on all aspects of African angel investing, particularly outside South Africa. The study of this phenomenon in the African context has the potential to transform our understanding of angel investing, as has been the case in other disciplines (Bates et al., 1993). Such research can also respond to recent calls for increasing contextualization of entrepreneurship research (Welter, 2011; Zahra and Wright, 2011). Much of what we do know about African angel investing is restricted to technology-based startups, which represent a small percentage of economic activity on the continent.

But why study angel investing in Africa in the first place? Africa provides a unique research setting likely to provide important theoretical insights about angel investing for five reasons:

- Our absence of knowledge about this phenomenon in general represents a powerful reason to study it in greater detail. Unlike in either the USA or Europe, it remains unclear if African angel investing is economically significant. We still know very little about the volume of money invested by business angels in Africa, the size and stage of investments being made, the extent to which angels add value in the African context and, if so, how, and the degree of investment by local investors as compared to cross-border investment and how the two activities may vary, if at all.
- Economic development is often stopped in developing economies by dominant elite coalitions who block innovations that can erode the rents on which social order depends (North et al., 2009). These elites are especially well entrenched in Africa, and the study of how innovators skirt their dead hand to launch scalable new ventures may help us to gain a better understanding of new venture activity in developed economies, where such elites are again reasserting their dominance (Wolin, 2010). As members of these elites considering investments in local startups, African angels face investment decisions driven as much by politics as they are by economics.
- African economic history has been characterized by extreme, but temporary, shocks in the form of commodity booms and busts, famines and migrations (Collier, 1993). These shocks shape and reshape the opportunity set that entrepreneurs can either discover

or create in ways that remain dimly understood. We know, for example, that demographic, technological and socio-economic changes yield discoverable new venture opportunities (Shane, 2003), but shocks – as a particular type of change – have not been well studied in entrepreneurship to date. Yet this shock-prone nature of economies remains common across all economies – developed, emerging and developing (Reinhart and Rogoff, 2009). African entrepreneurs have proven themselves adept at exploiting the opportunities created by this dynamism (*The Economist*, 2012a). How have angel investors adapted to this unstable macro environment?

- Africa's institutional diversity lends itself to comparative research strategies that are 'the economist's best substitute for the controlled experiment' (Collier, 1993, p. 58). Such settings are also ideal for extending old theories and developing new ones. As we shall see, angel investing varies significantly by economy in sub-Saharan Africa, offering the opportunity to tease out some of the institutional drivers of the phenomenon.
- Resources for entrepreneurship in Africa often are raised in a social environment, where social networks and family ties are important. Such a tradition may yield important insights for business angels in Western environments.

Research on angel investing began by focusing on the phenomenon of business angels investing in startups, seeking to understand the characteristics of business angels and the significance of the phenomenon. More recently, studies have begun to move from description to theory-building, for example, Florin et al. (2013). A similar evolution in research can be anticipated for African angel investing. Some possible research questions that could be pursued are as follows:

- Is angel investing a significant phenomenon in Africa, and what are its characteristics? Shane (2008) demonstrated that while angel investors may account for the bulk of startup equity financing, they are relatively few in number. We still have no accurate picture of how large the total stock of angel investment is across sub-Saharan Africa, the annual levels of investing activity and the proportion of angel investing within the larger informal investing phenomenon. We also need a much clearer picture of where 'friends and family' informal investing ends in Africa, and more arm's length angel investing begins. For example, to what extent are investments made by an investor in a startup with founders from the same tribe or ethnicity – but not the same family – to be considered angel investments? In what ways – if any – are these types of angels different from angel investments in other countries?

- What is an ABC (attitudes, behavior and characteristics) description of business angels in Africa?
- What are the similarities and differences in angel investing between sub-Saharan African and other emerging economies from which we have data, such as Southeast Asia (Scheela and Isidro, 2009; Scheela and Jittrapanun, 2012) and China (Li et al., 2014)?
- How do these investors structure their investments? For example, to what extent is debt used, rather than equity? What internal rates of return (IRRs) do angel investors seek in Africa, and what are the implications of these targets for how they structure their investments? To what extent is post-investment monitoring and support important in African angel investing, and are successful angel investments there more likely to provide such monitoring or support?
- In what ways do Africa's distinctive institutional environments shape angel investing activity? To what extent are angels a part of their economy's dominant elite coalition? How does the dominance of elite coalitions shape the types of investments angels pursue? In what ways – if any – have Africa's shock-prone economies influenced angel investing? How do differences in Africa's formal and informal institutions influence the level of angel investing activity?
- To what extent are African business angels effectual, and, if they are, do effectual angels in Africa make better investments? Wiltbank et al. (2006) demonstrated that effectual angels have lower levels of investment failure than those who rely on prediction in investment decision-making, while not experiencing a lower level of investment success.
- To what extent do connections between angels and venture capitalists (both domestic and foreign) exist in sub-Saharan Africa? How do these connections – or the lack of them – influence the emergence of angel investing? How does the recent increase in foreign private equity investment in Africa (*The Economist*, 2015b) influence these connections?
- How are angel investing markets organized in Africa?
- Given the dominance of strong personal ties in Africa, what influence do levels of generalized trust have on the likelihood that an angel will invest in a local startup? Kwon and Arenius (2008) suggest that residents of countries with high levels of generalized trust are more likely to invest in an entrepreneur with whom he has a weak

personal tie than with an investor from a country with low levels of generalized trust.

## 11.8 CONCLUSIONS

Angel investing in Africa may be a significant phenomenon, but as yet we know little concrete or specific about it. This chapter has attempted to sketch out the contours of our knowledge to date and suggest some directions for future research. The recent increase in GDP growth rates in several African economies, combined with a slow reduction in levels of violence across the continent, has contributed to an increase in entrepreneurial activity. To the extent that African economies follow patterns observed in the USA, UK and Europe, we can expect that angel investing will increase as a result. However, it seems unlikely that such activity will simply mimic that seen in developed economies. As African angels diffuse angel investing practices from elsewhere, they also will adapt these practices to local conditions and perhaps re-export the 'new and improved' product to Western societies, much as those innovators who brought us microfinance and products derived from *jugaad* innovation practices have done.

National levels of angel investing activity are likely to continue to vary, in part influenced by formal and informal institutions. While relatively high levels of angel activity are likely to continue in South Africa, the most interesting phenomenon to watch will be how angels in economies with angel-unfriendly institutional environments adapt investing practice to local conditions. Of those economies, Nigeria seems most likely to be an important laboratory for experimentation around this issue. The size and diversity of Nigeria's economy will likely permit significant stocks of opportunity-oriented entrepreneurs and angel investors (both local, cross-border and, as with India, returning expatriates) to arise and interact.

A significant wild card in African angel development is the role of government policy. If formal institutions improved more than expected and/or if proper angel investing incentives were designed and implemented by governments, then angel investing activity could increase significantly. In that regard, the large and increasing role of Chinese investment in some African economies could play a role. While much of that activity has involved large, state-controlled firms to date, smaller Chinese firms and investors are increasing their activity and may influence the evolution of policy.

Angel investing in Africa is a significant and interesting economic phenomenon in the process of formation. We have much to learn as this phenomenon develops.

# NOTES

1. This chapter focuses on sub-Saharan Africa. It does not consider angel investing in North Africa (Algeria, Egypt, Libya, Mauritania, Morocco, Sudan, Tunisia and Western Sahara).
2. Hofstede (2014) measures individualism, rather than collectivism. Li and Zahra (2012) measure collectivism as 100 – individualism.
3. The countries in Table 11.1 were those for which data on both formal and informal institutional development were available.
4. There is an inconsistency between the 27.2 percent 2010 figure quoted in Namatovu et al. (2010) and the 26.3 percent figure quoted for the same year in Table 11.3 from a 2014 study. These figures are based on different data, hence the discrepancy. The more recent data is more likely to be more accurate.

# REFERENCES

Abor, J. and N. Biekpe (2006), 'How are SMEs financed? Evidence from the Ghanaian nontraditional export sector', *Environment and Planning C: Government and Policy*, **24**(1), 71–81.

Aidis, R., S. Estrin and T. Mickiewicz (2008), 'Institutions and entrepreneurship development in Russia: a comparative perspective', *Journal of Business Venturing*, **23**(6), 656–72.

Allen, F., J. Qian and M. Qian (2005), 'Law, finance, and economic growth in China', *Journal of Financial Economics*, **77**(1), 57–116.

Bates, R.H., V.Y. Mudimbe and J. O'Barr (1993), 'Introduction', in R.H. Bates, V.Y. Mudimbe and J. O'Barr (eds), *Africa and the Disciplines*, Chicago, IL: University of Chicago Press, pp. xi–xiii.

Bruton, G.D. and D. Ahlstrom (2003), 'An institutional view of China's venture capital industry: explaining the differences between China and the west', *Journal of Business Venturing*, **18**(2), 233–59.

Bygrave, W. (2006), *2006 Financing Report*, Wellesley, MA and London: Babson College, London Business School and Kauffman Foundation.

Carstens, M. (2012), 'AngelHub: investors come together to foster startup growth', *Ventureburn*, 17 February, available at http://www.ventureburn.com (accessed 26 March 2014).

Collier, P. (1993), 'Africa and the study of economics', in R.H. Bates, V.Y. Mudimbe and J. O'Barr (eds), *Africa and the Disciplines*, Chicago, IL: University of Chicago Press, pp. 58–82.

*Economist, The* (2012a), 'Parallel players', *The Economist*, 23 June, available at http://www.economist.com (accessed 26 March 2014).

*Economist, The* (2012b), 'Angels in Lagos', *The Economist*, 28 October, available at http://www.economist.com (accessed 26 March 2014).

*Economist, The* (2015a), 'The twilight of the resource curse?', *The Economist*, 10 January, available at http://www.economist.com (accessed 30 January 2015).

*Economist, The* (2015b), 'A sub-Saharan scramble', *The Economist*, 24 January, available at http://www.economist.com (accessed 30 January 2015).

Falkena, H., I. Abedian, M. von Blottnitz et al. (2002), *SMEs' Access to Finance in South Africa: A Supply-side Regulatory Review*, Report by the Task Group of the Policy Board for Financial Services and Regulation, available at http://www.treasury.gov.za (accessed 26 March 2014).

Florin, J., R. Dino and M.N. Huvaj (2013), 'Research on angel investing: a multilevel framework for an emerging domain of inquiry', *Venture Capital*, **15**(1), 1–27.

Global Entrepreneurship Monitor Consortium (2014), *Key Indicators*, available at http://www.gemconsortium.org (accessed 26 March 2014).

Gordon, J. (2014), 'A stage model of venture philanthropy', *Venture Capital*, **16**(2), 85–107.
Graham, F. (2012), 'Filling Africa's technology skills gap', 13 August, available at http://www.bbc.com (accessed 26 March 2014).
Hearn, B. (2014), 'The impact of institutions, ownership structure, business angels, venture capital and lead managers in IPO firm underpricing across North Africa', *Journal of Multinational Financial Management*, **24**, 19–42.
Hofstede, G. (2001), *Culture's Consequences: Comparing Values, Behaviors, Institutions and Organizations Across Nations*, Thousand Oaks, CA: Sage.
Hofstede, G. (2014), 'Cultural tools: country comparison', available at http://www.geert-hofstede.com (accessed 26 March 2014).
Hoskisson, R.E., M. Wright, I. Filatotchev and M.W. Peng (2013), 'Emerging multinationals from mid-range economies: the influence of institutions and factor markets', *Journal of Management Studies*, **50**(7), 1295–321.
Kaufmann, D., A. Kraay and M. Mastruzzi (2007), 'Governance matters VI: aggregate and individual governance indicators 1996–2006', available at http://www.worldbank.org (accessed 26 March 2014).
Kaufmann, D., A. Kraay and M. Mastruzzi (2011), 'The worldwide governance indicators: methodology and analytical issues', *Hague Journal on the Rule of Law*, **3**(2), 220–46.
Kelly, P. and M. Hay (2003), 'Business angel contracts: the influence of context', *Venture Capital*, **5**(4), 287–312.
Khanna, T. (2008), *Billions of Entrepreneurs: How China and India are Reshaping their Futures –and Yours*, Boston, MA: Harvard Business School Press.
Kwon, S.-W. and P. Arenius (2008), 'Nations of entrepreneurs: a social capital perspective', *Journal of Business Venturing*, **25**(3), 315–30.
Lamprecht, S.J. and E. Swart (2010), *2010 SAVCA Venture Solutions VC Survey*, Houghton, South Africa: SAVCA.
Landström, H. (2007), 'Pioneers in venture capital research', in H. Landström (ed.), *Handbook of Research on Venture Capital*, Cheltenham, UK and Northampton, MA, USA: Edward Elgar, pp. 3–65.
Lerner, J. and J. Tåg (2013), 'Institutions and venture capital', *Industrial and Corporate Change*, **22**(1), 153–82.
Li, U. and S.A. Zahra (2012), 'Formal institutions, culture, and venture capital activity: a cross-country analysis', *Journal of Business Venturing*, **27**(1), 95–111.
Li, Y., S. Jiang, D. Long, H. Tang and J. Wu (2014), 'An exploratory study of business angels in China: a research note', *Venture Capital*, **16**(1), 69–83.
Mason, C.M. and R.T. Harrison (2000), 'The size of the informal venture capital market in the United Kingdom', *Small Business Economics*, **15**(2), 137–48.
Mason, C.M. and R.T. Harrison (2008), 'Measuring business angel investment activity in the United Kingdom: a review of potential data sources', *Venture Capital*, **10**(4), 309–30.
Namatovu, R., W. Balunywa, S. Kyejjusa and S. Dawa (2010), *GEM Uganda 2010 Executive Report*, available at http://www.gemconsortium.org (accessed 27 March 2014).
North, D.C. (1990), *Institutions, Institutional Change and Economic Performance*, New York: Cambridge University Press.
North, D.C., J.J. Wallis and B.R. Weingast (2009), *Violence and Social Orders: A Conceptual Framework for Interpreting Recorded Human History*, Cambridge: Cambridge University Press.
OECD (2011), *Financing High-growth Firms: The Role of Angel Investors*, Paris: OECD Publishing.
Okonji, E. (2013), 'Startup entrepreneurs compete for LAN investment support', *This Day*, 6 May.
Reinhart, C.M. and K. Rogoff (2009), *This Time is Different: Eight Centuries of Financial Folly*, Princeton, NJ: Princeton University Press.
Reynolds, P.D., W.D. Bygrave and E. Autio (2003), *Global Entrepreneurship Monitor: Executive Report 2003*, Wellesley, MA and London: Babson College, London Business School and Kauffman Foundation.

Scheela, W. and E.S. Isidro (2009), 'Business angel investing in an emerging Asian economy', *Journal of Private Equity*, **12**(4), 44–56.
Scheela, W. and T. Jittrapanun (2012), 'Do institutions matter for business angel investing in emerging Asian markets?', *Venture Capital*, **14**(4), 289–308.
Scott, W.R. (2008), *Institutions and Organizations: Ideas and Interests*, Thousand Oaks, CA: Sage.
Shane, S. (2003), *A General Theory of Entrepreneurship: The Individual-Opportunity Nexus*, Cheltenham, UK and Northampton, MA, USA: Edward Elgar.
Shane, S. (2008), *Fool's Gold? The Truth Behind Angel Investing in America*, Oxford: Oxford University Press.
Sohl, J.E. (2007), 'The organization of the informal venture capital market', in H. Landström (ed.), *Handbook of Research on Venture Capital*, Cheltenham, UK and Northampton, MA, USA: Edward Elgar, pp. 347–68.
Sudek, R., A. May and R. Wiltbank (2011), 'Angel investing: catalyst for innovation', Unpublished Working Paper, available at http://www.angelresource.org (accessed 20 August 2014).
Unsal, O. (2013), 'An angel at the entrepreneur's table', available at http://www.blogs.worldbank.org/psd (accessed 27 March 2014).
Van Vugt, B. (2012), 'Angel investing in Africa (case study part 1): Canadian investor Jerome Kisting and Kenyan based M-Kazi', available at http://www.vc4africa.biz (accessed 27 March 2014).
Welter, F. (2011), 'Contextualizing entrepreneurship – conceptual challenges and ways forward', *Entrepreneurship Theory and Practice*, **35**(1), 165–84.
Wiltbank, R., S. Read, N. Dew and S.D. Sarasvathy (2006), 'Prediction and control under uncertainty: outcomes in angel investing', *Journal of Business Venturing*, **24**(2), 116–33.
Wolin, S.S. (2010), *Democracy Incorporated: Managed Democracy and the Specter of Inverted Totalitarianism*, Princeton, NJ: Princeton University Press.
Zahra, S.A. and M. Wright (2011), 'Entrepreneurship's next act', *Academy of Management Perspectives*, **25**(4), 67–83.

# 12 Business angels in developing economies: the experience of Latin America*

*Gianni Romaní and Miguel Atienza*

## 12.1 INTRODUCTION

Over recent years, emerging economies such as Latin America are attracting the attention of foreign investors, not only because of the crisis that still persists in some economies in Europe and the United States, but also due to the stability and growth that some Latin American countries have achieved. These countries are heterogeneous in terms of their population, gross domestic product (GDP) per capita, inflation rates and level of development (see Table 12A.1 in the Appendix). There are, however, certain aspects common to all the countries of the region, among which the limited access to financing stands out. According to the World Economic Forum (2012), credit constraint is one of the top ten problems of Latin American economies regarding the creation of new businesses. Furthermore, entrepreneurship is characterized by the predominance of necessity entrepreneurship and the limited number of growth-oriented and innovative ventures (Kelley et al., 2011; Lederman et al., 2014).

The countries of the region are increasingly aware of the importance of entrepreneurship and innovation as engines of economic development and job creation (OECD, 2011). As a result, the majority of Latin American governments are fostering a series of programmes to encourage entrepreneurship, innovation, venture capital and even the creation of business angel networks – BANs[1] (Kantis and Federico, 2012). At the same time, the business class and many high net worth individuals (HNWI) are starting to invest in new enterprises in these countries. Empirical evidence about the importance of angel investors is fundamentally based on the experience of developed countries (Mason and Harrison, 1997; Aernoudt, 1999, 2005; Sohl, 2012).

Generally, the angel investors market is difficult to quantify accurately because most investors prefer to remain anonymous. This problem is even more acute in Latin America because the activity of angel investors is very recent and there is a severe lack of information. As a point of departure, it is important to consider the large differences that currently exist between the United States, Europe and Latin America in terms of the size of the angel investment market. Considering only the visible market, in the United States, where this activity started, there were around 340 angel investor groups in 2009 that invested USD 469 million in 2160 new ventures (OECD, 2011). In Europe, during the same year, there were 400 angel networks that invested USD 383 million in 1500 new ventures (OECD, 2011). In contrast, in Latin America and the Caribbean (LAC), 28 angel investor networks were identified, of which only 20 are operating. These networks invested in 99 new ventures from 2005 to 2011, and the total investment volume reached just USD 26 million (FOMIN/BID, 2013). The angel investment market in Latin America is very incipient, since 70 per cent of these networks have started their activity since 2008.

This chapter aims to fill the gap of information and the scarcity of research related to developing countries, particularly Latin America, where this type of financing could play a significant role in the promotion of innovative and value added business. We analyse the angel investment market indirectly by means of the evolution of angel networks, clubs or non-profit associations where this type of investor becomes more visible. We shall study the cases of Brazil, Chile, Colombia and Mexico considered by Lerner et al. (2013) as having the most developed venture capital ecosystem. We shall also analyse the case of Argentina whose experience is particularly representative of some of the main problems that the region is facing. Our analysis of these countries focuses on the study of their economic and entrepreneurial context, the development of angel investment and their main challenges. This analysis is based on secondary data and interviews with the founders and managers of some active networks across countries and other key informants.

The chapter is organized as follows. The next section gives an overview of the business angels market in Latin America. Sections 12.3 to 12.7 analyse the evolution of angel investment in the selected countries. Section 12.8 analyses the similarities and differences in angel investment across the countries. Finally, in the conclusion, we summarize our main findings and future lines of research.

## 12.2 AN OVERVIEW OF BUSINESS ANGEL[2] MARKETS IN LATIN AMERICA

It is important to notice that the number of members of the networks does not represent the total angel investors existing.[3] An approximation of this information can be obtained from the database of the Global Entrepreneurship Monitor (GEM), which enables identification of the informal investors[4] and more specifically the angel investors, defined as

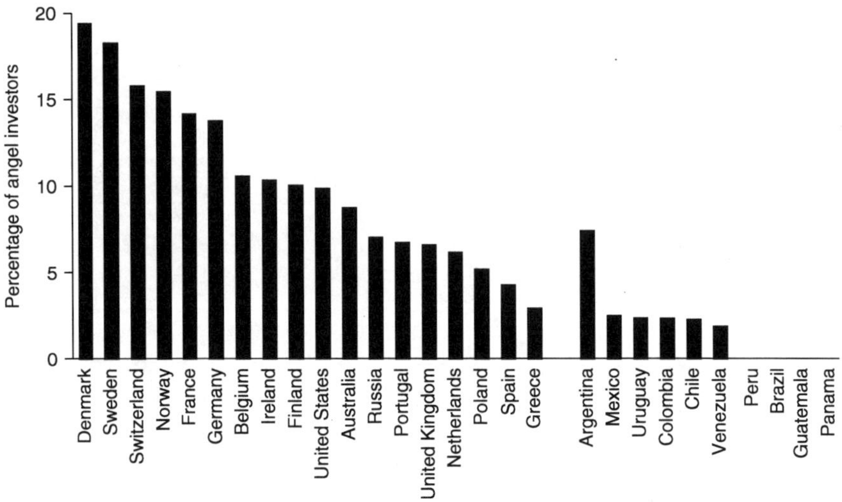


*Source:* Authors based on GEM database, 2011.

*Figure 12.1 Angel investors as a percentage of total informal investors*

individuals who invest at least one dollar in the business of strangers. Figure 12.1 shows angel investors as a percentage of total informal investors in the United States, Europe and LAC. The highest rates are found in Europe, especially the Nordic countries, where informal investors represent more than 10 per cent of total informal investors. In the United States the rate is 9.8 per cent, while in the UK angel investors represent 6.5 per cent of informal investors. With the exception of Argentina, angel investors in the rest of the LAC countries are less than 2.5 per cent of total informal investors. This low percentage of the prevalence of angel investors in the region once again shows the small size of their angel investors market, which manifests not only the emerging nature of this activity but also cultural and institutional differences that we shall analyse below.

Results change slightly when we consider the number of angel investors per 10,000 inhabitants (Figure 12.2). On average, the number of angels is higher in the United States and Europe than in LAC. There are, however, five Latin American countries, namely, Chile, Argentina, Mexico, Colombia and Uruguay, where the number individuals who invest in the business of strangers per 10,000 inhabitants is higher than in many European countries. This result shows that despite the small size of the angel investors market in Latin America, there is a potential number of investors who may become angels if the appropriate conditions are developed.

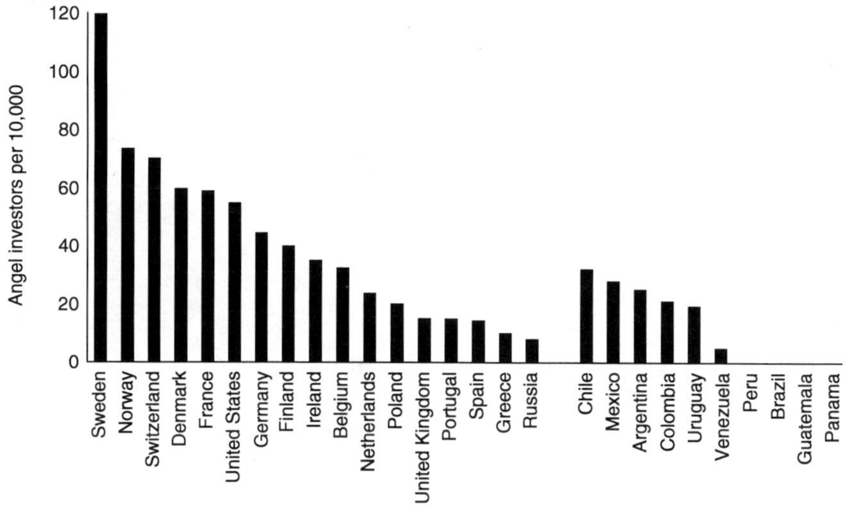


*Source:* Authors based on GEM database, 2011.

*Figure 12.2 Angel investors per 10,000 inhabitants*

The first angel networks in Latin America were created between 2002 and 2005 in Brazil, Chile and Argentina, and later, starting in 2008 in Mexico and in 2010 in Colombia and the rest of the countries in the region. In parallel, between 2005 and 2010 the Multilateral Investment Fund (MIF), a branch of the Interamerican Development Bank (IDB) developed a series of initiatives supporting entrepreneurship in the region, incorporating the creation of BANs in LAC countries. In May 2010, the Latin American Business Angels Association was launched, with the objective of fostering the creation and development of BANs throughout LAC; stimulating the exchange of experiences between the angel investor networks; and promoting the adoption of best practices, among others. However, it has not yet taken off (OECD, 2011). In any case, the interest that developing countries have in entrepreneurship and innovation as engines of economic development has brought angel investment to the political agenda as one of the main sources of financing of early stage activities and adding value to entrepreneurs, particularly innovative ones.

These pioneering efforts in the region have contributed to a timid growth of angel investment. However, the activity of networks is still not well known in that it has not had the expected results either in terms of investments made or the attraction of new investors (FOMIN/BID, 2013; Romaní et al., 2013). Many of the first networks created in Chile,

Argentina, Brazil and Bolivia are no longer active. At the same time, however, new networks have been emerging at a growing rate. The development of this market is quite heterogeneous and varies from country to country (FOMIN/BID, 2013).

In the next five sections, we analyse the evolution of angel investment in the selected countries, with a focus on the economic and entrepreneurial context, the development of angel investment and its main challenges.

## 12.3 ARGENTINA

### 12.3.1 Economic and Entrepreneurial Context

Argentina stands out as a frustrated experience in the development of angel investment despite the existence of a critical mass of entrepreneurs with innovative potential. The macroeconomic instability and lack of a secure institutional framework have been the main obstacles to consolidating this form of financing. The development of the angel market in Argentina was one of the earliest in the region and reached its highest development at the end of the decade of the 1990s, characterized by the strong growth of Internet companies. The start of the decade was marked by considerable foreign investment, benefitted by the policy of privatization of state utilities. By the end of 1997, there was a large presence of international venture capital funds that were looking for local partners. The foreign investors were interested in small companies and many of these investors partnered with local investors, causing a period of intense activity in venture capital investment (Carullo and Vismara, 2006).

From 1998 to 2000, the formal and informal venture capital market experienced a 'short spring' with the success of dot.com companies such as Sitio.com, which opened its capital on the Nasdaq in 1999; and Patagon.com, which was sold to Banco Santander for USD 750 million. The first angel investors appeared, such as Carlos Adamo who financed Office Net, Federico Agardy who financed the start of Patagon.com and Wood Staton who financed Core Security (Gonzalo et al., 2013). These initiatives were a model for other investors. According to Jacobsohn and Carullo (2005), that period had many investors with little experience, without knowledge of the market or the risk of their investments and, in many cases, invested without taking the precautions necessary to strengthen the viability of their projects.

In the mid 1990s, the government approved Law 23.877 on Promotion and Development of Technological Innovation, which gave rise to the creation of a Secretary of Science and Technology (SeCyt). This institution developed various instruments to encourage the creation of new, innovative technology-based businesses such as the 'Programme for Business Incubators and Technological Parks and Poles'. In addition, at the end of the 1990s the government proposed the Bill 25.548, the objective of which was to promote the emergence, development and strengthening of technology-based companies and the creation of a National Venture Capital System. This Bill was intended to facilitate the participation of private investors, favouring formal instruments. It granted public funds to create venture capital funds and established fiscal incentives for investors that operated through these funds. The Bill incorporated the figure of the 'angel investor' and included it among the potential beneficiaries of the fiscal incentives for investment. Unfortunately, the Bill was vetoed by the National Executive Branch, considering it incompatible with the existing constitutional framework and that it could generate duplicate efforts and conflicts between different public institutions (Carullo, 2002, p. 43).

The fall of the Nasdaq starting in March 2000 meant the start of a crisis of the venture capital market, both formal and informal, with a strong reduction of projects and the disappearance of the majority of the investors who supported it. This situation was aggravated by the social and macroeconomic crisis that Argentina underwent from December 2001, which caused a significant reduction in the activity of angel investors and the venture capital funds. According to Carullo (2002), before the crisis there were 41 active funds in the venture capital market, while by mid 2004 only four funds and few active angel investors remained (Jacobsohn, 2009). Pereiro (2001) shows that in those years 48 per cent of Argentine entrepreneurs used only one source of financing, and 36.7 per cent of the sample financed their start-up with personal savings and just 20 per cent used bank financing.

After the 2001 crisis, many initiatives were developed to promote the formation of a technological services market and reinforce the development of the venture capital industry. Most of these public initiatives were developed by the 'Programme of Venture Capital for Science, Technology and Productive Innovation Enterprises' (CREAR-CIT), created in 2002 and whose objective was to develop the venture capital industry, both formal and informal. In 2003, the government renewed the third version of the loan agreement with the IDB to finance a 'Technological Modernization Programme'. This programme included support for angel investors among its lines of action (Ferreira, 2008). Five years later, CREAR-CIT ended and was substituted by a group of different programmes basically oriented towards the promotion of formal venture capital. There have been no public programmes to foster angel investment to date.

The crisis of 2008 once again struck the Argentine economy and informal venture capital activity. However, in recent years, entrepreneurial activity has grown and given angel activity a new boost. Despite the ups and downs of the economy, Argentina has developed an emergent entrepreneurial ecosystem. For example, in Buenos Aires, 'Palermo Valley', founded in 2008 via Twitter, is a non-profit institution that connects the Argentine community with the high-tech business industry, both within Latin America and beyond. According to Essinger (2012), 'today Buenos Aires is bubbling away with activity, with many interesting tech start-ups and established companies, and a top notch talent pool'. In February 2014, the Ministry of Industry, by means of the Secretary of Small and Medium-sized Enterprise (SME), created the programme 'Incubar' to improve the growth and development of new firms using incubators as a way to improve the entrepreneurial ecosystem in the country. Incubated firms have access to non-reinbursable funds up to USD 18,733 to finance their business projects. At the same time, organizations supporting entrepreneurship receive a maximum of USD 375 every month over a period of 90 days as part of the incubating costs, as well as free information on topics such as bussiness plans development, cash flow statements, market research and commercialization. The pilot programme, which started in the last quarter of 2013, supported 39 new firms with subsidies of USD 10,241 on average (Orellana and Contreras, 2014). Despite this programme and many other initiatives oriented to improve the entrepreneurial activity as 'Buenos Aires Emprende', Argentina has lost seven positions in 2009 to 2013 in the dimension 'Entrepreneurial culture and deal opportunities', from 49 to 56 out of 118 countries (see Table 12A.2 in the Appendix) according to the Venture Capital and Private Equity Country Attractiveness Index 2013. It has lost positions in the dimensions related to 'Ease of starting and running a business', 'Simplicity of closing a business' and 'Corporate R&D'. In contrast, the 'Innovation' according to the 'Capacity of innovation' and the 'General index of innovation' has slightly improved from position 71 to 68 (Groh et al., 2013). Economic instability explains this situation, which also affects culture and entrepreneurial activity. In fact, the GEM Argentina report[5] shows that entrepreneurial activity in the early stages declined from 20.8 per cent in 2011 to 15.9 per cent in 2013. At the same time, the perception of good business opportunities in the region has decreased.

### 12.3.2 The Development of Angel Investment

The first BANs were private and appeared in 2005 around the city of Buenos Aires. The Club de Inversionistas Ángeles del IAE – Instituto de Administración de Empresas (Angel Investors Club of the Business

Administration Institute) was formed by a group of six former students of the Business School of the Universidad Austral. The idea was inspired by the angel groups of business schools in the United States, such as the Massachusetts Institute of Technology (MIT) and Stanford. The founders studied the functioning of these clubs, made contact with their members and adapted the model to Argentine characteristics. In 2014, this private initiative had more than 100 members and has invested USD 3.5 million in 23 projects. Its members invest between USD 50,000 and USD 150,000, and can reach USD 500,000 in special cases.

The same year, the Instituto de Emprendimientos Científicos y Tecnológicos (IECyT) (Institute of Scientific and Technological Ventures) was transformed into a civil, non-profit association that acts in the public and private sectors with various programmes for entrepreneurs and investors. In the private sector it manages its own network of investors called the Red de Inversionistas Angeles del IECyt (BAN of the IECyT). There is a low level of activity in this private network. To date, just three investments have been made.

Subsequently, other clubs have been created. There are currently at least three active investors clubs in the city of Buenos Aires: the Club de Inversionistas Angeles del IAE previously mentioned. The Club de Inversionistas EMPREAR has characteristics very similar to previous clubs regarding its target investor's profile, philosophy and goals, but in addition to regular meetings where projects are presented, it organizes training programmes for investors and entrepreneurs. Its investments are from USD 10,000 to USD 100,000. The Club de Inversores Angeles IG is an independent group comprised of 60 qualified investors. They have made more than five investments. There are also two networks: the Red de Inversionistas Angeles del IECyT mentioned above and Improver. According to Jacobsohn (2012), the operation of these networks has been very complex due to the inexperience of the investors, causing strain on the managers as well as on relations with the investors, and they have not achieved the expected results in the majority of cases. It is also known that there are networks operating outside the city of Buenos Aires but it has not been possible to identify them. Nor has it been possible to quantify the total volume of investment in the market, or the number of investments made.

In recent years, some business accelerators have appeared oriented towards the technological sector and that operate with private capital and from multilateral organizations. These include Wayra funded by Telefónica and NXTPLabs with local and international angel investors and the MIF/IDB. Both invest in early stages, with amounts from USD 15,000 to 70,000. Wayra supported more than 20 enterprises in 2012, while

NXTPLabs invested around USD 25,000 in approximately 32 enterprises (Jacobsohn, 2012).

### 12.3.3 Main Challenges

Argentina has had an irregular trajectory in angel investment, with some successful cases. It is one of the few countries in Latin America where activity was flourishing at the end of the 1990s. Although there is experience, the public and private initiatives and those of multilateral organizations in early stage financing have not been able to consolidate an efficient and articulated system for developing a strong angel investors market. The networks that currently operate in Argentina are all private and struggle to survive. They provide various services for entrepreneurs as well as investors, such as courses and workshops oriented towards the venture capital investment process. These services enable them to generate resources to cover their high operating costs. In addition, some have institutional support, whether from a private university or a foundation.

Although the country has the human resources, the entrepreneurial culture, the managerial capabilities and the strength of the scientific and technological system that favour venture capital investment, the current status of the legal situation, fiscal stability and the political and economic situation are the factors that most discourage investments in Argentina. These factors are the main obstacles for the development of angel investment in the country. Public policies to promote venture capital have not had continuity and have centred on venture capital funds, leaving angels aside. The debate on the Law of Technology Based Companies and the National Venture Capital System of 1999 demonstrated the lack of a homogeneous conceptual base among the institutional, public and private actors to establish a venture capital system adapted to Argentine characteristics. The Law approved by Congress established a model of intervention by the public sector that the subsequent veto from the Executive Branch put into question, creating a scenario of marked uncertainty (Carullo, 2002, p. 43).

Jacobsohn (2009) reveals that the actions that investors consider as priorities for developing a formal and informal venture capital market are the establishment of fiscal incentives, the inclusion of the topic of entrepreneurship in undergraduate and postgraduate education and the approval of appropriate legislation for this market. Furthermore, the analysis of Argentina reveals serious limitations in terms of access to and reliability of the information (Jacobsohn and Carullo, 2005).

## 12.4 BRAZIL

### 12.4.1 Economic and Entrepreneurial Context

In recent years, the impact of entrepreneurship not only on employment but also on innovation has become apparent in Brazil, and this is reflected in its efforts to support start-ups and encourage entrepreneurs. For example, the government agency, Financing Agency for Projects and Studies (FINEP), launched a significant project, 'PRIME', in 2009 to support start-ups. It aimed to supply around USD 65,000 to start-ups focused on innovation and to help 10,000 innovative companies over four years, thereby generating ten new jobs for each one directly created by each new company (Ortmans, 2012). In the same vein, the Brazilian government has introduced many incentives to attract business from the rest of the world. Through the *Lei do Bom* (Good Law), the government offers tax incentives to companies oriented towards technological innovation. From 2006 on, many technological parks have been created with the objective of promoting technological innovation that has been financed by their respective federal states, with various fiscal incentives for research and development (R&D).

In 2011, the 'Plano Maior' of Brazil was created, bringing together efforts to foster entrepreneurship and innovation. The objectives of this plan were to increase firms' average expenditure on R&D from 0.59 per cent to 0.9 per cent in 2014; to increase national value added; to increase the knowledge-intensive industry from 30.1 per cent to 31.5 per cent and the number of innovative small and medium-sized enterprises (SMEs) up to 58,000. For these purposes, several measures have been implemented among which the simplification of financing processes and the improvement of the regulation of innovation stand out. In 2013, the Ministry of Science, Technology and Innovation created the programme 'Start-up Brazil' to support techonology-intensive firms. This programme provides almost USD 90,000 in annual grants for R&D, formation and access to investors. Other new programmes are 'Inovativa Brasil' that trains and connects innovative business younger than five years old, and the investment fund Criatec, that provides seed capital to new firms (Orellana and Contreras, 2014).

All these efforts to boost the culture of innovation and entrepreneurship in Brazil promise to sustain its growth in the coming years. This situation, along with the good economic cycle that the country is experiencing, the increased use of the Internet by the population and major sports events (World Cup in 2014 and Olympic Games in 2016) have contributed to this country being considered as a hub in the areas of entrepreneurship and innovation in Latin America. It is important to note that the city of Sao Paulo holds 13th place in the world ranking of entrepreneurial ecosystems, and first place in Latin America, according to the *Startup Ecosystem Report 2012* (Startup Genoma and Telefonica Digital, 2012). In 2009 to 2013, Brazil has improved its position in the dimension 'Entrepreneurial culture and deal opportunities' of the Venture Capital and Private Equity Country Attractiveness Index, from ranking 61 to 52 out of 118 countries. Brazil is, however, in a worse position than Mexico, Colombia and Chile but better than Argentina (Table 12A.2). This result is positively affected by the position of Brazil in the index of 'Innovation' (38), the 'Scientific and technical journal articles' (15) and the 'Company spending on R&D and utility patents' (28). In contrast, Brazil has a low ranking (90 out of 118) in the 'Ease of starting and running a business' and 'Simplicity of closing a business' (Groh et al., 2013).

According to Gary Shapiro, founder of the Consumer Electronics Show (CES) technology fair, one of the largest in the world, and president of Consumer Electronic Association, an association that holds an annual event in Las Vegas, there is no better place than Brazil for a technology enterprise that wants to start up. Similarly, Professor Hashimoto of the Entrepreneurship Centre of the 'Fundacao Armando Alvarez Penteado' points out in an interview that the favourable economic situation that the country is experiencing has attracted many venture capital funds that are escaping from the European economies in search of greater capital gains. At the same time, falling interest rates favour risk investment as a viable alternative with elevated gains. This entire situation undoubtedly favours the resurgence of the angel market that had been practically inactive for almost a decade.

Brazil, along with Argentina, is a country where angel investor activity started a few years before the rest of Latin America. Its development was influenced by the institutionalization of what are called *Sociedades de Capital de Risco* (venture capital companies), at the end of the 1980s, through Decree of Law 2287 that regulates venture capital activity. However, there were already isolated experiences of groups operating with characteristics of venture capital funds since the end of the 1970s (Romaní, 1996). Public policy in the area of venture capital was oriented towards strengthening the formal venture capital market more than the informal market (Leamon and Lerner, 2012). For that reason, the angel investment market remained practically inactive, with some groups of private investors operating intermittently.

*Sociedades de Capital de Risco* moved into later stage investments 13 years after the institutionalization of the venture capital funds. Consequently, in 1999, the government agency FINEP, with support from the MIF/IDB, started the INOVAR programme with the objective of creating new venture capital funds that invest in early stages. This programme started in 2001 and included training for contributors of the funds, mainly pension funds, and for the managers through venture forums and venture capital training programmes.

### 12.4.2 The Development of Angel Investment

The INOVAR programme had to be restructured due to the persistent tendency of the funds to invest in later stages. New changes incorporated a stimulus for the seed stage and angel funds. So the 'Seed Forums' and 'BANs Initiative' programmes were born. INOVAR organized training workshops on legal and tax aspects only for angel investors with more than 150 total attendees. After attending the first workshop, one participant started an umbrella organization for Brazilian angel groups. It is important to point out that the networks that arose in Brazil did not have financial support from INOVAR or even enough to cover their administrative costs. INOVAR only provided them with training through workshops and in the seed forums (where the entrepreneurs presented their projects). The first BAN in Brazil was Gávea Anjos, a private, non-profit association created in 2002. This network has a limited number of members, including individuals and legal entities. It invests in companies geographically located within a radius of action of 200 kilometres around the city of Rio de Janeiro.

According to Leamon and Lerner (2012), five BANs had been established in Brazil, although the number of all existing networks is not known and could be more since they are distributed in different states of the country. After the creation of the Gávea Anjos network in 2002, Sao Paulo Anjos was created in the state of Sao Paulo; Bahia Angels in the northeast of the country; and Floripa Anjos in Florianópolis in southern Brazil. During recent years, with the emergence of numerous programmes of both public (INOVAR/FINEP, SEBRAE) and private institutions for the development of entrepreneurship and innovation, the figure of the angel investor is strengthened as a financing alternative. With the effervescence of entrepreneurship in Brazil and the need for financing, new private investor networks began to emerge, such as Anjos do Brasil in 2011. It is also important to mention that in November 2013, the first women's angel investor network, Mulheres Investidoras Anjos, was launched having the objective of encouraging the inclusion of women in the Brazilian angel market with three fundamental pillars: sensitize, invest and train. Despite the existence of these networks, this activity has not yet taken off.

In 2013, the Ministry of Development, Industry and Commerce signed an agreement to create public policies oriented towards the promotion of angel investment (Tanji, 2013). This agreement was signed during the first congress of angel investors organized by the network Anjos do Brasil on 2 July 2013. The objective of this agreement is to create a regulatory framework favourable to angel investment in the short and medium term. In March 2014, Bill No. 54/2014, which creates incentives for angel investors in Brazil, was sent to the Senate. Concretely, it proposes a deduction of 20 per cent of the total investment amount, with a limit of USD 34,174 (BRL 80,000) per year and applies to a total investment of up to USD 70,868 (BRL 400,000[6]) per year and per investor. It is expected that this pioneer project in Latin America will be approved and contribute to strengthening the angel investor market in Brazil.

Currently, Bahia Anjos and Sao Paulo Anjos are inactive, while Anjos de Brasil is the most active network in the country and has ten nuclei throughout Brazil and 80 members. The network has invested in 13 projects and its expected returns are between 40 and 60 per cent per year. The average investment by angels ranges from USD 21,884 to USD 43,768 and can reach USD 438,000 when the investment is by groups of investors (Vigna, 2013). It is considered a second generation network since it offers various services for both entrepreneurs and investors such as seminars for the diffusion of the activity and dissemination of know-how; meetings for the presentation of entrepreneurs' best projects; and ties with the ecosystem's principal actors.

In 2013, Anjos do Brasil published a report on the Brazilian angel market, showing the existence of 6450 angel investors who invest in start-ups. The number grew 21.7 per cent from 2010 when 5300 private investors were identified. The volume of investment also increased from USD 197 million (BRL 450 million[7]) to approximately USD 270 million (BRL 619 million) in the same period. Despite a 37 per cent increase, total investments in 2013 (USD 54 million) represented just 0.0024 per cent of Brazil's GDP. The average investment per investor is USD 41,860 (BRL 96,000). The report also reflects that 50 per cent of the angel investors are entrepreneurs, 29 per cent are company executives, 13 per cent are investors or managers and 6 per cent are independent professionals. Their main areas of interest are information technologies (75 per cent), mobile telephone services (56 per cent), health/biotechnology (44 per cent) and e-commerce (42 per cent). The average age of these investors is 44 years old and 98 per cent are male (Anjos do Brasil, 2013). Some of these characteristics are close to those of angels in other parts of the world.

### 12.4.3 Main Challenges

There are still many challenges for consolidating the angel market in Brazil. Among the main barriers that angel investors face is the tax burden (there are still no tax incentives for angel investors) and a lack of design of public policies favouring the development of the angel market. It is hoped that the proposed legislation on fiscal incentives for investors is one of many measures that can be implemented in order to consolidate the market. There is also a lack of co-investment funds and the need to train both entrepreneurs and investors. According to the director of Anjos do Brasil, many people with personal equity of over USD 438,000 do not even consider the possibility of becoming an angel investor, above all due to risk aversion, high taxation and the bureaucratic complexity of the processes. In the same vein, Professor Hashimoto (2013) points out that there is also an excess of prudence and caution on the angel investor's part. Even though it is called risk capital, risk is not what the investors want to assume. According to Hashimoto, this contradiction is due to the lack of maturity of investors in understanding what to 'assume risk' is when evaluating an opportunity. He also points out the lack of preparation of some entrepreneurs in presenting and negotiating projects, whereby the limitations of the entrepreneurs impede investors from going ahead with the process. The investors also pointed out the lack of good projects that tend to be non-innovative or are poorly presented, and the difficulty in the selling or exit of the investment. This latter point is not a minor matter because, depending on the type of exit, investors will obtain liquidity in their participation and if there is no appropriate exit, it could paralyse investors who will not be able to make new investments, a problem that many European networks currently face.

## 12.5 CHILE

### 12.5.1 Economic and Entrepreneurial Context

Chile was the first country in Latin America to develop government programmes specifically oriented towards the promotion of BANs, including the supply of subsidies during the first stages of these networks. Consequently, Chile is one of the countries where more BANs have been created in the region. At the same time, and despite macroeconomic and institutional stability, Chile is the country that shows the highest rate of discontinuance of BANs. In this sense, many lessons can be learned from its recent experience.

Chile is one of the LAC countries that has developed more programmes to foster the culture of entrepreneurship and innovation between 2002 and 2012 (Kantis and Federico, 2012). In fact, the government named the year 2012 as the 'Year of Entrepreneurship' and 2013 as the 'Year of Innovation'. One of the programmes that attracted most attention from global media coverage is 'Start Up Chile', launched in 2010, with a budget of USD 40,000 in funding for each entrepreneur willing to relocate to Chile to incubate their start-ups. By December 2013, more than 1400 entrepreneurs from 65 countries had participated in the programme and Chilean entrepreneurs can now apply to this programme. The participating entrepreneurs obtained USD 500 million in private funds and created 1025 jobs (Start Up, 2014). Successful cases have been identified and at least eight of the businesses created have already been acquired. While these cases are not mega successes like Google or Facebook, the programme has undoubtedly contributed to the development of the country's ecosystem for entrepreneurship and innovation, particularly in the capital city Santiago.

It is also important to point out the effervescence of entrepreneurial activity in recent years. According to figures from the GEM Chile report, the rate of early stage entrepreneurial activity has grown significantly from 12.9 per cent in 2008 to 24.3 per cent in 2013 (Amorós and Poblete, 2009; Amorós and Acha, 2014). Many private national and multinational companies have started to carry out a series of activities along with universities located in Santiago such as demo days, business plan competitions and others. All these activities have undoubtedly had an influence on Santiago, currently considered number 20 in the ranking of entrepreneurial ecosystems and holding second place within Latin America, according to the *Startup Ecosystem Report 2012* (Startup Genoma and Telefonica Digital, 2012). At the same time, between 2009 and 2013 Chile has maintained its ranking in the dimensions of 'Entrepreneurial culture and deal opportunities' of the Venture Capital and Private Equity Country Index 2013 (see Table 12A.3 in the Appendix). It is important to highlight the improvement in the category of 'Ease of starting and running a business', where Chile has moved from ranking 69 to 60 out of 118 countries. From January 2014, it is posible to create a business in one day (online) and close it in 12 months, according to the new bankruptcy law that came into force October 2014. Despite all these changes, Chile has lost positions in the dimension 'Corporate R&D' between 2009 and 2013, especially in 'Company spending on R&D and utility patents' (Table 12A.2).

Despite the advances in entrepreneurial culture, the GEM Chile report shows that while the number of entrepreneurs increased significantly between 2008 and 2013, the quality of these ventures, except for a few cases, remains precarious. Despite all the existing development programmes, the financing of entrepreneurship is still an unresolved issue. Furthermore, public policies since 1989, with the creation of the Investment Funds Law, and until 2005, focused on the promotion of formal venture capital, which has financed mainly companies that are already consolidated (Romaní et al., 2009).

### 12.5.2 The Development of Angel Investment

The development of angel investment in Chile goes back to 2004 with the creation of the first BAN, Red de Inversionistas Ángeles de Chile, with the support of a private university and the IDB (Romaní et al., 2009; Romaní et al., 2013). In 2005, CORFO,[8] through the 'Innova Chile'[9] programme, created a programme called 'Apoyo a la creación de redes de Angeles Capitalistas' (Support for the Creation of BANs) with the objective of 'increasing the investment opportunities of non-institutional investors, who are so important in the early phases of the creation of businesses, and to provide new alternatives for accessing to capital by entrepreneurs and small and medium enterprises (SMEs), in order to develop innovative businesses with high growth potential' (CORFO, 2006, p. 5).

This programme was modified over time and enabled the creation of 11 BANs. According to Romaní et al. (2013), in December 2010, there were around 210 private investors belonging to seven angel networks that invested an average USD 284,426 in 34 projects. However, in May 2012, only four active networks remained. By September 2013, another network had discontinued its activities, but three more networks had been created under the CORFO programme. Five BANs are active at the time of writing (2013) (Table 12.1).

*Table 12.1 BANs supported by Innova Chile and Innova BíoBío*

| BANs | Creation | March 2014 |
|---|---|---|
| Southern Angels | 2006 | Inactive |
| Incured S.A. | 2007 | Inactive |
| Angeles de Chile | 2008 | Inactive |
| Angeles DICTUC | 2009 | Inactive |
| Angeles del Sur | 2009 | Inactive |
| Chile Global Angels | 2009 | Active |
| Proyecta Chile | 2010 | Active |
| MCapital | 2012 | Active |
| Plataforma Electrónica de Inversión | 2013 | N.I. |
| Santiago Angels | 2013 | Active |
| DAD Neos | 2013 | Active |

*Note:* N.I. = no information.

*Source:* Authors from CORFO Innova information.

Between 2005 and 2012, the investment made by all the networks amounted to USD 15,282,375, financing 42 projects with an average investment of USD 355,404 and a median of USD 240,000. Just the investment made during 2012 amounted to USD 1,833,750,[10] which represented 0.001 per cent of Chilean GDP. Despite the programme's effort to encourage the creation of angel networks throughout the country, all are located in Santiago except for one that is already inactive (Romaní et al., 2013).

Currently, Chile Global Angels is the most active network in Chile, with 27 members who are mostly Chilean living outside the country. Since the creation of this network, 12 investments have been made in different sectors and the investment amounts range from USD 100,000 to USD 800,000. Chile Global Angels has alliances with networks from Mexico, Colombia and Peru for the exchange of experiences and good practices. This network has the support of the Fundación Chile, a private, non-profit institution, the principal members of which are the Chilean government and two important mining companies. In addition to the network, the Fundación Chile has an investment fund for early stages and a co-investment fund 'Fondo Subsidio Semilla de Asignación Flexible' (Flexible Assignment Seed Subsidy Fund). The network Proyecta Chile has ten investors and has made an investment of USD 500,000 where four of its members participated. MCapital is the first women's BAN in Chile. It has more than ten members and has not made any investments. Santiago Angels has 15 members. Investment amounts range from USD 25,000 to USD 500.000. It has not made any investments. DAD Neos is a network oriented towards financing technological endeavours. It is headquartered in Chile and its area of action is Latin America. The investments of this network range from USD 68,000 to USD 275,000. It has not made any investments.

Despite the existence of five active BANs, just two have made investments. This situation shows the precariousness of angel investment in Chile, where the public initiative has not been enough to promote the angel investment market, due, among other factors, to the focus of policies on the supply side of angel investment and lack of complementary measures oriented towards the creation of a venture capital culture, the financial sustainability of networks and the investment readiness of new ventures.

### 12.5.3 Main Challenges

The challenges for the development of BANs and the informal venture capital market in Chile are related to the sustainability of the networks, the development of training programmes for entrepreneurs and investors, tax incentives, lack of an institutional representation for the BANs, increase in the critical mass of angel investors and the need to raise awareness about the importance of early stage investments and venture capital concepts and modus operandi (Romaní et al., 2013).

The sustainability of the BANs is probably the main challenge of the Chilean angel market. The CORFO Innova programme for the creation of BANs provides financing for the activity of networks over three years. After that period, and depending on the results obtained, the subsidy can be renewed for three more years. After these six years the network should be self-sustainable. Unfortunately, the networks have had to date a low performance. Most networks stopped operating either because they did not meet the goals set by CORFO Innova or because, after six years, they were not able to self-finance their activities. The current networks are seeking the best business model to enable them to be self-sufficient after six years. In this sense, it is urgent to create training programmes for angel investors, as well as exchange experiences with investors from more advanced networks in order to generate a venture capital culture among them. In Chile, the majority of angel investors are entrepreneurs or professionals who are unaware of the peculiarities of the venture capital investment process and do not have a risk culture (Romaní et al., 2013), while there is a minority of investors who do know the peculiarities of venture capital investment but who do not dare to invest.

Public policy for the development of BANs in Chile has been oriented mainly towards the supply of resources. However, there is empirical evidence that the entrepreneurs who require those resources are not well prepared to present their projects verbally or in writing to the investors (Romaní et al., 2013). It is important to create 'investment readiness' programmes, continually evaluated and monitored (Lerner, 2010; Mason and Harrison, 2001; Mason and Kwok, 2010). Together with this training, it is also important to transfer know-how to entrepreneurs regarding the importance of innovation in their products or services. The promotion of entrepreneurship should be oriented towards innovative entrepreneurship with added value, both from the supply and the demand sides.

As in other countries, Chilean government policy was initially based on the promotion of formal venture capital. In this sense, the country has fiscal incentives for formal venture capital, but not for individual investors or members of the BANs. The Chilean Capital Market Reform project includes the incorporation of fiscal incentives for business angels, but it has not yet been approved. A system of tax incentives adapted to the country and with mechanisms to evaluate its impact could attract active angel investors to the market and avoid the attraction of 'dumb money' (Mason, 2009). In Chile, the number of angel investors linked to active networks is currently not more than a hundred. Creating incentives to increase the number of active angel investors is important in order to achieve an active angel investment market. Chile has 56,000 millionaires and 76,000 adults in the top 1 per cent of global wealth holders (Credit Suisse, 2013). These people could be potential angel investors and could be sensitized to the importance of early stage investing, showing cases of success and generating awareness regarding venture capital investment. Accordingly, it would also be convenient to create a national network that represents angels' activity; to raise awareness of the industry; to train the angel investors; to develop professional standards; and to collect data from members of the BANs, among others.

## 12.6 COLOMBIA

### 12.6.1 Economic and Entrepreneurial Context

Colombia is one of the LAC countries that has drawn much attention for the relevance that entrepreneurship and innovation have acquired in recent years. In August 2010, the new government, led by President Juan Manuel Santos, pushed forward an economic reform agenda through the 'Prosperity for All' national development plan for 2010–14. The goals for this plan are to reduce poverty, increase income, generate employment, improve security, ensure the sustainable use of natural resources and improve the quality of the business environment including those starting a business, paying taxes, protecting investors and resolving insolvency. Regarding the last point, we should remark that Colombia's insolvency reforms began almost two decades ago.

In February 2012, the government created an organization called Innpulsa Colombia[11] with the objective of supporting and promoting entrepreneurial growth through the generation of awareness and a change in the mindset of its inhabitants, the correction of market failures and the strengthening of the ecosystem's actors across the country. According to the report of this organization in July 2014, 18 new instruments of co-funding for early stage projects were created, promoting incubators that increased from 15 to 31 at the national level (Orellana and Contreras, 2014). In 2013, in a contest organized by the *Wall Street Journal* and City Group, Medellín was chosen as the most innovative city of the world from among a group of 200 cities, thanks to the progress achieved in terms of innovation and social transformation in recent years. According to the organizers of the contest, Medellín had positioned itself on the innovation map thanks to the boost of technological, educational and cultural projects that have awakened a vigorous entrepreneurial mindset in its inhabitants.[12]

All these measures have led to substantial improvements in the quality of the business environment and a more solid foundation for private sector development. It is important to remark that initially most of the regulatory reforms took place at the national level. However, as the business environment continued to improve, the reforms spilled over to the local level.

We can also observe a change in the ranking of Colombia from 51 to 48 in the dimension 'Entrepreneurial culture and deal opportunities' of the Venture Capital and Private Equity Country Attractiveness Index 2013. 'Innovation index' experienced the highest ranking improvement, specifically the dimension 'General innovativeness and capacity for innovation' that moved from ranking 64 to 55 in 2009 to 2013. Another important change is related to the 'Ease of starting and closing a business', especially the latter, where Colombia has moved from ranking 36 to 20 (Table 12A.2). From 2011, the time required to start a business has been reduced from 60 days to 14 days, the cost from 28 per cent of income per capita to 8 per cent and the number of procedures from 19 to 9. Furthermore, thanks to insolvency reforms, creditors' recovery rate rose from 56 cents on the dollar to 76 and the time to complete a liquidation proceeding fell from 3 years to 1.3 years.

According to the GEM Colombia report, Colombia is one of the countries that between 2008 and 2013 maintained a rate of early stage entrepreneurial activity equal to or greater than 20 per cent, reaching 23.7 per cent in 2013 (Bosma and Amorós, 2014). Despite this, access to financing is one of the main problems that entrepreneurs face. According to Matíz and Fracica (2011), the financial market for entrepreneurship and new enterprises is still embryonic. In Colombia, the financing of enterprises has basically come from the banking sector. One of the main barriers for Colombian entrepreneurs is related to aspects tied to the credit process, such as the high interest rates, the lack of credit experience and lack of real guaranties.

### 12.6.2 The Development of Angel Investment

Angel investment in Colombia is very recent. Its beginnings date from 2010 with support from MIF/IDB. This multilateral agency has contributed to the creation of two BANs. The first network, Angeles Inversionistas de Capitalia, was created in alliance with Capitalia Colombia[13] in Medellín. In the same year, the MIF/IDB, in an alliance with the Bavaria Foundation, created Angeles Inversionistas Bavaria in the capital city, Bogotá. Both networks have worked together in seeking projects and investors in the regions of Santander, the Atlantic Coast, the Coffee Belt and Bogotá, among others, with the support of the Ministry of Commerce, Industry and Tourism. In September 2011, Medellín was the host of the first Latin American meeting of angel investors, whose objective was to exchange experiences regarding entrepreneurship projects and to attract investment. In that meeting, the Colombian government set the ambitious goal of reaching 15 active networks in the country by 2014. The same number of BANs remained in Colombia to 2014 and in 2015 only one more BAN was created.

In December 2012, the government, through Innpulsa Colombia, incorporated a series of measures oriented towards the development of entrepreneurship and sources of financing, focused on the creation of angel investor networks. At that time, a national call was made for institutions to apply for resources for the training and start-up of BANs with national coverage. The network Angeles Inversionistas Bavaria was awarded the project and is currently working with various regional universities on the construction of a national network with initial branches in Bogotá, Cali and Barranquilla.

In 2013, there were three active investor networks in Colombia: two supported by the MIF/IDB – Angeles Inversionistas de Capitalia and Angeles Inversionistas Bavaria – and one of private origin – the network TIC HUBBOG, created in 2012. There are also other networks that are in the formation process. The active networks involve approximately 75 investors and the investments they have made amount to at least 2 million USD in 14 projects.

Angeles Inversionistas de Capitalia has approximately 30 active members and operates only in the department of Antioquia whose capital is Medellín. It invests in health sciences, biotechnology, environment, applied engineering, communication, information technologies and food technology. Its investment amounts ranging from USD 50,000 to USD 400,000. The amount invested has reached USD 1,650,000 in 11 projects, with an average investment of USD 150,000. In order to sustain its activities, this network charges its members an annual fee and also offers various services to entrepreneurs as well as investors, consulting and methodology transfer to groups or networks of investors existing or in the formation process, as well as courses and seminars on topics linked to the various aspects of venture capital. In addition to these services, it has the support of the Antioquia city hall through the Route N programme and the co-investment fund of that same programme. This BAN is a second generation network.

Angeles Inversionistas Bavaria has around 35 members and its investments have reached USD 400,000 in three projects. The investment amounts established by the network are between USD 25,000 and USD 2 million. Their geographic area of operation is Colombia but they have offices in Barranquilla and Cali and invest in all sectors. Currently, this network finances its activities with contributions from the MIF/IDB, the Bavaria Foundation and the Colombian government through the project it was awarded to create the national angel investors network.

The network TIC HUBBOG was created in 2012 by a group of eight young angel investors located in Bogotá and New York. This network is totally private and belongs to the HUBBOG group, created in 2010 as a campus for start-ups that offers, in addition to the network, various services such as co-working spaces, workshops for entrepreneurs and mentoring. The investment amounts range from USD 20,000 to USD 500,000, although its activity is recent and concrete statistics are not yet available.

### 12.6.3 Main Challenges

One of the main challenges that the angel market in Colombia faces is lack of awareness by the entrepreneurs of this type of investment. The vast majority of Colombian entrepreneurs are unaware of the existence of a chain of financing and the non-traditional alternatives such as BANs and venture capital funds (Matíz and Fracica, 2011). There have been significant efforts, both public and private, to promote informal venture capital during recent years. However, more dissemination is still necessary, not only to create a new investment market but also to change the existing mindset among entrepreneurs regarding the financing of their enterprises.

On the investors' side, the main problem is the strong risk aversion. According to key informants, investors have a mindset of 'investment bankers' and are not willing to lose. The timing of investment is another of the challenges that limit angel investment in Colombia. Investors are not patient and have a short-term view. Having to wait more than three years to recover the liquidity of their investment is something that discourages most investors. At the same time, investors are not capable of identifying business opportunities in traditional activities where the country has a comparative advantage and underestimate these projects. A venture capital culture has not yet been developed in the country, which is also manifested in the lack of professionalization of the investors. This limitation also exists, and perhaps with more severity, in the case of entrepreneurs, who show serious problems with investment readiness and awareness of corporate governance.

In addition to the cultural and formative aspect, the great challenge for all the active networks in Colombia is, as in the Chilean case, their permanence over time once state subsidies or the contributions from multilateral organizations end. In some networks, their members refuse to pay membership fees, while in others, these fees cover just a percentage of the BANs' operating costs. Consequently, the networks are currently in a process of diversification of activities and are seeking new business models to cover their high operating costs. Nevertheless, the consolidation of the existing networks cannot yet be guaranteed. In this regard, various interviewees have pointed out the importance that the establishment of fiscal incentives for angel investment by the government could have as a source for increasing the critical mass of active investors.

## 12.7 MEXICO

### 12.7.1 Economic and Entrepreneurial Context

Most people perceive Mexico as a country with many problems that could negatively affect the business arena. Problems such as the current violence in the country, which is fighting a war against organized crime, the poor infrastructure and a bureaucratic environment (Charvel, 2012a) could affect the development of angel investment. However, that negative perception is more external than internal. According to key informants, the local perception is favourable since the violence is concentrated only in some places. In fact, Mexico is experiencing an attractive economic situation for investors as shown by the Venture Capital and Private Equity Country Attractiveness Index (Groh et al., 2013). Since December 2012, the Mexican economy stands out regards structural reforms that have been discussed, passed or in the pipeline to be approved by both the Congress and Senate, which could fuel a 'Mexican moment'. According to Charvel (2013, p. 10), 'The reforms include labour, education, competition, telecom, finance, energy and fiscal constitutional and legal changes. These reforms will not only affect Mexico's economic core, but also come at a defining moment, a time of global uncertainty where few countries are being able to achieve change, helping to drive more foreign interest to the country.'

Towards the mid 1990s and until the middle of the first decade of the twenty-first century, a series of programmes were created to promote R&D and patent registration, without great results. Also, incentives offered by the Federal Government were created to promote the creation of investor clubs, business incubators, enterprise accelerators and other institutional schemes that did not achieve the expected results (Santillán-Salgado and Hernández-Perales, 2011).

Between 2010 and 2013, many important reforms took place related to the ease of starting a business. This affected the position of the country in the dimension 'Entrepreneurial culture and deal opportunities' of the Venture Capital and Private Equity Country Attractiveness Index 2013, where Mexico improved its position, and leading the group of countries studied (Table 12A.2). In 2009, to start a business it took nine procedures, 28 days, expenses of 12.5 per cent per capita income and a minimum capital of 11 per cent per capita income. In 2013, entrepreneurs only needed six procedures, nine days, expenses of 10.1 per cent per capita income and it was not necessary to have a minimum amount as capital. Mexico improved its ranking from position 71 in 2009 to 48 in 2013 out of 118 countries. In the rest of this index's dimensions, Mexico is always in a position lower than 40 out of 118 countries.

As part of Mexican economic policy to support entrepreneurs and micro and SMEs, the new government created the Instituto Nacional del Emprendedor – INADEM (National Entrepreneurs' Institute) in January 2013. INADEM is a public, decentralized organization of the Secretary of the Economy with the objective of 'arranging, executing and coordinating a national support policy including entrepreneurs and micro, SMEs, driving their innovation, competitiveness and projection in national and international markets to increase their contribution to economic development and social well-being, as well as co-assisting in the development of policies that encourage an entrepreneurial culture and productivity' (Article 57 bis. Internal Regulations of the Secretary of the Economy).

INADEM has four strategic lines, among which is the strengthening of the financing and promotion of a new national entrepreneurial and business culture. Various programmes have been created for each line, such as the creation of a financing culture, the support of high impact entrepreneurship and the professionalization of fund managers.[14] In August 2013, the Entrepreneurs' Support Network was created to link the various government and private sector policies and programmes to support entrepreneurs and micro SMEs by means of the strategy called 'Moving to Mexico Network and Points for Moving to Mexico' whose aim is the articulation and integral support for entrepreneurs. This strategy includes public as well as private programmes to create a favourable environment to transform good business ideas into successful enterprises. It is expected that all these measures will contribute to create an appropriate ecosystem of entrepreneurship and innovation in Mexico, including the development of a robust angel investors market.

All the reforms previously mentioned and the favourable economic performance that Mexico has recently experienced (Table 12A.1) have positively affected the domestic entrepreneurial environment. According to the GEM Mexico report 2013, the entrepreneurial activity in the early stages significantly increased between 2011 and 2013, from 9.6 per cent to 14.8 per cent of the adult population. Furthermore, more than 50 per cent of the adult population perceives that there are good business opportunities in the country to start a business. According to the experts intervewed in the report, the key factor to promote entrepreneurship is to make deep changes is aspects such as access to funding in order to consolidate the entrepreneurisl ecosystem (Naranjo et al., 2014).

### 12.7.2 The Development of Angel Investment

The angel investment market is still emerging in Mexico, despite the proximity to the largest angel market in the world, the United States, and the progress achieved in the development of formal venture capital and private equity activity (Charvel et al., 2006; Charvel, 2007, 2012b; Lerner et al., 2013). Some concrete actions oriented towards the development of the angel market were the government initiative for the creation of an Angel Investors Website[15] and the 'Entrepreneurs' and Investors' Support Programme' of the Mexican Development Bank (NAFIN) in 2004. The objective of the website was to contact investors interested in injecting fresh resources in productive projects. The education of investors was also contemplated. In 2007, the website had 2692 angel investors registered, who had a password to access a list of projects with the name of the company, the activity and the amount of capital required. Unfortunately, both the website and the programme stopped functioning in 2010.

In 2008, the Secretary of the Economy also started a programme to create angel investors clubs. According to the information compiled, several clubs were created in the country,[16] at least two of which are still active, Angel Ventures Mexico and Club de Inversionistas Innovateur managed by Innovateur Capital. At the end of the first decade of the twenty-first century there was an outbreak of angel activity in Mexico with an increase in the demand for angel capital by entrepreneurs as a result of the business acceleration programmes and domestic economic stability. In February 2014, at least five active groups of angel investors (networks, clubs and associations) were identified: Angel Ventures Mexico, Guadalajara Angel Investor Network – GAIN, MTY Global Ventures, Innovateur Capital and Fundación E. With the exception of Angel Ventures Mexico, information on the other groups is scarce and not very detailed.

According to key informants, the above-mentioned groups can be considered formal due to their visibility in the Mexican angel market. However, it is known that there are also around 13 closed groups formed by friends and former colleagues who invest in early stages. According to experts interviewed, there are currently around 300 angel investors linked to the formal networks. They estimate that the number of deals could reach 20 new ventures with an investment volume of approximately USD 14 million, that is, on average, USD 700,000 per project.

The most active BAN in Mexico is Angel Ventures Mexico. This network, created in 2008, is currently located in the Federal District, Puebla, Yucatán and Sonora (Angel Ventures México, 2010). To be a member of this network that operates as an investors club, an individual or corporate membership fee must be paid. The network has 200 members comprising individual investors and company representatives. Since its creation it has invested in 12 projects with a total of USD 12 million. It has also worked on the first co-investment fund for projects with high growth potential with qualified investors, which started operating in 2012. This network offers many services that enable it to be sustainable over time, which include training for investors and entrepreneurs, advising on business plans, legal advice for entrepreneurs and consulting. It also has collaboration agreements with networks from Chile, Colombia, Peru and Ecuador, among others, for the exchange of experiences and good practices.

The rest of the networks have a very diverse profile. Guadalajara Angel Investment Network – GAIN is a regional network that was created in 2008 and has 22 investors. GAIN is focused on technology projects in the region of Guadalajara, considered Mexico's most important technological cluster. Even though its geographic area is limited, it is open to considering proposals from any industry or geographic area of Mexico. MTY Global Ventures, located in Monterrey, is an association of people and independent fims whose objective is to provide capital, know-how, experience and abilities to develop and/or support processes, products or services typical of entrepreneurs. Angeles Inversionistas de la Fundación E was created in 2009 in an alliance with the Dutch Fundación BiD. The objective of this network is to match entrepreneurs and investors. Investment ranges from USD 100,000 to USD 1 million. This network is interested in investing in technological and sustainable projects and also in traditional sectors with value added. Innovateur Capital is a private institution for the support and development of venture capital. It has Club de Inversionistas Innovateur for early stage investments and manages the Fondo Innovateur for later stage investments.

### 12.7.3 Main Challenges

According to our key informants, one of the challenges faced by Mexican angel investors is basically the lack of fiscal incentives for individuals.

These incentives could contribute to increasing the critical mass of local angel investors. In that sense, the generation of awareness of this activity in the HNWI is also relevant. This would make it possible to incorporate more angel investors in the market.

The lack of professionalization of some investors also stands out, above all those who have not yet made investments. In this sense, programmes for training and the exchange of experiences with more active investors are fundamental. The literature reviewed shows that Mexican angel investors, in contrast to those from the United States, lack sector expertise. They do not have a clear exit strategy and do not trust entrepreneurs (Angel Ventures México, 2011). Despite this, the Mexican market is closely tied to Silicon Valley and in some cases the Mexican BANs are members of American angel networks. The proximity to the United States has been beneficial not only for the investors but also for the entrepreneurs, in the sense that they have a more global perspective since they have been able to act with ventures from Silicon Valley. Nevertheless, angel investors from the United States rarely invest in Mexico.

## 12.8 SIMILARITIES AND DIFFERENCES OF ANGEL INVESTMENT IN LATIN AMERICA

The previous sections have analysed the development of angel investment in the selected Latin American countries and manifest a high level of heterogeneity. In this section, we focus on the identification of similarities and differences among these countries in terms of the evolution and activity of the BANs, observing some of its characteristics. Before starting this analysis, it is interesting to describe the changes to the Venture Capital and Private Equity Country Attractiveness Index in the selected countries as a general framework of the advance in the conditions of venture capital investment and private equity in the group of countries analysed.

In 2009 to 2013, the countries studied in this chapter either maintained or improved their ranking in the Venture Capital and Private Equity Country Attractiveness Index. Among them, Chile is the most attractive country in the Latin American region and ranks 25 out of 118 countries in 2013, significantly improving its ranking in 2009 to 2013 (Table 12A.3). This result is fundamentally due to the macroeconomic stability, the depth of capital markets and tax reforms, all of these dimensions where Chile has experienced significant improvements. After Chile, Brazil stands out as the most attractive country for venture capital and private equity in Latin America and ranks 36 out of 118 countries, without any change in 2009 to 2013. Brazil is among the first 25 countries in 'Economic activity' and 'Depth of capital markets' but in other dimensions of the index ranks over 50. The third most attractive country in Latin America is Mexico. This country has improved its ranking in the dimensions 'Economic activity', 'Depth of capital markets', 'Taxation' and 'Entrepreneurial culture and deal opportunities', while it ranks over 50 in dimensions 'Investor protection andcorporate governance' and 'Human and social and environment'. Colombia has improved its ranking in eight positions during this period, especially in the dimensions 'Economic activity', 'Taxation', 'Depth of capital market', 'Investor protection and corporate governance' and 'Entrepreneurial culture and deal opportunities'. The only dimension where this country has lost position is 'Human and social environment'. Despite improving in eight positions in the Venture Capital and Private Equity Country Attractiveness Index, Argentina has the lowest ranking among the group of countries studied. This country ranks lowest in the dimensions 'Economic activity', 'Entrepreneurial culture and deal opportunities' and 'Depth of the capital market' (Table 12A.3). For the other dimensions, Argentina has relatively improved its ranking compared to 2009.

### 12.8.1 Evolution of Angel Investment in the Countries Studied

Brazil and Argentina are the countries with the longest trajectory, but the angel market is not consolidated in either of them. Argentina had a flourishing activity in the second half of the 1990s, with successful experiences and capital supply, mainly private, both national and foreign, in technological projects. However, its economic instability and an inappropriate institutional framework paralysed its development. Brazil started the activity at the beginning of the twenty-first century through public initiatives such as the educational workshops for angel investors in the INOVAR programme of FINEP and the formation of private groups of investors such as Gávea Angels. In Chile and Mexico, angel activity started around 2004. In Chile, the first angel investor network was created by a private university with the support of the World Bank. Later, the government supported the creation of BANs. In Mexico, the Angel Investors Website also had public support. In Colombia, the creation of angel networks started in 2010 with the support of the MIF/IDB and public and private institutions (Table 12.2). The origin of all these initiatives is very diverse according to the country: private local and foreign investors, universities, multilateral organizations, private and government institutions. Two extreme cases regarding the creation of BANs are Argentina and Brazil, on one side, and Chile, on the other. In the first two countries, private initiative predominated, while in the second, public programmes were the driving force of angel investment.

*Table 12.2 Characteristics of BANs in Argentina, Brazil, Chile, Colombia and Mexico*

| Characteristics of BANs | Argentina | Brazil | Chile | Colombia | Mexico |
|---|---|---|---|---|---|
| Origin and main support | 1998–2000 Private (local and foreign investors) | 2002 Private | 2004 Private and IDB 2005–13 Public | 2010 Private, public and MIF/IDB | 2004 Public (NAFIN) |
| Number of active BANs (including investor clubs) | 5 | 3 | 5 | 3 | 5 |
| Number of members (total approx.) | > 160 | > 100 | > 70 | 80 | 300 |
| Amount of investment by angel (approx.) | Min: USD 50,000 Max: USD 600,000 | Min: USD 22,000 Max: USD 500,000 | Min: USD 25,000 Max: USD 800,000 | Min: USD 20,000 Max: USD 500,000 | Min: USD 50,000 Max: USD 1,000,000 |
| Average investment (approx.) | USD 152,000 | N.A. | USD 350,000 | USD 150,000 | USD 700,000 |
| Number of investments (approx.)[a] | < 50 | N.A. | < 50[b] | 14 | 20 |
| Geographical localization | Concentrated predominantly in Buenos Aires | Relatively dispersed (Sao Paulo, Rio de Janeiro, and other main cities) | Very concentrated (only Santiago and Chile) | Dispersed (main cities such as Bogotá, Medellín, Cali, Barranquilla) | Dispersed (Federal District, Guadalajara, Monterrey and offices in main cities) |

| | | | | | |
|---|---|---|---|---|---|
| Geographic scope | The BANs located in Buenos Aires invest locally | There are regional BANs that invest in the regions where they are located. Most active BAN has national scope | The BANs' investments are predominantly in the Metropolitan Region (Santiago de Chile) | BAN Capitalia: regional scope<br>HUBBOG: only Bogota<br>BAN Bavaria: national scope | The most active BAN invests in many regions. The rest are regional BANs |
| Gender composition | The members of the BANs are mostly men | Members are mostly men but there is a BAN formed only by women | Members are mostly men but there is a BAN formed only by women | The members of the BANs are mostly men | The members of the BANs are mostly men |
| Type of BAN | First and second generation | First and second generation | Predominantly first generation | Second generation | Predominantly first generation but there are also second generation |
| Sectors | All the sectors with focus on ICT | All the sectors with focus on ICT | All the sectors with focus on ICT | All the sectors. One BAN is focused on ICT | All the sectors. One BAN is focused on ICT |

*Notes:*
[a] There are many BANs that remain non-visible and it has not been possible to identify them. Many of these networks are formed by groups of friends, business school alumni and work colleagues who invest in the early stage. For example, in Mexico there are at least 13 informal groups compared to five formal groups.
[b] Since the networks were created in 2005–12.
N.A. = not available; ICT = information and communications technology.

*Source:* Authors.

In all the countries analysed, public intervention was focused initially, between the end of the 1980s and 1990s, on the regulation and creation of programmes to support formal venture capital. In this sense, the institutional framework at the beginning of this century was not prepared for the development of angel investment. In fact, Chile is the only country in Latin America where the government created a programme exclusively for the creation of BANs. During the last decade, the governments of the region have increased the number of programmes aimed at creating an ecosystem favourable for innovation and entrepreneurship, incorporating a series of initiatives for the SMEs, entrepreneurs and investors oriented towards training and the generation of awareness, such as 'Start up' in Chile; 'Buenos Aires Emprende' in Argentina; 'INOVAR' in Brazil; the Instituto Nacional del Emprendedor in Mexico; or Innpulsa in Colombia. In all these cases, angel investment is incorporated with a secondary role in the supply of funds and the education of investors. However, up to the present, only Brazil has considered regulatory changes such as the creation of fiscal incentives for angels in its Bill No. 54/2014 sent to the Senate in March 2014.

It is important to point out the role that some multilateral organizations have played in promoting angel investments in some countries of the region such as Colombia. The IMF/IDB launched a platform for catalysing early stage investment, Xcala, on 10 April 2014. During the second half of 2014, the call for business angels' projects was launched. The IMF/IDB provides partial support over a four-year period to encourage the creation of BANs and professionalize the management of the existing networks. The MIF/IDB contributes up to USD 200,000, while the counterpart networks contribute between 30 per cent and 50 per cent of the total. According to the programme executive, 24 projects received financial support as well as other benefits such as free workshops and training in 2015. The programme also accompanies entrepreneurs and investors in the investment process, particularly in the negotiations and agreements to close the deals. This business model pursues the economic self-sustainability of the networks through a high orientation towards commercial management. What is interesting about this programme, in addition to the education for entrepreneurs, investors and managers, is that the business model enables them to interact with almost all the components of the entrepreneurship ecosystem (Lerner et al., 2013), with the exception of the 'legal and regulatory environment'.

### 12.8.2 The Activity of BANs in Selected Countries

The activity of the BANs shows very uneven levels of investment by country, ranging from an average of USD 150,000 in Colombia to USD

700,000 in Mexico. The number of networks in each country is very small, not more than five active networks, with investments in a small number of projects that are predominantly in the field of information technologies (Table 12.2).

The business models of the networks are also very diverse and do not follow a national pattern. There are networks that are exclusively websites for investment, such as Angeles Inversionistas in Mexico; others, such as Proyecta Chile, are first generation networks and only do the matching between entrepreneurs and investors through the Venture Forum. The majority, however, are second generation networks that, in addition to matching entrepreneurs and investors, offer training services for investors and entrepreneurs, such as the networks Angeles Inversionistas de Capitalia and Anjos do Brasil. The most advanced networks also have co-investment funds, such as Angel Ventures México, and make alliances with the entrepreneurship and innovation ecosystem actors. The networks that have been able to remain active for three or more years have diversified their activities, offering various services and many of them belong to foundations or private corporations that provide them with financial backing. This is the case of Chile Global Angels, supported by the Fundación Chile and Bavaria and Angeles Inversionistas de Capitalia in Colombia. The first operates with the support of Fundación Bavaria, while the second is managed by Capitalia Colombia.

The geographic scope of the networks varies among countries according to their size and the administrative organization of the state. The networks of the biggest countries with a federal structure, especially Brazil and Mexico, operate in various regions, above all in the largest cities, and have even developed regional networks. The same occurs in Colombia, despite having a smaller market size. Despite its size, Argentina is an exception and shows a strong concentration of the networks and investment around the city of Buenos Aires. In any case, the most concentrated market is Chile, where the BANs are located and invest predominantely in the capital, Santiago.

## 12.9 CONCLUSIONS AND FUTURE RESEARCH

Despite the current scarcity of information, the aim of this chapter has been to introduce the reader to the current situation of angel investment in the main Latin American countries where development is still incipient. In Colombia the activity has just started, while in other countries such as Argentina, Brazil, Chile and Mexico with a longer trajectory, their consolidation has not yet been achieved. The development of informal venture capital in Latin America is influenced by the experience of successful companies in the United States such as Amazon and Google, initially financed by angel investors. In contrast to the United States, the origin of angel investment in some Latin American countries has had significant public support and from multilateral organizations such as the MIF/IDB. Nevertheless, the region does not yet have a critical mass of angels, although there are sufficient HNWI that could contribute to activating the market. Just as an example, in 2012, 165,300 HNWI were identified in Brazil (Anjos do Brasil, 2013). Why, when the majority of the region has achieved certain macroeconomic stability and shows high levels of growth, do only a low proportion of these HNWI becomes angel investors?

Even in the most stable countries in the region that have the most favourable ecosystem for investment, the experts interviewed point out the importance of the culture as a key dimension for understanding the weakness of the angel market in Latin America. As indicated in various studies (Inglehart and Welzel, 2005; Inglehart and Carballo, 2008), the experts also point out the lack of trust as a trait of the region. The fear of being deceived makes difficult the relationship between investors and entrepreneurs and the formation of networks capable of collaborating, and becomes an obstacle for the development of angel investment.

The lack of long-term vision and the risk aversion of Latin American investors are other cultural traits that have limited angel investment. Inmediate returns are expected, and the uncertainty inherent to innovative businesses is not tolerated. The preference for fixed income securities is still predominant in the region due to the recent development of the capital markets and lack of financial education of the population. New generations could help to overcome these cultural barriers. In fact, many of the existing networks were created by young investors. In order to promote a cultural change, awareness of the importance of informal venture capital needs to be raised in the population through public programmes and changes in the educational system.

During the last two decades, changes in the institutional framework of the Latin American countries have contributed, in the majority of cases, to greater political and economic stability. However, the lack of clarity in defining the rules of the game can still constitute one of the biggest obstacles for the development of the angel investment market in the region, as shown by the experience of Argentina. Two points are highlighted in this regard by the experts interviewed: first, the continuity and coordination of public policies and programmes; and second, the creation of fiscal incentives for angel investment. In most Latin American countries, programmes are only vigent during the government administration that implements them. These programmes disappear with the incoming administration that proposes new and sometimes contradictory initiatives. Public programmes are not coordinated and rarely subjected to impact evaluation, so a long-term perspective is lost. Similar problems are repeated on occasions in the investment regulatory framework, which in addition has not fully recognized the figure of the angel investor and maintains a focus centred on formal venture capital. Consequently, to date, the creation of fiscal incentives to drive the development of the angel market has not been proposed, except in Brazil.

Institutional stability is a necessary but not sufficient condition for the development of BANs, as shown by the experience of Chile. One of the major problems of angel networks in Latin America has been its lack of sustainability. The scarce experience and professionalization of investors has been recognized by the experts interviewed as one of the causes of this problem. The experts also mentioned the lack of sufficiently attractive projects and the weak education of entrepreneurs in the presentation of their projects. Consequently, the training of investors and entrepreneurs becomes a key measure for strengthening the activity of the networks. At the same time, it would be appropriate to reinforce the collaboration between starting and existing networks. Furthermore, public programmes and those of multilateral organizations must consider a more gradual exit since many networks disappear suddenly when their support ends.

Due to the recent development of angel investment in Latin America, it has not yet attracted the attention of the scholars, and at the same time opens a broad field of research possibilities. The progress of this activity in the region also depends on how much we know about it. Future lines of research should be oriented, in a first stage, to filling the current gap of information and raising awareness in the region about this activity. In fact, the study of angel networks is only the tip of the iceberg. In that sense, the case study methodology is an interesting alternative to start; on the one hand, case studies linked to the development of BANs are welcome and also related to business models and the best practices of the most active networks as in the case of Angel Ventures from Mexico as an interesting example of a successful network; on the other hand, case studies related to successful investees are also important, as in the case of Globant in Argentina, the Buenos Aires-based software development giant that has become one of the top success stories, creating over 3000 jobs across 15 countries since it was founded in 2003. This company celebrated its US initial public offering (IPO) on 18 July 2014, raising nearly USD 59 million. This IPO marks a major milestone for angel investment in Argentina.

Another line of study of special interest for the region is the analysis of the discontinuity of angel networks, its causes and potential viable alternatives, especially in the case of Chile where many BANs were created and also many discontined their activities. A deeper understanding of the experience of current BANs could help better design public policies oriented to the sustainability of angel network in developing countries. At the same time, due to the public nature of many programmes applied in some countries, their impact needs to be evaluated to contribute to the design of future programmes in order to improve the efficiency of these programmes.

Another potential line of research could focus on cultural aspects of angel investment. One is the low propensity to invest in other people;s businesses in Latin America. In this field, it is key to analyse trust, the way it is created and affects angel investment, particularly in developing countries where the levels of trust are especially low. Furthermore, as in Latin America fiscal incentives for angel investment do not exist, it is important to explore to what extent this kind of incentive can have any effect on the behaviour of potential investors. Fiscal incentives could trigger the investment of the group of HNWI that exist in Latin America and contribute to the launch of this activity.

Unfortunately, the difficulty in identifying and contacting angel investors limits the knowledge of the total population of angels and makes extremely complicated the possibility of quantitative studies based on statistically significant samples. An alternative in this field is qualitative research based either on particular angel investors or groups of them in order to analyse their attitudes, motivations and behaviour. This would be an important contribution to the literature on angel investment in Latin America, where angels still play a secondary role. In this respect, universities and research centres should make alliances with angel networks as a means to not only foster new business but also promote research in this topic.

The late stage of angel investment is one of the areas that has received least attention in this field. An additional line of research could be focused on the disinvestment processes and the role of angels and networks in the post-investmente stage. This will be possible in the short term because many networks have made investments that have already matured, so the analysis of exits becomes imperative, especially in Latin American countries where the capital markets are not fully developed and where it is very difficult for an investee to make an IPO. Furthermore, in the future, when time series of sufficient length are available to perform longitudinal studies that analyse the behaviour of groups of investors according to the characteristics of the networks in which they participate, this will help in understanding the different strategies of networks and the determinant of changes in their investment decisions.

Comparative studies are another alternative on the recent development of angel investment in Latin America. This comparison can be made among countries of the region, and also with more developed countries. In many cases, Latin American countries seem to follow the same path already walked by Europe and the United States and to make the same mistakes. Finally, the analysis of the geography of angel investment is particularly interesting in Latin America due to the high degree of spatial concentration of the population that characterize this region and the differences existing in the levels of fiscal, administrative and political decentralization in each country.

## ACKNOWLEDGEMENTS

The authors acknowledge and are grateful for the information provided by Elard Arévalo, Jaime Geiseke, Silvia Carbonell, Gabriel Jacobsohn, Hernán Fernandez, Roberto Charvel, Juan Pablo Neira, René Rojas, Izaias Martins, Maria Rita Spina and Marcelo Roca.

## NOTES

* The chapter was written during 2013 and some information was later updated to March 2014.
1. In this chapter, we use BAN and network interchangeably.
2. In this chapter, we use business angel and angel investor interchangeably.
3. According to the Organisation for Economic Co-operation and Development (OECD, 2011), the angel networks represent 3 per cent of total angel investment in the United States, 7 per cent in the European Union and 12 per cent in the United Kingdom.
4. Informal investor includes money invested in the business of family, friends, neighbours, work colleagues and strangers (Bygrave and Quill, 2007).
5. Personal communication, GEM Argentina, March 2014.
6. The exchange rate is BRL 1 = USD 0.42717 (9 March 2014).
7. The exchange rate is BRL 1 = USD 0.43768 (17 September 2013).
8. The Productive Development Corporation is the public institution responsible for promoting national productive development in Chile since 1939.
9. Innova Chile was created by CORFO to promote innovation and technology transfer activities.
10. Information provided by CORFO Entrepreneurship Division, 9 September 2013.
11. http://www.innpulsacolombia.com.
12. http://www.urnadecristal.gov.co/gestion-gobierno/por-qu-medell-n-es-ciudad-m-s-innovadora-mundo.
13. Capitalia Colombia is a firm of financial solutions and services specialized in new enterprises and SMEs.
14. For more details see http://www.inadem.gov.mx.
15. http://www.elsiglodetorreon.com.mx/noticia/308893.impulsa-nafin-a-emprendedores.html.
16. There is no precise information on the number of investors clubs created.

# REFERENCES


Aernoudt, R. (1999), 'Business angels: should they fly on their own wings?', *Venture Capital*, **1**(2), 187–95.

Aernoudt, R. (2005), 'Business angels: the smartest money for starters? Plea for a renewed policy focus on business angels', *International Journal of Business*, **10**(3), 271–84.

Amorós, J.E. and A. Acha (2014), *Global Entrepreneurship Monitor GEM Reporte de Chile 2012*, Santiago de Chile: Universidad del Desarrollo.

Amorós, J.E. and C. Poblete (2009), *Global Entrepreneurship Monitor GEM Reporte de Chile 2008*, Santiago de Chile: Universidad del Desarrollo.

Angel Ventures México (2010), 'Inversionistas Ángeles en México', available at http://www2.esmas.com/emprendedor/articulos/emprendedores/148142/angel-investors-inversionistas-angeles-mexico-angel-ventures-me (accessed 27 August 2013).

Angel Venture México (2011), 'Presentación Especial: Angel Ventures México', available at http://imef.org.mx/wp-content/themes/imef/img/grupos/sonora/AVM2011.pdf (accessed 5 March 2014).

Anjos do Brasil (2013), 'O Investimento Anjo Pode Fazer a Diferenca Para a Inovacao Brasileira', available at http://www.anjosdobrasil.net (accessed 5 March 2014).

Bosma, N. and J.E. Amorós (2014), *Global Entrepreneurship Monitor 2013 Executive Report*, available at http://www.gemconsortium.org (accessed 15 March 2014).

Bygrave, W. and M. Quill (2007), *Global Entrepreneurship Monitor. 2006 Financing Report*, Babson Park, MA and London: Babson College and London Business School.

Carullo, J.C. (2002), *El capital de riesgo en Argentina: Surgimiento, crisis, experiencias y propuestas*, Final report, available at http://www.improver.com.ar/archivos/capital_de_riesgo_en_argentina_II.pdf (accessed 14 March 2014).

Carullo, J.C. and F. Vismara (2006), 'Venture capital in Argentina: public policies and cooperation between public and private sector', *International Journal of Entrepreneurship and Innovation Management*, **6**(4/5), 326–40.

Charvel, R. (2007), 'A comprehensive look at private equity industry in Mexico (1990–2006)', *Journal of Private Equity*, **10**(4), 42–53.

Charvel, R. (2012a), 'Is private equity in emerging markets coming of age? Evidence of the Mexican private equity market', in D. Klonowski (ed.), *Private Equity in Emerging Markets. The New Frontiers of International Finance*, New York: Palgrave Macmillan, pp. 249–60.

Charvel, R. (2012b), 'The road map for private equity, venture capital and hedge funds in Mexico: alternative assets as an accelerator credit to firms in emerging markets', *Journal of Private Equity*, **15**(2), 53–62.

Charvel, R. (2013), 'Mid-year review shows 2013 may be Mexico's PE/VC moment', Venture Equity Latin America, Annual Report, XII (18)1, 10–14, available at http://www.ignia.com.mx/bop/uploads/media/VELA_2013-11153.pdf (accessed 19 February 2014).

Charvel, R., L. González and D. Olivas (2006), 'The unfullfilled need of venture capital in Mexico', *International Journal of Entrepreneurship and Innovation Management,* **6**(4/5), 303–25.

CORFO (2006), 'Línea de Financiamiento Apoyo a Redes de Capitalistas Ángeles. In Bases Administrativas', mimeo, Corporación de Fomento de la Producción CORFO Innova Chile, CORFO, Santiago de Chile.

Credit Suisse (2013), *Global Wealth Report 2013*, Research report, available at http://images.smh.com.au/file/2013/10/09/4815797/cs_global_wealth_report_2013_WEB_low%2520pdf.pdf?rand=1381288140715 (accessed 4 March 2014).

Essinger, J. (2012), 'Latin America creates rival for Silicon Valley', available at http://www.worldfinance.com/inward-investment/americas/latin-america-creates-rival-to-silicon-valley (accessed 5 January 2014).

Ferreira, M. (2008), 'Políticas Públicas para el desarrollo del Capital de Riesgo en Argentina', Fundación Empresa Global, FOMIN/BID, available at http://www.feg.org.ar/archivos/Informecapitalderiesgo.pdf (accessed 5 September 2013).

FOMIN/BID (2013), *Las Redes de Inversionistas Ángeles en América Latina y el Caribe*, available at http://www5.iadb.org/mif/en-us/home/knowledge.aspx (accessed 15 August 2013).

Gonzalo, M., J. Federico, S. Drucaroff and H. Kantis (2013), 'Post-investment trajectories of Latin American young technology-based firms: an exploratory study', *Venture Capital*, **15**(2), 115–34.

Groh, A., H. Liechtenstein and K. Lieser (2013), *The Global Venture Capital and Private Equity Country Attractiveness. 2013 Annual*, available at http://blog.iese.edu/vcpeindex/files/2013/08/VCPE-Index-2013-Annual-HD.pdf (accessed 15 March 2014).

Hashimoto, M. (2013), 'Os desafios do investimento anjo no Brasil', available at http://revistapegn.globo.com/Revista/Common/0,,EMI327008-17141,00.html (accessed 5 September 2013).

Inglehart, R. and M. Carballo (2008), 'Existe Latinoamérica? Un análisis global de diferencias transculturales', *Perfiles Latinoamericanos*, **16**(31), 13–38.

Inglehart, R. and C. Welzel (2005), *Modernization, Cultural Change, and Democracy: The Human Development Sequence*, New York: Cambridge University Press.

Jacobsohn, G. (2009), 'Informe del Observatorio de Capital de Riesgo', mimeo, Buenos Aires.

Jacobsohn, G. (2012), 'Angeles Inversores: Un estudio de Casos en Argentina', available at http://idem.uab.es/GabrielJacobsohn_TI_2012.pdf (accessed 12 December 2013).

Jacobsohn, G. and J.C. Carullo (2005), 'Capital de Riesgo en Argentina: Diagnóstico, Necesidades y Políticas', available at http://www.improver.com.ar/archivos/capital_de_riesgo_en_argentina.pdf (accessed 14 March 2014).

Kantis, H. and J. Federico (2012), 'Entrepreneurship policy in Latin America: trends and challenges', in R.A. Blackburn and M.T. Schaper (eds), *Government, SME and Entrepreneurship Development. Policy, Practice and Challenges*, Surrey: Gower Publishing, pp. 49–64.

Kelley, D., N. Bosma and J.E. Amorós (2011), *Global Entrepreneurship Monitor 2010 Executive Report*, available at http://www.gemconsortium.org (accessed 15 March 2014).

Leamon, A. and J. Lerner (2012), 'Creating a venture ecosystem in Brazil: FINEP`s Innovar Project', Harvard Business School, Working Paper 12-099, available at http://lavca.org/wp-content/uploads/2013/12/Creating-a-Venture-Ecosystem.-FINEP%E2%80%99s-INOVAR.pdf (accessed 10 March 2014).

Lederman, D., J. Messina, S. Pienknagura and J. Rigolini (2014), *Latin America Entrepreneur Many Firms but Little Innovation*, Washington, DC: The World Bank.

Lerner, J. (2010), *Boulevard of Broken Dreams: Why Public Efforts to Boost Entrepreneurship and Venture Capital Have Failed – and What to Do about It*, Princeton, NJ: Princeton University Press.

Lerner, J., A. Leamon and S. García-Robles (2013), *Best Practices in Creating a Venture Capital Ecosystem*, available at http://lavca.org/wp-content/uploads/2013/12/Best-Practices-in-Creating-a-VC-Ecosystem.pdf (accessed 10 March 2014).

Mason, C. (2009), 'Public policy support for the informal venture capital market in Europe: a critical review', *International Small Business Journal*, **27**(5), 536–56.

Mason, C. and R. Harrison (1997), 'Business angel networks and the development of the informal venture capital market in the UK. Is there still a role for the public sector?', *Small Business Economics*, **9**(2), 111–23.

Mason, C. and R. Harrison (2001), 'Investment readiness: a critique of government proposals to increase the demand for venture capital', *Regional Studies*, **34**, 663–68.

Mason, C. and J. Kwok (2010), 'Investment readiness programmes and access to finance: a critical review of design issues', Working Paper 10-03, Hunter Centre for Entrepreneurship, University of Strathclyde, Glasgow.

Matíz, F.J. and G. Fracica (2011), 'La financiación de nuevas empresas en Colombia: Una mirada desde la demanda', *Revista Economía Administración y Negocios*, **70**, 118–31.

Naranjo, E., I. Lucatero, M. Campos, M.A. Flores and N. López (2014), *Monitor Global de la Actividad Emprendedora México 2013*, available at http://www.gemconsortium.org/docs/download/3368 (accesed 31 July 2014).

OECD (2011), *Financing High-growth Firms: The Role of Angel Investors*, available at http://www.eban.org/wp-content/uploads/2013/03/OECD-Angel-Financing-Publication.pdf (accessed 24 May 2013).
Orellana, F. and F. Contreras (2014), 'Brasil, Colombia y Chile lideran impulsos para porenciar el emprendimiento y la innovación', available at https://www.df.cl/noticias/empresas/innovacion-y-sustentabilidad/brasil-colombia-y-chile-lideran-impulsos-para-potenciar-el-emprendimiento-y-la-innovacion/2014-09-05/215855.html (accessed 8 September 2014).
Ortmans, J. (2012), 'Start-ups continue to bloom in Argentina', available at http://www.entrepreneurship.org/resource-center/q/StartUps%20Continue%20to%20'Bloom'%20in%20Argentina.aspx (accessed 5 March 2014).
Pereiro, L. (2001), 'Tango and cash: entrepreneurial finance and venture capital in Argentina', *Venture Capital*, **3**(4), 291–308.
Romaní, G. (1996), 'A Situacao das companhias de capital de risco no Brasil: Um estudo exploratorio', Master's dissertation, Universidade de Sao Paulo, Brazil.
Romaní, G., M. Atienza and J.E. Amorós (2009), 'Financing entrepreneurial activity in Chile: scale and scope of the public support programs', *Venture Capital*, **11**(1), 50–70.
Romaní, G., M. Atienza and J.E. Amorós (2013), 'The development of business angel network in Latin America: the ase of Chile', *Venture Capital*, **15**(2), 95–113.
Santillán-Salgado, R.J. and N.A. Hernández-Perales (2011), 'Generalities on private equity and venture capital funds: a current review of the industry and its environment in Mexico', available at http://mpra.ub.uni-muenchen.de/27815/ (accesed 24 February 2014).
Sohl, J. (2012), 'The changing nature of the angel market', in H. Landström and C. Mason (eds), *Handbook of Research on Venture Capital: Volume 2*, Cheltenham, UK and Northampton, MA, USA: Edward Elgar, pp. 17–41.
Start Up (2014), 'The entrepreneurial Revolution Start Up Chile', mimeo, Santiago de Chile.
Startup Genoma and Telefonica Digital (2012), *Startup Ecosystem Report 2012 – Part One*, available at http://multisite-blog.digital.telefonica.com.s3.amazonaws.com/wp-content/uploads/2013/01/Startup-Eco_14012013.pdf (accessed 2 September 2013).
Tanji, T. (2013), 'Governo assina acordo para estimular investimentos en startups', available at http://info.abril.com.br/noticias/carreira/2013/07/governo-assina-acordo-para-estimular-investimentos-em-startups.shtml (accessed 31 July 2013).
Vigna, R. (2013), 'Investimentos-anjo podem atingir R$ bilhoes em 2014', available at http://jcrs.uol.com.br/site/noticia.php?codn=133049 (accessed 16 August 2013).
World Economic Forum (2012), *The Global Competitiveness Report 2011–2012*, available at http://www3.weforum.org/docs/WEF_GCR_Report_2011-12.pdf (accessed 10 December 2013).

# APPENDIX

*Table 12A.1 Macroeconomic indicators of Latin American countries analysed, 2013*

| Data | Argentina | Brazil | Colombia | Chile | Mexico |
|---|---|---|---|---|---|
| Currency | Argentine Peso | Brazilian Real | Colombian Peso | Chilean Peso | Mexican Peso |
| Language | Spanish | Portuguese | Spanish | Spanish | Spanish |
| Population (million) | 41.9 | 193.7 | 47.6 | 17.4 | 113.3 |
| GDP (USD billon) | 471.5 | 2,263.7 | 370.5 | 264.9 | 1,193.9 |
| GDP per capita(USD) | 11,252 | 11,686 | 7,783.6 | 15,224 | 10,537 |
| GDP growth 2004–12* | n.a. | 3.9 | 4.8 | 4.5 | 2.8 |

*Sources:* The Venture Capital and Private Equity Country Attractiveness Index, 2013 Annual; * World Bank.

*Table 12A.2 Entrepreneurial culture and deal opportunities dimension of the Venture Capital and Private Equity Country Attractiveness Index, ranking 2009–13**

| Dimension | Argentina | | Brazil | | Chile | | Colombia | | Mexico | |
|---|---|---|---|---|---|---|---|---|---|---|
| | 2009 | 2013 | 2009 | 2013 | 2009 | 2013 | 2009 | 2013 | 2009 | 2013 |
| Entrepreneurial culture and deal opportunities | 49 | 56 | 61 | 52 | 41 | 42 | 51 | 48 | 38 | 36 |
| Ranking Index | | | | | | | | | | |
| Innovation | 71 | 68 | 34 | 38 | 48 | 46 | 64 | 55 | 66 | 66 |
| Scientific and technical journal articles | 32 | 32 | 15 | 15 | 40 | 39 | 52 | 52 | 27 | 30 |
| Ease of starting and running a business | 105 | 108 | 118 | 116 | 69 | 60 | 77 | 73 | 71 | 48 |
| Simplicity of closing a business | 66 | 68 | 95 | 98 | 77 | 77 | 36 | 20 | 28 | 31 |
| Corporate R&D | 43 | 46 | 29 | 28 | 38 | 44 | 57 | 59 | 39 | 35 |

*Note:* * The index is calculated for 118 countries.

*Source:* Authors based on Groh et al. (2013).

*Table 12A.3* *Venture Capital and Private Equity Country Attractiveness Index, ranking 2009–13**

| | Argentina | | Brazil | | Chile | | Colombia | | Mexico | |
|---|---|---|---|---|---|---|---|---|---|---|
| | 2009 | 2013 | 2009 | 2013 | 2009 | 2013 | 2009 | 2013 | 2009 | 2013 |
| VC/PE Index | 56 | 48 | 36 | 36 | 34 | 25 | 47 | 39 | 42 | 38 |
| Economic activity | 14 | 37 | 4 | 24 | 46 | 16 | 44 | 27 | 17 | 8 |
| Depth of capital market | 41 | 46 | 13 | 22 | 48 | 16 | 44 | 37 | 32 | 27 |
| Taxation | 71 | 60 | 85 | 78 | 41 | 14 | 58 | 47 | 96 | 57 |
| Investor protection and corporate governance | 99 | 98 | 64 | 68 | 26 | 27 | 76 | 67 | 59 | 59 |
| Human and social environment | 70 | 67 | 51 | 51 | 20 | 16 | 44 | 50 | 96 | 96 |
| Entrepreneurial culture and deal opportunities | 49 | 56 | 61 | 52 | 41 | 42 | 51 | 48 | 38 | 36 |

*Note:* * The index is calculated for 118 countries.

*Source:* Authors based on Groh et al. (2013).

# PART IV

# POLICY ISSUES

# 13 The effectiveness of tax incentives for business angels

*Cécile Carpentier and Jean-Marc Suret*

## 13.1 INTRODUCTION

Several governments have implemented various programs, including tax incentives, intended to increase the number of business angels (BAs) and foster their activity. These programs exist in numerous jurisdictions and represent tax expenditures of several hundred million US dollars each year, yet their economic benefit is largely unknown. The findings of the few analyses available are mixed. Programs can be clear failures (Carpentier and Suret, 2007; Hu, 2007) or provide governments with limited (EDR Group Inc., 2014) or huge benefits (Brander et al., 2005). This situation results from the lack of data and the difficulty of measuring direct effects and economic impacts of such programs (Aernoudt, 1999; Loritz, 2008; Pierrakis, 2011). It can also be traced to the different hypotheses and methods used by the researchers. Thus, opinions on the effectiveness of tax incentives for BAs largely differ among BAs, policymakers and the public. As underlined by Chris Hayter, 'even angels are in disagreement as to the economic growth benefits of tax credits.'[1] To feed this debate, we propose a survey and an analysis of the evaluations of these programs. This approach limits the breadth of our analysis because most of the available studies focus on front-end tax incentives, and several interesting programs have not been studied yet. We are consequently restricted to a subsample of disparate programs. However, we can contribute to the debate by summarizing what we know about these incentives, along with the knowledge gaps, and by suggesting some research avenues. This type of analysis is useful to determine to what extent the differences in the program evaluations result from their design or from the methodological choices and hypotheses retained by the authors.

The chapter is structured as follows. Section 13.2 presents the reasons justifying implementation of policies that favor BAs, and outlines the types of actions observed worldwide. A sample of programs based on tax incentives is briefly summarized. Section 13.3 is devoted to the analysis of expected effects and potential drawbacks of this type of incentive. Section 13.4 provides a summary of the various tax incentive schemes around the world that have been analyzed in depth. Section 13.5 considers the methodology for assessing the impact of such schemes (and the associated challenges) and presents the available empirical evidence. The final section presents our conclusions and suggests avenues for future research.

## 13.2 INCENTIVE PROGRAMS: OBJECTIVE AND CHARACTERISTICS

### 13.2.1 Rationale

To foster small business financing, governments have generally favored venture capital (VC) funds (Lerner, 2010). These actions are grounded in a double assertion. First, innovation and job creation largely depend on the activities of a small group of young innovative companies (Shane, 2008; Stangler, 2010; Le Moign and Passet, 2011; Mason and Brown, 2013). These firms play a key role in employment, economic growth and prosperity. Second, new technology-based firms (NTBF) face a strong equity gap because of their high risk level, large proportion of intangible assets and associated information asymmetry (Revest and Sapio, 2012). Insufficient funds could impede the development of new innovative firms and reduce innovation capacity and job creation. Accordingly, the early-stage VC market is characterized by serious and persistent market failures (Mason, 2009; Dagnino et al., 2010) that justify public interventions.

A growing number of programs target BAs, for four main reasons. First, early-stage financing is mainly provided by private investors, while VC funds finance a small number of firms at a later stage. The move of the VC industry toward later stages of financing has intensified since the latest financial crisis (Mason et al., 2013). There is a persistent and increasing lack of BAs and other seed investors, in part because of low returns, which makes early-stage investments unattractive (European Commission, 2009). Second, BAs bring more than money to the investees. They are seasoned hands-on investors and provide the firms with strategic guidance, network access and expertise – valuable resources for early-stage entrepreneurs. Third, there is a common wisdom that a large pool of inactive and potential or 'virgin' BAs exists (Aernoudt et al., 2007). Incentives are assumed to increase the number of active BAs. A fourth reason for the increase in programs targeting BAs is related to the geographical dimension of BA investing. In the USA, 60 percent of VC is concentrated in California and Massachusetts (Kellogg, 2013). The early-stage equity gap could be more significant in rural regions than in metropolitan areas, leading several US states to implement incentives (Heard and Sibert, 2000;

Wessner, 2013). Promoting BA investment is considered an efficient way to close the regional equity gap (Mason and Harrison, 1995). The reasons cited when the programs are proposed generally refer to at least one of the arguments listed above.[2]

### 13.2.2 Types of Incentives

A popular approach to stimulate BA activity consists in changing the risk-return of angel investing, in the hope that more funds will be attracted by this type of investment. A second approach entails reducing impediments to BA investment.

To change the risk-reward characteristics of a given type of investment, policymakers could implement three types of measures. First, they could reduce the net acquisition cost of business equity using a tax credit. This front-end tax incentive is by far the most common type of intervention. It offers taxpayers a credit ranging from 10 percent to 100 percent of their qualified investment in a target firm. The characteristics of these credits and the maximum annual amount that can be claimed for a given firm vary across jurisdictions, but the general idea is to decrease the net cost of the investment to increase investors' expected return.[3] Second, the government can offer a preferential tax rate applicable to capital gains on small businesses. This mechanism increases the after-tax rate of return of successful investors, but provides nothing to investors who sustain a loss. A variation of this approach is the rollover provision, which defers the tax on gains realized on such investments when the proceeds are invested in other qualifying small businesses. Third, policymakers can opt to reduce investment risk. Preferential fiscal treatment of losses lets investors deduct their capital loss from ordinary revenues (Barkoczy and Sandler, 2007). Loss insurance programs also exist in some countries. Participants can sometimes benefit from both front-end and back-end incentives, as in the UK Enterprise Investment Scheme (EIS). We are not aware of any comprehensive analysis of back-end incentives.

The market for informal investment is constrained by several inefficiencies, namely, the invisibility of BAs and the high search costs of angels trying to find investment opportunities and entrepreneurs seeking investors (Mason and Harrison, 1995). Moreover, individual BAs are restricted in their capacity to analyze innovative projects and to reinvest in later rounds. Mason and Harrison (1995) contend that the most cost-effective means of closing the equity gap is for the public sector to underwrite the operating costs of business introduction services designed to overcome these sources of inefficiency. Governments have implemented monetary support for angel syndicates that improve BAs' visibility and allow pooling of resources. They have also financed matching funds dedicated to investing jointly with BAs and increasing their capacity to undertake follow-on investment. Evidence related to these programs is limited.

In this chapter, we focus on front-end tax incentives. Our objective is to summarize previous analyses of incentives dedicated to BAs, and previous research is restricted to this type of program.

### 13.2.3 Survey of Programs

We analyzed 53 programs implemented worldwide. We obtained a detailed description of each program, generally found on the websites of the administering authorities and in the fiscal regulation. We constructed detailed tables including the implementation, closing or modification dates, the fiscal rules related to the credits, including limits and possible carry-back or -forward, the types of taxpayers, firms and sectors targeted, and the budget available. We tabulate the tax incentive programs in Table 13.1 along two dimensions: target investors and target firms. Singapore, Malaysia, Portugal and Michigan restrict the tax incentives to BAs certified by a BA syndicate or governmental agency.[4] In Wisconsin, investors must be able to get involved in the investees and to analyze the investments (WEDC, 2012). Seven programs enable qualified investors, as defined by the securities regulation, to get the tax credit. Qualification definitions refer to individuals' wealth or revenues, but do not consider their capacity to act as hands-on investors in an entrepreneurial venture. Most programs are available to any taxpayer. Private placements must satisfy the local securities regulations, but the program manager does not check the investor's status.

Target firms are generally defined by a size limit that can be very high. For example, the EIS applies to firms with gross assets of up to US$25 million[5] before any share issue and with fewer than 250 full-time employees. Such firms can hardly be described as early-stage ventures. The most restrictive programs target small innovative firms exclusively, using a qualification process to assess the firm's innovation capacity. Although innovative firms are not solely high-tech firms, reports available in Wisconsin and Louisiana indicate that high-tech sectors represent most investments when innovation criteria apply.

Of the 53 tax incentives implemented to promote BA investment in innovative high-growth firms, only four active programs are specifically dedicated to BAs, as defined in this volume, and to innovative firms. Generally, the programs are available to all taxpayers or qualified investors, even if BAs make up only a small subsample of informal or qualified investors (Sørheim and Landström, 2001). Only one program targets

NTBF and requires that both investors and investees be qualified by a BA network.[6] Policymakers generally do not differentiate among BAs, informal investors and qualified investors. There is a puzzling mismatch between program objectives that focus on BAs and innovative firms and the rules that generally make tax credits available to every taxpayer financing a very large set of firms without considering innovation and growth potential. However, Table 13.1 seems to indicate that most US programs show a much more focused approach toward firms than non-US programs.

## 13.3 EXPECTED OUTCOMES

A policy analysis process should begin with forecasting the expected policy outcomes (Dunn, 2012). The objective of incentives dedicated to BAs can be stated in terms of equity provision, and promotion of firm growth or overall economic development. There are several reasons why it is very difficult to assess the effectiveness of tax incentive programs. They include lack of precise objectives, lack of data and the superposition effect. Moreover, incentives can have negative effects that should be considered.

Several programs have loosely defined objectives, like 'encourage taxpayers to invest capital in businesses that are in the early stages of development' or even 'fostering economic growth'. Evaluating a program with such vaguely defined targets is difficult. Further, the objectives are often defined within a short-term perspective; long-term effects are not considered. The observation of an increase in investment in emerging firms could be seen as a positive outcome of the program. It can also indicate a poor allocation of funds in the economy if the investees generally fail or simply post economic performance that is poorer than that of comparable firms.

The second impediment to program analysis is the lack of accurate data. The program design tends to lack clear requirements for evaluation and data collection. Analysts of BA-dedicated programs generally cannot access the lists of investments or investors. The analysis of the fate of the financed firms is then out of reach, as is the estimation of the investors' rate of return or simply the rate of successful exits.

The superposition effect refers to the fact that tax credits for BAs are often part of a larger strategy based on several complementary programs (Cheney and Ozawa, 2011). For example, firms targeted by the Wisconsin Angel Tax Credit can also benefit from Venture Fund Credits (WEDC, 2012). The Ohio Third Frontier program includes tax incentives (Ohio Technology Investment Tax Credit), pre-seed and seed funds, and the VC funds-of-funds mechanism to increase early-stage investing (Cheney and

*Table 13.1 Distribution of the angel investors' tax credit programs by eligible investors and firms*

| Eligible investors | Eligible firms | | | |
|---|---|---|---|---|
| | Small high tech | Small targeted | Small | All targeted |
| Business angels with record | Malaysia | Singapore<br>**US Wisconsin** | | Portugal |
| Business angels | | US Michigan (old) | | |
| Qualified investors | US Connecticut<br>US Kansas<br>US Ohio<br>**US Minnesota** | US Georgia<br>**US Louisiana**<br>US South Carolina | | |
| All investors | US Maryland<br>US Arkansas<br>US New Jersey<br>US New York<br>US Virginia<br>US West<br>Israel | US Arizona<br>US Colorado<br>**US Illinois**<br>US Indiana<br>US Iowa<br>US Maine<br>US Nebraska<br>US New Mexico<br>US North Carolina (old)<br>US Rhode Island<br>**Canada BC**<br>**UK;** *UK (3)*<br>Canada Manitoba<br>Canada NF<br>Canada Yukon<br>*Singapore*<br>*USA* | France<br>Canada NB<br>Canada NS<br>**Canada QC** (old)<br>Finland<br>*Australia (2)*<br>*Canada (3)*<br>*USA (2)*<br>*Italy* | **US Hawaii** (old)<br>US North Dakota |

*Notes:* Back-end tax credit programs are in italics. Front-end tax credit programs with available evaluations are in bold. 'Old' means that the program has been repealed.

Program names: USA: Arizona Angel Investment Tax Credit (ITC); Arkansas Equity ITC; Colorado Advanced Industry ITC; Connecticut Angel TC; Georgia Angel Investor TC

*Table 13.1* (continued)

| |
|---|
| Hawaii High Technology Business ITC; Illinois Angel ITC; Indiana Venture Capital ITC; Iowa TCs for Investment in Qualifying Businesses; Kansas Angel Investors TC; Louisiana Angel Investor Rebate Program; Maine Seed Capital TC; Maryland Biotechnology ITC; Michigan Small Business ITC; Minnesota Angel ITC; Nebraska Angel ITC; New Jersey Angel Investor TC; New York Qualified Emerging Technology Companies; New Mexico Angel ITC; North Carolina Qualified Business ITC; North Dakota Seed Capital ITC; Ohio Technology ITC; Rhode Island Innovation TC; South Carolina Angel Investor Act; Virginia Qualified Equity and Subordinated Debt Investment Credit; West Virginia High Growth Business ITC; Wisconsin Angel Investor TC; Canada: BC Eligible Business Corporation; Manitoba Small Business Venture Capital TC; NF Direct Equity TC; NB Small Business Investor TC; NS Equity TC; QC: Quebec Business Investment Company; Yukon Small Business ITC; Malaysia Angel Tax Incentive; France Tepa Law; Ireland Employment and Investment Incentive; Israel Angels' Law; Portugal Qualified Venture Capital Investors TC; Singapore Angel Investors Tax Deduction; UK Enterprise Investment Scheme (EIS) and Seed Enterprise Investment Scheme (SEIS). |
| Australia (2): Small business concessions; small business rollover; Canada (3): Lifetime capital gains exemption; capital gains deferral for investment in small business; business investment loss; USA (2): Gains on the sale of small business stock; Small Business Jobs Act; Italy: Private investors' capital gain tax exemption; UK (3): Capital gains tax exemption; capital gains tax deferral relief; share loss relief; Singapore: Enterprise Investment Incentive; USA: Rollover of gains on qualified small business stock. |

Ozawa, 2011). When the whole effect of a multi-dimensional development strategy is attributed to a single component of the strategy, this artificially increases its perceived effectiveness. This problem has generally been neglected.

### 13.3.1 Expected Effects

Front-end tax incentives are designed to increase the expected rate of return by decreasing the after-tax cost of the investment. Policymakers thereby expect to stimulate investments associated with the credit, by several means. Existing active BAs can increase the amount invested in each deal or finance more firms. Previously inactive BAs may become involved because of the change in the perceived risk-return reward. Informal investors without any knowledge of business or investment can be attracted by the tax credit. Most programs neglect this dimension, although Gompers and Lerner (2010, p. 208) stress that the challenge for public policymakers is how to ensure the involvement of BAs who can add the most value. The literature indicates that BAs face a shortage of good projects. If, as asserted by Mason and Kwok (2010), firms' access to finance is constrained by demand-side weaknesses, BAs will not be very sensitive to tax dimensions. In this situation, the increase in investment can mainly come from unskilled investors, who cannot select projects wisely but who are attracted by tax credits. As a result, the program will not meet the challenge raised by Gompers and Lerner. The type, knowledge and capacity to act as a hands-on investor of the individuals attracted by tax credits have been neglected by previous research.

Tax incentive programs are generally devoted to stimulating firm growth. This objective is particularly difficult to study because it requires longitudinal data that are usually not collected. Moreover, classical growth indicators most often make little sense when estimated for nascent firms, because the initial values are close to zero. Several analyses of tax incentives use the increase in invested funds as a measure of success. From an economic standpoint, the increase in invested equity can be an indicator of success only if this financing goes to high-growth and ultimately successful firms (Brown and Mason, 2012). Evidence of this program outcome is extremely scarce.

Analysts can also study the programs from a global economic viewpoint, by comparing the tax expenses and benefits. The programs induce direct and indirect economic effects through new salaries and expenses. In turn, this increases the tax revenues for the government: new workers can be hired, and firms and new employees buy goods and services. Macroeconomic analysis should use a model and a large set of hypotheses to link the increase in activity at a small sample of firms to the overall economy and to tax revenues. Researchers refer to a multiplier effect. This is a perilous exercise, providing different results depending on assumptions about the way the government finances the program. A correct estimation of this type of effect considers the alternative use of funds. Had the government spent an amount equivalent to the tax expenditure in an investment or overall tax cuts, this could have generated direct and indirect effects that should be considered.

### 13.3.2 Potential Drawbacks

Tax incentives can have several drawbacks: public policies dedicated to small business financing have generally failed because of poor conception or implementation (Lerner, 2010). This is particularly true of front-end incentives; several programs have missed their target (Sandler, 2004, p.498). Keuschnigg and Nielsen (2004, p.371) demonstrate that this type of program results in a global welfare loss because these subsidies are not related to success. Accordingly, they erode the incentives for effort. The drawbacks concern non-angels, experienced angels and the economy. First, tax incentives can attract inexperienced investors to a type of high-risk investment that they cannot correctly appraise. As Gompers and Lerner (2003) underscore, 'Encouraging individuals to make such small investments may be counter-productive and socially wasteful if the financial returns are unsatisfactory and the companies financed are not viable.' Between 40 percent to 60 percent of firms financed by skilled angels ultimately generate negative or tiny rates of return (DeGennaro, 2012). The probability is high that unskilled investors will participate in less promising ventures, lose much of their investment and become trapped in illiquid placements in small private firms. However, as the SAGPA report (2013) asserts, eligibility criteria for tax breaks make it difficult to target 'real' angels without making rules too complicated. Exit is a real challenge, even for skilled investors, and may be impossible for naïve investors.[7] Second, whereas tax incentives could raise the number of investors, BAs already do not receive enough deal propositions that meet their investment criteria (Mason and Harrison, 2001; Mason and Kwok, 2010). In such a situation, the tax credit might increase the value sought by the entrepreneur and decrease the expected rate of return, creating an implicit tax rate effect.[8]

Third, from an economic standpoint, tax incentives distort resource allocation in that some activities are favored not because they are more economically productive but because they provide a tax credit (Zee et al., 2002). Incentives constitute a tax expenditure that reduces revenues. Moreover, as Zee et al. (2002) argue, abuse and leakage are perennial problems with tax incentives and warrant administrative resources. The distortion problem is particularly important when the eligibility rules allow the taxpayer to receive credits for any kind of investment in a large set of industries. Such loosely defined eligibility rules appeared in the first version of incentive programs in Sweden and the Netherlands (Centre for Strategy and Evaluation Services LLP, 2012). In the UK, both the EIS and the Business Expansion Scheme, which was the predecessor of the EIS, have had the same problem of defining which type of firms and sectors should be excluded.

## 13.4 PREVIOUS ANALYSES AND PROGRAMS

### 13.4.1 Analyses

We identified 53 tax incentive programs for BAs. For each jurisdiction, we carefully scanned the websites of entities managing the program and local tax authorities to detect all analyses and reports. We also surveyed the academic literature. We found six programs analyzed with sufficient data and methodological rigor to use in our survey.[9] We detail these programs in the next subsections. The EIS in the UK (Boyns et al., 2003; Cowling et al., 2008) is generally considered a success, and the Angel Investment

Program in Illinois (VanMetre, 2012) has a low positive marginal effect. The Angels Tax Credit in Minnesota provides a modest increase in employment (98 direct jobs over three years) and rewards the state with earnings of US$0.61 for every US$1 it forgoes in revenues (EDR Group Inc., 2014). The Hawaii 100 percent QHTB Investment Tax Credit is generally considered inefficient based on the observed decrease in high-tech employment and evidence that firms exploit several loopholes (Sakai and Bird, 2005; Hu, 2007; Kato et al., 2009). The analysis of the French incentive program leads to similar conclusions (NEOVIAN, 2012; Levratto and Tessier, 2016). Brander et al. (2005) look at the Canadian British Columbia (BC) Equity Capital Program and conclude that it is much too early to assess the performance of the program regarding the creation of successful companies.[10] However, their results suggest that the tax revenue effects of the program are modest and should not be viewed as a primary justification for the program. Hellmann and Schure (2010) analyze the Venture Capital Program in BC, but BAs constitute only a small component of this complex program. Carpentier and Suret (2007) conclude that the Quebec Business Investment Company (QBIC) program failed to attract BAs. In addition, firms financed through the program exhibit very poor performance.

### 13.4.2 Equity Investment Scheme

The EIS was introduced in 1994.[11] It provides 30 percent tax relief (20 percent before 2011) to investors (individuals only) with direct equity holdings in qualifying companies. The credit may be carried back for up to one year. Shares must be held for three years. No capital gains tax is payable on disposal of shares after three years. If EIS shares are disposed of at a loss, such loss can be offset against the investor's capital gains or income in the year of disposal. Both front-end and back-end tax incentives are available for a single investment. There are few restrictions on investors, except that individuals must have no connection with the company issuing the shares. This program is not dedicated to BAs. The maximum annual tax reduction per investor is US$500,000.[12]

This program is not focused on high-growth innovative firms, but notably excludes real estate, financial and legal and accountancy services. Recent data indicate that high-tech firms comprised 28 percent of firms benefiting from the program and received 20 percent of investments from 2009 to 2013.[13] Even firms listed on the Alternative Investment Market can participate in the program, but must be 'small companies' as measured by their gross assets (no more than US$25 million) and number of employees (fewer than 250).

### 13.4.3 French Tax Incentives

The French government has provided tax incentives to BA investments for years. First, an income tax break for small and medium-sized enterprise (SME) investment is available, although the rate was reduced from 25 percent to 18 percent in 2012 and the maximum reduced from US$35,000 to US$14,000. Individuals who can act as BAs are generally eligible for a wealth tax that applies to people owning assets in excess of US$1.1 million in 2010. This tax is reduced by 75 percent of the total amount invested in SMEs within the limit of US$70,000. This tax reduction was reduced in 2012 to 50 percent of the total amount invested within the limit of US$62,000. There are no restrictions relative to the industry, innovation or stage of development. Any investment in non-listed companies qualifies for the credit, and any taxpayer can obtain it. The French incentives available are untargeted credits. Many angel groups in this country have created collective investment vehicles for BAs (SIBAs) to group taxpayers attracted by tax credits.

### 13.4.4 Minnesota Angel Tax Credit

The Minnesota Angel Tax Credit was introduced in 2010.[14] It provides a 25 percent credit (refundable) to investors (or investment funds) financing high-tech start-ups. Investors need to hold the investment for three years, and investors (firms) must report annually for three (five) years. Investors must have sufficient knowledge and experience in financial and business matters to evaluate the merits and risks of a prospective investment. They must be accredited by the Department of Employment and Economic Development (DEED) before investing. Non-residents (including foreigners) are eligible. The available annual amount of credits is capped at US$15 million from 2014 to 2016 (US$12 million before). The maximum annual credit is US$125,000 per investor. The minimum qualifying investment is US$10,000 for investors and US$30,000 for funds. The maximum total credit per business is US$1 million.

Firms must be mainly active in the state (headquarters and 51 percent of employees and payroll), have fewer than 25 employees and be less than 10 years old (20 years for medical devices or pharmaceuticals). Their securities may not be traded on a public exchange. Previous private equity should be lower than US$4 million. Firms must be qualified by the DEED before investment. They must be engaged in technological innovation; real estate and several other sectors are excluded.

From 2010 to 2013, the program issued credits for US$46.6 million, and 425 businesses were financed through it. It is clearly dedicated to innovative firms, and provisions regarding investors indicate a preference for angel-type investors. However, until 2014, insiders and their family were allowed to participate if they did not (collectively) receive more than 50 percent of their gross income from the investee. For 2015 and 2016, insiders (officers, principals and 20 percent owners) and their families will no longer be eligible for the credit.[15]

### 13.4.5 The Illinois Angel Investment Credit Program

The Illinois Angel Tax Credit was introduced in 2011.[16] It shares several characteristics with the Minnesota program. Increasing jobs and capital investment in the state is an important consideration. It provides a 25 percent credit to investors (individuals, corporations, partnerships, limited liability companies) in a qualified new business venture (QNBV). Investors need to hold the investment and report annually for three years. The credit may be carried forward for up to five years. The available annual amount of credits is capped at US$10 million from 2011–16. The maximum annual investment is US$2 million per investor. The maximum total investment per business is US$4 million.

Firms must register with the Department of Commerce and Economic Opportunity for each taxable year to get QNBV status. Firms must be mainly active in the state (headquarters and 51 percent of employees), have fewer than 100 employees and have operated for less than ten years prior to certification. Previous private equity should be lower than US$10 million (US$4 million for investments qualifying for tax credit). Firms must be principally engaged in innovation, and have the potential to create jobs or capital investments.

### 13.4.6 Hawaii

The Hawaii High Technology Business Investment Tax Credit was introduced in 1999. The program was intended to encourage the growth of high-tech firms. This program, the most generous in the USA, was closed in 2010.[17] The tax credit was granted to eligible taxpayers (individuals, LLC or partnership investment entities) at a decreasing rate for each year following investment in a qualified high-tech business (QHTB). In years 1, 2, 3, 4 and 5 the credit percentage was, respectively, 35 percent, 25 percent, 20 percent, 10 percent and 10 percent. Over the five years, the total credit was thus equal to 100 percent of the amount invested. This non-refundable tax credit could be carried forward in subsequent years until it was exhausted. The maximum annual investment was US$2 million per investor.

A QHTB was a business with capital, property or an office in Hawaii. Qualified research had to constitute more than 50 percent of the firm's activities, and more than 75 percent of qualified research had to be done in Hawaii. QHTBs derived more than 75 percent of their gross income from qualified research. Gross income came from products (services) made in, sold from or manufactured (performed) in Hawaii. QHTBs had to carry out qualified research such as software development, biotechnology, sensor and optic technologies, ocean sciences, astronomy or non-fossil fuel energy-related technology. Qualified research also included performing arts such as film production.

### 13.4.7 British Columbia

As described by Brander et al. (2005, p. 10), the Venture Capital Program comprises three distinct programs, one for labor-sponsored VC corporations (employee VC corporations), one for VC corporations (VCCs) and one for eligible business corporations (EBCs). Eligible small businesses (ESB) can be funded by BAs, friends and family, EBC, the Governmental Equity Capital Program and by VC funds (VCCs). Two categories of VCCs coexist. Retail funds sell shares to the public; they include labor-sponsored funds. Non-retail funds are financed by accredited investors. Hellmann and Schure (2010) study the various types of financing, but provide separate analyses for non-retail VC-funded firms (NRVCF), where the relative proportion of BAs cannot be determined. We use NRVCF-related information nonetheless, because it is the only available information.

The program for EBC was introduced in 2003.[18] An ESB can register as an EBC, which allows the ESB to get directly funded without having to implement a VCC. The primary function of the program is to increase access to capital for small businesses, but it is not specifically dedicated to early-stage or innovative firms. It provides a 30 percent (non-refundable) tax credit to BC investors (individuals or corporations) making eligible investments. Investors need to hold the investment for five years. The credit may be carried forward for up to four years. The available annual amount of credits is capped at US$6.4 million. The maximum annual tax credit is US$56,000 per investor. The maximum total investment per business is US$4.7 million.

Firms must be corporations, mainly active in BC (permanent establishment, at least 80 percent of their assets and 75 percent of employees), be substantially involved in manufacturing, processing or export of value-added goods produced in BC, tourism, development of interactive digital new media products, cleantech or research and development of proprietary technologies. They must have no more than 100 employees at the time of the initial investment and equity capital of at least US$23,500.

### 13.4.8 Quebec Business Company

The Quebec Business Investment Company (QBIC) program was introduced in 1985. Designed to attract outside investors in small businesses, the program consists in creating a QBIC: a private company whose sole activity is to make minority investments in qualified corporations (QCs). The QBIC must remain a minority shareholder in each QC and maintain the investment for 24 months. The QBIC is therefore an intermediate structure between investors and a QC. Because most QBICs have only one investee and are managed by the investee team, we can consider this program similar to the other tax incentives for BAs. Investment Quebec registers the QBICs, authorizes each investment and gets information from QBICs up to five years after their last investment. The program was closed in 2004. Investors get a deduction applicable to their provincial taxes of up to 150 percent of their holdings in qualifying investments made by a QBIC, capped to 30 percent of the investor's annual total income. The credit may be carried forward for up to five years.

To qualify for investment from a QBIC, a corporation must be a Canadian-controlled private corporation, operating mainly in Quebec (head office and 50 percent of employees), with assets totaling less than US$47 million. It must not have made significant disbursements of funds to shareholders or investors in the past 24 months. There are no restrictions on the type of activity, except for natural resources. Between 1985 and 2003, 664 QBICs were completed, for total investments of US$275 million.

## 13.5 WHAT DO WE KNOW ABOUT EFFECTIVENESS OF TAX INCENTIVES FOR BUSINESS ANGELS?

The analysis of incentive programs addresses the following questions. First, what is the net effect of the incentive on the target firms' supply of equity? Second, what is the net direct effect of the program at the firm level, including investment, profitability, employment and growth? Lastly, what are the consequences at the macroeconomic level? A classical perspective involves estimating the increase in economic activity due to the program, then estimating the associated increase in tax revenues. There is no easy way to answer each question because the effect of the program is the difference between the actual situation and the one that would have prevailed without the program. Data needed to quantify the actual situation are often missing or incomplete. Further, the situation without the program cannot be observed, and the conclusions of the analysis depend on the hypothesis related to this 'no program situation'.

### 13.5.1 Effect on Equity Supply

Even if taxpayers claim a tax credit for investing US$10 million, this amount cannot be considered as the program's net impact on equity offering. Part of this amount would have been invested anyway. A fair analysis of the program's effects should estimate the additionality of the program. If US$6 million had been invested without the program, the additionality is only 40 percent of the reported investments. To estimate additionality, analysts rely on surveys sent to investors. The survey results are then extrapolated to the whole population. This method generates potential biases. Investors expecting to benefit from the program are more likely to report that they would not have invested without a tax credit, while experienced BAs, assumed to be less affected by tax incentives (Paul et al., 2003), would probably not answer the survey.

Additionality is the key value to determine the first-level benefit of a program. A careful reading of the available analyses indicates large variations in the reported values, and in the estimation hypotheses. It is striking that researchers conclude differently on additionality even when the surveys provide similar ranges of values.[19] Reported additionality ranges from 53 percent in Minnesota (EDR Group Inc., 2014) to 53 percent to 87 percent in the UK (Boyns et al., 2003) and 60 percent in Canada. Overall, the front-end tax incentive increases investment by about half of the amount reported by the programs. However, an important question is: to what extent are experienced BAs or financial investors more prone to be attracted by tax credits? Answers to this question are very scarce. In BC, Hellmann et al. (2010) report that 11.9 percent of BAs would not invest at all if the tax incentive were removed, and 23.8 percent would reduce their investment by 60 percent in this case. In Illinois, 66.7 percent of the surveyed BAs claim that they would have made the same investment without the tax credit. Additionality seems lower for hands-on investors (experienced angels) than for financial investors (Boyns et al., 2003, p. 165).

The proportion of hands-on investors among the investors attracted by the credit is estimated at 20 percent. In Minnesota, 80 percent of surveyed investors were new to angel investing (EDR Group Inc., 2014, p. 19). In the UK, 26 percent of the investors are considered as hands-on investors (Boyns et al., 2003, p. 52). Generally, studies in BC report that tax incentives have had a strong impact on angel activity. However, according to a report on the visible angels' market in Canada in 2012, only 15 percent of Canadian investments are located in the four western provinces, including BC (NACO, 2013). The impact of tax incentives on the population of the members of angel groups thus remains to be demonstrated.

The leverage effect refers to the funds that firms receive from other sources following a tax incentivized investment. Leverage should be assessed through surveys, and evidence is scarce. EDR Group Inc. (2014) reports a leverage ratio for equity of 16 percent in the manufacturing sector and 36 percent for non-manufacturing firms. BC studies report a huge leverage effect of 373.18 percent for NRVCFs. This can be partially attributed to the fact that numerous government-backed programs are likely to participate in the financing of the same small business, including VC companies, retail funds, friends and family, the Community Venture Capital program and the New Media Venture Capital program, as illustrated by Brander et al. (2005). The extent to which participating small businesses leverage private funds that do not provide tax credits remains to be determined. To summarize, front-end tax incentives dedicated to BAs attract new investors, but about 40 to 50 percent of the funds invested would have been injected in SMEs without the programs, and the proportion of skilled angels attracted by such programs is largely unknown.

### 13.5.2 Firm-level Effect

The two main questions addressed by previous research are related to employment and financial performance of firms financed by the program, and the estimates are generally extrapolated from surveys. This method is likely to produce biased estimates, which can be illustrated as follows: the death rate reported by the EIS firms themselves in Boyns et al. (2003) is 12.1 percent (p. 101), but investors estimated this rate at 17.5 percent (p. 102). The data indicate a short-term death rate of 24.8 percent and a ten-year death rate of 40 percent (Cowling et al., 2009). Real data on participating firms constitute the sole source of accurate estimates, but such data are generally not available.

Several analyses consider that the firms in question would not have existed without the program. For example, the tax revenues of the BC programs are estimated based on total BC income tax generated by the companies (Hellmann and Schure, 2010, p. 14). The implicit assumption in this method is that all jobs in target firms exist because of the program for BAs, even when the firm has received only a small amount from a BA and a large amount of equity from another program or other investors (WEDC, 2013). The assumption that the firms would not have existed without the program is not realistic, mainly when the firms operate in traditional sectors where the equity gap is less important than for innovative firms. As Zee et al. (2002, p. 1501) contend, the most profitable projects could have been undertaken even if there had been no tax incentives. Accordingly, the results of cost–benefit analyses strongly depend on the assumption made on this dimension. In a few cases, a displacement ratio is considered. This ratio is the amount of activities and sales that would have occurred without the credit. This practice is not generalized, although some analyses show that the displacement effect can reach 67 percent (VanMetre, 2012, p. 69). This indicates that without the incentive, 67 percent of the observed investment would have been made by the firms. Any estimate that does not include the displacement effect overvalues the program's impact (Sakai and Bird, 2005). This is the case for most of the analyses reported in this chapter.

**Employment**

The total number of jobs attributed to the program is often reported, but analysts generally estimate the tax cost by job initially created. Depending on the study, this tax cost ranges from US$1500 to US$70,000. EDR Group Inc. (2014) presents a comprehensive analysis of the incremental effect of the program on employment. First, surveyed firms were invited to estimate the number of new jobs they created through the program. The survey's results were cross-checked with reported employment in the program database. The results were extrapolated to the whole sample. A similar procedure has been used to estimate the increase in non-salary expenses. Overall, 186 jobs are attributed to the tax program, for a qualified investment ratio of US$280,798 per job and a tax cost of US$70,000 per job. Using total jobs in lieu of incremental jobs, the Wisconsin report suggests a fiscal cost of US$8174 per job. In Hawaii, Sakai and Bird (2005, p. 57) report that the growth rate in private technology jobs targeted by the program was one-quarter of the growth rate in all private non-technology jobs. However, even modest growth in employment is questionable in this program because of the high frequency of loophole exploitation that includes the creation of subsidiaries by large firms to capture the credit, and short-term film projects. In Quebec, detailed data on job creation are not available. However, the QBIC program has probably not created many jobs, because only 39 percent of the financed firms survive, and their profitability and growth is lower than those of comparable firms. Job creation is reported for EIS based on self-reporting. In 2003, firms reported net job creation of 11.4 jobs per firm associated with the program, and Boyns et al. (p. vi) infer a cost of approximately US$25,000 per job. According to Hellmann and Schure (2010), the annual growth rate in employment for NRVCFs is 1.08 percent per year. Accordingly, the authors assess an astonishing program performance of 2.15 jobs per US$9400 of credit, for a tax cost of approximately US$1500 per job. Several factors can explain this result. First, the authors do not consider additionality or displacement: the entire increase in firms' activity is attributed to the program, and without the program, not a single dollar is considered to be invested. Second, many firms started the program in 2007–09 (p. 13), and the analysis ends in 2008. Most of the firms were very early stage at the time of the analysis; it is unlikely that the job creation rate persisted during the bad economic conditions that followed. Indeed, figure 1 of the report evidences a reduction in employment in 2008. The estimates provided in BC probably favor the programs because of the methodological choices.

To summarize, there is limited accurate evidence that tax incentive programs dedicated to BAs have a significant and durable effect on employment. The two analyses that report a low tax cost per employment consider the total number of jobs in financed firms as an outcome of the program; the additionality and substitution effects are neglected.

**Operational and financial performance of financed firms**

In theory, firms financed by tax incentives for BAs should exhibit stronger performance than comparable firms, for two main reasons. First, they benefit from an equity injection that allows investment and enables them to operate on a larger scale (Cowling et al., 2009). Second, they have been selected and monitored by BAs. Observations generally refute this hypothesis.

Comparative analysis of firm performance and growth exists for four programs. EIS schemes generally have little discernible impact on gross profit margins. There is robust evidence that EIS investments are negatively associated with firm profit margins and overall performance (Cowling et al., 2009). This study also suggests that EIS has a small positive effect on employment, but the model is not specifically dedicated to the analysis of employment. In France, tax incentives could partially explain the growth in the number of angels and angel syndicates. According to the France Angels website, 1600 angels active in 30 of the 38 syndicates have invested US$22 million in 2005, and 4292 angels active in 82 syndicates invested US$56 million in 2012. The SAGPA report (2013) assesses that these syndicates used to be based on government subsidies. Levratto and Tessier (2016) compare the dynamics of companies backed by BAs with companies that are not, using 300 French companies financed by BAs with similar firms matched by size, age, industry and location. The dependent variables are the growth rate in employment, assets and revenues over two years. The authors observe a significant effect of angel involvement only on investment. However, such an effect could be traced to the comparison of firms that seek and get outside equity with firms that generally do not issue new shares.[20] Overall, the results are very similar to those reported by Cowling et al. (2008) in the UK. In France, the lack of significant effect of the tax incentives can probably be traced to the very loose eligibility rules. As mentioned by SAGPA (2013, p. 93), the French scheme is used by a wide array of different people and for other purposes than classical angel investment. This could explain why entrepreneurs financed by BAs in this country are disappointed by the very low involvement of these investors in their firm development (NEOVIAN, 2012). Carpentier and Suret (2007) evidence that companies financed by the QBIC program are of mediocre quality. Participating firms' growth is weak post-financing, and their operational performance is significantly inferior to that of companies of comparable size and sector. In sharp contrast, the 205 NRVCFs in BC exhibit a compound annual growth rate in revenue of 188.66 percent (Hellmann and Schure, 2010, p. 26). This astonishing result can probably be traced to the fact that several firms reported no revenues at all at the first financing time, as the authors acknowledge (p. 26).[21] The study also reports a huge compound annual growth rate in assets of 46 percent. However, for the whole period the firm assets increase by US$1.13 million, an amount close to the financing inferred from the data reported by Brander et al. (2005). The very high growth rate reported in BC for NRVCFs mainly comes from the fact that financed firms were often early-stage pre-revenue firms. No other information on the performance of NRVCFs is available, but returns are available for the retail funds that are part of the VC program. Even if firms financed by these funds exhibit a compound annual growth rate in revenues of 54.91 percent (Hellmann and Schure, 2010, p. 26), the funds' average rate of return is clearly negative, at −57.2 percent for five years. Accordingly, the high growth rate of firms' revenues is a puzzling observation.

Another perspective about financed firm performance consists in checking positive investor exits, namely by initial public offerings (IPOs) and trade sales. In BC, the proportion of NRVCFs that exit through an IPO is 0.52 percent, and 2.86 percent of firms were acquired. This can be traced to the fact that NRVCFs are small and early stage, but Hellmann et al. (2010) acknowledge that exit remains a significant challenge. Exit is not explored in the other studies. Boyns et al. (2003, p. 162) report that the proportion of exited investors is lower than 18 percent. Hands-on investors made a substantial profit in 35 percent of the exits, compared with 12 percent for non-hands-on investors. Overall, 1.69 percent of investors report exiting with substantial profits.

Tax incentives can foster firm growth in the short run, by the mechanical effect of equity injection. However, there is no evidence that such programs have a long-run significant impact on growth, productivity and positive liquidity event frequency. The two studies that use benchmark firms evidence that financed ventures perform worse than comparable firms.

### 13.5.3 Macroeconomic Effect

Previous research has adopted two perspectives. In classical cost–benefit analysis, tax expenditures are compared with first-level tax revenues directly generated by the program. However, other researchers consider that the contribution to overall economic growth, generation of employment opportunities, effects on individual income (including returns to investors associated with the program) and effects of new innovative products on general welfare are more important than tax effects (Brander et al., 2005). However, measuring these dimensions objectively is a challenge. Moreover, users of this approach generally fail to consider the alternative use of tax expenditures. For example, if it does not implement the incentive, the government can invest corresponding amounts in education or in the wealth system, thereby creating a direct or indirect revenue effect.

The cost–benefit approach entails estimating the incremental effect of programs on salaries and other expenses of financed firms. The direct and indirect taxes paid by the firms, their employees and the other firms that benefit from this first-level activity can then be determined. The results depend mainly on the accuracy of the determination of the additionality and displacement effects and on the model used to estimate the tax revenues. The other approach consists in estimating the increment in small business finance compared with benchmarks in other jurisdictions.

The cost–benefit approach has been used by Hellmann and Schure (2010) in BC, EDR Group Inc. (2014) in Minnesota and with limited data but careful analysis in Hawaii (Sakai and Bird, 2005). Boyns et al. (2003) and Pierrakis (2011) restrict the cost–benefit analysis to an estimation of the amount of tax credits needed to provide one unit of additional funds to a target firm.

In Minnesota and Hawaii, the authors conclude that tax benefits do not compensate for tax expenditures. In the first case, the author assesses that a benefit could occur in the long run, but the program will not pay for itself within ten years. Both studies that fail to demonstrate tax benefits consider additionality and/or displacement effects. In BC, Hellmann and Schure (2010) assume that firms' activities are totally attributable to the program, even if they acknowledge that many of the companies that benefited from the program would have been active without the programs (p. 14). They also neglect the additionality effect. Accordingly, each dollar invested and all of the firms' operations and employment are credited to the program in the estimation of tax revenues. All categories of taxes are considered. NRVCFs generate direct and indirect tax revenues well over the tax expenditures: every US$1 of BC tax credit generated US$1.41. However, if one applies an additionality factor of 50 percent, the tax multiplier falls to 0.70, in the same range as that reported in Minnesota. For EIS, the estimated cost in terms of tax forgone is US$0.55–0.66 for every additional US$1 invested through it (Boyns et al., 2003; Pierrakis, 2011). Such an indicator is not, however, a clear sign of the scheme's success. If the funds are mainly invested in low performing firms that never reach the status of local leaders, the program becomes a tool for ineffective allocation of funds in the economy.

## 13.6 CONCLUSIONS AND DISCUSSION

Our knowledge of the effectiveness of tax incentives for BAs is indeed very limited. The failure of most programs to collect and provide the data needed to evaluate the programs is a major impediment to the development of comprehensive analyses. Moreover, program objectives are generally loosely defined, which complicates the work of researchers who perform a cost–benefit analysis. The review of previous analyses finds very limited evidence that tax incentives for BAs are effective: tax expenditures are generally higher than tax revenues when the additionality and displacement effects of the incentives are considered. The programs' failure seems clearer for poorly designed programs, as evidenced in Quebec and Hawaii. Well-designed programs that have been revised several times produce a cost–benefit ratio in the vicinity of one. The BC program seems to be an outlier, but a careful reading of the report indicates that the results in this province are largely dependent on methodological choices and hypotheses. More in-depth analyses using more insightful indicators than the number of financed firms or total invested amounts are required.

The lack of clear evidence of the effectiveness of incentives can be explained by the types and characteristics of the firms that benefit from the programs. They generally exhibit modest performance, but pertinent evidence is very scarce. Nonetheless, such evidence is central to assessing the effectiveness of tax incentives dedicated to BAs. We can expect more research based on filings by recipients and on thorough comparative analyses of performance and growth of financed firms. Future research should first address the methodological dimension. Existing studies diverge in the estimation of additionality and displacement, and in the methodology applied to estimate tax benefits of programs. The lack of a clear methodological framework across the various studies makes comparison difficult.

Three important questions not addressed by the literature point to fruitful avenues of future research. First, even if the tax incentive programs attempt to improve investors' rate of return, little is known about whether this objective has been reached. Data related to the exit of the investors involved in this type of program are extremely scarce. The immediate objective of tax incentives is to improve after-tax returns for investors (Boyns et al., 2003, p. 3). Accordingly, the performance of financed firms and the related rates of return experienced by investors attracted by tax credits deserve attention. Exiting is difficult even for skilled angels, and the likelihood that inexperienced investors remain locked in private companies is great. The extent that this objective has been reached was analyzed by Boyns et al. (2003), but more research is needed. The scant data on the extent to which tax-subsidized investments have resulted in successful 'exits' such as acquisitions or IPOs, or in the creation of a high growth firm, indicate a success ratio in the vicinity of 1 percent to 2 percent. This is a very important point because the conceptual literature indicates that tax incentives could be detrimental for investors. The Expert Group notes the risk that a flow of short-term 'dumb' money can lead to inflating company valuations, with too much money chasing too few suitable investment opportunities (European Commission, 2012). This proposition should be explored.

Second, the programs we describe in this chapter are officially dedicated to BAs, but they are generally open to all taxpayers or qualified investors. The programs' impact on BAs, defined above, thus remains largely unexplored. Research should examine the type of investors attracted by tax incentives. Because value-added investors have a significantly higher impact on new venture success than informal investors, they should be the main target of tax incentives. Only one study provides information on this point. If, as suggested by previous research, active BAs face a shortage of good projects, providing a tax credit will not change their capacity to invest. The tax credit does not influence the probability that the project will fail.

Third, the long-run effects of programs have not been investigated. The ultimate objective of programs is to foster economic activity, a result largely dependent on the survival and development of high-growth firms. Given that the available analyses focus on short-term effects, we know little about the performance, survival and success of firms financed by tax credits.

It is often assumed that back-end incentives provide the most positive outcome and are less costly than front-end incentives (Barkoczy and

Sandler, 2007). The effectiveness of such back-end incentives deserves attention and is a promising, albeit difficult, research topic. One possibility is to compare jurisdictions that have made opposite choices in terms of providing support for BAs.

## NOTES

1. Chris Hayter, *State Strategies to Promote Angel Investment for Economic Growth*, NGA Center for Best Practices, available at http://www.nga.org/files/live/sites/NGA/files/pdf/0802ANGELINVESTMENT.PDF. See also S. Shane, 'The problem with tax credits for angel investors', *Bloomberg Business Week*, 20 August 2010, http://www.businessweek.com/smallbiz/content/aug2010/sb20100820_461551.html; Jeff Cornwall, 'Not a fan of angel investment tax credits, the entrepreneurial mind', http://www.businessinsider.com/not-a-fan-of-angel-investment-tax-credits-2011-4; C. Mason, Does tax relief tempt angels?', *Financial Times*, 20 April 2012, http://www.ft.com/cms/s/0/ae61feda-7509-11e1-90d1-00144feab49a.html; 'Should angel investors get tax credits to invest in small businesses?', *Wall Street Journal*, Debate, http://online.wsj.com/news/articles/SB10001424052702304459804577283420497271022; R. Boettcher, 'Angel investors share mixed feelings on new tax credit', http://www.omaha.com/apps/pbcs.dll/article?AID=/20110825/MONEY/708259893/1026927.
2. In Illinois, the purpose of the Angel Investment Program is to attract and encourage investment in early-stage innovative companies. In Nebraska, the program is aimed at angel investors who provide capital for risky businesses involving new technology. The stated objective of the New Jersey Angel Investor Tax Credit is to spur job creation and growth in the state's current and next generation of high-skill, high-wage emerging technology industries. In the UK, the measure is designed to encourage private individuals and companies to invest in smaller, unquoted, high growth potential companies to grow their businesses into sustainable, profitable enterprises.
3. Program descriptions are available in EBAN (2009), Carpentier and Suret (2013) and Williams (2008). Several programs channel the tax advantaged investment through funds. We exclude these programs from the analysis because their participants do not invest directly in unquoted business, as specified in the definition of BA.
4. In the UK, the government suggested a more restrictive definition of BAs, 'to ensure that the additional relief was only available to those providing both finance and the benefit of their business acumen' (HM Treasury, 2011, p. 14). However, this provision has not been implemented.
5. All amounts have been converted to US$ based on the Bank of Canada exchange rate on 31 December 2013.
6. Announced by the prime minister in the 2013 Budget, The Malaysian Angel Tax Incentive is administered by the Angel Tax Incentive Office, which delegates investor and investee qualification to the Malaysian Business Angel Network. See http://www.mban.com.my/investors/ or the Angel Tax Incentive Fact Sheet, available at http://www.digitalnewsasia.com/sites/default/files/files_upload/Angel%20Tax%20FAQ.pdf.
7. Indeed, angel syndicates can help unskilled investors invest wisely. However, there is generally a large gap between the number of active investors in an angel group and the number of users of tax incentives. According to Mason and Harrison (2010), 590 angel group members invested in the UK in 2008–09 while 37,135 subscriptions are reported in the EIS program. Even if several subscriptions can be done by a single investor, such numbers indicate that a very large proportion of EIS users are not considered as members of an angel group and could not receive advice and mentoring from seasoned angels.
8. If a given investment has an expected value of 120 in one period with a required rate of

return of 20 percent, its value on the market should be 100. If the investors are granted a tax credit of 25 percent when they buy the stock, they will push the price up to 133 (100/0.75). The rate of return without the tax credit becomes negative, and the after-tax rate of return stays at 20 percent. The reduction in the rate of return implied by the tax incentive is the implicit tax rate.

9. We also use the results of two partial reports available for the Louisiana and Wisconsin programs.
10. The authors mention that the analysis of the program's effects on increasing tax revenues and on the performance of supported firms is beyond the mandate and scope of their study.
11. The government changed the rules of the program to increase the tax credit. It also introduced the Seed Enterprise Investment Scheme (SEIS) dedicated to very early-stage companies by offering 50 percent tax relief to investments made on or after 2012. http://www.hmrc.gov.uk/seedeis/background.htm.
12. A detailed description of the program is available at http://www.hmrc.gov.uk/eis/part1/1-2.htm.
13. See https://www.gov.uk/government/publications/companies-and-amount-of-investment-by-industry.
14. A detailed description of the program is available at http://mn.gov/deed/business/financing-business/tax- credits/angel-tax-credit/index.jsp.
15. http://mn.gov/deed/images/Angel_Tax_Credit_Fact_Sheet.pdf.
16. A detailed description of the program is available at http://www.illinois.gov/dceo/ExpandRelocate/Incentives/taxassistance/Pages/AngelInvestment.aspx.
17. http://law.justia.com/codes/hawaii/2013/title-14/chapter-235/section-235-110.9.
18. http://www.mit.gov.bc.ca/ICP/VCP/EligibleBusinessCorp/index.htm.
19. Two studies use similar methods but reach different conclusions about additionality. In Minnesota, 18 percent of investors would have made the same investment without the credit, 13 percent would have made a smaller investment, situated at between 50 percent and 100 percent of the current investment, and 48 percent would not have invested at all. In the UK, the corresponding numbers are 34 percent for full investment, 9 percent for a 50 percent to 100 percent investment and 37 percent for non-investing. Additionality seems higher in Minnesota, but the authors suggest an estimation of 52 percent in this state (EDR Group Inc., 2014) and of 53 percent to 87 percent in the UK (Boyns et al., 2003). In BC, surveyed investors assess that 50 percent of relevant equity would have been raised without the tax credit. Further, 60 percent to 70 percent of the co-investors (friends and family) would have been interested even without the tax credit (Brander et al., 2005, p. 82). Additionality could then be estimated at around 40 percent. However, the authors include the answer for VC company investors and get an estimation of 60 percent.
20. There is no control for this dimension in the selection of the matching firms.
21. Moreover, the reported averages are based on the distribution of growth rates estimated for each firm and each available pair of years.

# REFERENCES

Aernoudt, R. (1999), 'European policy toward venture capital: myth or reality?', *Venture Capital*, **1**(1), 47–58.

Aernoudt, R., A. San José and J. Roure (2007), 'Executive forum: public support for the business angel market in Europe – a critical review', *Venture Capital*, **9**(1), 71–84.

Barkoczy, S. and D. Sandler (2007), 'Government venture capital incentives', Research Study No. 46, Australian Tax Research Foundation.

Boyns, N., M. Cox, R. Spires and A. Hugues (2003), *Research into the Enterprise Investment Scheme and Venture Capital Trusts*, PACEC Report for Inland Revenue, available at http://www.hmrc.gov.uk/research/report.pdf (accessed 1 December 2014).

Brander, J.A., E.J. Egan and A.E. Boardman (2005), *The Equity Capital Program in British Columbia: An Assessment of Capital Availability, Program Efficiency, and Policy Alternatives*, Report, available at http://evc.sauder.ubc.ca/downloads/ECPApril2005.pdf (accessed 1 December 2014).
Brown, R. and C. Mason (2012), 'Raising the batting average: re-orientating regional industrial policy to generate more high growth firms', *Local Economy*, **27**(1), 33–49.
Carpentier, C. and J.-M. Suret (2007), 'On the usefulness of tax incentives for business angels and SME owners: an empirical analysis', *Venture Capital*, **9**(1), 1–22.
Carpentier, C. and J.-M. Suret (2013), 'Incitatifs fiscaux pour les anges investisseurs', *Canadian Tax Journal*, **61**(1), 79–157.
Centre for Strategy and Evaluation Services LLP (2012), *Evaluation of EU Member States' Business Angel Markets and Policies*, Final report, Sevenoaks.
Cheney, D. and J. Ozawa (2011), 'Evaluating Ohio's portfolio of technology programs', *Research Evaluation*, **20**(4), 293–303.
Cowling, M., P. Bates, N. Jagger and G. Murray (2008), *Study of the Impact of the Enterprise Investment Scheme (EIS) and Venture Capital Trusts (VCTs) on Company Performance*, Report researched by the Institute for Employment Studies, HM Revenue and Customs Research, No. 44, available at http://www.hmrc.gov.uk/research/report44.pdf (accessed 1 December 2014).
Cowling, M., G. Murray and P. Bates (2009), 'Promoting equity flows into smaller businesses: the UK Enterprise Investment Scheme and Venture Capital Trusts', in R. Baptista and J. Leitao (eds), *Public Policies for Fostering Entrepreneurship: A European Perspective*, New York: Springer, pp. 207–30.
Dagnino, G.B., R. Faraci and M. Sorrentino (2010), 'Mobilizing capital for fostering the early growth of firms: the role of business angels in nascent European entrepreneurship', *Frontiers in Entrepreneurship Research*, Babson College, **26**, 109–24.
DeGennaro, R.P. (2012), 'Angel investors and their investments', in D. Cummings (ed.), *The Oxford Handbook of Entrepreneurial Finance*, Oxford: Oxford University Press, pp. 392–423.
Dunn, W.N. (2012), *Public Policy Analysis*, 5th edn, Upper Saddle River, NJ: Pearson.
EBAN (2009), *Compendium of Fiscal Incentives Available to Business Angels in Europe*, Brussels: European Business Angels Network.
EDR Group Inc. (2014), *Evaluation of the Minnesota Angel Tax Credit Program: 2010–2012*, Report for the Minnesota Department of Revenue, Economic Development Group, Boston, MA.
European Commission (2009), 'Financing innovation and SMEs', Commission Staff Working Document, available at http://ec.europa.eu/enterprise/policies/innovation/files/swd_financing_innovation.pdf (accessed 1 December 2014).
European Commission (2012), *SME Access to Finance Report of the Chairman of the Expert Group on the Cross Border Matching of Innovative Firms with Suitable Investors*, Brussels: Directorate-General for Enterprise and Industry, European Commission.
Gompers, P. and J. Lerner (2003), 'Equity investing', in Z.J. Acs and D.B. Audretsch (eds), *Handbook of Entrepreneurship Research*, Dordrecht: Kluwer Academic Publishers, pp. 267–98.
Gompers, P. and J. Lerner (2010), 'Equity financing', in Z.J. Acs and D.B. Audretsch (eds), *Handbook of Entrepreneurship Research*, New York: Springer, pp. 183–214.
Heard, R.G. and J. Sibert (2000), *Growing New Businesses with Seed and Venture Capital: State Experiences and Options*, Washington, DC: National Governors' Association.
Hellmann, T. and P. Schure (2010), *An Evaluation of the Venture Capital Program in British Columbia*, Report prepared for the Ministry of Small Business, Technology and Economic Development, Vancouver.
Hellmann, T., I. Ilyaszade and T. Lee (2010), 'Angels in British Columbia: preliminary survey results', Working Paper, University of British Colombia.
HM Treasury (2011), 'Tax-advantaged venture capital schemes: a consultation', Consultation

paper, available at http://www.hm-treasury.gov.uk/d/consult_condoc_tax_advantage_venture_capital.pdf (accessed 1 December 2014).
Hu, D.H. (2007), 'Seed capital is not enough: lessons from Hawaii attempt to develop a high-technology sector', *University of Hawaii Law Review*, **30**, 401–22.
Kato, A., S.L. Croix and J. Mak (2009), 'Small state, giant tax credits: Hawaii's leap into high technology development', Working Paper No. 09-1, available at http://www.economics.hawaii.edu/research/workingpapers/WP_09-14.pdf (accessed 1 December 2014).
Kellogg, D. (2013), 'Information and observations on state venture capital programs', available at http://www.treasury.gov/resource-center/sb-programs/. . ./VC%20Report.pdf (accessed 1 December 2014).
Keuschnigg, C. and S.B. Nielsen (2004), 'Taxation and venture capital backed entrepreneurship', *International Tax and Public Finance*, **11**, 369–90.
Le Moign, C. and O. Passet (2011), 'Business angels and venture capital in France: tax challenges', Centre d'analyse stratégique, Note d'analyse 237.
Lerner, J. (2010), *Boulevard of Broken Dreams: Why Public Efforts to Boost Entrepreneurship and Venture Capital Have Failed – and What to do About It*, Princeton, NJ: Princeton University Press.
Levratto, N. and L. Tessier (2016), 'La croissance des PME est-elle favorisée par les Business Angels? Une analyse à partir du cas français en 2008 et 2009', *Innovations, Revue d'économie et de management de l'innovation*, **49**(1), 141–76.
Loritz, J. (2008), 'State strategies to promote angel investment for economic growth', NGA Center for Best Practices, available at http://www.nga.org/files/live/sites/NGA/files/pdf/0802ANGELINVESTMENT.PDF (accessed 1 December 2014).
Mason, C.M. (2009), 'Public policy support for the informal venture capital market in Europe: a critical review', *International Small Business Journal*, **27**(5), 536–56.
Mason, C. and R. Brown (2013), 'Creating good public policy to support high-growth firms', *Small Business Economics*, **40**(2), 211–25.
Mason, C. and R. Harrison (1995), 'Closing the regional equity capital gap: the role of informal venture capital', *Small Business Economics*, **7**(2), 153–72.
Mason, C.M. and R.T. Harrison (2001), 'Investment readiness: a critique of government proposals to increase the demand for venture capital', *Regional Studies*, **35**(7), 663–8.
Mason, C. and R. Harrison (2010), *Annual Report on the Business Angel Market in the United Kingdom: 2008/09*, Department of Business, Innovation and Skills, HM Revenue and Customs.
Mason, C. and J. Kwok (2010), 'Investment readiness programmes and access to finance: a critical review of design issues', *Local Economy*, **25**(4), 269–92.
Mason, C., T. Botelho and R. Harrison (2013), 'The transformation of the business angel market: evidence from Scotland', Working Paper, University of Glasgow and Queen's University, Belfast, available at http://ssrn.com/abstract=2306653 (accessed 1 December 2014).
NACO (2013), *Report on Angels Investing Activity in Canada in 2012*, Toronto: National Angel Capital Organization.
NEOVIAN (2012), *Performance des Anges en France*, Paris.
Paul, S., G. Whittam and J.B. Johnston (2003), 'The operation of the informal venture capital market in Scotland', *Venture Capital*, **5**(4), 313–35.
Pierrakis, Y. (2011), *Incentivising the Supply of Finance for Early Stage Business Through Tax Schemes: A Preliminary Analysis of the Impact of EIS, VCT and CVS*, London: The National Endowment for Science Technology and the Arts.
Revest, V. and A. Sapio (2012), 'Financing technology-based small firms in Europe: what do we know?', *Small Business Economics*, **39**(1), 179–205.
SAGPA (2013), *Business Angel, Co-investment Funds and Policy Portfolios*, Stockholm: Swedish Agency for Growth Policy Analysis.
Sakai, M. and B. Bird (2005), 'Measuring the costs and benefits of Hawaii's Qualified High Technology Business (QHTB) Investment Tax Credit', Appendix B of the Tax Review Commission.

Sandler, D. (2004), *Venture Capital and Tax Incentives: A Comparative Study of Canada and the United States*, Toronto: Canadian Tax Foundation.
Shane, S. (2008), 'Why encouraging more people to become entrepreneurs is bad public policy', *Small Business Economics*, **33**(2), 141–9.
Sørheim, R. and H. Landström (2001), 'Informal investors – a categorization, with policy implications', *Entrepreneurship and Regional Development*, **13**(4), 351–70.
Stangler, D. (2010), *High-growth Firms and the Future of the American Economy*, Kauffman Foundation Research Series: Firm Formation and Economic Growth Volume 2, Kansas City.
VanMetre, B. (2012), 'Entrepreneurial activity in Illinois: investigating the impact of tax incentive developmental programs', Mercatus Policy Essay, available at http://grad.mercatus.org/sites/default/files/VanMetre_MPE%2011.pdf (accessed 1 December 2014).
WEDC (2012), *Act 255: Early Stage Business Investment Program 2012*, Annual report, Wisconsin Economic Development Corporat.
WEDC (2013), *Annual Report on Economic Development*, Madison, CT.
Wessner, C.E. (2013), *Best Practices in State and Regional Innovation Initiatives: Competing in the 21st Century*, Washington, DC: National Research Council Committee on Competing in the 21st Century.
Williams, J. (2008), 'Tax credits and government incentives for angel investing in various states', Belmont University Working Paper, available at http://www.angelcapitalassociation.org/data/Documents/Public%20Policy/State/Tax%20Credits%20-%20Jeffrey%20 Williams.pdf (accessed 1 December 2014).
Zee, H.H., J.G. Stotsky and E. Ley (2002), 'Tax incentives for business investment: a primer for policy makers in developing countries', *World Development*, **30**(9), 1497–516.

# 14 Business angel networks: a review and assessment of their value to entrepreneurship

*Tom Lahti and Henrik Keinonen*

## 14.1 INTRODUCTION

Entrepreneurs with young innovative companies that are looking to grow their business may be unable to raise funding from banks and venture capital funds. Such companies often have few tangible assets and with little that can be used as collateral banks often deduce that these companies are too risky to fund. Venture capitalists for their part are rarely prepared to invest less than €200,000 in a business. Many of the costs are fixed that arise from due diligence and monitoring of investments, which makes such investments uneconomical (Mason, 2009). However, business angels defined herein as 'individuals, acting alone or in a formal or informal syndicate, who invest their own money directly in an unquoted business in which there is no family connection, and who after making the investment, takes an active role in the business, in the hope of financial gain' (for example, Avdeitchikova et al., 2008; Mason and Harrison, 2008) may provide a perfect partnership for these entrepreneurs. In many cases they provide more than just funding, as they can also be a source of valuable business experience and provide a network of business and industry contacts (for example, Ardichvili et al., 2002; Politis, 2008).

For entrepreneurs on the lookout for funding, business angels may be hard to find, particularly those with experience and competences compatible with the venture's specific needs. The investment market is virtually invisible, as there is no record of active angel investors, which makes it difficult for an entrepreneur to identify business angels (for example, Wetzel, 1983). In an effort to overcome this obstacle, business angel networks (BANs) were born. BANs are designed to function as financial intermediaries. They enable and facilitate trading between investors and capital seekers, but do not invest any funds themselves (Knyphausen-Aufsess and Westphal, 2008). They can be considered similar to 'dating agencies' – providing a channel of communication that enables entrepreneurs seeking financing to gain the attention of business angels. What is more, BANs make it a point to inform angel investors of investment opportunities with no compromise to the investors' privacy (Mason and Harrison, 1996; Mason, 2009). BAN facilitation reduces the costs of searching for the perfect fit for all parties involved.

Yet, increasing numbers of BANs are now expanding their role beyond that of providing a communication channel. This is typically the case in BANs where the angel investors are themselves actively involved in planning and governing the network's activities, usually via board membership. In an effort to meet the demands of a variety of business angels with heterogeneous expectations and investment experience, the networks engage in supplementary activities, like educating less experienced members or using their social capital to attract competent lecturers for BAN events. Some networks also actively recruit new angel investor members, as many are attracted by the idea of co-investing with other prominent business angels. In countries where governmental support for BANs is on the wane, it is important that BAN offerings are made sufficiently attractive, so as to provide the network with a steady income. Income is normally derived from membership, registration and success fees, that is, the percentage of the investment paid to the network. In order to establish and maintain sufficient activity, BANs need to appeal to both angel investors and entrepreneurs.

The first aim of this chapter is to provide an overview of the BANs currently operating in Europe and the USA. In particular, we focus on describing the evolution of BAN activity in European countries. Our second aim is to reflect on the socioeconomic value of BANs by reviewing extant research evaluating their benefits and drawbacks. Researchers have disagreed on the question of whether government should support BAN establishment and operations, as both positive and negative evidence has been found for their role in stimulating investment activity.

In his work, US researcher Jeffrey Sohl (2007) coined the term 'angel portal' to depict various communication channels that exist between entrepreneurs and angel investors. This chapter specifically focuses on 'matching network' BANs, one of Sohl's portal modes. A matching network is a BAN that on one hand provides investors with a mechanism for evaluating opportunities, and on the other hand provides entrepreneurs with a means to gain access to angel investors (Sohl, 1999). This is done via a database, matching investment preferences with summaries of entrepreneurs' business plans. In addition to this connecting function, matching networks also commonly provide venture forums and educational events (see Sohl, 2007). Sohl's other modes of angel portals are also touched on briefly herein.

The chapter begins with an introduction to the BAN function. This is followed by a description of the various BAN types, an overview of the BANs currently operating in Europe and the USA, and a discussion on BAN performance measurement. After this, we review the extant material assessing the networks' socioeconomic contributions, followed by a discussion section summarizing the main points and outlining suggestions for policymakers. This chapter ends with a proposal for future avenues of research.

## 14.2 FUNCTIONS OF BUSINESS ANGEL NETWORKS

The core function of a BAN is to provide a communication channel that allows angel investors to examine investment proposals. In some BANs, the administrator screens the submitted proposals to ensure that the deal flow the angels encounter is of sufficient quality in terms of growth potential, for example. BANs can also tailor the deal flow to meet the individual preferences of the investors or specific requirements of the entrepreneurial ventures. Communication between investors and entrepreneurs typically takes place either electronically via the internet, and/or in investment forums, where entrepreneurs make presentations to a potential investor audience (for example, Gullander and Napier, 2003). The communications do not always concern financial investments, however, as some BANs also facilitate service-for-equity investments, whereby investors assume managerial and board positions in the ventures – offering their expertise, experience and effort in exchange for ownership (for example, Lange et al., 2003).

In cases where several angels indicate an interest in investing in the same venture, BANs also provide opportunities for investment syndication (Mason and Harrison, 1997). On occasion BANs also facilitate the search for lead syndicate investors, that is, angel investors who agree to assume the main responsibility for managing the investment, as they commonly hold the most relevant knowledge and experience for the investment in question. This deal-brokering capacity is often complemented by other services, including investment readiness training for the entrepreneurs, training for the investors, standardized contract models for use in business angel investor-entrepreneur negotiations and affordable advisory services to all parties (see Gullander and Napier, 2003; Aernoudt et al., 2007).

Low investment readiness implies that an entrepreneur is not ready to receive business angel funding. It may stem from shortcomings in the written and/or oral material that is targeted toward the investors (for example, Mason and Harrison, 2001; Mason and Kwok, 2010). BANs can improve investment readiness by either helping entrepreneurs directly or by referring them to affordable advisory services. Among other things, these services can help polish up a business plan, tweak a revenue model or coach towards the perfect sales pitch, thereby reducing information asymmetries about the quality of the business opportunity (for example, Lahti, 2014). Business angel training and coaching help in increasing the additionality of angel investments by lowering the entry barriers into the business angel market. Potential and inexperienced investors are provided with the tools and knowledge to manage angel investments (for example, Christensen, 2011). An underlying objective is also to increase overall awareness about angel investing. By promoting business angel activity, BANs can also play an important role in enhancing market development. The model contracts offered by BANs reduce costs and save time by reducing the need for legal expertise.

## 14.3 DIFFERENT KINDS OF BUSINESS ANGEL NETWORKS

There are several different kinds of BANs operating in today's market. Lange et al. (2003) developed the following typologies for differentiating between them.

- private vs. public
- for-profit vs. not-for-profit
- early stage focused vs. all stages
- specialist investors vs. generalists
- active screening and support vs. passive
- regional or local geographical reach vs. national or pan-national
- introduction services only vs. a broader range of services offered.

Table 14.1 illustrates these typological dimensions, providing brief descriptions of their implications and demonstrating examples of different BANs from the European Business Angels Network's (EBAN) membership information (see EBAN, 2008, 2014a). EBAN is an organization whose mission is to represents the interests of the European BANs, most of whom are members of EBAN.

It is worth noting that the modus operandi of private, for-profit BANs is to generate a profit, and hence these types of networks offer very active screening and support along with a broad range of services. They also often facilitate investments in later stage ventures and management buyouts (Mason and Harrison, 1997). As these are typically large investments, a success fee tied to the investment size makes these investments more profitable than fees collected from early stage companies.

*Table 14.1 Typological dimensions of business angel networks*

| Typological criteria | | Description | | Description |
|---|---|---|---|---|
| Financial mode | Private | These BANs are self-sufficient and finance their operations from sources of income such as registration fees, success fees and sponsorship.<br>*Success fees* are commonly 1–2% of the invested capital (e.g. NeBIB in the Netherlands, BAF in Finland) | Public | Public funding is obtained from organizations that seek to spur economic development such as local authorities, government agencies, universities, science parks and business incubators (e.g. Macedonian Business Angels Network, Serbian Business Angels) |
| Profit orientation | For profit | Commercial BANs are established to provide profits for their founders. Socioeconomic benefits are secondary in importance (e.g. Brains ToVentures in Switzerland, BAF in Finland) | Not-for-profit | To obtain public sector funding and/or sponsorship from corporations, BANs have a not-for-profit status (associations). Socioeconomic benefits are highlighted (e.g. FiBAN in Finland, Almi in Sweden). |
| Preferred financing stage | Early stage preferred | Emphasis on the pre-seed, seed, start-up and the early stage (e.g. Angels Den in the UK, BE ANGELS in Belgium) | All stages | Considers all stages of development, and even sometimes investments in management buyouts (e.g. the Informal Investors Network in the Netherlands, BCN Business Angels in Spain) |
| Preferred industry sector | Specialist | May focus on only two industry sectors, such as. Biotech and Telecommunication (e.g. Cyban in Cyprus, Amber Network in Poland) | Generalist | Considers investments in many different industry sectors (e.g. Business Angels Network Vlaanderen in Belgium, IESE in Spain) |

| | | | | |
|---|---|---|---|---|
| Screening and support | Active | BAN manager has an active role, screens out investment opportunities of low quality, and provides support functions to angels and/or entrepreneurs (e.g. FiBAN in Finland) | Passive | BANs provide limited support and do not actively engage in screening of investment opportunities (e.g. Huban in Hungary, Ukrainian Business Angel Network) |
| Geographical reach | Regional or Local | Limited geographical scale, serves local angels and entrepreneurs (e.g. the Cambridge Angels in the UK, Maxwell Group in the Netherlands, Sting Business Angels in Sweden and Malaga Business Angels in Spain) | National or pan-national | Geograpic scale in national BANs is a single country (e.g. Lab-X in Turkey, CatCap GmbH in Germany and Bulgarian Business Angel Network), in Pan-National BANs the scale is two or more countries (e.g.Δ BiD Network in the Netherlands and Go Beyond Ltd; in Switzerland) |
| Types of Services offered | Introduction services only | Introduce investment opportunities, but do not engage in other functions (e.g. Venture Bonsai in Finland, Huban in Hungary) | Broad range of services offered | Provide a broard range of services, such as business angel training and services that seek to improve investment readiness (e.g. ESTBAN in Estonia, BANC in Spain) |

*Sources:* Adapted from Lange et al. (2003); examples from EBAN (2008, 2014a).

As we mentioned earlier, Sohl (2007) has coined the term 'angel portal' to categorize the various communication channels between business angels and entrepreneurs. The main features of all six of Sohl's portals in the following list are briefly described in Table 14.2:

- matching networks
- facilitators
- informal angel groups
- formal angel alliance
- electronic networks
- collection of individual investors.

European countries have adopted the 'matching networks' portal. By and large, most BANs provide the three core functions of a matching network, that is, a matching database, an investment forum and educational seminars. These functions have also been the foundation for the most recent BANs launched in emerging business angel markets in Eastern Europe, in countries like Estonia and Latvia. The development in the USA has followed very different lines, as the 'matching network' is not the typical angel portal. Informal angel groups and formal angel alliances enjoy much wider popularity. The next two sections look at the evolution of BANs in Europe and the USA.

## 14.4 AN OVERVIEW OF BUSINESS ANGEL NETWORKS IN EUROPE

The earliest BANs were established in the UK in the early 1990s, followed by the Netherlands (NEBIB) in 1995, Finland (the SITRA Matching Service) in 1996 and Belgium (the Vlerick Business Angels Network) in 1999 (Mason, 2009). The number of BANs in Europe has increased over time. Figure 14.1 shows the European development from 1999, when there were only 66 BANs in Europe, to 2013, when the corresponding number was 468 (EBAN, 2014b).

Figure 14.2 demonstrates the number of BANs currently operating in different European countries, comparing 2013 figures with those from 2007. In some countries, like the UK, Belgium and Germany, the number of BANs has remained relatively stable during this time period, but when examined from a long-term perspective a decline in all three countries is evident (for example, EBAN, 2008). From 2003 to 2004, the number of BANs in the UK dropped from 51 to 35, while in Germany the number of BANs peaked in 2005 at 40. In Belgium, there were seven BANs in 2003.

*Table 14.2 Different angel portals*

| Portals | Matching Networks | Facilitators | Informal angel groups | Formal angel alliance | Electronic networks | Collection of individual investors |
|---|---|---|---|---|---|---|
| Description | Based on four fundamental principles: need to protect investor anonymity, to provide access to capital for entrepreneurs, to have an efficient mechanism for business angels to screen investment opportunities and the importance of face-to-face interaction between business angels and entrepreneurs. Three tiered approach: (1) matching database, (2) the venture forum format, and (3) educational seminars. | Facilitators maintain a list of interested participants, including private investors, entrepreneurs and service providers. Organize events on specific issues, such as valuation, term setting and organizing a business plan. Least organized form of angel portals, considered as event planners. | The informal angel groups consist of a membership that typically ranges from a handful of business angels to 50 business angels. Members themselves bring in the business opportunities 'perform the backoffice functions'. The venture forum format is the predominant mechanism for assessing investment opportunities. | Have a larger membership per group than the informal angel groups and a higher visibility. As its name indicates, its organisational structure is more formal than in facilitators and informal angel groups. As the deal flow is substantial staff is hired to conduct the 'back office' work. Have typically a board of directors and an executive director. Have criteria for membership and annual membership fees. Membership might imply group decision-making and sufficient investment activity. | An internet platform that enables accredited investors to identify investment opportunities. Entrepreneurs need to submit a two-page summary of their business proposal. An efficient method for deal screening, but investment decisions require face-to-face interaction Mostly an unsuccessful investment portal. | The least organized of the angel portals. Individual investors that are not directly affiliated with any angel portal. Draws on referral sources such as trusted friends and business associates to obtain deal flow. |

*Sources:* Adapted from Sohl (2007, 2012).

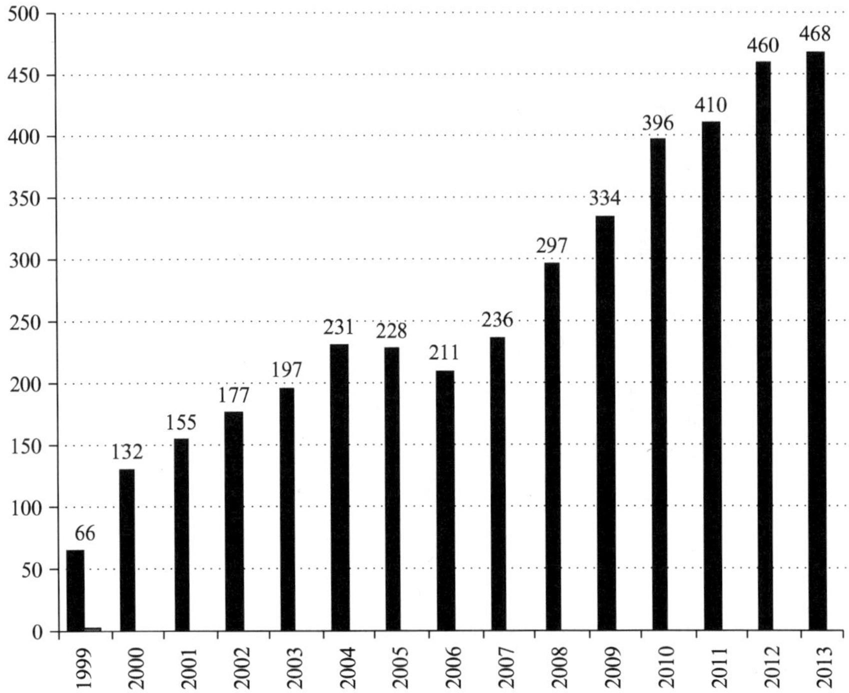


*Source:* EBAN (2014b).

*Figure 14.1 The number of BANs in Europe during the time period 1999–2013*

The strong decline in non-commercial BANs in the UK and Germany has been influenced by reduced public sector support (Mason, 2009).

In contrast, Figure 14.2 shows that the number of BANs has grown in Finland, Spain and France. This reflects a spike in regional BANs, as these large nations have angel investors spread throughout the country who prefer to invest locally. In Finland, many of the regional BANs were only recently established. The Finnish Business Angel Network (FiBAN) has launched affiliate BANs in many of the country's major cities. At the same time, the number of BANs has declined in Sweden and Norway. Finland and Sweden organize their business angel networks in a similar fashion. In both countries, there is a strong national actor – Connect in Sweden and FiBAN in Finland – and there are several regional affiliates.

Since 2007, BANs have been established for the first time in many Central and Eastern European countries. These countries include Estonia

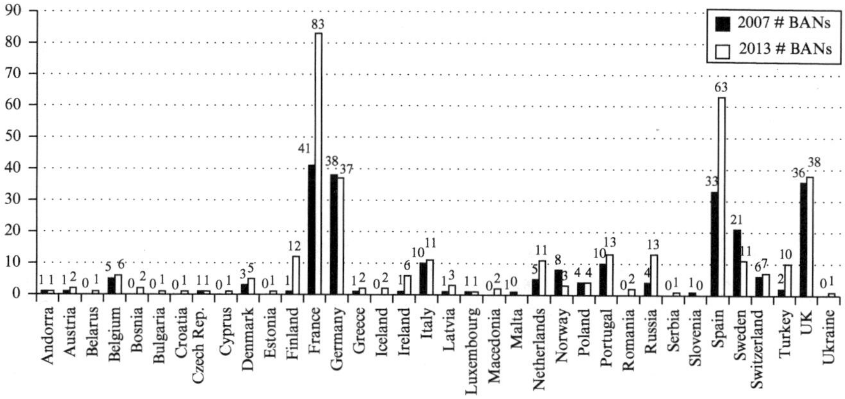


*Sources:* EBAN (2008, 2014b).

*Figure 14.2 Number of BANs in different European countries*

(EstBAN), Serbia (SBAN), Croatia (CRANE), Cyprus (CYBAN), Romania (Finantare) and Ukraine (UBAN). In these countries business angel activity is still in its infancy. Estonia's EstBAN, founded in 2012, has been the most active of these recently established networks. It collaborates with FiBAN in Finland and SOBA in St Petersburg, Russia and has had the opportunity to learn from their best practices. This collaboration also enables investments from Finnish and Russian angels to reach Estonian startups. It partly explains why 82 ventures have already received network funding – a considerable amount when EBAN statistics report that only 52 angels investors are active in Estonia (EBAN, 2014b).

Figure 14.3 provides an estimate of the number of BANs per business angels in some of the European countries. The estimates for the number of business angels have been adopted from EBAN's 2013 survey on business angel activity (EBAN, 2014b). While the business angel market in the UK is by far the largest in Europe, there is less than one BAN per 100 angel investors. When examining this figure, however, one needs to consider the uniqueness of BANs in the UK. In Scotland BAN activity is concentrated in one big public actor, Local Investment Networking Company (LINC). LINC adopted the strategy of aggregating local enterprises into one national BAN (Sohl, 2007). This large nationwide BAN contains not just individual angels but also a large number of angel syndicates with up to 70 members (see Mason and Harrison, 2010, 2011). Thus, there are many angel groups organized within a single BAN. As these angel groups are not counted as BANs, the number of BANs may not give an accurate picture

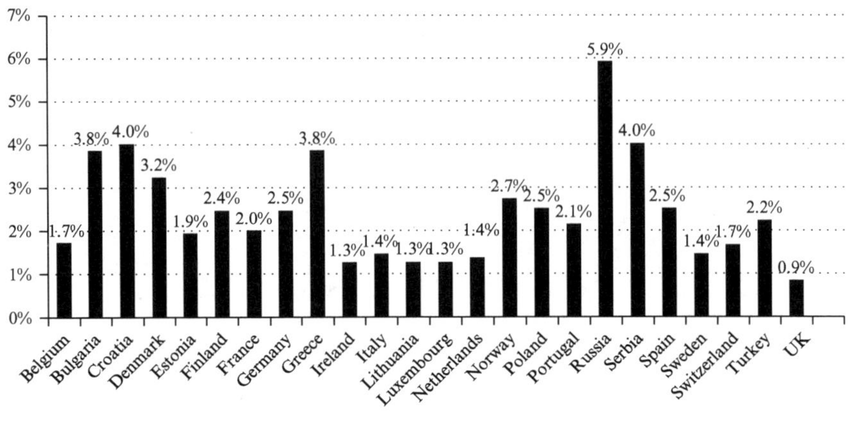


*Source:* EBAN (2014b).

*Figure 14.3 Number of BANs as a percentage of the number of business angels*

of the organization of the angel market in the UK. In England, Wales and Northern Ireland most of the BANs are members of the British Business Angel Association.

Although Russia has 13 BANs, it is estimated that there are only 220 business angels living in the country. The low amount of business angels in Croatia and Serbia also places them high in the Figure 14.3 comparison. It is important to bear in mind that in many countries like the UK, Germany, Sweden and Belgium, the trend has been a decline in the number of BANs as the market matured. A large number of BANs are set up with public sector support during the early development of a market, to create visibility for the operation and open up the market. Many of these are reliant on public support to finance their operations. This support may not be warranted in situations where angel investors can encounter superior quality deal flow outside a BAN, or when BANs are not able to provide increased funding additionality. In a country such as Russia, where there is plenty of untapped potential to expand the pool of angel investors, efforts to establish BANs are likely to produce good results.

Figure 14.4 shows the sources of funding for European BANs; 20 percent of the funding comes from parent organizations, as many of the BANs are affiliated with a private or public sector actor that aims at promoting entrepreneurship. Another 28 percent is generated by membership fees and success fees. These numbers indicate that BANs are quite hard-

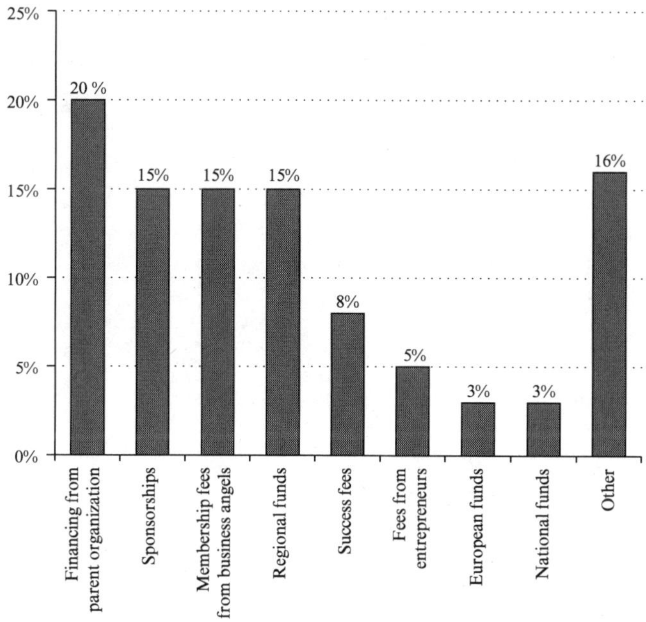


*Source:* EBAN (2014b).

*Figure 14.4 Sources of income for European BANs*

pressed to cover their expenses with revenues from their business activities. Public sources of funding from European funds, national funds and regional funds account for 21 percent of the funding. It would seem that sponsorship would be a suitable source of funding for BANs, but it may be difficult for commercial BANs to rely on sponsorships, as corporations tend to be more willing to associate themselves with non-profit-oriented activities. Based on the figures, it is difficult to extract the relationship between private and public sector funding, just as it is hard to determine the extent to which 'funding from parent organization' is public or private. Public funding may be injected indirectly, as the parent organization may obtain support for setting up the BAN. Sponsorships can also be had from both private and public sector sources.

Figure 14.5, illustrates the services provided by BANs. It shows that the European BANs contain the elements required of the aforementioned 'matching network'. Almost all of them feature an educational element as well as forums for company presentations.

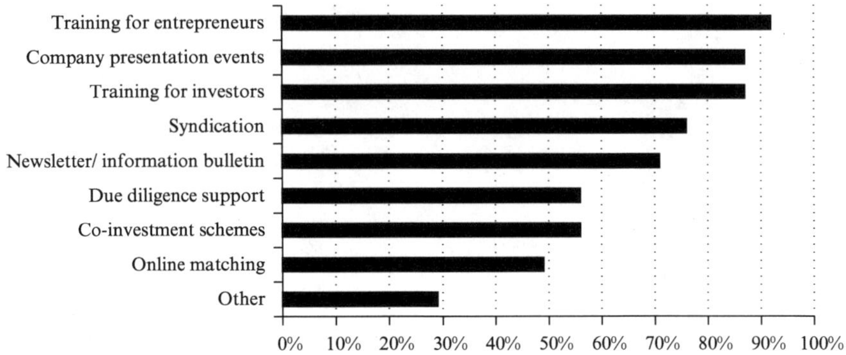


*Source:* EBAN (2014b).

*Figure 14.5 Services for BAN members*

## 14.5 AN OVERVIEW OF BUSINESS ANGEL NETWORKS IN THE USA

The first BAN in the USA was, Venture Capital Network (VCN), founded in 1979 at the University of New Hampshire (Sohl, 1999). It was based on the four fundamental principles of a matching network: (1) the need to protect investor anonymity, (2) the necessity of providing access to capital for entrepreneurs, (3) to create an efficient mechanism for business angels to screen investment opportunities and (4) the importance of face-to-face interaction between business angels and entrepreneurs (Sohl, 2007). VCN maintained a confidential database with information on investment opportunities submitted by entrepreneurs and interest profiles submitted by investors. Business introductions were provided when investment opportunities met the investors' investment criteria (see Wetzel, 1987). VCN complemented this matching service with educational seminars and venture forums. The network targeted entrepreneurs and investors from a variety of states in the USA, and while many business introductions were made relatively few deals were signed (Wetzel, 1987).

Another early effort to create a widespread appeal for BANs and increase business angel activity in the USA was the establishment of the ACE-Net in 1996. ACE-Net was an internet-based listing service that brought together entrepreneurs and business angels. Like VCN information services, ACE-Net operators were affiliated with universities and state-based organizations, reliant on public sector support and ran on a not-for-profit basis (see Acs and Tarpley, 1998). ACE-Net operated on a national scale and its business model relied on the assumption that if investors were provided with sufficient information on investments they would be willing to invest outside their local region. As it has ceased to exist due to the low number of deals made, this could suggest that angels were not attracted by long-distance investments at this time (Harrison et al., 2010).

As indicated earlier, most 'matching networks' have vanished from the US market. Only 13 of the roughly 200 BAN members of the Angel Capital Association, the leading professional and trade association for US business angels, are 'matching networks', while the rest are angel groups (ACA, 2014). Those few matching networks that still exist have evolved into electronic networks that lack physical presence (Sohl, 2012). However, as business angels' investment decisions require face-to-face interaction such electronic platforms have been relatively unsuccessful in meeting their needs. Matching networks in the USA use the internet as their matching mechanisms, while the European ones make use of investment bulletins and investment forums (Mason, 2006).

There are institutional reasons why traditional BANs are not well suited to the US market. First of all, a potential BAN investor needs to be accredited. To certify as an accredited investor in the USA, these individuals need to display expertise in financial and business matters, a net worth of more than $1 million and an income of more than $200,000 in the last two years. These regulations as specified in the US securities laws and regulations (Wetzel, 1987; Acs and Tarpley, 1998) limit the pool of angel investors that are available to invest through a BAN.

Second, the Securities Exchange Act (SEC) restricts the scope of BAN managers' involvement in BAN transactions. Persons running the BAN cannot, for instance, provide advice about the merits of the investment opportunities, receive compensation from BAN users, participate in negotiations between investors and entrepreneurs or assist in the completion of any transaction (Acs and Tarpley, 1998). This means that BAN managers are not able to actively help angel investors in their selection of business opportunities, and their incentive to do so is also hampered by the fact that they cannot receive compensation. For informal angel groups and formal angel alliances these restrictions are not problematic, as the evaluation, due diligence and negotiations are performed by the angels themselves. As Table 14.2 indicates, any personnel are mainly hired for back office work (see Sohl, 1999, 2007).

## 14.6 MEASURING PERFORMANCE OF A BUSINESS ANGEL NETWORK

There are many different ways in which the performance of a BAN can be assessed. The primary objective of a BAN is to enable investments, and therefore a successful BAN is one in which many entrepreneurial projects secure funding. Thus, the key measure of a BAN's performance is the number of investments it facilitates, the amount of invested capital and the amount of matches that are made. Research may then be undertaken that looks into the long-term effects of the BAN-facilitated investments. Perhaps the best measure of these long-term effects is the number of new jobs created in the BAN funded ventures. This number is of particular interest in research that assesses the benefits and drawbacks of public support for BANs.

Deal flow size may not be the best BAN performance indicator. For instance, a study from Mason and Harrison (2010) of UK BANs found no correlation between the number of business plans received and the number of investments made. Here the four largest BANs, that accounted for 67 percent of all business plans received, accounted for only 44 percent of the companies generating funding. A large component of the BAN deal flow may be of insufficient quality to be of any real interest to business angels. For similar reasons, the number of investor members in the BAN is also not the best performance measure.

Mason and Harrison (2010) indicated that successful BANs are those that yield investment opportunities of such high quality that they can be presented to the investors. A strong relationship was discovered between the number of proposals presented to the angel investors and the number of deals. For example, a total of 233 companies secured their funding through the UK BANs. While this figure is only 2.8 percent of all the companies seeking funding, it accounts for 28 percent of those that were eventually presented to investors. As Mason and Harrison (2010) suggest the key differentiation between networks appears to be in the process used to whittle down the business plans received in order to select the companies that are ready to be presented to the investors. They add that once the investment opportunities are presented, the success rates in securing financing are broadly similar among the BANs. A conclusion could be drawn that it would be meaningful to assess the performance of BAN investment readiness services. Mason and Harrison (2010) compare BANs that provide investment readiness training to other BANs in the marketplace. The success ratio in the former was much higher than in the latter. In BANs offering investment readiness training 36 percent of the entrepreneurs that pitched their business idea obtained funding, while the corresponding figure for the other BANs was 23 percent. This would imply that the actual performance of a BAN is best measured in how well they perform services that increase entrepreneurial readiness. This same investment readiness training increases investment activity. Mason and Harrison (2004) argue that business angels are turned off by entrepreneurs unable to provide sufficient information on their business opportunity or tell a compelling story during their pitch. BANs that provide readiness training can help entrepreneurs to overcome these shortcomings and with that improve their chances of obtaining funding. Given that business angels increase their funding to entrepreneurial ventures if they encounter a deal flow of sufficient quality, measures that improve readiness are effective for increasing angel investment additionality.

BAN-performance is not only reflected in the quality of their investment readiness training, but also in the quality of BAN's other services, like angel investor education, forum events, syndication practices and matchmaking platforms. Through all of these, BANs can increase the number of investments and the amount invested. Hence, it can be deduced that, these are determinants that influence the quality of a BAN and contribute to its actual performance.

## 14.7 AN EVALUATION OF THE IMPACT OF BANS

This section is divided into two subsections. The first provides an overview of research that shows evidence of positive socioeconomic effects of BANs. The second shows evidence of negative socioeconomic effects.

### 14.7.1 Positive Evidence

Aernoudt and Eriksson (2007) argue that public sector support to BANs is often intended to cover costs arising from efforts to (1) enhance the entrepreneurial culture; (2) recruit new business angels; (3) seek and evaluate entrepreneurs willing to work with a business angel; and (4) match business angels with entrepreneurs. Christensen (2011), Knyphausen-Aufsess and Westphal (2008) and Collewaert et al. (2010) are examples of recent studies that empirically evaluate whether governments should support BANs. Pioneering research on the theme was made by Mason and Harrison (1997) who investigate whether commercial for-profit BANs replace the need of publicly funded BANs. Data were gathered from 17 BANs in the UK that provided information on 100 investments made in 1993–94 and 1994–95. Significant differences were found between investments that were made through publicly funded and commercial BANs.

The commercial BANs were involved with larger investments, later stage deals including management buyouts (MBOs) and 'low-tech' manufacturing. Consequently, it would seem that publicly supported BANs do not compete for the same deal flow as commercial BANs. This suggests that the establishment of commercial BANs does not necessarily eliminate the need for publicly supported BANs. They also do not provide a solution to the equity gap that public BANs aim to bridge. Commercial BANs might in fact be more inclined toward bridging a so-called second equity gap arising in situations where seed funds and business angels have commonly exhausted their funds, and yet the company is still too small to attract venture capital (for example, Harrison and Mason, 2000). Moreover, they found that the commercial BANs were not active in the same regions as the publicly funded BANs, which provided further indication of a lack of overlap. The diversity in terms of regions covered by commercial and publicly supported BANs is advantageous as Avdeitchikova (2009) among others suggests that metropolitan areas often attract the vast majority of capital, while a large number of peripheral regions are virtually deprived of investments.

Collewaert et al. (2010) evaluate whether public sector intervention through the subsidizing of BANs enhanced regional economic growth in Flanders, Belgium. The data in the study build on 55 interviews with entrepreneurs and business angels, in addition to a quantitative performance assessment of 34 companies that have obtained funding through a BAN in comparison with 50 companies that obtained angel funding through another channel. Four publicly supported regional BANs were represented in the quantitative assessment. The BAN-backed companies were matched with non-business angel-backed companies for the variables age, industry and size. The study investigates how well the BANs achieve their objective of reducing market failures by increasing access to angel investments. As indicated in the introduction, young innovative companies suffer from financial constraints because they have difficulty obtaining funding from banks, as their value is rarely dependent on tangible assets that can be used as collateral for a loan. Collewaert et al. (2010) show that ventures obtaining funding through the BAN are primarily young high-tech companies that pose great financial risk. The research suggests that BAN funding assists companies that tend to suffer from financial constraints and thus helps in bridging equity gaps. Furthermore, it demonstrates that the entrepreneurs and business angels would not have known about the other without a BAN. This indicates that the BANs increase transparency in the market and generate additionality in funding.

Quantitative assessment suggests that companies seeking funding through BANs are not riskier, nor do they grow less or have lower post-investment returns than companies that obtained angel funding through other channels. It also shows that for every euro spent on government subsidies, €85.39 is obtained in value added. Value added is measured as the return on assets of the companies in year four. It is notable that the value added of the companies that obtained business angel funding is higher than for those that did not. Moreover, results demonstrate that 102 net jobs (187 jobs created minus 85 jobs destroyed) were created in the BAN-backed companies from the year of the business angel investments. Given an estimate that only considers the increase in jobs in the companies in question each job created equals a subsidy of €8399. Under a very positive assumption that considers all 495 jobs in the BAN-backed companies as additional, the subsidy per job drops to €1731. The study compares the cost-efficiency to other public sector initiatives aiming to promote entrepreneurship. Given this positive assumption it compares well with other public sector initiatives. For example, in the 'European business incubators initiative' the figure for subsidy per job was €4000 (European Commission, 2002). Similar to many BANs, European incubators are typically recipients of public support.

Christensen (2011) provides further justification for public sector support of BANs, drawing on an in-depth observation study of the life cycle of a national BAN – the Danish Business Angel Network – and compares it with a similar national BAN in Wales. The main argument is that any evaluation of the effects of public sector BAN support should consider not only direct socioeconomic effects, but also the indirect effects that materialize. The direct effects include the creation of new jobs and the fueling of innovation and economic growth. A valuable indirect effect is the training they provide for their members. This education is important for the value added, measured in Collewaert et al. (2010) as the return on assets, to emerge. With sufficient training business angels can provide a value-added contribution from their hands-on involvement (for example, Mason and Harrison, 2000). Educating entrepreneurs on how to improve investment readiness and on what it means to obtain business angel funding is another important contribution of BANs.

Other important indirect effects of BANs that were addressed in the study were the screening of investment opportunities, the continuous improvement of BAN practices, the creation of awareness regarding angel investing and, their coordinating function and network development. BAN managers' screening of projects saves time and expenditures for angel investors and is also beneficial for entrepreneurs who get notified about business proposal shortcomings. BANs continuously seek to improve their services based on member feedback. As stated earlier, the BANs also contribute to raising awareness of business angel investing.

This is important for many reasons: it encourages individuals to become business angels, promotes business angel activity through policy measures and reduces equity aversion amongst potential recipients of business angel investments. Equity aversion arises when entrepreneurs do not have a sufficient understanding of the different forms of equity financing, leading to a decreased flow of investment opportunities (for example, Mason and Harrison, 2001). Increased awareness of business angel investing from BANs helps to plug this knowledge gap (Harding, 2002). Yet another BAN contribution is substantiated by Christensen (2011), who argues that BANs substantially reduce aggregate transaction costs in a society by virtue of 'drawing up standard legal documents, codes of conduct, and providing guidance on questions such as tax problems and so on' (p. 345). Actions such as these add to entrepreneur and investor knowledge, and are particularly beneficial for those with limited experience. Finally, membership in BANs helps business angels to leverage their social network. Virgin angels, making their first investments learn both from the education programs and from syndicating investments with more experienced investors. Events and meetings organized by BANs provide business angels with opportunities for partnering not only with other investors, but also with different stakeholders affiliated with the network, such as intellectual property experts, solicitors, accountants and consultants.

In summary, evidence points to the socioeconomic benefits of BANs. For this reason, Collewaert et al. (2010) suggest that public support for BANs is a cost-efficient measure to create new entrepreneurship.

### 14.7.2 Negative Evidence

Knyphausen-Aufsess and Westphal (2008) criticize public sector intervention in BANs. They build a case for why the drawbacks outweigh the benefits. Their empirical analysis is based on the data from one German BAN, The Northern Bavarian Business Angels. First, they argue that the services provided by BANs are often of insufficient quality, as they are dependent on BAN manager competencies. Therefore, they argue, they may not meet the needs of business angels. Accordingly, this lack of BAN manager competence results in services being standardized rather than tailored to the needs of the various members. The study suggests that BAN services result in a one-sided advantage for young, technology-based ventures, with experienced business angels obtaining few benefits from membership.

Second, they question BAN ability to screen investment opportunities. It is advocated that BAN managers commonly do not have the competences to assess the quality of investment opportunities, which makes it hard for them to distinguish between high and low quality. This would reduce the value of BAN managers' pre-screening that is intended to mitigate the risks of adverse selection and help business angels select less risky projects. It is suggested that BAN managers particularly lack the competences of evaluating investment opportunities where the level of innovativeness is substantial.

Third, Knyphausen-Aufsess and Westphal (2008) claim that BAN services increase rather than decrease the risk of adverse selection. The first argument for this is that services aimed at increasing investment readiness tend to homogenize the offerings that business angels encounter. BAN help to polish business plans may make it more difficult for business angels to assess entrepreneurs' ability level and the quality of their investment opportunities. BAN help is especially valuable for entrepreneurs unable to come up with material of adequate quality themselves, so consequently, instances may occur where a business angel selects a weak project over a good one. The second argument is that these services tend to increase the valuation by creating false value. If window dressing performed by the BAN services increases the perceived quality of an investment opportunity, a business angel may end up paying a high price for an investment opportunity that is in fact of poor quality.

Fourth, the results support findings from Mason and Harrison (2000) that suggest that BANs do not attract the highest quality investment opportunities. The closed marketplace of a BAN creates fees that angel investors and entrepreneurs can avoid if they carry out transactions in the open market. Given that the value of BAN-services is limited to experienced entrepreneurs and business angels, they are more likely to find each other in, for example, public business plan contests.

Finally, it is argued that contracts imposed by BANs are more comprehensive than ones business angels would use without BAN involvement. This contrasts with the 'incomplete contracts approach' that characterizes the business angels' style of managing investments (see Van Osnabrugge, 2000), where the focus is on post-investment involvement as opposed to comprehensive contracting. If emphasis in the investment process is shifted toward contracting, it might reduce the value added that is transferred through the angel investor's hands-on involvement.

In summary, it can be argued that given that BANs benefit mainly technology-based ventures their socioeconomic benefits are scarce. According to Knyphausen-Aufsess and Westphal (2008), obtaining investment opportunities through BANs can have immediate negative consequences. In light of their findings, government intervention to support the establishment of BANs and their operations is not motivated.

## 14.8 DISCUSSION AND SUGGESTIONS FOR POLICY-MAKERS

There is no conclusive answer as to whether there is a need for public sector BAN support. As the preceding section reveals, evidence and opinions are mixed. This chapter, however, provides some food for thought for policy-makers that strive to promote entrepreneurship through suitable measures.

First, when evaluating whether the state should intervene by supporting BAN activity one has to consider the development of the angel investor market. In countries where the market is underdeveloped, as in many of the Eastern European and some of the Central European countries, there might not be sufficient private-sector initiatives to build a well-functioning BAN. In such a context public sector intervention in the angel market reaps the most benefits. There is also a need to increase awareness of business angel investing in general in these instances. For instance, Russia's population is greater than the UK's, yet EBAN statistics indicate that the number of business angels in Russia is 5 percent of that in the UK (EBAN, 2014b). This implies there is a lot of growth to be achieved in terms of angel investment additionality before the market reaches a point of maturity. As in the example of EstBAN, when new BANs are set up, there is much to be learned from existing ones. This may help in identifying best practices in BAN operations. However, Russia is characterized by an environment with institutional weaknesses such as corruption, weak property rights enforcement and negative informal values toward entrepreneurship (Aidies et al., 2008). In such an environment, trade credit substitutes for bank credit and reinvestment of profits for outside equity (Aidies et al., 2008). BANs establishment could contribute to enhancing the entrepreneurial culture and as such may change the way entrepreneurship is perceived in society. However, the legal system still provides a challenge as there is limited support for broken contracts. This may hold back the development of angel investor activity in Russia.

Second, the cost-efficiency of public sector support for BANs should be compared to that of other public sector initiatives to support entrepreneurship, as was the case in Collwaert et al. (2010). While the study in question suggests that public sector support of BANs was cost-efficient in the region of Flanders, Belgium, this was dependent on the assumption that companies that obtained funding through the BAN would not have survived without the investments. In a more conservative estimate considering only the net job growth created after the investments, cost-efficiency in terms of jobs per subsidy decreases markedly. It is important for policy-makers to ensure that that any BAN public funding is injected into a productive use, where researchers are able to evaluate its direct and indirect effects.

Third, as found in Mason and Harrison (2010), it is meaningful to assess BAN service performance for its help in converting BAN deal flow into presentable investment opportunities. It is invaluable for BANs to involve the angel investors in developing these services. Experienced angel investor knowledge helps to ensure that investment readiness programs, angel training and deal-brokering platforms meet the needs of angel investors in the market. This helps to overcome the problem illustrated in Knyphausen-Aufsess and Westphal (2008) whereby BAN services do not appeal to large parts of the angel investor population. To avoid this, policy-makers should promote models where business angels share responsibility with the BAN management in the organization of key tasks. Successful European BANs are acquiring features of angel groups, where angel investor involvement is substantial and BAN management's role is fairly limited.

Finally, one could suggest that public sector intervention in a market should decrease as time passes and eventually be terminated. Successful BANs are able to develop services that their members are willing to pay for and have the potential to cover their expenditures with internally generated funds and sponsorships from corporations. Their less-successful counterparts may fail to attract high-quality investment opportunities and/or improve the investment readiness of their deal flow, limiting the number of deals that are made. In a situation where public sector support is terminated only the most competitive BANs will remain in the marketplace. For policy-makers it is important to ensure that these remaining BANs contribute to bridging the equity gaps that exist in the market.

In summary, extant research on BANs is scarce and concentrates on assessing whether the government should support BAN activity. This means that there is a lot of scope for future research. The following section provides four suggestions for future BAN research.

## 14.9 AVENUES FOR FUTURE RESEARCH

First, one of the suggestions made in this review, and also in Knyphausen-Aufsess and Westphal (2008) for that matter, is that the human capital of those that actively contribute to BAN activities has a great impact on its success in creating socioeconomic value. The human and social capital of BAN management greatly affects the quality of the services provided. An interesting avenue of future research would be to study whether the level of experience that a BAN can draw upon influences its success. Success in this scenario could be both short-term goals like recruiting new business angel members and creating funding additionality, and long-term goals like creating added value in terms of new employment and profitable growth. This kind of analysis would require an access point to the data of several BANs.

Second, Mason and Harrison's (1997) investigation of publicly supported and private BANs goes back more than 15 years. This implies that there is a need for an up-to-date picture on the differences between the roles and activities of publicly supported and private BANs.

Third, research needs to examine how the maturity of a market affects the types of BANs in the marketplace and their performance. As was indicated in the earlier discussions, BANs can significantly increase the additionality of angel investments in a market that is underdeveloped, expanding the number of BAN members and the number and worth of investments made. In more mature markets, angel investor groups and clubs may emerge from outside the BANs and replace them. Consequently, the number of BAN-facilitated deals may decline over time. The number of commercial networks tends to increase with a market's development. It is also worth investigating how business angel involvement in BANs is influenced by the maturity of a market. With the passage of time, the need for a strong public BAN may be eliminated, as angel investors are able to self-organize to promote their interests.

Finally, the effects of public support for BANs should be compared to that of tax breaks for angel investors. Tax breaks exist in the USA and many European countries, such as the UK, Ireland and Luxembourg. The two policy-measures have the goal of increasing venture growth. It may be relevant to make a comparison of how well they achieve their objectives and cost-efficiency. However, these are not competing public initiatives. While tax incentives may increase the additionality of angel funding, they do not enable business angels and entrepreneurs to connect (Mason, 2012). Hence, tax incentives are no substitute for the BANs, even if they so increase investment activity.

## ACKNOWLEDGMENTS

The authors would like to acknowledge Director Luis Galveias and Office and Membership Manager Pablo Garrido from EBAN and Mr Ari Korhonen for their valuable help in providing data for the chapter.

# REFERENCES


ACA (2014), *ACA Member Directory*, available at http:// angelcapitalassociation.org/directory/ (accessed 15 December 2014).

Acs, Z. and F. Tarpley Jr (1998), 'The angel capital electronic network (ACE-Net)', *Journal of Banking and Finance*, **22**, 793–7.

Aernoudt, R. and T. Eriksson (2007), 'Business angel networks: a European perspective', *Journal of Enterprising Culture*, **10**(3), 177–87.

Aernoudt, R., A. San José and J. Roure (2007), 'Executive forum: public support for the business angel market in Europe – a critical review', *Venture Capital*, **9**(1), 71–84.

Aidies, R., S. Estrin and T. Mickiewicz (2008), 'Institutions and entrepreneurship development in Russia: a comparative perspective', *Journal of Business Venturing*, **23**, 656–72.

Ardichvili, A., R.N. Cardozo, K. Tune and J. Reinach (2002), 'The role of angel investors in the assembly of non-financial resources of new ventures', *Journal of Enterprising Culture*, **10**(1), 39–56.

Avdeitichikova, S. (2009), 'False expectations: reconsidering the role of informal venture capital in closing the regional equity gap', *Entrepreneurship and Regional Development*, **21**(2), 99–130.

Avdeitchikova, S., H. Landström and N. Månsson (2008), 'What do we mean when we talk about Business Angels? Some reflections on definitions and sampling', *Venture Capital*, **10**(4), 371–94.

Christensen, J. (2011), 'Should government support Business Angel Networks? The tale of Danish Business Angel Network', *Venture Capital*, **13**(4), 337–56.

Collewaert, V., S. Manigart and R. Aernoudt (2010), 'Assessment of government funding of Business Angel Networks in Flanders', *Regional Studies*, **44**(1), 119–30.

EBAN (2008), *European Directory of Business Angel Networks in Europe*, Report by the European Business Angel Network Secretariat, Brussels.

EBAN (2014a), *European Directory of Business Angel Networks in Europe*, Report by the European Business Angel Network Secretariat, Brussels.

EBAN (2014b), Statistics Compendium 2014, Report by the European Business Angel Network Secretariat, Brussels.

European Commission (2002), *Benchmarking Business Incubators*, Report by the European Commission.

Gullander, S. and G. Napier (2003), *Handbook in Business Angel Networks – The Nordic Case*, Report by the Stockholm School of Entrepreneurship, Stockholm.

Harding, R. (2002), 'Plugging the knowledge gap: an international comparison of the role for policy in the venture capital market', *Venture Capital*, **4**(1), 59–76.

Harrison, R.T. and C.M. Mason (2000), 'Venture capital market complementarities: the links between business angels and venture capital funds in the United Kingdom', *Venture Capital*, **2**(3), 223–42.

Harrison, R.T., C.M. Mason and P. Robson (2010), 'Determinants of long-distance investing by business angels in the UK', *Entrepreneurship and Regional Development*, **22**(2), 113–37.

Knyphausen-Aufsess, D. and R. Westphal (2008), 'Do business angel networks deliver value to business angels?', *Venture Capital*, **10**(2), 149–69.

Lahti, T. (2014), 'The value-added contribution of advisors in the process of acquiring venture capital', *International Small Business Journal*, **32**(3), 307–26.

Lange, J., B. Leleux and B. Surlemont (2003), 'Angel networks for the 21st century: an examination of practices of leading networks in Europe and the US', *Journal of Private Equity*, **6**(2), 8–28.

Mason, C.M. (2006), 'Informal sources of venture finance', in S. Parker (ed.), *The Life Cycle of Entrepreneurial Ventures, Volume 3*, New York: Springer, pp. 259–99.

Mason, C.M. (2009), 'Public policy support for the informal venture capital market in Europe: a critical review', *International Small Business Journal*, **7**(5), 536–56.

Mason, C.M. (2012), 'Does tax relief tempt angels?', *Financial Times*, Weekend Money Section, April, 21–2.
Mason, C.M. and R.T. Harrison (1996), 'Informal venture capital: a study of the investment process, the post investment experience and investment performance', *Entrepreneurship and Regional Development*, **8**, 105–25.
Mason, C.M. and R.T. Harrison (1997), 'Business Angel Networks and the development of the informal venture capital market in the UK: is there still a role for the public sector', *Small Business Economics*, **9**, 111–23.
Mason, C.M. and R.T. Harrison (2000), 'Barriers to investment in the informal venture capital sector', *Entrepreneurship and Regional Development*, **14**, 271–87.
Mason, C.M. and R.T. Harrison (2001), 'Investment readiness: a critique of government proposals to increase the demand for venture capital', *Regional Studies*, **35**(7), 663–8.
Mason, C.M. and R.T. Harrison (2004), 'Improving access to early stage venture capital in regional economies: a new approach to investment readiness', *Local Economy*, **19**(2), 159–73.
Mason, C.M. and R.T. Harrison (2008), 'Measuring business angel investment activity in the United Kingdom: a review of potential data sources', *Venture Capital*, **10**(4), 309–30.
Mason, C.M. and R.T. Harrison (2010), *Annual Report on the Business Angel Market in the United Kingdom: 2008/2009*, Report by the Department for Business Innovation and Skills, London.
Mason, C.M. and R.T. Harrison (2011), *Annual Report on the Business Angel Market in the United Kingdom: 2009/2010*, Report by the Department for Business Innovation and Skills, London.
Mason, C.M. and J. Kwok (2010), 'Investment readiness programmes and access to finance: a critical review of design issues', *Local Economy*, **25**(4), 269–92.
Politis, D. (2008), 'Business angels and value added: what do we know and where do we go?', *Venture Capital*, **10**(2), 127–47.
Sohl, J.E. (1999), 'The early stage market in the US', *Venture Capital*, **1**(2), 101–20.
Sohl, J.E. (2007), 'The organization of the informal venture capital market', in H. Landström (ed.), *Handbook of Research on Venture Capital*, Cheltenham, UK and Northampton, MA, USA: Edward Elgar, pp. 347–68.
Sohl, J.E. (2012), 'The changing nature of the angel market', in H. Landström and C.M. Mason (eds), *Handbook of Research on Venture Capital: Volume 2*, Cheltenham, UK and Northampton, MA, USA: Edward Elgar, pp. 17–41.
Van Osnabrugge, M. (2000), 'A comparison of business angel and venture capitalist investment procedures: an agency theory-based analysis', *Venture Capital*, **2**(2), 91–109.
Wetzel, W. (1983), 'Angles and informal risk capital', *Sloan Management Review*, **24**, 23–34.
Wetzel, W. (1987), 'The informal venture capital market: aspects of scale and market efficiency', *Journal of Business Venturing*, **2**, 299–313.

# PART V

# NEW DEVELOPMENTS

# 15 Crowdinvesting: angel investing for the masses?

*Lars Hornuf and Armin Schwienbacher*

## 15.1 INTRODUCTION

This chapter introduces crowdinvesting as a new source of entrepreneurial finance. Crowdinvesting (also referred to as investment-based crowdfunding,[1] securities-based crowdfunding[2] or equity crowdfunding[3]) denotes the Internet-based investment in startup companies by the crowd with the intention to obtain some residual claim on future cash flows of a firm.[4] While in the past transaction costs made it unlikely that such small amounts would be offered to the general public, the Internet now provides opportunities to accomplish just this (Friedman, 2005; Schwienbacher, 2013). As a consequence, crowdinvesting has become a viable alternative form of entrepreneurial finance, even for firms that are excluded from venture capital, angel finance, government programs or friends and family (2Fs).[5]

While crowd*funding* primarily but not exclusively targets projects in art and music as well as social activities, crowd*investing* deals with the financing of corporate growth and innovation (see for example, Bradford, 2012; Klöhn and Hornuf, 2012). Therefore, crowdfunding depicts a broader activity, as it also encompasses donations, pre-purchase and other reward-based forms of funding by the crowd. Crowdinvesting is a sub-category of crowdfunding in which firms issue securities in order to satisfy their financial needs. The capital raised goes directly to developing a sustainable firm and is not necessarily restricted to a particular product. Our analysis in this chapter is limited to this specific form of crowdfunding.[6]

These new developments raise the question of whether crowdinvesting makes the crowd become small business angels, generating a fuzzy boundary between crowdinvestors and business angels.[7] The objectives of this chapter are, first, to describe the function of crowdinvesting and, second, to analyze differences and similarities between crowdinvesting and angel investing. Similarities result from the fact that the crowd partly resembles business angels purchasing securities via the Internet. Differences stem from various sources, such as variations in financial contracting, differences in securities regulations, active involvement of investors, the resulting degree of information asymmetries as well as potential exit strategies. This approach enables us to offer an answer to the important follow-up question of whether crowdinvesting will replace conventional angel investing. In the conclusion, we shall argue that, in many cases, crowdinvestors are likely to complement rather than substitute business angels or venture capital funds either because they fill funding gaps or co-invest in the same round with professional investors.

The chapter is structured as follows. Section 15.2 presents important aspects of securities regulation relevant to crowdinvesting. Section 15.3 describes how crowdinvesting works in some of the most developed markets. In Section 15.4 we compare crowdinvesting to angel investing and illustrate similarities and differences. Section 15.5 deals with the question of whether crowdinvesting and angel finance are complements or substitutes. Section 15.6 provides avenue for future research.

## 15.2 CROWDINVESTING AND SECURITY REGULATION

Crowdinvesting offerings in the form of debt and equity finance typically involve financial securities and are thus subject to securities regulation (see Bradford, 2012; for crowdinvesting contracts that are not classified as securities, see Hornuf and Schwienbacher, 2016). As a general rule, securities laws protect investors against fraudulent offerings through adequate disclosure by the issuer (Brandeis, 1914; Hazen, 2012). For instance, the United States (US) Congress voted the Securities Act of 1933 and the Securities Exchange Act of 1934 as a response to the stock market crash of 1929. The legislation was meant to mitigate the information asymmetries between securities issuers and investors, with the main objective to regulate how and when securities can be offered and sold to the general public. Among other provisions, the Securities Act requested compulsory information disclosure, which is necessary to make sound investment decisions on the securities offered. Prior to general solicitation, information disclosure by the issuer requires a registration statement validated by the Securities and Exchange Commission (SEC).[8] The registration statement is identical to the prospectus issuers provide to investors. According to §12(a)(2) of the Securities Act, the issuer would be liable for the completeness and accuracy of the information supplied in the registration statement. This would eventually offer greater investor confidence and protect the general public from fraudulent behavior. Other countries around the world adopted similar approaches, generally also in response to financial crises or scandals related to securities sold to the general public. At the same time, this securities legislation generates costs for businesses seeking to raise finance, which may become uneconomic for small amounts of finance.

Investors who are able 'to fend for themselves'[9] may ask to opt out of the general solicitation and become 'accredited investors' or 'qualified investors.' In this way, entrepreneurs can make private offerings to investors without a registration statement. Securities regulators would authorize private individuals to become accredited investors if they meet certain conditions on personal wealth and experience.[10] Many business angels comply with these conditions. Shane (2008) reports that 23 percent of US business angels seek accreditation from the SEC, which disburdens the issuer from registering a costly prospectus (for the costs of a prospectus, see Bagley and Dauchy, 2003; Prifti, 2010).

The emergence of crowdinvesting has recently challenged this regulation. For instance, in the member states of the European Union (EU) companies are not requested to comply with the prospectus and registration requirements at the national securities regulator if a public offering does not exceed €100,000 within a 12-month time interval.[11] Other exemptions in the EU refer to the maximum number of investors to whom the offer is made, the minimum contribution imposed on investors, the minimum denomination of the securities offered as well as whether the offer is made to qualified investors only.[12] As a consequence, crowdinvesting has become a viable alternative form of entrepreneurial finance. In the US, the JOBS Act will offer similar opportunities. As soon as the new regulation comes into force, crowdinvesting will no longer be restricted to accredited investors.

## 15.3 HOW CROWDINVESTING WORKS?

In many countries crowdinvesting took off (Hornuf and Schwienbacher, 2015a), with issuers offering financial securities to investors and thus granting returns in the form of interests, dividends and/or parts of the earnings of the business. Today, a large range of portals has been set up to facilitate the matching between entrepreneurs and the investing crowd (Figure 15.1).

At first blush, the financial operation of crowdinvesting seems to be very similar to that of angel investing. After all, both investment activities match the financial needs of an entrepreneur with the speculative desire of one or more investors, who are willing to bear the business risk of a startup company. Nevertheless, the structures of the financial transactions differ to a great extent.

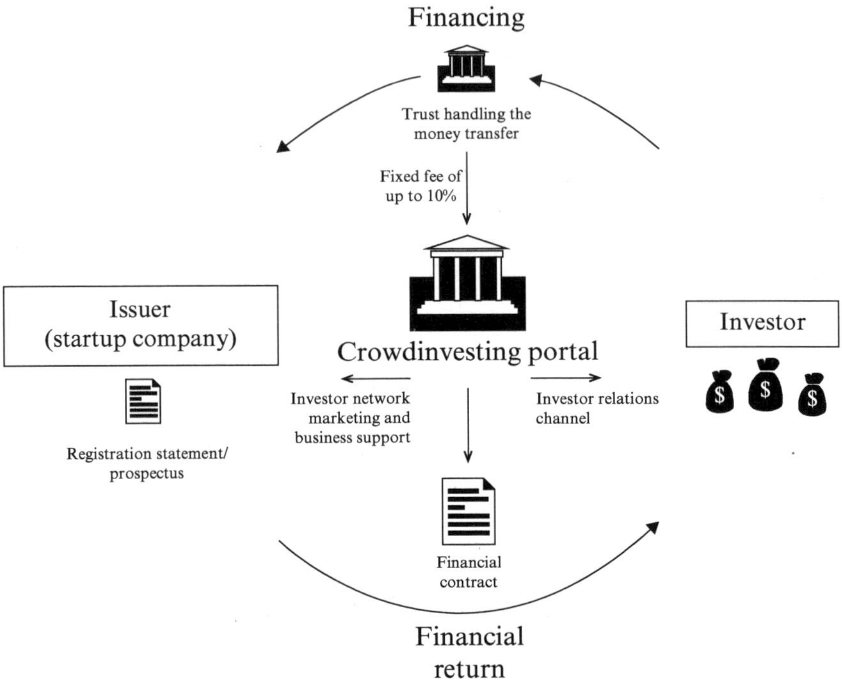


*Figure 15.1 Structure of crowdinvesting transactions*

Crowdinvesting transactions rely on crowdinvesting portals as intermediaries (Figure 15.1), which in some jurisdictions are even mandated by law.[13] Among other things, the crowdinvesting portals offer standardized financial contracts to the issuer, provide marketing and business guidance to the entrepreneur and offer an investor network by advertising the securities on the portal website and in newsletters.[14] In return for these services, portals obtain a previously determined success fee of up to 10 percent of the transaction value. In many countries, the money is wired via a trust that earns up to another 2 percent of the transaction value. In case a certain minimum funding threshold cannot be reached during a prespecified funding period, investments are generally returned to the investor.[15] Only if the minimum funding threshold is reached or exceeded, the funds and the fee are respectively channeled to the entrepreneur and the portal. While the wiring of funds as well as the matching of entrepreneurs and investors rely on an intermediary, it is worth noting that the financial contracts are ultimately struck between the issuer and investors. In order to facilitate future exits, some portals pool the crowd together by having it invest in a special purpose vehicle that in turn invests in the startup. That way, future buyers face a single counter party (that is, the holding company) instead of a large number of very small investors.

Another difference between business angels and financiers investing through crowdinvesting portals is that the latter do not have to register as accredited investors, while some business angels do. This is because the issuers typically offer securities to the general public by relying on small offering exemptions from the registration requirement.[16] As a result, crowdinvesting is available to a much broader but on average less wealthy investor base. Some portals such as Fundsters or Companisto permit virtually everyone to make an investment starting from €1 or €5, respectively. This is not yet the case for US crowdinvesting portals such as CircleUp and FundersClub, whose offers are still restricted to accredited investors. They will only be accessible to a larger crowd of investors after the SEC has implemented the JOBS Act. On the other hand, many European portals erect natural entry barriers that restrain the crowd by selling minimum investment tickets with very high denominations. For instance, the Italian portal SiamoSoci repeatedly sold minimum investment tickets of €50,000; German Innovestment requested at least €25,000 in one of its auctions. Similarly, the startup company Urban Suspects was looking for a maximum of four active investors on the French portal Fondatio, with each investing at least €50,001 in exchange for shares in the company and a seat on the board of directors.

Not surprisingly, those entry barriers influence the composition of the crowd that issuers are reaching out for. According to a survey by Klöhn and Hornuf (2012), the 1422 registered users of Innovestment were on average willing to invest up to €124,100 on the portal and up to €59,500 per startup firm. The majority of them reported to be working in information technology, consulting or finance, with many being self-employed. Moreover, 82 percent of the crowd had already invested in company shares on the regular stock market. This is in line with observations by the Financial Conduct Authority, which reports that crowdinvestors 'tend to be high-net worth individuals with investment experience' (FCA, 2013, p. 37). Based on detailed information on all the members of the largest crowdinvesting portal in France, Hervé et al. (2016) conclude that the bulk of crowdinvestors are not that different from retail investors in other financial markets in terms of gender representation and age. In this sense, it appears that crowdinvestors are indeed small business angels. In some cases, the amounts that crowdinvestors are willing to provide do not differ from those offered by 'true' business angels, at least for portals such as SiamoSoci and Innovestment. Sophisticated business angels invest on average $150,000, with a median of $25,000 (Goldfarb et al., 2013).

Moreover, many business angels are members of angel networks (Mason and Harrison, 1997) that are similar to crowdinvesting portals, as they enable entrepreneurs to find investors, sometimes even via the Internet.

## 15.4 COMPARING CROWDINVESTING TO ANGEL INVESTING

This section discusses similarities and differences between crowdinvesting and angel investing along several dimensions, each of which are dealt with in separate subsections.

### 15.4.1 Financial Contracting

The market structure of crowdinvesting already suggests that the way financial contracting takes place must differ from angel investing. While crowdinvesting largely relies on standardized contracts that are provided by the portals and leave no space for negotiations or amendments in the offer,[17] private ordering as described by Williamson (2002) has been a keystone of the US angel investing and venture capital market (Gilson, 2003).

Not only the way financial contracting takes place differs to a great extent, but also the substance of the securities offered. Venture capitalists and business angels use various covenants in the contracts they sign with the entrepreneurial firm. These include anti-dilution provisions that protect against down-rounds, tag-along and drag-along rights that facilitate exit opportunities, and liquidation preferences that secure higher priority in the distribution of value (Kaplan and Strömberg, 2000; Wong et al., 2009). Moreover, business angels sometimes stage their provision of capital, notably as a way to reduce their risk exposure. In the context of crowdinvesting, tailor-made contractual arrangements and stage financing are difficult to implement, as they require negotiations, as well as strong monitoring and oversight of the entrepreneurial firm, which are burdensome to accomplish with hundreds of parties at stake. While firms may raise follow-up capital by going a second time to a crowdinvesting portal,[18] staged finance is not used as a control mechanism as in the case of angel investments.

Along the same vein, business angels often refrain from buying common shares (Wong et al., 2009), as sometimes practiced in crowdinvesting (mostly by English portals such as Crowdcube and Seedrs as well as German Bergfürst). Even worse, the crowd usually buys profit participating loans without any voting rights that rank last in case of bankruptcy (Klöhn et al., 2016). By contrast, business angels may opt for securities such as convertible preferred shares that give them higher priority if the firm fails. This eventually leaves the crowd with relatively little protection through private ordering and potentially at the mercy of fraudulent behavior (Griffin, 2013).

### 15.4.2 Investor Protection

If investors are not in the position to protect themselves *ex ante* through tailor-made financial contracts and/or cannot *ex post* fend for themselves, securities laws have to step in to protect them. As a general rule, security offerings in the US have therefore been subject to a ban on general solicitation.[19] Furthermore, entrepreneurs issuing financial securities had to provide either detailed information and register with the SEC or qualify for an exemption from the registration requirement. Many US startup companies attracted business angels by using Rule 506 of Regulation D, which provides a 'safe harbor' for the private offering exemption of §4(2) Securities Act. This exemption allows for securities issues to an unlimited number of accredited investors as well as up to 35 other investors. In the EU, similar exemptions exist for small offerings (see Section 15.2; Hornuf and Schwienbacher, 2016).

Natural persons whose net worth exceeds $1,000,000 at the time of the purchase or who had an individual income in excess of $200,000 in each of the two most recent years could qualify to become accredited investors and were thus always able to engage in crowdinvesting activities. Crowdinvesting by a larger crowd of unsophisticated individuals is prohibited in the US until the SEC finally implements concrete rules on the JOBS Act of 2012. Once effective, startups will be able to collect up to $1,000,000 without registration if funds are collected via a 'funding portal' or broker-dealer and specific information is disclosed to the market. Moreover, there is a limited aggregate amount that a single investor can spend on crowdinvesting. If either the annual income or net worth of an investor is less than $100,000 the financier can invest the greater of $2000 or 5 percent of her annual income or net worth. If either the annual income or net worth of an investor exceeds $100,000 the financier can spend 10 percent of her annual income or net worth up to a maximum amount of $100,000.

Statutory law thus provides an alternative route of investor protection, which does not rely on tailor-made financial contracts or staged finance. Most notably, the maximum amounts that qualify for somewhat more lax disclosure rules and thus potentially allow issuers to commit securities fraud more easily are limited to $1,000,000 in the US and range from €100,000 to €5,000,000 in Europe.[20] Moreover, many jurisdictions protect investors by establishing a gatekeeper (that is, offerings must occur via a crowdinvesting portal), by requiring initial and annual disclosure from the issuer as well as by not permitting the advertising of crowdinvesting offerings (except for limited 'tombstone' notices). Furthermore, crowdinvesting portals in the US must register with the SEC and the Financial Industry Regulatory Authority (FINRA), provide investors with education materials and are prohibited from having a financial interest in the issuers. Summing up, crowdinvestors have a smaller capacity to protect themselves through financial contracts, but receive a considerable degree of protection under statutory securities laws.

### 15.4.3 Double Trust Dilemma of Innovation

Among many other factors, an entrepreneurial firm often requires a revolutionary idea as well as sufficient capital to turn the mere idea into a sellable product or service. To raise funds for an innovative venture, the entrepreneur has to disclose the idea to an investor. No investor is willing to provide funds for an entrepreneurial firm without first determining its value. After disclosing a groundbreaking idea, the investor might, however, use the information without compensating the innovator. As a consequence, entrepreneurs might not reach out for the funds they require to develop their business. That is what Cooter and Edlin (2013) call the double trust dilemma of innovation.

When approaching an angel investor, entrepreneurs can solve the double trust dilemma by having the potential financier sign a non-disclosure agreement (NDA). If the angel investor breaches this contract, the entrepreneur may sue out injunctions to prevent future exploitation of her innovation. Furthermore, the angel investor may be subject to monetary damages or equitable relief. Even if no NDA is signed, the fact that angel investors are not anonymous may further help solve the double trust dilemma. Indeed, the angel investor could still suffer severe reputational damage if she steals or leaks a groundbreaking idea, which provides her with good incentives to attract innovative ideas in the first place. Crowdinvesting cannot solve the double trust dilemma in such a way, because the innovation of the fund-seeking venture is publically disclosed and advertised on the portal's website. As a consequence, only particular firms can raise capital via crowdinvesting: either their business ideas are per se very difficult to replicate, for instance, because they are highly dependent on the founder's personality, or the innovation is not worth copying. If the latter were true, the crowdinvesting market might suffer from an adverse selection bias.

### 15.4.4 Investor Behavior and Investor Relation

While angel investors are increasingly organized as groups of individual financiers pooling their financial and informational resources, crowdinvesting is by definition a phenomenon of the masses. The investment behavior of the crowd might therefore differ significantly from that of angel investors – at least in two important respects. On the upside, the crowd potentially benefits from what has become known as the 'wisdom of crowds' (Surowiecki, 2005). While the investment decisions of angel investors might suffer from individual decision-making biases, crowdinvestors can make efficient investments because individual decision-making errors cancel each other out on the aggregate. This hypothesis is borne out by empirical studies analyzing traditional capital markets (Kelley and Tetlock, 2013), which provide evidence that retail investors contribute to capital market efficiency by providing novel information. On the downside, investment decisions by the crowd can suffer from groupthink (Janis, 1972) and herd behavior (Hornuf and Schwienbacher, 2015b; Vismara, 2015). As a result, the crowd might make foolish investment decisions that a single investor (for example, business angel) would not have made. More precisely, the crowd may provide funds to entrepreneurial firms only because their peers do so. If the crowd behaves in such a way, financial resources may not be invested in the most profitable ventures.

Another difference between business angels and crowdinvesting may result from the means by which funding is attracted. In the context of crowdinvesting, the portal and/or the entrepreneur are required to interact with the crowd in a way that is different from traditional shareholders such as business angels (Belleflamme et al., 2014). Crowdinvestors expect to be kept informed, even though the channel of communication is not directly the board of directors as in the case of business angels. Moreover, the motivation of the crowd is also borne by the feeling of support and participating in the development of new products and companies (Jeppesen and Frederiksen, 2006; Gerber et al., 2012). While empirical evidence stems from other forms of crowdfunding, it seems plausible that similar motivations also drive crowdinvestors, although presumably to a lesser extent. As a result, investment decisions made by the crowd are also affected by non-pecuniary benefits. This may affect the choice of investments made and investor behavior once the company has raised the capital needed.

### 15.4.5 Information Asymmetry and Funding Risk

One benefit of crowdinvesting is that the entrepreneur obtains information on potential market demand under crowdinvesting *if* interest of crowdinvestors is correlated with market demand (Schwienbacher, 2015). This may occur if crowdinvestors are also consumers. The fact that the investor base in crowdinvesting is larger than under angel finance would lead to a noisy signal of market potential, reducing the information asymmetry between the entrepreneur and consumers. This ultimately reduces uncertainty for the entrepreneur who can decide to pursue or stop the project based on the information collected in the course of the crowdinvesting campaign. Such information cannot be obtained under angel finance.

However, crowdinvesting can generate higher operating risk, since the project may fail if the entrepreneur does not estimate capital needs well. Under crowdinvesting, no due diligence is conducted beyond the limited one done by some of the portals. Under angel finance, an extensive due diligence is performed and stage finance allows additional capital injection when needed and worthwhile. Investors not involved in the firm's business operations (that is, not sitting on the board of directors) can hardly assess whether the extra capital requested by the entrepreneur is truly needed. Firms that rely on crowdinvesting may eventually exhibit different characteristics due to their funding source and thus evolve differently in the future.

Schwienbacher (2015) shows that firms funded by the crowd may generate different forms of operating risk than firms funded by equity investors, such as business angels. First, firms funded by the crowd are not screened by professional investors and their business plans are not shopped around as done for angel finance. Thus, estimation of production costs and operating efficiency is solely based on the founders' appreciation. This creates higher operating risk than under angel finance. Second, business angels are more likely to inject further funds if costs turn out to be higher than expectations. Under crowdinvesting, firms can only raise subsequent funding when more tangible results can be shown, since the crowd is not a true insider to the firm. As a result, firms funded by the crowd may turn out to have different risk-return profiles than angel-backed firms.

### 15.4.6 Exit and Return

There is empirical evidence that venture capital also requires a well-developed stock market (Black and Gilson, 1998; Da Rin et al., 2005) because venture capitalists appreciate the opportunity to exit an entrepreneurial firm through an initial public offering (IPO). Furthermore, IPOs provide an opportunity for a successful entrepreneur to reacquire control of her firm from the venture capitalist (Gilson and Black, 1999). These arguments hold in a similar vein for angel investors. Entrepreneurial firms that are financed via crowdinvesting are often too small for an IPO on the stock market.[21] Exit opportunities are thus restricted in crowdinvesting. Yet, angel investors and venture capitalists can themselves provide an exit opportunity for the crowd as was the case with the German startup Gini (previously Smarchive), which acquired follow-up funding from venture capitalist fund T-Venture. Moreover, a second generation of crowdinvesting portals might provide an even better exit opportunity for early crowdinvestors. One example is the German portal Bergfürst that has established a secondary market allowing for IPOs in the range €2,000,000 to €10,000,000.

Only very recently scholars have started to study returns generated from crowdinvesting (Hornuf and Schmitt, 2016; Signori and Vismara, 2016). Similarly, little is known about the riskiness of these investments. The main reasons for this lack of knowledge are data availability and sample size. Indeed, most of the investments have been made in the last two years and failures will probably materialize sooner than successes. However, the market is expanding quickly and is likely to become large as soon as the JOBS Act becomes effective in the US. This will facilitate the study of risk and return of crowdinvesting. Since crowd investments in startups resemble deals also made by venture capitalists and business angels (but earlier and at a smaller scale), we may expect high failure rates.

## 15.5 ARE CROWDINVESTORS SMALL BUSINESS ANGELS?

The question of whether crowdinvestors and business angels substitute or complement each other cannot be answered unambiguously, as there is a vague boundary between the two types of investors. On the one hand, there will be crowdinvesting portals offering minimum investment tickets in the size of angel investments. In this sense, crowdinvesting and angel finance might be substitutes and the former will ultimately drive down the returns of the latter. On the other hand, there may be scenarios where crowdinvestors and business angels complement each other, in particular, as some of the latest crowdinvesting portals are hybrids. The second generation of portals, which is currently being set up, is the result of inefficiencies due to the differences discussed above. For instance, several portals are now more closely integrated in the financial landscape as they work with more traditional investors, including business angels. Two examples of the latter are the UK-based portal Syndicate Room and the Belgian portal MyMicroInvest, where the crowd co-invests with business angels. Such co-investments have several benefits. One advantage is that the crowd may rely on the financial contracting skills and monitoring abilities of business angels, which further provide hands-on advice and lend their reputation to the entrepreneurial firm (Hsu, 2004; Ferrary and Granovetter, 2009). Business angels could in turn benefit from the participation of the crowd that may complement what angel investors can contribute. Moreover, the wisdom of the crowd may reveal novel information to the benefit of traditional investors.

Nevertheless, crowdinvesting and angel investing can be distinguished along two major lines. First, crowdinvesting by definition gives entrepreneurs access to a large investor base (that is, the crowd), which can only be accomplished if crowdinvesting portals do not erect natural entry barriers, for example, through large minimum investment tickets. Second, if the crowd invests amounts as little as €5, financiers are not likely to engage in any form of financial contracting because transaction costs outweigh the potential gains arising from a tailor-made financial contract. As a result, crowdinvesting portals provide boilerplate contracts to investors and entrepreneurs. In this way, the fuzzy boundary between crowdinvesting and angel investing can be disentangled: crowdinvesting portals allow for small investment tickets to attract a large crowd and in return provide boilerplate contracts (bottom left corner in Figure 15.2), while business angels buy large investment tickets and benefit from customized contracts as the gains from financial contracting outweigh their negotiation and drafting costs (top right corner in Figure 15.2).

Finally, the extent to which crowdinvestors become small business angels also depends on how securities regulation will evolve, in particular, whether exemptions to registration and prospectus requirements will facilitate crowdinvesting. Under the new legal exemptions specifically tailored to crowdinvesting activities financiers are less protected. One immediate reason is that firms issuing securities under the available exemptions disclose less information, while crowdinvestors are somewhat less sophisticated and may in some instances not be able to fend for themselves. Moreover, the securities that many crowdinvesting portals offer often rank last in bankruptcy. The problem is even more severe, as the crowd cannot protect itself by actively engaging in financial contracting (for example, through covenants or staged finance). In contrast, angel investors purchase securities in firms that either comply with the general securities regulation or negotiate tailor-made contracts that offer more adequate protection. Whether investors ultimately suffer extensive financial losses by engaging in crowdinvesting remains to be seen. During the first five years crowdinvesting existed in Germany, 13 percent of the successfully funded startups filed for bankruptcy or were liquidated right away due to lack of insolvency assets (Hornuf and Schmitt, 2016). However, this comparatively low failure rate might only be the result of cherry picking in the early phase of the market.

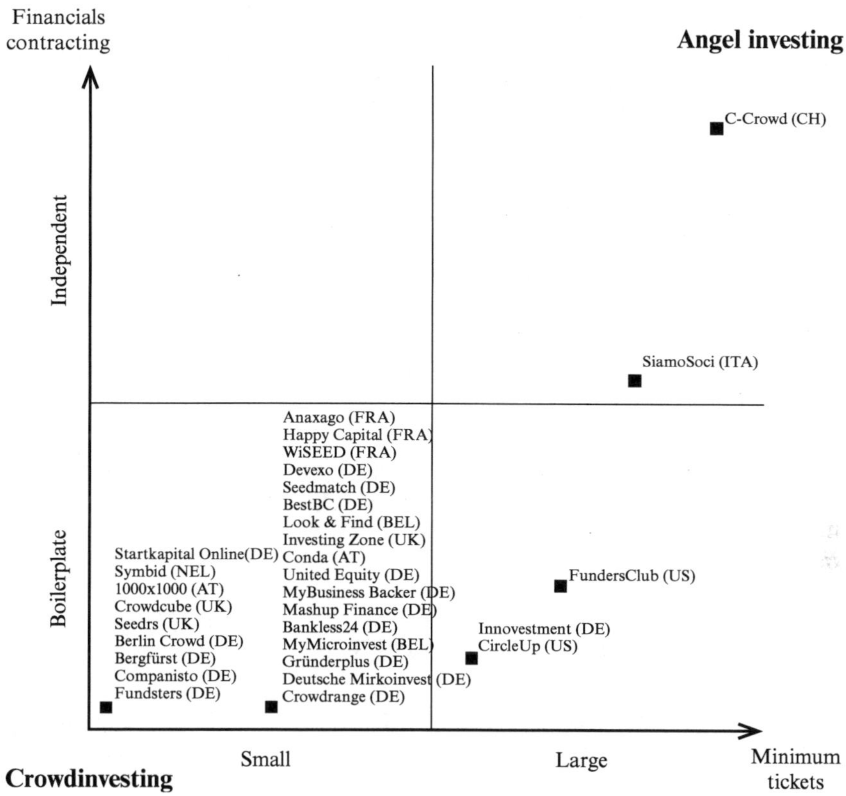


*Figure 15.2 Fuzzy boundary between crowdinvesting and angel investing*

## 15.6 AVENUES FOR FUTURE RESEARCH

The discussion provided in this chapter raises interesting follow-up questions that offer potentially worthwhile avenues for future research. At this point, very little is known about crowdfunding, but even less about crowdinvesting. The main reason is clearly the lack of data. An immediate research question worthwhile exploring concerns the risk and expected return of crowdinvesting for the crowd. Relatedly, what types of firms are created by crowdinvestors? Are they viable? Moreover, what are realistic exit routes for crowdinvestors? Similar to business angels and venture capitalists, entrepreneurs will need to offer exit opportunities to their investors. For crowdinvesting, these issues remain largely unresolved.

Another set of research questions pertain to the crowd more directly.

For instance, what motivates the crowd to invest in startups? Are their motivations different from business angels? Given the size of investments they make, it appears likely that motivations of crowdinvestors are quite similar to business angels. However, the geographical proximity to the investee company is likely to be less relevant. Similarly, while professional investors (business angels and venture capitalists) typically invest in startups within their own area of expertise, crowdinvestors are likely to prefer startups with which they share the same affinity.

Taking a different perspective, interesting research questions relate to the structure of platforms and contracts. Do some contract forms attract more investors and thereby potentially larger funds? Do investor restrictions imposed by platforms such as high minimum ticket size or pooling of the crowd into a financial vehicle affect crowd participation?

Finally, an open question is to what extent does crowdinvesting facilitate and make more difficult follow-up funding? For instance, Leavitt (2005) argues that the presence of business angels in some startups may make access to venture capitalists more difficult for funding future investment rounds, since business angels invest in earlier stages where risk is larger and for which they secured significant control rights that they may at times be reluctant to give up. It is likely that such tensions in the context of stage financing may occur also with crowdinvestors. This issue has not been tested empirically so far. Given the contracting differences between crowdinvesting and angel investing, the source of such conflicts may differ. Crowdinvestors generally have very little control rights in the startups; however, the fact that they are many may create tensions and ultimately free-rider or hold-up problems.

## NOTES

1. See the Financial Conduct Authority Consultation Paper CP13/13, 'The FCA's regulatory approach to crowdfunding (and similar activities)'.
2. See Knight et al. (2012) as well as the Securities and Exchange Commission's (SEC) Proposed Rules.
3. See Bradford (2012) as well as Ahler et al. (2013). The JOBS Act merely uses the term 'crowdfunding' for transactions involving the offer and sale of securities.
4. We refer to this activity as 'crowdinvesting' as it can come in either way – debt or equity finance – and may in some jurisdictions not necessarily involve a financial contract that falls under the legal definition of a security. See Klöhn and Hornuf (2012) who define the term in a similar way.
5. The crowd could be seen as belonging, at least in part, to the third 'F'; that is, 'fans.' However, the crowd is generally composed of more than fans, such as pure consumers for rewards-based crowdfunding or investors for crowdinvesting.
6. Other forms of crowdfunding are discussed and studied, among many others, by Mollick (2014) and Agrawal et al. (2013).

7. Some portals actively advertise to their investors that they can 'benefit like business angels through early investments in corporate growth!' ('*wie ein Business Angel durch Ihr frühes Investment vom Unternehmenswachstum profitieren!*'), see http://www.seedmatch.de/fuer-investoren#sogehts (accessed 10 February 2014).
8. The SEC was set in place by the Securities Exchange Act of 1934.
9. *SEC v. Ralston Purina*, 346 US 119, 125 (1953) as well as Rule 506(b)(2)(ii) of Regulation D Securities Act.
10. See Rule 501(a) of Regulation D Securities Act.
11. According to Directive 2010/73/EU national legislators have discretion to raise this ceiling up to €5,000,000, which some countries did (see Hornuf and Schwienbacher (2016) for an international analysis and the impact of securities regulation on crowdinvesting).
12. Directive 2010/73/EU, Article 3(2).
13. See §4(6)(C) Securities Act for the US.
14. According to §4A(b)(2), Securities Act US issuers will not be allowed to 'advertise the terms of the offering, except for notices which direct investors to the funding portal or broker.' In stark contrast, English and German crowdinvesting portals send out regular newsletters advertising the startup companies looking for funding.
15. See §4A(a)(7) Securities Act as well as the business model of many German crowdinvesting portals.
16. Directive 2010/73/EU, Article 3(2)(e) and Title III of the JOBS Act.
17. A notable exception is the Swiss portal c-crowd, which leaves the drafting and negotiation of contracts to the parties.
18. Firms that have raised two or more rounds on the same crowdinvesting portal include LeaseRad, Front Row Society, Honestly, Refined Investment, miBaby, foodieSquare, easyPEP and Paymey. Firms that have raised two or more rounds on different crowdinvesting portals are Ludufactur and swabr.
19. See Cable (2010–11, p. 154ff.) with a focus on business angels of what constitutes a general solicitation in the US.
20. Assmann et al. (2010), section 1 'WpPG', n. 4.
21. Carpentier and Suret (2010, p. 43, f.n. 5) report that the new markets in Europe, which were established to foster growth companies, required minimum gross proceeds of around €5,000,000 from potential issuers.

# REFERENCES


Agrawal, A.K., C. Catalini and A. Goldfarb (2013), 'Some simple economics of crowdfunding', *Innovation Policy and the Economy*, **14**, 63–97.

Ahler, G.K.C., D. Cumming, C. Günther and D. Schweizer (2013), 'Equity crowdfunding', *Entrepreneurship Theory and Practice*, **39**(4), 955–80.

Assmann, H.-D., M. Schlitt and W. von Kopp-Colomb (2010), *WpPG VerkProspG*, 2nd edn, Köln: Verlag Dr Otto Schmidt.

Bagley, C.E. and C.E. Dauchy (2003), *The Entrepreneur's Guide to Business Law*, 3rd edn, Eagan, MN: Thomson West.

Belleflamme, P., T. Lambert and A. Schwienbacher (2014), 'Crowdfunding: tapping the right crowd', *Journal of Business Venturing*, **29**(5), 585–609.

Black, B.S. and R.J. Gilson (1998), 'Venture capital and the structure of capital markets: banks versus stock markets', *Journal of Financial Economics*, **47**, 243–77.

Bradford, S. (2012), 'Crowdfunding and the federal securities laws', *Columbia Business Law Review*, 1–150.

Brandeis, L.D. (1914), *Other People's Money and How the Bankers Use It*, New York: Frederick A. Strokes Company.

Cable, A.J.B. (2010–11), 'Fending for themselves: why securities regulation should encourage angel groups', *University of Pennsylvania Journal of Business Law*, **13**, 107–72.

Carpentier, C. and J.-M. Suret (2010), 'Entrepreneurial equity financing and securities regulation: an empirical analysis', *International Small Business Journal*, **30**(1), 41–64.

Cooter, R. and A. Edlin (2013), 'The double trust dilemma: combining ideas and capital', in R. Cooter (ed.), *The Falcon's Gyre: Legal Foundations of Economic Innovation and Growth*, Berkeley Law Books, available at http://scholarship.law.berkeley.edu/books/1 (accessed 30 May 2016).

Da Rin, M., G. Nicodano and A. Sembenelli (2005), 'Public policy and the creation of active venture capital markets', ECB Working Paper Series No. 430.

Ferrary, M. and M. Granovetter (2009), 'The role of venture capital firms in Silicon Valley's complex innovation network', *Economy and Society*, **38**(2), 326–59.

FCA (Financial Conduct Authority) (2013), 'The FCA's regulatory approach to crowdfunding (and similar activities)', Consultation Paper CP13/13, available at http://www.fca.org.uk/your-fca/documents/consultation-papers/cp13-13 (accessed 30 May 2016).

Friedman, T. (2005), *The World is Flat: A Brief History of the Twenty-first Century*, London: Penguin Books.

Gerber, E.M., J.S. Hui and P.-Y. Kuo (2012), 'Crowdfunding: why people are motivated to post and fund projects on crowdfunding platforms', in *Proceedings of the International Workshop on Design, Influence, and Social Technologies: Techniques, Impacts and Ethics*, ACM, available at http://www.juliehui.org/wp-content/uploads/2013/04/CSCW_Crowdfunding_Final.pdf (accessed 30 May 2016).

Gilson, R.J. (2003), 'Engineering a venture capital market: lessons from the American experience', *Stanford Law Review*, **55**, 1067–103.

Gilson, R.J. and B.S. Black (1999), 'Does venture capital require an active stock market?', *Journal of Applied Corporate Finance*, **11**(4), 36–48.

Goldfarb, B., G. Hoberg, D. Kirsch and A. Triantis (2013), 'Are angels different? An analysis of early venture financing', Robert H. Smith School Research Paper No. RHS 06-072, available at http://ssrn.com/abstract=1024186 (accessed 30 May 2016).

Griffin, Z.J. (2013), 'Crowdfunding: fleecing the American masses', *Case Western Reserve Journal of Law, Technology & the Internet*, **4**, 375–410.

Hazen, T.L. (2012), 'Crowdfunding or fraudfunding? Social networks and the securities laws – why the specially tailored exemption must be conditioned on meaningful disclosure', *North Carolina Law Review*, **90**, 1735–70.

Hervé, F., E. Manthé, A. Sannajust and A. Schwienbacher (2016), 'Investor motivations in investment-based crowdfunding', Working Paper, available at http://ssrn.com/abstract=2746398.

Hornuf, L. and A. Schwienbacher (2015a), 'The emergence of crowdinvesting in Europe: With an in-depth analysis of the German market', *LMU Discussion Paper*, **43**, available at http://ssrn.com/abstract=2481994.

Hornuf, L. and A. Schwienbacher (2015b), 'Portal design and funding dynamics in equity crowdfunding', *Research Papers in Economics, No. 9/15*, available at http://ssrn.com/abstract=2612998.

Hornuf, L. and M. Schmitt (2016), 'Success and failure in equity crowdfunding', *CESifo DICE Report*, **14**, 16–22.

Hornuf, L. and A. Schwienbacher (2016), 'Should securities regulation promote equity crowdfunding?', *Small Business Economics*, forthcoming.

Hsu, D. (2004), 'What do entrepreneurs pay for venture capital affiliation?', *Journal of Finance*, **59**, 1805–44.

Janis, I. (1972), *Victims of Groupthink: Psychological Study of Foreign-policy Decisions and Fiascos*, 2nd edn, Boston, MA: Houghton Mifflin.

Jeppesen, L.B. and L. Frederiksen (2006), 'Why do users contribute to firm-hosted user communities? The case of computer-controlled music instruments', *Organization Science*, **17**, 45–63.

Kaplan, S.N. and P. Strömberg (2000), 'Financial contracting theory meets the real world: an empirical analysis of venture capital contracts', *Review of Economic Studies*, **70**, 281–315.
Kelley, E. and P. Tetlock (2013), 'How wise are crowds? Insights from retail orders and stock returns', *Journal of Finance*, **68**, 1229–65.
Klöhn, L. and L. Hornuf (2012), 'Crowdinvesting in Deutschland: Markt, Rechtslage und Regulierungsperspektiven', *Journal of Banking Law and Banking*, **24**(4), 237–66.
Klöhn, L., L. Hornuf and T. Schilling (2016), 'Crowdinvesting-Verträge – Inhalt, Entwicklung und praktische Bedeutung', *Journal of Banking Law and Banking*, **27**(3), 142–78.
Knight, T.B., H. Leo and A.A. Ohmer (2012), 'A very quiet revolution: a primer on securities crowdfunding and Title III of the JOBS Act', *Michigan Journal of Private Equity and Venture Capital Law*, **2**, 135–53.
Leavitt, J.M. (2005), 'Burned angels: the coming wave of minority shareholder oppression claims in venture capital start-up companies', *North Carolina Journal of Law and Technology*, **6**(2), 223–88.
Mason, C.M. and R.T. Harrison (1997), 'Business Angel Networks and the development of the informal venture capital market in the UK: is there still a role for the public sector?', *Small Business Economics*, **9**(2), 111–23.
Mollick, E. (2014), 'The dynamics of crowdfunding: an exploratory study', *Journal of Business Venturing*, **29**(1), 1–16.
Prifti, W.M. (2010), *Securities: Public and Private Offerings*, 2nd edn, New York: Clark Boardman Callaghan.
Schwienbacher, A. (2013), 'Financing the business', in T. Baker and F. Welter (eds), *The Routledge Companion to Entrepreneurship*, London: Routledge, pp. 193–206.
Schwienbacher, A. (2015), 'Entrepreneurial risk-taking in crowdfunding campaigns', Working Paper, available at http://ssrn.com/abstract=2506355.
Signori, A. and S. Vismara (2016), 'Returns on investments in equity crowdfunding', Working Paper, available at http://ssrn.com/abstract=2765488.
Surowiecki, J. (2005), *The Wisdom of Crowds*, New York: Anchor Books.
Wong, A., M. Bhatia and Z. Freeman (2009), 'Angel finance: the other venture capital', *Strategic Change*, **18**, 221–30.
Vismara, S. (2015), 'Information cascades among investors in equity crowdfunding', Working Paper, available at http://ssrn.com/abstract=2589619.
Williamson, O. (2002), 'The lens of contract: private ordering', *American Economic Review*, **92**, 438–43.

# Index